CURRICULUM INNOVATION

THE OPEN UNIVERSITY
FACULTY OF EDUCATIONAL STUDIES

The Curriculum Design and Development Course Team

Robert Bell
Dennis Briggs
Sheila Dale
Robert Glaister
Michael Golby
Jane Greenwald
Alan Harris
Donald Holms
Margaret Johnson
Martin Lawn
Ken Little
Robert McCormick
John Miller
Caroline Pick
William Prescott (Chairman)
Diana Roantree
David Seligman
Ruth West
Heather Young

Consultants

Clem Adelman (University of East Anglia)
Ray Bolam (University of Bristol)
Keri Davies (University of Stirling)
John Elliott (University of East Anglia)
Philip Gammage (University of Bristol)
Eric Hoyle (University of Bristol)
David Jenkins (University of East Anglia)
Denis Lawton (London Institute of Education)
Barry MacDonald (University of East Anglia)
Harry McMahon (New University of Ulster)
Dudley Plunkett (University of Southampton)
Richard Pring (London Institute of Education)
John Reynolds (University of Lancaster)
Peter Scrimshaw (Homerton College of Education)
Malcolm Skilbeck (New University of Ulster)
Hugh Sockett (New University of Ulster)
Rob Walker (University of East Anglia)

✓

Curriculum
Innovation

Edited by
Alan Harris, Martin Lawn
William Prescott
at The Open University

A HALSTED PRESS BOOK

JOHN WILEY & SONS
New York   Toronto

Library of Congress Cataloging in Publicating Data

Main entry under title:

Curriculum innovation.

    "A Halsted Press book."
To accompany the teaching materials for the course
Curriculum design and development, prepared by the
Curriculum Design and Development Course Team of the
Faculty of Educational Studies at the Open University.
    1. Curriculum planning – Addresses, essays, lectures.
I. Harris, Alan Edward, 1936-   II. Lawn, Martin.
III. Prescott, William, 1939-   IV. Open University.
Curriculum Design and Development Course Team.
LB1027.C94   375'.001   75-22488
ISBN 0-470-14086-0

Printed in Great Britain

CONTENTS

FOREWORD

INTRODUCTION

1. Innovation — bandwagon or hearse? *John Nisbet*   1

I Styles of Curriculum Development
2. The state of the art of curriculum development
   Tony Becher and Stuart Maclure   15
3. Curriculum development in England *J.G. Owen*   30
4. Curriculum development in Northern Ireland *H.F. McMahon*   47
5. Curriculum development in Scotland *John Nisbet*   52

II Curriculum Development at National Level
6. DES Ministers and the Curriculum *Gerry Fowler*   59
7. The Schools Council in Context *Geoffrey Caston*   72
8. Teachers and the Schools Council *Anne Corbett*   87
9. The Schools Council and Examinations *Stuart Maclure*   95
10. The G.C.E. Examining Boards and Curriculum development
    T.S. Wyatt   104
11. The examination system and a freer curriculum
    Henry G. Macintosh and Leslie Smith   115

III Curriculum Development at Local Level
12. Local curriculum development *Allan Rudd*   127
13. The Malmö Region   138
14. Staff development: the league model *John I. Goodlad*   143

IV Innovation and the School
15. Open Schools, Open Society *Basil Bernstein*   155
16. Open Space — Open Classroom *Clem Adelman and Rob Walker*   162
17. The Evolution of the Continuous Staff Conference
    Elizabeth Richardson   170
18. Planned Change and Organizational Health: Figure and Ground
    Matthew B. Miles   192

V Innovation and the Teacher
19. Understanding life in classrooms *Philip W. Jackson*   205
20. The teacher in the authority system of the public school
    Howard S. Becker   217
21. Innovation and the authority structure of the school
    Dan Lortie   230

22. How can the teaching profession be improved? *R.G. Corwin*   242
23. Full-time people workers and conceptions of the 'professional'
    William S. Bennet Jr. and Merl C. Hokenstad Jr.   250

VI Strategies of Innovation
24. The management of educational change towards: a conceptual
    framework *Ray Bolam*   273
25. Planned organizational change in education *Eric Hoyle*   291
26. The utilisation of educational research and development
    Ronald G. Havelock   312
27. The creativity of the school in Britain *Eric Hoyle*   329

VII Case Study
28. Countesthorpe College *Gerald Bernbaum*   347

    INDEX

FOREWORD

Two companion volumes of readings, *Curriculum Design* and *Curriculum Innovation,* have been prepared for the course, Curriculum Design and Development (E203), offered by the Faculty of Educational Studies at the Open University.

Curriculum Design is in two parts: Perspectives on the Curriculum, and Issues in Curriculum Design. Among the issues discussed are objectives for the whole curriculum, curriculum organisation, approaches to planning, and curriculum evaluation. *Curriculum Innovation* includes the following sections: styles of curriculum development, curriculum development at national and local levels, innovation and the school, innovation and the teacher, and strategies of innovation.

The Readers form one component of the course, which also includes correspondence texts, radio and television programmes, personal tuition and a number of prescribed texts. In order to avoid duplication we have deliberately excluded from the Readers any material which will appear in one of the other components of the course. This accounts for the non-appearance of some familiar names which might otherwise be expected to appear in such Readers.

The Editors wish to acknowledge the help of the consultants to the course team in compiling these Readers.

The texts have been reproduced with their original spelling and punctuation, though the use of quotation marks and the treatment of headings have been standardised throughout. Obvious misprints have been corrected. Numbered notes have been put at the end of each chapter (renumbered sequentially if necessary), followed by any further references. Asterisked notes are at the foot of the page, and a small number of these have been omitted where they refer to deleted material. Editorial omission or interpolations are indicated by the use of square brackets and the editor's introductions to each chapter are set inside square brackets.

INTRODUCTION

If the 1960s represented the period of optimism for curriculum innovation in Britain, then the 1970s may represent a move towards realism, perhaps even pessimism. The breezy confidence of the early curriculum projects has given way to a more tentative and cautious search for solutions. Even among the most active of curriculum developers, innovation is now regarded as a mixed blessing. Schools, it is now widely conceded, must learn not only how to adopt innovations — but also how to *reject* them. This is the spirit in which this collection of readings has been brought together.

The Reader begins with a wide-ranging article by Nisbet in which he considers some of the problems involved in innovations, which are in fact some of the main themes running through this collection of readings. He suggests that we might build on the good will which now exists towards introducing change by concentrating not on the isolated superficial innovations of recent years but on the more fundamental aspects of change. These include the attempt to gain a better understanding of the nature of educational innovation, the development of the necessary support structures, and the realisation that the school or college or university must develop a capacity for self-renewal.

The four articles that follow review different approaches to curriculum development in Europe and North America. Becher and Maclure make the point that in all countries the curriculum is subject to control, and not simply left to teachers to decide. Sometimes the control is centralised; at other times it is a more complicated network of formal and informal controls exercised at various levels of the system. How a country develops the curriculum will be closely related to this system of control. Owen's article echoes some of the warnings about innovation found in Nisbet. So far as England is concerned he is very cautious about the prospects for major change in the next decade. McMahon however appears rather more hopeful that some of the blind alleys down which curriculum developers scurried in the 1960s may be avoided by those now active in Northern Ireland. Nisbet's second article on Scotland seems to confirm some aspects of the Becher and Maclure analysis: the Scottish approach is very different from the English, and reflects the approach to the control of the curriculum which has developed in Scotland.

Section II includes a number of articles on national agencies which affect curriculum change. Fowler, formerly a junior Minister in the Department of Education and Science, questions the dogma that the government does not, and should not interfere in the curriculum. He maintains that there is much more intervention than is commonly supposed. His views form an interesting contrast with those of Caston, which follow. Caston is anxious to emphasise that though the Schools Council is a centralised agency for curriculum development, it is committed to pluralism (by which he means the dispersal of power in education) and the support of the teacher's professional autonomy. The Council may receive half its funds from the central government, but it is free from interference. Anne Corbett's article questions the Council's commitment to teacher autonomy. She claims that the teacher representation on the Council is dominated by the teachers' professional associations, whose principal concern is with the working conditions and status of their members rather than with curriculum development. The Council, therefore, as at presently constituted, is not providing the kind of support for the innovating teacher that it should. Maclure's discussion of the Schools Council and examinations picks up the point which he made in the earlier extract about the relationship between curriculum development and the control of the curriculum. The examination system in England exercises a powerful control over the curriculum, and there are many people who do not wish this situation to change. The only person who could authorise a change is the Secretary of State for Education. We are brought back to Fowler's comments on the importance of central government. Wyatt's article is a reminder that changing the examination system is a formidable task. Not only is it difficult to make rapid changes, but as Maclure pointed out, the examination system exists to serve a number of functions, and there are many people who would resist any changes which would prevent it from carrying out these functions. The last extract in this section, however, takes a more radical look at the possible role of examination boards. The authors recognise the importance of examination boards and suggest ways of using their central position to encourage and consolidate innovation rather than to prevent it.

Section III offers an intriguing comparison of styles of development at the local level. Rudd describes some aspects of the North West Regional Curriculum Project, emphasising the two critical elements of local teacher initiative and co-operation of interested groups. The Malmö study confirms the impression gained from the Becher and Maclure review that the Swedes do not see centralised curriculum decision-making as removing the need for local development. Where however the North West project finds itself responding implicitly to the central-government decision to raise the school-leaving age, Malmö is quite explicit in attempting to find new and better ways of interpreting the national guidelines. Both projects therefore reveal in their own ways how curriculum decisions contain a strong political element involving central government, but there is a recognition that if decisions are to be implemented at the school level, teachers must be involved. The article by Goodlad echoes some of the points made by Rudd, but in an American context. The work of the League of Cooperating Schools is based on the assumptions that the school must be regarded as the largest organic unit for educational change, but that the individual school is not sufficiently strong to overcome the barriers to change without the help of outside agencies.

Goodlad's article forms an appropriate bridge between Sections I-III, which concentrate on styles of development and supporting agencies, and Sections IV and V which emphasise the importance of schools and colleges as social systems, and the crucial role of the teacher in innovation. Bernstein traces the implications for schools of the move towards greater 'openness'. He emphasises particularly the threat to the established order represented by the move away from specialist in-depth subject teaching to a broader integrated approach to the curriculum. We are once again reminded of Nisbet's initial warning about the dangers of attempting innovation. Adelman and Walker continue the theme of openness. They stress the importance of the quality of the interaction in open and closed classrooms, and would wish to play down some of the more superficial aspects such as the architectural features.

The extract from Elizabeth Richardson's book on Nailsea school underlines the crucial importance of two aspects of the school as a social system. The first is the quality of the human relationships within the school, and the second is the need for a sufficient understanding of school management techniques. In this extract we see how one particular school developed a machinery for staff consultation and decision-making. The contrast with the case-study of Countesthorpe is very marked. The last article in Section IV by Miles, although very different in style from Elizabeth Richardson's study, is surprisingly close to it in its concerns and in some of its conclusions. The target for those promoting innovation should be not short-term innovations but the general 'health' of the educational institution.

No educational innovation can hope to succeed without some measure of co-operation from the teaching profession. So what sort of people are teachers? Philip Jackson's study emphasises the teachers' preoccupation with the immediacy of the classroom, the reliance upon intuition rather than research, the willingness to accept simple causal explanations for complex events, and an inability to envisage radical educational change. As Jackson points out, some of these characteristics may develop as a response to the everyday problems of coping with a large class of children. Life in classrooms may indeed demand characteristics of this kind. Whatever the explanation, the thought is a sobering one for the proponents of revolutionary change. Becker considers the way in which the teacher maintains what she regards as her legitimate sphere of authority in the face of possible challenges, particularly from parents. Although teachers may welcome the co-operation of parents, they feel their authority may be threatened if 'outsiders' become too deeply involved in the work of the school. Seen in this light, community schools pose a particular threat and presumably require a very different conception of the teacher's role.

The extract from Lortie is also concerned with the teacher's authority. He speculates on how a particular innovation, team teaching, might affect working relationships between teachers. The extract offers a particularly good summary of some of the possible implications of educational change. It is interesting to note that although the innovation he discusses might be regarded as a move towards 'open education', he examines the possible strengthening of the hierarchical control that might result. The complexities of an innovation may be heightened still further if the reform involves the co-operation of a number of institutions. Corwin looks at the Teacher-Corps experiment in which reform-minded young people were encouraged to help in a programme directed towards the education of low-income children. The different ideologies and perspectives of university teachers, school teachers and young volunteers indicate just how difficult co-operation may become. It may be that the emotive element in this reform — the education of low-income children — virtually guaranteed that the relationship would be stormy, but whatever the reason, it offers an interesting complement to the discussion of co-operative approaches to innovation earlier in the Reader (12 and 13).

The last article in Section V considers the future of a number of professions, including teaching and social work. Bennett and Hockenstad consider that these professions will move away from the image of the traditional professions (such as law or medicine) and become increasingly conscious of the political nature of their work. These are merely hunches which are being explored in this article, but they raise interesting questions about the possible conflicts in the teaching profession between those who would like to build up the traditional professional image and those — like the deschoolers — who regard this image as harmful. And what of those like some of the teachers' professional associations who wish to retain their political character but at the same time build up their professional image?

Section VI considers strategies of innovation. Here some of the significant elements discussed separately in other parts of the Reader are brought together. Bolam, for example, suggests that it is useful to distinguish between four major factors in any innovation: the innovator (or change agent), the innovation itself, the person or institution who is to use the innovation, and the process of innovation over time. It is therefore possible to see a number of the contributions to this volume within the context of this framework, and indeed several of the contributors are located within the text. But there is a further purpose. Many innovations fail because significant factors are overlooked. The article therefore is an attempt to provide guidelines for the management of innovation.

Hoyle's article on planned organisational change discusses in detail some of the themes introduced by Nisbet, in particular the need to change *people* if curricular change is to be successful, and the need to provide them with adequate support. Havelock also considers the problem of support services. He sees the need for linking agencies which will bring together the resources and the users.

Hoyle's paper on the creativity of the school raises the dilemma that curriculum innovation requires changes in the internal organisation of the school, and a change in the internal organisation is itself a major innovation. He concludes that a school which is free to establish its own staff-staff relationships, forms of pupil-grouping, and arrangements for teaching and curriculum, is more likely to innovate than a school which does not have this autonomy. It is important to bear in mind that Hoyle is discussing the creativity of the school *in Britain*. The description earlier in the Reader by Becher and Maclure of other approaches to curriculum innovation is a useful reminder that not every country relies quite so heavily on the autonomy of the school and the teaching profession.

Finally, there is an independent study of Countesthorpe College in Leicestershire. Although the school had only recently opened when the study was made, it is still possible to identify some of the critical areas which reoccur with such frequency throughout the Reader: the importance of outside support — in this case the Local Education Authority — and particularly the Director of Education; the key role of the head, acting as a change agent, bringing in ideas culled from sources outside the school like the Nuffield Projects; the need to reconcile the different perspectives of staff, parents and children; the implications for the role of the teacher of many of the innovations which were introduced. Those who have followed the subsequent history of Countesthorpe and are familiar with the problems which have arisen will perhaps appreciate Barry Macdonald's warning quoted in Nisbet's introductory article to the Reader that anyone contemplating jumping on the bandwagon of innovation should consider its potentialities as a hearse.

1 INNOVATION — BANDWAGON OR HEARSE?

John Nisbet

The Frank Tate Memorial Lecture on Wednesday 3rd July, 1974, by John Nisbet, Visiting Professor in the Faculty of Education, Monash University. First published in *Bulletin of Victorian Institute of Educational Research*, 33, 1–14, 1974. Copyright John Nisbet.

[Innovation inevitably brings with it problems — problems of extra workload, loss of confidence, confusion and the threat of backlash. The task is to gain a better understanding of the dynamics of change and to develop structures which will promote innovation within the educational system, so that the system itself can be self-renewing. The school must develop the capacity to adopt, adapt, generate or reject innovation. Three significant requirements for successful innovation are described: support services, the involvement of teachers and parents in the process of innovation, and the provision for evaluation.]

Education, like politics, is too much influenced by slogans. Certain phrases or words become fashionable from time to time, and they may have a powerful influence on policy, and then they fade away in popularity. The astute educationist, whether administrator or teacher, learns to develop a sensitivity to the swings of fashion in the vocabulary of education. A few years ago, 'manpower planning' and 'management' were popular ideas in education; but the words acquired unpleasant overtones, seeming to imply the clever manipulation of individuals by power groups out of self-interest, and now they are out of fashion. The word 'clever' itself is rather under a cloud at present. The words 'research' and 'experiment' could formerly be used to persuade anyone to accept some change in educational practice; but there has been an anti-scientific swing in public opinion, and today, if you want to justify some departure from established practice, you have to use the word 'innovation'.

Perhaps already the word has begun to lose some of its initial glossy attractiveness, and soon it may become a sad word, or a bad word, like other terms which have followed the same cycle of popularity and disillusionment. There is a danger that 'innovation' in education may come to mean

something cheap, meretricious and gimmicky, undertaken rashly without adequate resources to see it through, as a protest arising out of frustration and impatience.

That is not the definition you will find in the dictionary for 'innovation'; but I think there is a risk that the meaning of 'innovation' may become tarnished by cynicism in this way. It would be unfortunate if this happened

1

John Nisbet

— a great opportunity for reform would have been missed or mishandled. For schools and colleges and universities have been slow to change in the past; but at present we have a new climate of opinion which is aware of the urgent need for change, a new willingness to accept the idea of a search for new and better methods of education. My aim in this lecture is to defend innovation, not to attack it, and I use the word 'innovation' to refer to any new policy, syllabus, method or organisational change which is intended to improve teaching and learning.

There is no shortage of examples — recent innovations which have been tried or proposed include: new syllabuses in science and mathematics, new devices for improving reading, language laboratories, the development of educational technology involving the use of television or computer-aided instruction, resource centres, team teaching, the employment of teacher aides, open schools and new architectural designs, ungraded or non-streamed classes, vertical grouping, the abolition of grading and examinations, greater use of guidance and counselling staff, power-sharing and the devolution of authority within schools, the greater involvement of parents, community schools, and so on. The range and variety is impressive, and though much of it is froth on the surface, there is an underlying ferment of ideas in education which is in sharp contrast to the placid complacency of twenty years ago.

Innovation has become something of a bandwagon. Many teachers and administrators in education would like to have the reputation of being innovators, especially if they are ambitious and want to get on. To be an innovator is to have the image of being up-to-date, efficient, responsive, professional — and definitely superior to the mass of common conventional people. Many of us who are cautious and sensible and have our feet firmly on the ground (or at least that is how we see ourselves) would like to have the image without the reality: the image of being up-to-date without the reality of having to struggle with the problems and stresses which result from any change in practice. To want this is to ask for *innovation without change* — that is, innovation within the established framework. As one administrator said to me, 'The trouble with your new ideas is that they don't fit our existing policies: you're out of touch — you're living in an ivory tower.' What he was asking for was some innovation which did not threaten any of the established practices. But this just will not do. Any proposal for change is seen as a threat by those who rely on established practices; and we all rely on established practices to some extent. Thus, innovation always has an undercurrent of threat, below the popular and acceptable image on the surface.

There are others who see innovation in a different way, as a means of undermining the assumptions which in their view, have dominated our educational thinking for too long. (This is what the French call 'l'innovation sauvage', or wild innovation.) Their true aim is to destroy the citadels of reaction, to clear the ground for the building of a new and better structure of education, and a new and better society. But they are not prepared or equipped for the effort of building a permanent system to replace the one they destroy, and consequently the initial enthusiasm dwindles away and the initial achievements come to nothing in the end.

This is why I suggest to anyone who plans to jump on the bandwagon of innovation, that he should also consider its potentialities as a hearse. For anyone who embarks on any innovatory experiment in education encounters a number of problems which may prove disastrous not only to his experiment but also to himself and to his colleagues in the experiment. It is well to be realistic about these problems. I shall group them under four headings, corresponding to four waves of difficulty which the innovator must survive.

The first of these is an increase in everyone's work load. The most immediate effect to be noticed when anyone introduces some new procedure is that everyone has to work harder. The change is initially stimulating — there is certainly no risk of boredom — but the stage of novelty, like the honeymoon, has to give way to a firm working arrangement. In the new situation, there are no familiar routines to fall back on; and the activities which normally look after themselves, which are carried out routinely and automatically, have to be planned consciously and deliberately. Teachers and students no longer have well-understood roles to perform, and one cannot assume that others will do precisely what one expects them to do. So special attention has to be given to communication and discussion, and this eats into the already precious spare time. The potential for misunderstanding and disagreement is greatly increased. Consequently, it may be very unwise for a school to attempt an experiment as a solution to some crisis. If there is already a feeling of tension among the staff, or between staff and students, you can be sure that this will be aggravated and not eased as the experiment gets under way. The school which is well placed to try out a new idea is one in which there are, already existing, good channels of communication, understanding between colleagues, a well-organised system which has some slack to take up, and the capacity to bring problems out into the open. A school in crisis seldom has these qualities.

If the first effect of innovation is to increase the pressure of the work load, the second effect, which becomes evident almost as quickly, is a loss in confidence and an increase in anxiety. Initially, the effect of innovation is to destroy the teacher's competence. What I mean is that a trained and experienced teacher has built up an impressive range of information and skills for dealing with all sorts of day-to-day problems which crop up, and this becomes the basis of his confidence in withstanding the stresses of responsibility and decision. But any substantial change makes his existing skills inapplicable in the new situation. Thus innovation 'de-skills': it makes experience irrelevant. It is hardly surprising that it is the younger and less experienced teachers who are usually the strongest advocates of reform: they have, as it were, least to lose. Thus, anyone who embarks on

3

innovation should be prepared for anxiety, in himself and in his colleagues. In some circumstances, the anxiety of colleagues may grow into suspicion – suspicion of the motives of the innovating group – and emerge as hostility, because they see the innovation as a threat to their own professional standards. This is especially likely to happen in a secondary school where some form of integrated syllabus is introduced, cutting across the conventional subjects of the curriculum. For many secondary school teachers, including some of the most gifted, the conventional subjects are specialised disciplines which have become, for them, the core of their personal identity. This is the centre of their professional interest: they see themselves as historians, geographers, scientists, mathematicians, linguists; and an integrated curriculum removes from them this distinctive personal role.

A common strategy adopted by hostile colleagues for handling an innovatory group in a school is to try to isolate the group in circumstances where the innovators have low status and little influence. A member of staff who lacks prestige is put in charge; the group is given inferior or makeshift accommodation; and naturally they cannot expect to be given any extra share of finance or facilities which they may need to develop their new programme. Under these circumstances, the innovation can safely be left for a year or so, to wither away and die what seems to be a natural death. The host body has dealt effectively with the infection. (There is an interesting parallel with immunology and the capacity of an organism to isolate, immunise and reject a graft or transplant which it identifies as having come from a body other than its own.)

The third 'wave' of difficulty in the process of innovation can be described as 'confusion'. A period of some confusion is, I think, inevitable in any educational innovation, sooner or later – and unfortunately we do not know enough about the process to be able to predict when to expect this, but it is the most vulnerable moment, and it is necessary to be ready for it. The sequence of events is fairly predictable. The first steps in any new venture are planned with some care, but beyond that it is impossible to forecast what will happen. Because the situations are novel, unanticipated problems arise. New developments call for difficult decisions, and new directions have to be worked out to meet the developments as they occur. Some ideas work, others do not; some move quickly, others slowly; and things get out of phase. Education is a system, and we cannot change one part of a system without associated changes in other parts of the system. New roles and boundaries of responsibility have to be defined: human beings are territorial animals, and in the absence of clearly defined boundaries of responsibility, some people trespass on areas which others regard as their own, and some areas are covered by no one because each person assumes that they are someone else's responsibility.

One or other of two things may happen at this stage. The confusion may slip into chaos, or the whole project may be halted by disillusionment.

Chaos can come in a variety of ways: an attempt by a leader to impose order or structure on a group of people who do not accept his authority or his judgement; rash extemporisations to deal with problems piecemeal — rash because the work load of the innovators is already as much as they can carry; or wild extravagances in an attempt to maintain the impetus of the initial creative idea.

Alternatively, there is disillusion: the fun goes out of the adventure and exhaustion sets in. People begin to have misgivings, but sensible criticisms are seen as a betrayal of loyalty. Elizabeth Richardson in Bristol, who recently published a report of a three-year study of the process of change in an English secondary school,[1] defined 'loyalty' in this context as

> the conspiracy to maintain the pretence of omniscience in the leader.

Undoubtedly, one of the qualities needed in an innovatory group is the capacity to survive these periods of confusion, the capacity to tolerate uncertainty. But even though the group may be able to tolerate this stage, it cannot be assumed that other colleagues, or the pupils, or their parents, will be willing to accept that this is a natural stage in the process, that the darkest hour is before the dawn, that this is how solutions have to be worked out. Parents in particular cannot be ignored. In my own home town, within the past three months, an innovating headmaster, R.F. Mackenzie, author of *State School, A Question of Living* and other internationally famous books, survived the opposition of half of his staff but was eventually halted by the hostility of a group of parents, and he has been suspended and replaced.

The stage of confusion thus is often followed rapidly by the next stage, the backlash. Some event or crisis sparks off a public challenge, and the whole venture is suddenly on trial. The Russians launched Sputnik 1 in 1957, and the progressive movement in American education found itself under attack. An international evaluation survey might report, for example, that Australian education has lower standards than other countries, or a Commonwealth survey reveal differences between states; or, as has happened in Britain, a reading survey suggests that standards of reading have not improved over the past ten years and may even have declined; or a distinguished academic figure complains that his students are not as well prepared as they used to be; and the witch hunt is on. In a crisis, we look for persons to blame, and innovators are an obvious target for criticism. It is their own fault if they are not ready for this. Anyone who embarks on an innovation must think ahead to the time when he will be called to account. The challenge is inevitable in the long run, and he must be ready with his answer. It is therefore essential to build in from the beginning some system of recording what is happening, and some evaluation as a check on the effects. Generally, innovators tend to be suspicious when one talks of the need for evaluation. Educational experiments seldom have the dramatic pay-off which one can get in medical research with new drugs, or in scientific or technological research. The critical questions are: what form will the evaluation take? at what stage will it be applied? by what criteria will the decision be made?

So far, I have been trying to analyse the process of innovation, to anticipate the problems which it brings, and I have suggested four main waves of difficulty — the effort required, the anxiety aroused, the confusion created, and the backlash which follows. In this analysis, I have in fact already identified what I think are the three main requirements if we are to have successful innovation in the schools: support, involvement and evaluation. These are the three headings for the remainder of this lecture.... [However] it may already be too late. As I said in my opening remarks, there are signs that the attitudes of the public and of the teaching profession may be beginning to change, and that too many ill-considered experiments have drained away goodwill. There are symptoms (at least in Britain and USA) of 'innovation fatigue' among teachers. Constant attacks on conventional procedures have undermined teachers' confidence in their capacity to teach, and may even have weakened public confidence in teachers. The capacity for self-criticism is a valuable academic quality but it can be interpreted by the public as a confession of incompetence. The additional burden of constant changes may be the last straw in breaking the back of an overstrained and undersupported teaching profession. Somehow, we must build a provision for change, a capacity for growth, into our educational system. We are in the middle of a period of substantial and far-reaching educational change, and the question is not 'when will it stop?', but 'How can we ensure that the process of change is successful and not disastrous?' Innovation is not some troublesome irritant which will eventually disappear if we ignore it: it is our means of survival in a rapidly changing environment. Without change, unless we sustain an evolutionary growth in education, our schools will be like the dinosaur, unable to survive because it was unable to adapt.

The first part of the task, I think, is for us to understand better the dynamics of change. Understanding the dynamics of change will help us to manage the process more effectively. At present, we innovate in the dark. We know little about the impact of the changes we make — even less about whether that impact will endure.

The second part of the task is to develop structures which will promote innovation within the educational system, so that the system itself can be self-renewing. Some sociologists and some political thinkers will say that this is impossible, that any institutional system is inevitably reactionary and resists change. However, it is the quality of a living organism that it has this capacity to adapt; and this is the style of system towards which we have to work. To use the terminology of a recent OECD seminar in Lisbon, we are concerned to develop the 'creativity of the school', that is, its capacity to adopt, adapt, generate or reject innovations. (The word 'reject' was not included in the first draft of the definition, but was added later.) To be able to adopt new practices, to adapt them to suit the special circumstances of the school, to generate new ideas, and also to resist or reject those changes which are in conflict with the school's aims or unsuited to its conditions of working: what are the factors which determine the capacity of a school to do these things?

This is, in fact, a topic of world-wide concern, and it marks a significant change in the whole style of educational research. In Britain, both in England and Scotland, in USA, and Canada, in the Council of Europe, in Sweden and Norway, in UNESCO and OECD, as well as in Australia and New Zealand, the question of how to promote innovation in education has become a central concern of educational research. Instead of asking merely 'What kinds of innovation are needed?', we are asking 'How do we create systems which will generate innovations?', and 'How can we equip new ideas for survival, so that they can genuinely be implemented in the schools?'

I have suggested three headings: support, involvement and evaluation. Of these, support is the most important. Any human enterprise, if it is to flourish, needs a carefully planned basis of support services — funds, equipment, buildings, institutional arrangements, personnel, training, and so on. In the field of air transport, it is just over seventy years since the Wright brothers succeeded in lifting their bicycle-like contraption into the air for a brief minute; but today there are thirty flights a week between Australia and Europe, and twenty transatlantic flights daily from London. This is possible not only because of technical developments in aircraft design, but also because of the development of an intricate and sophisticated infrastructure of support service: airports, terminals, timetables, travel agencies, training programmes for staff, radar, air traffic control, international legislation, and, of course, the general public acceptance of the idea of air travel. In the RAF, in wartime days, we used to be told that it took ninety-nine ground staff to put one pilot in the air. How many supporting services are available to back up one teacher in his teaching role? In education we are at the stage of the Wright brothers, bicycle mechanics trying to get our contraptions airborne for long enough to demonstrate that their design is sound, and we need not be surprised that the onlookers are sceptical and show little enthusiasm for entrusting themselves to our products.

So, when the question is asked, 'Why does it take so long for ideas in education to be implemented?', or 'Why is there such a gap between theory and practice?', I suggest that it is because it takes time to develop the infrastructure which is essential to support innovation, and in education we have failed to pay sufficient attention to the development of supporting services. The term 'infrastructure' is borrowed from economics, but the metaphor is architectural. In education we have given too much attention to the design of the top floor, and it is time that we paid attention to other

7

parts of the structure.

We train people for educational research, and we train people for teaching, but between the two there is a 'middleman' role which has been seriously neglected. The whole process of research and development in education must be viewed as a complete and integrated system. If we consider the numbers of people involved and the expenditure of money and effort at each level, from research through innovation to diffusion and adoption, the structure should be pyramidal. At present there is a group of research workers at one extreme, the body of teachers at the other end, and very few people, stretched beyond their capacities and insufficiently supported by resources, in between. It is this gap that has slowed the pace of development, and has left us with feelings of ineffectiveness, isolation and frustration.

The weak link at present is in the middle, where a support system will need to be developed, with resources, personnel and provision for training. The three elements are interrelated: resources need personnel to operate them, and at all levels of education there is a need for training in the proper use of resources. The first function for a resource centre is to make teachers aware of what is already available, of the wide range of new materials and the very considerable experience that has already accumulated of how to use them and the problems which are likely to arise. This has to be done by personal contact and discussion, not just by books and newsletters: the situation of each school is different. There is fairly general agreement that resource centres for schools fully justify the expense of setting them up. Teachers are after all the key element in the process, and they are also the most expensive element: any provision which develops their effectiveness is the most economic form of investment in education. But though the idea of resource centres commands wide support, there is little agreement on what form they should take, the storage, maintenance and cataloguing of materials, their accessibility, how many centres are needed, where they should be located, how they should be staffed and who should control them. We have really made little progress beyond talk.

Within the school, the responsibility for the curriculum is the principal's and he must be helped to discharge this responsibility, firstly by appropriate training, and also by the provision of appropriate administrative support to deal with the routine clerical duties which at present absorb so much of his time. Again the situation is different for different schools, for large schools and small schools, primary schools and secondary schools, city schools and rural schools, schools with experienced staff and schools with high turnover, schools with disadvantaged children, and so on, My own view is that the principal's role is a key one, and the major problem is to persuade him (or to make it possible for him) to delegate some of his present managerial and public relations functions in order to leave time for this more important role. For this, he may need a different style of authority; but I shall come to that in a moment.

There still remains a need for other personnel for the special task of helping with the problems of innovation. The Americans have suggested the use of specialised consultants with research training and a university background; but it is too easy for such people to be out of touch with the real problems of a school. In Britain, the practice is to use local advisers or inspectors in a new role: there are far too few of such people to give real support, and sometimes they give it in the wrong way — or are interpreted as giving it in the wrong way. The danger is one that I suspect is familiar to you, that advisers may push their advice until it becomes concealed coercion. Naturally, advisers are anxious to justify their role, and they may see their function as converting teachers to the new orthodoxy which they think is favoured by the administrative directors. If so, they may be counter-productive, especially if they are part of the authority structure and have a say in promotions: then their effect is to weaken the school instead of supporting it. Their job is to strengthen the school's capacity for change, not to tell them what to do.

But I have already moved into the second of my three points, the involvement of teachers and of parents in the process of innovation.

If an innovation is to have any hope of being anything more than a passing novelty, then the teachers concerned must be involved from the start. And their involvement must be genuine, not just a matter of their being told what to do and why, but a proper participation in the planning and decisions. It is easy to say this, and commonplace nowadays, but actually to do it is a much harder matter. Teachers are not trained to take part in the planning of innovation; authority structures within schools usually limit the possibilities of delegation; and administrative procedures also apply severe constraints on what a school can do. We are beginning to learn how to provide for full involvement of the staff of a school, or at least to understand the problems in trying to secure it. I mentioned earlier the recent report by Elizabeth Richardson of a study of the response to change in a school where all the staff were involved in the project from the start;[2] and the evaluation of the Humanities Project of the Schools Council[3] suggests that the success of an innovation depends more on the relationships within a school than on the actual quality of the innovation itself.

The Karmel Report is less ambitious (possibly more realistic) in dealing with the question of involvement: it says:

> The effectiveness of innovation, no matter at what level it is initiated in a school organisation, is dependent on the extent to which the people concerned perceive a problem and hence realise the existence of a need, are knowledgeable about a range of alternative solutions, and feel themselves to be in a congenial organisational climate.[4]

This is a useful set of preconditions for success: recognition of the need for change, knowledge of alternatives, and confidence in relationships. I refer back to what I said at the beginning about the danger of using innovation as a solution to a crisis in a school. (Perhaps one might generalise to a warning against looking to innovation in schools for a solution to a crisis of authority in society.)

I also mentioned earlier how an innovation may destroy an experienced teacher's confidence and create anxiety. One reason for involving the teacher from the start in decisions and planning is that this preserves confidence and diminishes anxiety. Others have made the point more firmly — for example, Owen, former secretary of the Schools Council in England:

> The new idea which teachers think is peddled by the theorist or enthusiastic devotee for his own seemingly unintelligible ends, meets with coolness, suspicion and sometimes hostility. That which teachers make their own, on the other hand, quickly puts out strong roots and equally quickly flourishes in a variety of ways which go well beyond their originator's conception.[5]

This is a popular line of talk, but it glosses over the difficulties. As a recent New Zealand report observes:[6]

> Greater responsibility and freedom for teachers may mean a greater need to cooperate with other staff and with students and consequent loss of some traditional freedom. Relaxation in relationships between one teacher and his students creates a pressure on other teachers, and change in one school alters the status quo at another. It is necessary to try to anticipate the side effects of any particular innovation in order to maintain control over the situation and lessen the likelihood of tension and upset.

The solution, the report suggests, lies in 'the ability to ask for and take criticism', and in 'systematic well-planned provision to ensure interchange of ideas so that comment, judgment, condemnation or modification does not appear too threatening or destructive'. This is asking quite a lot. This is why the school must be the unit of innovation, and why the principal's role and the nature of his authority and relationships with his staff are so crucial.

There are obviously problems in providing teachers with the freedom to pursue their own ideas and their own initiative, and yet to incorporate this freedom within a responsible structure of an education service. There are even greater problems in securing the involvement of parents, but so little has been done in this respect that almost any progress at all would deserve the description of a 'breakthrough'. There is enough evidence — I have quoted one example earlier — to prove that any educational experiment must have the support of the community, or at least must command a sympathetic understanding from parents. The problem is that parents are generally a conservative — even reactionary — influence in education. I suspect that here we are up against a crisis in society, something far beyond the scope of the school, whether one calls it 'the generation gap' or 'the crisis in authority', a fear of loss of control over the powerful forces of youth.

The school is traditionally seen by many adults as a restraining influence; the principal should be a deterrent figure, a remote authority to stop youth from running berserk. Once we begin to analyse the dynamics of change in the school, we begin to open up some of the powerful tensions in the dynamics of social change, and this too is a problem which we have to examine, which will not go away if ostrich-like we merely shut our eyes to it.

Finally, there is the question of evaluation; and many of you who are familiar with the topics I have been discussing will know that this is the really controversial issue. I have no doubts myself on this: any innovation which does not include systematic provision for checking and reporting what has happened is pointless, a mere expression of protest against the establishment. The poor quality of evaluation is the weakest aspect of most of the present schemes for innovation, and, using the metaphor of the hearse, I think it may prove a fatal weakness for many of these schemes.

It should not be necessary to spend much time on why evaluation is necessary: the real issues are what kind of evaluation, what form should it take and who should do it. Why is evaluation important? Briefly, it provides a vital feedback of information to the innovating team on their strengths and weaknesses. It provides the basis for discussion; it strengthens the group's capacity for planning. Obviously also, other teachers should have access to evidence from which they can form a judgment on the worthwhileness of the idea: colleagues will not be persuaded by mere affirmations of faith. Parents too have a right to information: schools should be willing to undertake periodic stock-taking and make public the results.

What form should evaluation take? I know that the fervent campaigners for change and reform are suspicious of evaluation, and perhaps they have good cause to be. Evaluation in the past has often been applied in the wrong way, at the wrong time and with the wrong criteria. But there are new styles of evaluation which are being developed, and the attempt to devise a form of evaluation which can deal adequately with the assessment of innovation is currently one of the major areas of interest in educational research in Europe and North America as well as in Australia.

There is no single correct style of evaluation, but a basic principle is that those who devise and carry out a new idea should share in deciding how it should be evaluated. I think we can safely discard as inappropriate the original American model of precisely defined behavioural objectives, measurable outcomes, standardised tests and elaborate statistical analysis.

11

This was summative external evaluation: summative in that it was applied at the end (or sometimes only at the end of the initial stage); external in that it was done by a group separate from the innovators, supposedly neutral but often unsympathetic. Instead, we need a continuous or ongoing evaluation, built into the innovatory programme as an integral part of the team work. This is the model which was developed in the Schools Council Science 5–13 Project, and the Humanities Curriculum Project. The evaluator is an important member of the team, and he has one of the most difficult jobs to do. He is involved throughout, in the planning (to ensure that evaluation is possible), during the programme (to ensure that relevant records are kept), and at the end of each stage (to provide feedback to the team on their strengths and weaknesses). It is a pattern of formative or responsive evaluation.

Perhaps this may seem to allow too much freedom to the innovators. How do we deal with those who say, 'It is clear that there has been a change, we believe that it is a change for the better', or, 'We know from our day-to-day contact that the children are learning more effectively, and our statement of that conviction is the only valid evidence'? This is certainly part of the evidence, but the weakness of this style is that it denies to others the right to use their judgment — it withholds evidence. Evaluation is not only a judgment: it also sets out the evidence and reasoning which led to that judgment; and if evaluation is to be accepted as valid, we need to be sure that the evidence reported is a fair sample, and that the reasoning from it is logical, and that alternative interpretations have been considered and disproved. There is no necessity for statistics: recently published evaluations have included case studies, transcripts, specimens of pupils' work and so on. Evaluation is a form of communication, a sharing of the experience with others. Nowadays, expeditions into high mountains or jungle include a cameraman in the team: the choice of cameraman may be an important factor in winning public sympathy with the aims of the expedition.

There is a good summary of these points in the New Zealand report on curriculum change to which I referred earlier:[7]

When curriculum change is planned, is being implemented or is complete, it is inevitable that questions will arise: Will it work? How is it going? Was it successful? Evaluation is a complex process which not only involves comparing outcomes with intention during and after the change, but is also essential at the beginning . . . Evaluation is aimed at improving the curriculum and should be a continuous process present at every stage of curriculum development.

The road to reform is always uphill, but this particular road is steeper and rougher than most. The metaphors of the bandwagon and the hearse with which I started are both inappropriate. Change at one school alters the status quo at another, and nowadays communication recognises no national or state boundaries. Innovation is here to stay, and we must come to terms with it; and no one should underestimate the challenge and the difficulties which it presents.

I would like to conclude with two quotations. The first is from the Karmel Report, and it provides an effective summary of the argument:[8]

> If the nation's schools are to bear the responsibilities which seem . . . to be inescapable in a society such as ours, then many innovations will have to be made in the organisation and conduct of learning . . . The traditional process of change in Australian schools is seen by the Committee to have been characterised by the imposition of new policies from above on schools across-the-board. Pupils, parents, teachers, employers and the community at large . . . have played generally minor roles in the process. Emphasis has been placed on the substance of the change and on the conditioning of participants to accept its consequences, rather than on the enhancing and exploiting of the capacities of committed people to generate their own improvements. This widespread lack of concern with the dynamics of change . . . has led to a neglect of the fact that expensive resources — time, facilities and skills — must underpin the planning, implementing and consolidating phases of projects undertaken to improve schooling.

The final quotation is from another political adviser. In 1513 Machiavelli wrote:

> There is nothing more difficult to carry out, nor more doubtful of success, nor more dangerous to handle, than to initiate a new order of things. For the reformer has enemies in all who profit by the old order, and only lukewarm defenders in all those who would profit by the new order. This lukewarmness arises partly from fear of their adversaries, who have law in their favour, and partly from the incredulity of mankind who do not truly believe in anything new until they have had actual experience of it.

This 450-year old quotation shows that the problems of innovation are not so new after all. But perhaps, within the next few years, we may be better able than our predecessors to develop innovation as an integral part of the self-renewal of the educational system.

[The author wishes to acknowledge his debt to Barry Macdonald of the University of East Anglia for ideas included in the first half of the paper.]

John Nisbet

NOTES

1. See the extract from this study in this Reader, p. 170ff.
2. E. Richardson, *The Teacher, The School and the Task of Management,* Heinemann, (London, 1973).   1973).
3. B. Macdonald, *Beyond Evaluation,* Centre for Applied Research in Education, (Norwich University, 1974).
4. Australian Schools Commission, *Schools in Australia* (Canberra, 1973), p. 125.
5. J. Owen, *Education for Teaching* (1970).
6. *Improving Learning and Teaching* (Educational Development Conference, Wellington, 1974) p. 144.
7. Ibid., pp. 135—6.
8. Australian Schools Commission, loc. cit., p. 126.

The title and many of the ideas in the first part of this lecture were borrowed from the writing and conversation of Barry Macdonald of the University of East Anglia. The author acknowledges this debt and is grateful to him for permission to use these ideas here.

Part I

STYLES OF CURRICULUM DEVELOPMENT

2. THE STATE OF THE ART OF CURRICULUM DEVELOPMENT

Tony Becher and Stuart Maclure

From *Handbook on Curriculum Development* (unpublished mimeograph 'CERI/OECD' 1974).

[Becher and Maclure attempt to identify links between the techniques and organisation of curriculum development adopted by various countries and the systems for controlling the public curriculum which have been inherited from the past.]

Control of the public curriculum differs in important respects from one country to another. In the United States and Canada control of the school curriculum is decentralised to the local school board or in some cases the states. In the Continental European countries there are formal controls over the curriculum exercised by central government education ministries or, in the case of West Germany, the Länder education ministries. In England and Wales a complicated system of formal and informal constraints apply, with legal control vested in local government authorities and the voluntary (i.e. Church) bodies, who in turn have effectively resigned their controlling powers to the head teachers. They, in their turn, are limited in the exercise of their freedom by external examinations linked at the end of the secondary course to admission to higher education. And in many places there are still examinations at the end of the primary school which are used for deciding to which kind of secondary school children should be allocated.

Where the school curriculum is laid down centrally (whether by the State, province, local authority or school board) the formal document setting down the official programme may go into considerable detail (as in Norway and Sweden) or be limited to an outline syllabus (as in some of the German Länder). It will usually prescribe the number of timetable hours to be devoted to each subject and may, as in Scandinavia and lately in France, deliberately provide for a limited period of the week to be at the elective disposal of the school or the local school board.

It may prescribe the textbooks and other teaching material or set down a list of approved books and teaching aids from which schools can choose, with or without a further set of constraints being exercised at the local school board or local authority level on grounds of cost. Important indirect controls on the curriculum may be exercised in this way, especially if there is a division of financial responsibility between central and local government which provides — say — for teachers' salaries to be a charge on central government while books and equipment have to be paid for out of local funds.

It is usual for there to be a system of examination or grading by teachers at the end of the secondary school, linked to access to higher education. This, too, is a form of curriculum control, even if it is administered internally by the school. Because of the importance of the results — with competitive entry to more favoured faculties and institutions — the secondary leaving examination may also prove to be the point at which parents and the local community bring pressure to bear and exercise a conservative influence on the curriculum.

Many of the informal controls also apply to a country like England where, nominally, the curriculum is not subject to central government influence. The choice of books lies firmly with the teachers, but limitations on the amount of money made available by local authorities in the form of capitation allowances for the purchase of books and equipment, in themselves restrict the extent to which teaching materials can be changed at any specific time, and therefore the range of new materials which it is practicable to produce in connection with a curriculum development project.

For obvious reasons the techniques and organisation which a country chooses for curriculum development are closely related to the system for controlling the public curriculum which has been inherited from the past. There are discernible differences in curriculum development organisation between the countries with clear-cut systems for central control of the curriculum at national or provincial government level, and those where curricular decision-making is more diffused.

A series of groupings can be identified.

Scandinavia

Though there are important distinctions of emphasis and practice to be made between educational administration and curriculum development in Finland, Norway and Sweden, the points of similarity outweigh them to a marked degree, and it is fair to talk generally of a Scandinavian approach. In the first place, these are countries where curriculum development is seen as an integral part of a larger policy of educational reform.[1] The social and political objectives of this educational reform are determined by Parliament; they, in their turn, are part of a larger policy for the transformation of society as a whole.

All this means that the objectives of curriculum development, like the objectives of the schools and the curriculum generally, are outside the development process (though it may cause them to be refined in particular respects from time to time). It also means that there can be no sharp distinction between curriculum development and changes in the internal organisation of the school or the framework of relationships between institutions within which the school operates: hence in Sweden for instance,[2] a concern to study all the 'frame factors' which delimit what happens to a child's learning and social development; hence also a Government Commission now deliberating on the internal organisation of schools which, while not nominally about curriculum development, will become deeply involved in many of the matters which concern curriculum developers.

All three countries have a system of curriculum guidance which leads to the production of very full documents which are sent to individual schools and which constitute for them the public curriculum. In Finland inspectors are employed to supervise the application of the public curriculum within the schools, which are inspected at regular intervals to ensure that the official policy is being carried out. In spite of a shortage of inspectors, schools can expect to be inspected one year in three. In Norway and Sweden there are differences in the degree of detail in the different parts of the *Mønsterplan* or *Läroplan,* and differences, too, in the extent to which teachers feel bound by them. Some sections of the Läroplan have parliamentary authority and are mandatory upon the schools; others are advisory, expressing the conventional wisdom of the elite group of teachers on whom the National Board of Education rely. No doubt teachers find scope within these copious handbooks for selective quotation to support those aspects of official policy they prefer.

The published curriculum documents are the main instruments by which changes in the curriculum are, as it were, formally registered and transmitted to the schools. This would be so, were there no formal methods of curriculum development, as opposed to curriculum change.

The curriculum development function, therefore, has been integrated within the organisation of the government department responsible for the administration of the schools and the curriculum. In Finland the Experiment and Research Office is an integral part of the National Board of Schools. For evaluation purposes it calls on the Institute of Educational Research at the University of Tyvaskyla. In the case of Norway, the National Council for Innovation in Education is affiliated to the Norwegian Education Ministry.[3] It provides a separate administrative structure to take responsibility for approved experimental and innovative developments which would not otherwise be permitted under the administrative regulations of the Ministry. When and if an experiment or an innovation graduates to the status of an established practice, the ordinary regulations are revised to accommodate it and the first stage of the process of development is complete.

In this way the organisational and curricular changes implicit in the introduction of the comprehensive school were undertaken. Now the centre of gravity has shifted to the upper secondary school. It can be seen that a system of this kind is not without tensions between the NCIE and the rest of the Ministry — for example those which arise out of the attempts to innovate in the upper secondary school and their effect on the Council for Upper Secondary Schools, the traditional arbiters of secondary school policy (ex-teachers, now ministry officials, selected by the Minister). But the system has the merit of institutionalising these tensions and permitting movement to take place piecemeal, a useful device if the strain of whole-sale change is great.

In Sweden the process of curriculum development is inextricably caught up in the administrative techniques of the National Board for supervising the curriculum at every level. 'Heuristic' development leading to new curriculum materials takes place alongside the formulation of new syllabuses by simply assembling views — of inspectors on short-term attachment, of employers and trade unionists, of teachers and of academic observers. In-service training of teachers is closely linked to this — though not by any means only to this.

A bureau in the National Board is concerned with research and development and much of its programme is directed towards curriculum development, including sophisticated, social-science based studies designed to refine the process by which the larger aims of the curriculum are translated into the specific objectives of the subject curricula.

But while curriculum development projects of the conventional Research and Development kind, leading to the production of new curriculum materials (e.g. IMU mathematics), are an important — though perhaps decreasing — element in the Swedish system, this is by no means to be regarded as the 'typical' Swedish method. New curricula are as likely or more likely to be generated by a systematic and recurring process of taking thought, and by culling curriculum materials from a wide variety of already available sources, as by the production of new.

In the end, the Mønsterplan and the Läroplan become the curriculum brief and as important as such for the educational publishers as for the teachers. Once the brief is published, another round of curriculum development takes place on traditional lines as the publishers analyse it and seek authors capable of preparing attractive and popular text books in conformity with it.

More recently there has been an attempt in Sweden to decentralise some of the curriculum development activity. The mechanism for this has been for the NBE and local school boards jointly to set up 'development blocks' within groups of schools, involving a supporting team from a university or college of education. The block provides a means of trying out new methods, new materials, new ways of deploying time and resources — as, for example, in the Skellefteo projects on social studies, natural science and Swedish. These have worked on changes in class hours, the size of the teaching group, the introduction of extra teachers and visiting lecturers, and the mobilisation of additional, extra-scholastic, resources. The development block aims to spread the best practice by example, by staff movement and by the proselytising work of inspectors and consultants. Changes having been initiated in school practice, the expectation is that the materials will take care of themselves as publishers adapt to the demands of the market.

There is also an interest in decentralisation in Norway where the fact that there are no central government school inspectors in itself means that the 'public' curriculum is not 'policed' as closely as it might be. The Swedish 'development blocks' represent an attempt to bridge the gap between the 'public' curriculum and what teachers and their pupils actually pursue. They involve the teachers more directly in the process of development and they are as much concerned with dissemination and implementation as they are with the earlier stages of development. They are not exclusively concerned with the curriculum, as narrowly defined.

To sum up, therefore: the Scandinavian model of curriculum development organisation has the following characteristics.[4]

(i)   Curriculum development takes place within a more or less well-understood framework of socio-political objectives for educational reform as a whole.

(ii)   Curriculum development is therefore a subsidiary activity, geared to already determined objectives, and part of a comprehensive pattern of educational reform which is also concerned with the organisation of the school and the articulation of one institution with another in an educational system.

(iii)   Curriculum *development* takes place within a central government department, or similar body, which also has responsibility for the *control* of the curriculum.

(iv)   Curriculum development uses a mixture of experimental methods, *a priori* reasoning, negotiation and bargaining, and the collection of opinions from interested parties.

(v)   A need is recognised for a measure of decentralisation in educational administration including curriculum development, and this is leading to the creation of other centres of curriculum development located closer to the schools and involving teachers more directly.

France, Belgium, Austria and Spain

A second group of countries can be identified which have certain characteristics in common in respect of their forms of curriculum development organisation, present or putative. The limits of generalisation are quickly reached: it is not suggested that their education systems or the societies they serve are without important differences which affect curriculum development. In some of these countries self-conscious curriculum development activities are only in their infancy.

Tony Becher and Stuart Maclure

In France, on the other hand, a sophisticated organisation exists, staffed by a cadre of highly trained inspectors who have strong ideas about how the curriculum should develop and clearly-defined administrative techniques to carry out these ideas.

The overall control of the school curriculum in France lies firmly with the Minister of National Education. The national curriculum guidelines in each subject are drafted by a series of curriculum commissions, which now include (beside the specialist administrative staff and the Inspecteurs Generaux themselves) selected senior teachers and – in the case of upper secondary curricula – subject specialists from universities. The draft guidelines are referred for informal consultation, before final Ministerial endorsement, to relevant interest groups such as teachers' and parents' associations: but once endorsed, they are binding on all schools in the public sector. The guidelines include specifications of content to be taught, recommended teaching methods and approaches and the time to be allocated in the school's weekly timetable.

This bald description makes the system of curriculum control sound more rigid than it is in practice. There is certainly no truth in the *canard* that at any given moment, the Minister of Education will know by looking at his watch precisely which grade of pupils all over France will have reached which particular page in which standard textbook. The French, besides their reputation for Cartesian logic, have another (and contrasting) reputation as a nation of confirmed individualists. So while the overall curricular pattern is expected to be adhered to in general terms, there is room in practice for a good deal of individual variation in style from school to school and teacher to teacher.

Curriculum development, however, is not readily distinguishable from curriculum specification and control. Development normally takes place at national level through the work of the specialist curriculum committees, in the form of periodic revisions to the guidelines published for each sector of the system and for each subject (or, in the case of primary schools, broad grouping of subjects) taught in that sector. But the commissions themselves are not of course impervious to outside forces; it is always possible for an active pressure group (such as the syndicate of mathematics teachers), or even an active and influential individual, to bring about an eventual change in the way a subject is taught.

But since in France the educational system is indissolubly bound up with the political system, any organised attempt to modify the *status quo* is liable to get caught up in political controversy. Many of the movements for educational reform are seen as having left-wing affiliations: if the Minister shows too much sympathy with them, he is attacked on his right flank. On the other hand, if he proceeds on his own initiative, the innovative-minded teachers see this as an incursion on their jealously guarded autonomy. Although there are numerous pressures for change, they stem from diverse and conflicting ideologies, and tend to be cancelled out by the pressures of conservatism. The teachers' unions argue that better pay and conditions for their members are the sole prerequisites for educational improvement; most ordinary teachers prefer to avoid traumatic change by sheltering behind the real or imagined restrictions on their freedom (while nevertheless complaining bitterly about them); the treasury officials are reluctant to devote public funds to controversial innovations; and the political leaders hesitate to open the floodgates of change for fear that they will thereby unleash forces beyond their control.

Meanwhile, it is generally agreed that the schools are in a state of crisis, and that attempts have somehow to be made to work out a new structure within which educational researchers, policy-makers and teachers can work together in achieving agreed ends. A first step towards this new structure was taken in 1970, when the INRDP, the main official agency for curricular and other innovation was formed (together with OFRATEME, the national organisation for educational technology) out of the subdivision of the Institut Pédagogique Nationale. Its main function is research and documentation of a descriptive or evaluative kind: in this it collaborates with university-based research teams as well as with the administration and the inspectorate. It has also, however, taken a more active, developmental role, especially in connection with the major organisational reforms of the primary and the early secondary stages. The INRDP is itself a branch of the Ministry, and its task is therefore to help implement, rather than to question or challenge, official measures of reform.

The main challenges to national curricular assumptions come less from the INRDP than from the strong, and growing, private sector, or from grass roots consortia of state schools organised on a local or national basis — of which the long-established group of Freinet schools provides the most striking example. But, as in the Scandinavian group of countries, there is now a move away from immediate implementation of change on a nation-wide basis (where the consequences of any major decisions are so momentous that all but the most politically courageous of Education Ministers will shrink from taking them) to a more cautious and piecemeal approach. Thus, the INRDP is associated with a network of Centre Régionaux de Documentation Pédagogique, and with the evaluation of a number of pilot experiments in individual schools or experimental regions, as well as with the detailed implementation of reforms on a national scale.

This is probably the nearest French approach to the heuristic, as opposed to the traditional development model. For the most part, the task of spelling out national curricular guidelines in detailed classroom terms is left to the textbook publishers and their commissioned authors (usually experienced teachers, including some of those who serve on the relevant curriculum commissions). Teamwork in preparing curricular materials is still relatively rare, and trial of draft publications and revision in the light of classroom feedback is seldom systematically incorporated into the development process.

The average classroom teacher, although in theory free to develop his own approach within the framework provided by the national curricular guidelines, is usually content to accept the pattern worked out in one of the standard textbooks. There is — in contrast to the other countries in this group — no central list of 'approved texts', but the constraints of approval of each school's programme by the regional inspectorate ensure that all textbook publishers and authors adhere closely to the spirit of the Ministerial decrees. Indeed, these decrees are more studiously scanned by educational publishers than by teachers themselves, whose main concern is usually with the requirements laid down for the annual school examinations rather than with the curriculum itself. These examinations in their turn exercise a powerful constraint on the teachers' room for manoeuvre within the curricular guidelines.

The lack of an active and critical force for curriculum reform based on the teaching profession is a current cause of concern. Hence the move towards greater devolution of responsibility from the Ministry at the core of the system to the teachers at its operating surface. An example of this is the increased allowance of discretionary time within the weekly timetable — and the accompanying growth of interest at the Ministry in initial and in-service training provision. In the same spirit, the Minister of Education has decided recently to initiate a series of major consultations — involving educational researchers, teachers, administrators, parents and pupils — on the reform of secondary education.

The situation in Belgium is much the same as that in France, since the two countries share many of the same cultural traditions. The issues here are complicated by the language divide, which results in two virtually separate systems — the Flemish and the Walloon — existing side by side. But apart from the Catholic schools — which form the large majority of the state-supported 'free school' sector, and enjoy a certain measure of freedom for curricular experiment within the limitations of the state requirements for examinations — the educational provision is reasonably uniform between the two language groups. Women dominate the teaching profession in Belgium to a greater extent than elsewhere and, so it is said, are less inclined to take an active careerist stance than their male or female counterparts in less prosperous or less uxorious countries. Comprehensive reorganisation has been slower to take root here than in many other European systems, and the profession as a whole seems to have taken a relatively inactive part in planned curriculum change.

This is not altogether surprising, given that the traditional philosophy — a purer version of its French counterpart — holds the only worthwhile development to be that undertaken by the individual teacher. The curricular guidelines having been set by central committees of experts, the teacher is expected to adapt them to his or her personal interests and the needs of his or her own students. So every piece of curriculum innovation is by definition *ad hoc*, dependent on a particular context, and hence unique.

In accordance with this tradition, there is little systematic attempt by Belgian educationalists (many of whom are of international standing) to undertake curricular research and development. There is no equivalent to the French INRDP, regional centres or experimental schools.

The major current reform — related to the move to introduce a common curriculum at the early secondary level so as to defer selection by levels of academic ability — is sponsored by the Central Reform Commission of the Ministry for French-speaking schools, chaired by the Minister himself or his chosen nominee. This programme, in which schools enlist on a voluntary basis (though well over half the French-speaking secondary state schools, together with a substantial number of private and state-supported 'free schools', have enrolled since the scheme began in 1969) involves an active programme of teacher development through meetings, publications and collective discussions of educational aims, and is designed to encourage schools to take increasing responsibility for determining their own curricula. Another reform, initiated by the Ministry for Flemish-speaking schools, is concentrating on major changes in primary education. This programme, steered by a twelve-man commission (including inspectors and representative teachers from catholic, state and municipal primary schools) is now trying out and evaluating a variety of different teaching approaches in schools in four different regions of the country. In terms of curricula for individual subjects, the major reforms have stemmed from active academics and lively teacher associations in mathematics and modern languages.

Austria and Spain are currently at an earlier stage of the development process. In both countries — as in France and Belgium — the overall responsibility for defining the school curriculum rests with the Ministry of Education, which also controls the allocation of resources and authorises the textbooks and teaching materials which may be used by teachers in following the national curriculum guidelines.

In Spain, some measure of decentralisation has been introduced by setting up institutes for educational study (ICEs) in a number of universities. The task of the ICEs is twofold: to provide in-service training for teachers and to develop prototype curriculum materials. Both activities are, of course, pursued within the broad framework of ministerial policy. Attempts to reorientate the curriculum of the Basic School (giving greater emphasis to social goals and to the development of expressive and creative abilities), and to introduce more integrated secondary curricula in science and social studies, are in their early stages. Progress is likely to be gradual, since teachers are not accustomed to taking curricular initiatives and educational agencies at present lack the facilities and know-how to embark on substantial development programmes.

Austria is the subject of a more detailed case-study in Chapter 3 of this volume, so only brief reference need be made here to the current situation. The main innovative agency is the Ministry's Centre for School Experiments and School Development, set up on the recommendation of a

School Reform Committee appointed in 1969. The Centre has so far concentrated its attention on a comparative study of comprehensive and traditional forms of school organisation. This study has involved the development of teacher support materials in German, English and mathematics for pupils with a comprehensive range of abilities. The ministry is also carrying out a project whose purpose is to specify in more detail the objectives of vocational secondary education. The recently formed Klagenfurt Institute of Educational Sciences (an institute of higher education) is intended to become a major innovative agency, but is still in a developmental stage. There is at present no incentive for the majority of the teacher profession to participate effectively in the process of organized curriculum change.

In summary, the organisation of curriculum development in this group of countries has the following main features:

(i)   Curriculum development takes place within the central government education department which also has responsibility for the control of the curriculum.

(ii)   Curriculum development is regarded as an integral part of educational planning and therefore as subordinate to the overall planning objectives of the education system. But the social and political aims of education are not so clearly defined as in Scandinavia, and the connection between educational reform and the reform of society is less easy to discern.

(iii)   As compared with Scandinavia, there is less emphasis on experimental methods and more on *a priori* reasoning and on the collective wisdom of experienced people within the system.

(iv)   Textbook publishers play an important part in the development process, the published curriculum being in essence the brief used by publishers to produce teaching programmes. Team-based projects leading to the production of tested teaching materials constitute only a very small part of the total effort invested in curriculum development.

(v)   The inspectorate and specialist consultants play a central role in the traditional forms of dissemination and implementation.

Western Germany, the Netherlands, the UK, Canada and the USA

The differences between the educational systems of this group of countries are more immediately obvious than their likenesses. Each of the eleven West German Lander has its own system, organised along somewhat similar lines to those of Austria, France, Belgium and Spain. Many of the Provincial Authorities in Canada and of the local School Boards in the USA represent a fair degree of centralisation within a highly decentralised structure. In the Netherlands, a theoretically uniform national system is fragmented and weakened by strong religious and political divergences among the schools themselves. In the UK, a diversified system is bound together by a powerful network of external school-leaving examinations.

But sketchy caricatures of this kind conceal a number of significant similarities. These, taken together, constitute a strong family resemblance, at least in respect of the organisation of curriculum development.

To an outside observer, perhaps the two most striking characteristics of the German school system are on the one hand, the fierce suspicion shown by the Lander of any form of federal intervention in the educational process, and on the other, the high degree of respect accorded by society at large to academic research institutions.

Although the policies of the different Lander are to some extent harmonised by the Joint Conference of Ministers of Culture, they vary from one another in several important points of detail. For example, Hessen and the City-States of Berlin and Hamburg are politically committed to the comprehensive reorganisation of secondary schools; the other Lander are either equivocal or firmly opposed to such changes. Each state ministry has its own set of curriculum guidelines. In some the discretion allowed to teachers is relatively small; in others it is much greater.

Special agencies for research into curriculum or other innovations abound: some free-standing and supported by a mixture of federal, state and private funds; some based on universities; and some more directly under state ministry control. In many such institutes, the creation of academic theories is given greater emphasis than the conduct of practical experimentation.

In consequence of the first of these features — a jealously guarded state autonomy — the influence of the Bund (Federal) Ministry is largely limited, as it is in the USA, to the injection of additional funds to promote such innovations as may attract political favour at the national level. The amount of central funding is substantial and steadily increasing: in 1973 the total amount available for federal support of innovative educational programmes was DM70 million. Expenditure is in practice constrained, since each allocation has to be matched on a 50-50 basis by the Land ministry concerned. Nevertheless, a sizeable number of development agencies, experimental schools and individual curriculum programmes have been funded in this way.

In consequence of the second feature — the traditional Germanic esteem for academic research — the large majority of teachers are inhibited from direct participation in the development process. Anyone wishing to embark on curriculum change feels obliged first to pick a way through the dense and luxuriant forest of theoretical speculation — and this seems to deter all but the most determined explorers.

But although 'grass roots' development is discouraged not only by a traditional distrust of pragmatism but also by the growing recognition on the part of State curriculum agencies that their power may in this way be gradually eroded, a few outstanding local development groups survive. The most impressive and best known of these is probably the Bielefeld team, working under the direction of Professor von Hentig in the planning, staffing and organisation of a new comprehensive Laborschule, linked closely with an upper secondary Oberstufen-Kolleg. But many other experimental comprehensives now exist in various parts of the country: the main problem appears to be that their staffs have developed such a high degree of autonomy that it is difficult to encourage mutual co-operation between them on shared curricular problems.

As in the UK, the independent foundations — and especially the Volkswagenwerk Foundation — have played an important pump-priming role. A number of the institutes and programmes now supported by federal and state funds owe their existence to private funding of this kind. For example, a major secondary school science project based on Kiel University, and a highly sophisticated primary mathematics curriculum scheme under Professor Heinrich Bauersfeld at Frankfurt benefited from initial Volkswagen support. The same foundation, though now gradually withdrawing from the field of curriculum development, is currently supporting a variety of innovative programmes at the primary level, including one under Professor Klaffki at Marburg on the development of social attitudes, one under Professor Tütgen at Götingen on an integrated approach to science, and others concentrating mainly on the problems of socially deprived children.

Despite this considerable range of national and local activities — a recent survey by the UNESCO Institute at Hamburg identified well over 100 schemes of development of various kinds — there now seems to be a general air of disenchantment with curriculum development in Western Germany. This may result in part from the fact that many enterprises were set upon too small a scale to achieve an effective 'critical mass', and that others embraced with excessive enthusiasm the notion of 'teach-proof' curriculum materials. In any event, the present backlash takes the form (almost certainly over-idealistic in the national tradition, where teachers have little experience of freedom in curricular decision-making) of a vogue for open-ended, school-based experimentation supported by a new structure of local teachers' centres. One positive consequence of this change of fashion is a greater concentration than in the past on schemes for the professional development of teachers, both pre-service and in-service. The attendant danger may be that this becomes regarded as an adequate substitute for any critical attention to the curriculum itself or to the creation of learning materials other than those already produced by one or two enterprising and efficient publishers on the basis of a series of centrally-prescribed state curricular plans. The political impossibility of setting up any national co-ordinating and sponsoring agency for curriculum development may well aggravate this danger.

In the Netherlands, the national Ministry of Education — unlike that in England and Wales — issues general curriculum guidelines, albeit of a rather broad and permissive kind. It also centralises, through the Inspectorate and the official testing agency, CITO, the national system of school-leaving examinations. But the tradition of teacher autonomy is strongly entrenched, and the profusion of different curriculum agencies (subject-based national curriculum reform committees, separate national pedagogical centres for protestant, catholic and state schools, the national agency for educational research, the new regional pedagogical centres, and various university-based development teams) ensures that no one voice dominates the babel of developmental activity. When, in addition, it is remembered that the schools are divided at both the primary and secondary levels into three separate networks (state or municipal, catholic, and protestant), and further subdivided at the secondary level into vocational, normal, and academic sectors, it is scarcely surprising that curricular decision-making tends to become somewhat diffused.

The Ministry of Education is the main financial sponsor of curriculum development, though its activities in this respect are more reminiscent of the Scottish Education Department or the Schools Council in England and Wales than of, say, their French or Belgian counterparts. In other words, it tends to respond to initiatives within the system rather than prefer to take them itself. The influential primary mathematics programme, WISKOBAS, established in 1968 and based on the Institute for the Development of Mathematical Instruction — IOWO — at Utrecht (which was in turn initiated by active teachers and academics on the mathematics reform commission) provides one example of an officially-funded but semi-autonomous development. The more recent projects as in secondary school biology and physics — again deriving from the reform commissions in those subjects — offer further instances. (The physics project initiated in the autumn of 1972, is in fact funded by SVO, the official education research agency in the Netherlands.)

However, some major enterprises with a somewhat more theoretical and less pragmatic approach (such as the LEDO project in secondary school social education, based on Gröningen and Amsterdam, and the LOLA project, based on Utrecht) owe their support to university institutes of education. Others adopting a more market-orientated stance are wholly financed by major educational publishers such as Wolters-Noordhoff.

The growing Netherlands interest in heuristic curriculum development is reflected in a new concern with initial and in-service teacher education (though the organisational structure of the system has not yet adequately adapted itself to this), and in a sustained national debate on the various proposals put forward by the Commission on the Organisation of Curriculum Development (COLO) in 1971. The Commission suggested three alternative means of simplifying the fragmentary and unco-ordinated national pattern of development. Because of the multiplicity of vested interests involved, it seems probable that the weakest model — that of a loose federation of specialist committees and existing agencies — is the one

Tony Becher and Stuart Maclure

most likely to prove politically acceptable. But the prospect of any form
of national agency (inevitably calling for additional resources) may remain
in the balance throughout the present cut-back in the national educational
budget, which accounts for some 9 per cent of the GNP – the highest proportion in Western Europe.

Canada, the USA and the UK present a similarly untidy picture. In
marked contrast with the more orderly approach of the Scandinavian and
Latin countries (of which Austria appears to be an unofficial member),
there is a profusion of sources for curricular innovation and a corresponding profusion of educational goals. To take the Canadian province of
Ontario as an example, the Ontario Institute for Studies in Education
(OISE) acts as one major development agency, but the Ontario Ministry
in addition maintains ten regional offices staffed by professional 'program
consultants' who work with school boards in carrying out the provincial
curriculum guidelines. Many school boards also employ their own curriculum specialists; specialist teachers' associations play an independent role
in materials development; and private foundations such as the Canadian
Studies Foundation sponsor development in specific aspects of the curriculum.

As a result, teachers in this group of countries tend to be used to exercising some choice among a variety of alternative possibilities. Where they
lack the professional skills to do so wisely, attempts are made (often on a
better-late-than-never basis) to reinforce such skills by some form of
associated in-service training.

To conclude, despite the marked differences between their various educational systems and national traditions, this group of countries has the
following common characteristics:

(i)   The administration of curriculum development is not located
within the central education ministry. Curriculum development agencies are, for the most part, independent or quasi-independent of the
national or state education ministry, while drawing on central and local
government and foundations for their resources.

(ii)   This diffusion of curriculum development often coincides
with diffused curriculum control – the sharing of control with examination bodies and higher education institutions and the resulting increase in the number of points of entry into the curriculum development process.

(iii)   North America offers the supreme example of multiple goals
in educational reform, giving rise to multiple agencies for curriculum
development. Most of these agencies extend far beyond the jurisdiction
of any single school board. Every known approach can be found in one
U.S. or Canadian model or another, without any clear consensus about
objective.

(iv)   In all these countries the objectives of curriculum change are not pre-determined by nationally defined objectives for social reform though they will certainly reflect heightened national concern about topical issues — for example inner city problems, or racial strife, or community development. In contrast with the Scandinavian and Latin traditions, curriculum development is, in the main, a response to a generalised dissatisfaction with the failure of what the schools do now. That is to say, curriculum development is a stimulus to educational reform rather than the product of it.

(v)   Both heuristic and traditional techniques can be found operating side by side, with relatively more examples of heuristic, project-type essays in curriculum development than in the other two groups of countries. Production of teaching materials has been an important part in this development, alongside the activities of educational publishers with a keen eye to the directions in which development projects point.

(vi)   The UK has produced in its Schools Council[5] a compromise within this general pattern — a central agency for curriculum development, controlled by interlocking committees which reflect the distribution of power over the curriculum in the schools. This is connected to the main instrument of curriculum control, the examination system, but is precluded by convention from backing the products of its development work with any more authority than the schools themselves give them on their merits.

NOTES

1. See P. Dalin, *Strategies for Innovation in Education* (CERI) for a full discussion of the process of innovation and the relationship of curriculum development to other aspects of education reform.
2. See Sixten Marklund, *The Role of the Teacher in Educational Innovation in Sweden* (CERI).
3. See Sixten Marklund and Eskil Bjorklund, *National Council for Innovation in Education* (CERI).
4. This account seemed too tidy and idealised for one Norwegian expert who writes: 'There is some lip service in the Northern countries to the idea that educational reform should serve the purpose of changing society, maybe most marked in Sweden. Yet, looking at what really happens to the curriculum in this process, I think the most one can say is that there is an attempt to correct some of the most obvious biases inherited from the past, in order to reduce somewhat the distance between reality as conceived by most people today, and the picture of reality provided by the school. There is a long way to go even to cope with the task of catching up.

    Many of us would like to be radical, but the relatively few instances of genuine radicalism in the Scandinavian school systems are nearly always locally inspired, and somewhat embarrassing for the "middle of the road" policy followed by official authorities. In an international comparison, this may of course be something, but too much emphasis on the "changing society" policies of the Scandinavian countries could be rather misleading.'
5. See John Nisbet, *Schools Council* (CERI).

3. CURRICULUM DEVELOPMENT IN ENGLAND

J.G. Owen

From P.H. Taylor and M. Johnson (eds.), *Curriculum Development* (N.F.E.R., 1974).

[Owen, in reviewing curriculum development in England, posed four questions: who are the people who bring about any development within the curriculum? what kind of decisions do they make? how do they implement their decisions? what might prevent certain decisions from being put into effect? Owen is cautious about the extent to which the curriculum may be changed in the next decade.]

History lends depth to any description of the process, purposes and problems of curriculum development. The longer the time-scale, the clearer is the picture of differing influences which move the work of schools in specific directions from age to age.

In England, those influences on curriculum which can be identified are a mixture of certain kinds of thinking by individual philosophers, of good practices by particular teachers and of the regulations of central government.

Not all the forces which have had weight are visible; immeasurable and virtually unverifiable effects such as those of parental expectation or the requirement of employers or the even vaguer needs of particular communities and of the larger entity of society — these, too, have left their mark.

Each influence has in one way or another contributed to the meaning which is attached to curriculum in England at the present time. This amounts to saying that a hidden ideology is at work. Within this are included the effects of a long culture of education, of a broad range of definitions of human happiness and a readiness to accept the private nature of life — or at least to accept modes of living which do not have to conform to explicitly defined norms or to highly specific requirements laid down within regulations of state.

The ideology, whether hidden or not, is indefinable but all-permeating. It allows deviance within recognisable limits; it helps to produce, in the end, a near uniform sense of Englishness. Yet in England the idea that curriculum might be totalitarian is something to shudder at. How can you, after all, have sameness, or even random comparability in the curriculum of schools in which the constant boast is that teachers are autonomous?

The answer lies in the probability that behind the English illusion the facts are rather different. Reality is most clearly seen when one looks at the way in which teachers receive their professional education. For instance, those who train teachers can never give completely free rein to their own ideas. They are limited by the things that English society expects a school

— and a teacher — to achieve. Teachers have to prepare children to pass examinations, to become good citizens, to become employees who work hard and who become part of a social scene where honour and truthfulness, loyalty and love, trustworthiness and reliability are qualities of value.

Teachers have also to try to ensure that children are helped to become — or are not hindered from becoming — adults who have sensitivity, political balance, sound ethical judgement, wit, courtesy and honesty.

At the same time schools are expected to promote children's respect for the spiritual and religious values of their society as a whole as well as of individual members of that society; they are expected to affect their pupils in a manner which diminishes bigotry and prejudice, which promotes tolerance while not encouraging excessive permissiveness and which continually requires children to learn how to test the limits of their experience and their feeling. Teachers, in short, must help children in a great variety of ways to grow — socially, spiritually and intellectually.

Although it must try to take account of each of these needs, the process of professional preparation also has to recognise the importance of the personality and intellect of individual teachers, their maturity and their capacity to interpret their experiences. But at the same time these factors belong to the realm of human nature and are influenced less by training than by the mere passage of years.

In England the emphasis on the personal nature of a teacher's contribution to his job affects the definition which is given to curriculum. Because official requirements are not codified there is a natural temptation to assume that the teacher's own choice of what to teach and how to teach is all-important.

But teachers change from generation to generation; yet the curriculum of English schools is something which is considered to be highly stable. From this we have to assume at the very beginning of any definition that autonomy, freedom of choice and the muted nature of official voices do not have the dominance which is sometimes claimed.

Go back, then, to history. The official voice was first heard in the 1830s, in matters affecting central government grants to denominational schools. Grants were made on specific conditions. In the 1860s, these were spelled out more clearly. In the 1870s the requirements, although they were less explicitly stated, had a broader effect; it was from that time that the major effort dated to devise a system of compulsory education.

In the first decade of this century, the official definition of what schools were expected to do extended from elementary schooling to the beginnings of secondary education. By 1920, the influence of officialdom — although not stated in that way — was stronger because it had begun to express itself through the medium of syllabuses for public examinations. Then, until the 1940s secondary school curriculum ran the risk of having life choked out of it as syllabuses became more refined, more demanding and less open to individual interpretation. At the same time primary schools, too, were subjected to tight demands of examinations for the purpose of supporting the selection of pupils for one or other of three classes of secondary school.

When the major English statute was enacted which governs present-day education (the Education Act of 1944), educational thinking had nearly succumbed to the idea that three types of secondary school meant that there were three intrinsically different types of child — and that there were not only three types of intelligence but also a category of curriculum to match each one.

From 1950 until the present day, movements of change in secondary education have produced the idea of a comprehensive secondary education which matches the comprehensive (that is, undifferentiated) nature of English primary schools. As the programme of switching to comprehensive secondary education has gained ground, so has the meaning of curriculum changed.

It has not changed in a way which is altogether radical. Rather, it has transformed itself in the education of children aged eight to sixteen years into something which is comparable to the curriculum which has, since the 1920s, applied without challenge to the education of children aged five to seven years. It has, in brief, reverted to a pattern which above all attempts to recognise potentials and differing stages of readiness for the next phase of learning.

Like any swing in fashion, the movement of curriculum towards a largely child-centred view of the school world has, in some definitions, gone too far. It has gone far enough, for instance, to ignore (or forget) that education until mid-adolescence or late adolescence is a matter of initiation. Adults in their own way know what their world will require of those who are growing up. Unavoidably, that part of compulsory education which is concerned with initiation into the adult world has to be adult-centred. An all-encompassing attempt at child-centredness in the curriculum is therefore likely to be illusory.

[Sections I and II omitted]

III

Differences in the approach to an activity create distinctions of style. Style in itself is a label which carries a load of vagueness. Admittedly what is vague can be refined if a number of more specific questions can be answered. Who are the people who bring about *any* development within the curriculum? What kind of decisions do they make? How do they implement their decisions? What might prevent certain decisions from being put into effect?

These four questions in themselves deserve several large studies to be devoted to them. But more brief answers must be attempted: who, first, are the people who bring about any development of curriculum?

The answer, in England, starts in a deceptively simple way. The teacher is the major figure. But the way in which he changes what he does day by day (which amounts to a crude and simple but perhaps accurate definition of curriculum development) depends on his own experience and on what other people will expect of him. Like any other professional whose training is bound (in the process of teaching him to work with people rather than with things) to overlook, leave out or simply not think of certain human situations, he will sometimes feel that his training was incomplete. He will seek models of what to do. The most reasonable model lies within his own experience. His own teachers and tutors, the methods by which he learned or by which he was instructed — these will be the paradigms to which he will first turn.

If the teacher looks for models or for guidance in the present day rather than in his past experience he will pay attention to what others expect of him. What others expect can be expressed in a number of ways — by the head of a school, by the head of a subject department or by parents.

Parents are only slowly becoming respectable in the sense of being allowed to ask questions about curriculum. But they have, of course, been arbiters for a long time of the repute of a school and of particular teachers. And whether or not they are openly acknowledged, parents are certainly visible out of the corner of the eye of the average teacher in England.

Less openly acknowledged is the influence of the employer; perhaps the acknowledgement is less open because it is less readily recognised. For if education after all lacks a specific purpose in training for a job or for filling a niche in society or for fulfilling a particular role in the state's pattern of manpower demand, it is excusable that the employer should be regarded as an outsider. But this is, of course, precisely what the employer is not — at least once the formal business of education is over. He himself can be open to the pressing demands and recriminations of commercial customers, trade unions and government boards. But in turn he wields a predominant influence over individual lives. And he casts his shadow before: in anticipation of the employer's actual demands children will (through what has been said to them largely by their families) expect their work to need certain qualities, skills and attitudes.

As formative as the demands of employers are those of whatever happens to be the next stage of education. If the pupil stays at school beyond the minimum leaving age in England, he usually enters the Sixth Form, that is the sixth and seventh years of secondary schooling. He stays on in school either in order to gain an examination qualification of the elementary type (Certificate of Secondary Education or General Certificate of Education at Ordinary Level which he failed at the age of fifteen years) or to push his qualifications further in order that he might qualify for entry to a university, or to a course of teacher education, or to certain courses for a higher accreditation in polytechnic colleges or colleges of further education.

These latter qualifications are, at school, usually enshrined in syllabuses for the General Certificate of Education at Advanced Level. The syllabuses (in the same way as those at the younger and more elementary stage) make up the curriculum of pupils at school. In addition to a collection of syllabuses their education does, of course, include more. But the core of expectations which teachers have to satisfy at these stages is made up of syllabus demands which are imposed by other people.

Part, then, of the answer to the question of who are the people who bring about development within the curriculum lies amongst parents, amongst those who themselves taught the teachers in an earlier generation, those who are employers and those who make up the examination boards which define syllabuses for differing stages of qualification.

Qualifications and examinations are inseparable in any attempt to define the style (and the style-makers) of curriculum in England. An elitist, sharply differentiated society which survived beyond the Second World War has gradually given way to a supposedly broader development of popular democracy, of mass information and of pretensions to mass participation in matters which affect government, public expressions of taste and broad-ranging expectations of social behaviour. But behind the popular image of present-day English society it is noticeable how well-guarded are the doors to positions of power, influence and cleanly-earned money.

The history of academic examinations in England — as a procedure of administration and as a means of producing a series of graduated hurdles — is well documented (Wiseman, 1961). At this point all that needs to be said is that the teacher as a participant in curriculum development is much affected in the secondary school by those requirements which are laid on him in the name of examinations.

Are there other, less obvious requirements imposed on the major participant in curriculum development? Yes, and in the name once more of external influence.

In addition to public examinations, the range of constraints laid on teachers in secondary schools includes the influence of central government in matters which, at first sight, do not bear on curriculum. [The influence of central government over the curriculum is more fully discussed in the article by Fowler, page 59.] For instance, the physical state of a school — its area and juxtaposition of classrooms, workshops and other teaching spaces — can have a significant effect on curriculum construction. Another influence, which can sometimes act as a constraint but at other times be totally constructive, is that of the number of teachers who can be employed.

Both the physical dimensions of schools and the number of teachers who work within them (and hence the size of pupil-groups) are matters which markedly affect how a curriculum is constructed. The effect is certainly indirect since government policies which control school building programmes and teacher supply are affected by economic as well as by political considerations: these factors are seldom regarded as directly relevant to education in a broad sense or to particularities of curriculum. What else is affected by central government? Most obviously the items of schooling which can be quickly changed are those which are amenable to alteration by regulation. If the government of the day wishes to alter the shape, colouring or emphasis of schooling it issues official guidance, usually in the form of a document which is circulated to all local education authorities. Such circulars carry high potency. Thus, when in 1965 one government asked local education authorities to produce schemes of comprehensive secondary education, a sharp change of policy in terms of curriculum as well as of school organisation was the consequence. A *volte face* by another government — in 1970 — reversed this process and placed yet another influence on curriculum.

In 1973 one circular asked local education authorities to produce schemes for a large-scale provision of nursery education. This means that primary education needed to change its centre of gravity: instead of a six year curriculum, schools now had to re-jig their programmes of early learning — and particularly of reading and of early maths — in order to take account of the flying start which the majority of children would have by entering nursery education on a part-time basis at the age of 3½ years.

Equally important in effect on curriculum was another circular of guidance in 1973 which defined methods for implementing another central government policy, this time for the expansion of educational opportunities into the university sector beyond the age of eighteen years. Here again, by retaining certain minimum qualifications of entry into post-school courses at the same time as it broadened the range of non-degree work which would be available to 18-year-olds and 19-year-olds, the government of the day placed new curricular responsibilities on schools. And the teacher as a participant in the process of development again became the servant of other people's policies.

To change the organisation of schooling and to alter the type of accreditation course which might, at the college stage, follow schooling has a more or less direct effect on what is taught. But methods of teaching can also be touched by policies of central government: to teach in a capacious, well-equipped school of modern design is sometimes thought to be more conducive to experiment and novelty in the curriculum than the task of teaching in a physical setting which is older and less blessed with the presence of modern aids.

This argument can be over-played but there is still much truth in it. If a new curriculum calls for something other than the rigid timetabling of teachers to fit classrooms which in turn are to fit fixed sizes of pupil-group, difficult and compartmentalised buildings will be a hindrance. Thus the physical envelope of teaching, within which many factors of time, light, space and noise matter almost as much as the question of whether there is simply enough room, can affect a school's curricular energy.

The same can be said of the teaching ratio. Although the sorting out of pupils and teachers is ultimately a matter for the head of school, the possibility of running a system in which small groups, mass lectures, seminars, individualised learning and large group work came together within one school day depends on how many teachers are available overall to individual schools. If the supply of teachers is not adequate to allow flexibility in deciding the size of pupil-groups (or if there is not enough accommodation to fit a variety of methods of teacher deployment), experiment in curriculum can be held up. To delay experiment might, in the longer view, be beneficial. But in short-term and medium-term policies of trial and error, limitations of space and of the number of trained teachers can be a considerable impediment. Again, the teacher cannot be entirely free from central government policies – however indirectly they might touch the daily task of teaching.

Equally indirect in its effect on curriculum change in England is the shift which can be seen from decade to decade in policies of teacher-training. These policies are by tradition better known to colleges of education, university institutes and departments of education than to schools and schoolteachers. Nevertheless, decisions, for instance, to concentrate effort on the training of teachers of junior pupils (eight to eleven years) and secondary pupils (eleven to sixteen) can react unfavourably on the supply of teachers of infants (five to seven years) if the concentration of resources starves other training courses. Too few teachers might be trained or their training might be less than adequate.

Again, to try to concentrate resources of teacher training in such a way as to counteract a professional shortfall amongst teachers, for instance, of mathematics or of religious studies creates another type of distortion in teacher supply. The effects are, once more, indirect but the position of the teacher as a controller of curriculum development might clearly be altered by shifts in large-scale training policies.

The participants in change go, then, well beyond the teacher himself. Curriculum in England is indirectly affected by tradition, public expectation, government policy and government economics. But curriculum is also affected by such ready-made teaching materials as are available to the teacher. That which is commercially published, its cost and its manner of presentation matters a great deal. Thus, publishers and their textbooks, writers and their experimental materials, school suppliers and their own policies of selection also matter. Indirectly, they too become participants in the process of change. They are free from official structures; their choices of what to make available to teachers are governed by the market.

In contrast to these random, sometimes unplanned and often inconsequential activities, the teacher occasionally hears the voice of the speaker of supposedly pure truth from the research field. In England that voice is seldom loud. Research is not broadly commended and it is perhaps even more a matter of surprise that it does not often advocate its own credibility. But it exists and it is generally well written-up. That it lacks influence may lie less in its self-commendatory nature than in the difficulty which teachers find in having access to it.

IV

The nature of decisions which are taken about curriculum development has five aspects: the political, state-originated alteration which swings curriculum in the direction of favouring younger children or of expanding higher education speaks for itself. The nature of decision-making is part-political, part-economic, part-social and part-pedagogic. The nature of the decision could, presumably, be more exactly described in light of the advice or influence which led to the first formulation of the policy. This, however, is generally concealed.

Secondly, decisions about curriculum which indirectly stem from policies about teacher supply or about the economics of university-based as against non-university expansion of post-eighteen education – these could be claimed to be political but more obviously economic in their origin. Economics here would be brought into play on a large, national scale.

Third, there are social decisions. To raise the school leaving age might be an economic or a political decision (to take young workers out of the labour market, to reduce competition for jobs and to allow national statistics of unemployment to appear less grim), but it could also affect the degree to which future generations of parents would be better educated – and hence better capable, one would hope, of giving their own children fuller support in the process of being schooled. To create a new curriculum for those who might, in the first years after the compulsory raising of the school leaving age, be reluctant to stay in school, presents a fresh challenge to re-awaken interest, to provoke the involvement of pupils and to reveal the significance which schooling might have for a child's later life.

A fourth range of decision is connected with this same idea that curriculum development might re-awaken an interest in learning. But instead of reluctance, here we might see curriculum development as harnessing itself to the enlargement of educational opportunities for those who, either in themselves or through their parents' eyes, *wish* educational opportunity to be enlarged. To provide a new curriculum for those in the sixth and seventh years of secondary schooling in England (that is, in the Sixth Form) calls less for inventiveness or fresh interest than for a capacity to lead a larger number of young people through to the lucrative opportunities which lie before them in institutions of higher education.

Fifth and last come those decisions about curriculum development which have their roots not in politics or economics, not in social improvement and in the enlargement of opportunities but, instead, in the pedagogic ingenuity and insight of teachers. In contrast to those large-scale decisions which fall into the first four categories, the attempt to develop an improved curriculum at the teacher's own level is a matter of individual decision. The nature of decisions in this domain is coloured by the needs and capacities of individual pupils, by the situation of (and support locally given to) particular schools. At this level, the nature of decisions about curriculum change depends above all on the quality both of the leadership which a Head can give to an individual school and on the quality of individual teachers.

Within these five broad categories of decision, those nuances of curriculum development which, perhaps, matter most in England are more firmly connected with the means by which improvements are implemented than with their points of origin.

V

The implementation of any plan for curriculum development is a process which is often described as clean and orderly, with aims which are clearly delineated and results which are accurately verified.

Not surprisingly this type of description is sometimes too clinical. It misses the confusion, irresolution, uncertainty and carelessness of human activity. It also misses what has come to be known as style — and the differing styles which belong to the personalities of people who are involved in the job of development. Because differences of style make an inevitable impression it is fallacious to presume much for the perfection of models or to pretend that the people who are involved in development can ever be less than predominant in their influence — whether for success or for failure.

Plans nevertheless have to be laid; they have to assume that those who put them into practice are rational and well-intentioned, that they understand what plans are for and that they have the intelligence and will-power to ensure that things do not go too wrong. On this basis are laid the variety of strategies, programmes and schemes which are made by those agencies which are involved in reform.

The major distinction which is drawn in the implementation of reform lies between national and local effort. On a national scale, the impact of improvement stems from several sources. It can come from advisory publications of the Department of Education and Science (aimed at schools) or from stronger directives of guidance from the same source (aimed at Local Education Authorities). It can emerge from surveys of current practice in schools — conducted by national inspectors of schools and again published by the central ministry. Or, again, it can result from social surveys of the practices of school and of the expectations of parents, teachers and children — surveys which although they are conducted by a central agency which is not controlled by the Department of Education and Science nevertheless carry, in integrity and forcefulness, considerable persuasiveness.

In national terms, too, centrally-initiated projects of the Nuffield Foundation or of The Schools Council have a broad effect, directly on schools. Here the force of persuasion is not that of official *fiat* but of well produced, heavily researched and widely tested materials and teacher guides. No commercial interest is involved other than that of the publishers of the materials. Another form of influence comes from the British Broadcasting Corporation through schools broadcasts (television as well as radio). In these there is a distinctive element of helping, and perhaps of retraining, the teacher. There are also series of combined radio-television programmes which are aimed directly at teachers, for the purpose of in-service training. The Independent Broadcasting Authority and the commercial companies also transmit child-aimed school programmes.

The BBC in particular clearly combines the job of publishing with that of devising new approaches and materials which can have a substantial effect on curriculum.

This is roughly the same position as the Department of Education and Science holds. The Department surveys certain parts of the curriculum field and issues survey reports which are formative as well as informative. It also makes regulations and publishes circulars of guidance to local education authorities about school building programmes, about the number of teachers to be employed, about the pay of teachers and about large innovations such as the introduction of broad-scale nursery education. Each of these can create alteration in curriculum and can act as a force in the process of development.

A different position is held by commercial publishers: they may indeed publish for Nuffield and for The Schools Council. More often they will publish the work of private people — in the form of textbooks, non-book teaching materials, guides for teachers. They will act within the process of implementing improvement because they hold England's longest tradition as diffusers and because they are acknowledged and trusted by schools for the materials which they market.

The means of implementing change lies partly, then, within nationally handled schemes of research and publication; points of origin may be ministerial, reform-orientated (Nuffield) or commercial. Also on a national scale, the work of certain voluntary associations of teachers is important in implementing change. The National Association for the Teaching of English, the Association for Science Education, one or two powerful groups in the maths world — these too have an admittedly less formal but still deeply felt effect on the thinking and on the practices of teachers.

Associations are not likely to attempt large-scale strategic change but their own surveys, courses, and publications will be devised in such a way as to shape a programme. And programmes or packages of new work which have clear purposes and a step-by-step approach to the teacher now stand a better chance of being taken up than the isolated textbook. Thus, the commercial publisher is involved in putting out material which is programmed rather than random and concerned as much with a worked-out educational purpose as with commercial speculation.

But to implement an improvement depends on needs, more than on publication. Teachers will alter, develop and change their practices more readily and efficiently only if they believe in what they are doing and if they have been given the chance to become involved in bringing about that stage of change which lies within their own schools and their own class-rooms. This requires schemes of training — and of retraining — in new materials. It also means that teachers should be given the chance to think about what they are doing and what they might do as a new alternative.

If a new approach to moral education is put forward by, for instance, The Schools Council, teachers who are involved in those subjects which bear on religion and social education, on history and on literature need to satisfy themselves on the judgments and assumptions about values which a new project will entail.

But questions of value enter less obviously into a project for the improvement of, for instance, technical studies or of elementary engineering in schools — or at least *moral* values are not so heavily involved. Other values have still to be weighed: the teacher has to balance known benefits against potential gains before he alters his teaching. Values have to be assessed which are connected with the purpose of learning. A judgment once more has to be made — based on factors which relate directly to the job of teaching and less directly to the personal beliefs and personal style of thinking of the teacher himself. But whichever kind of judgment has to be re-assessed, whatever stimulus or purpose is involved in the judgment, a course of in-service training assists the teacher by reducing his isolation and by letting him learn from the mistakes as well as the successes of other people.

Implementation of curriculum development in England relies heavily, then, on retraining. This takes many forms — arranged by national inspectors, by local inspectors or advisers, by university schools of education, by colleges of education, by local teachers' centres, by the professional associations of teachers, and by project teams within the large development programmes of The Schools Council. Courses vary in length and in method. They employ differing types of experts and tutors. They involve teachers to differing degrees in their own training. And, of course, they differ very much in the way they are regarded by teachers: there are few common criteria for assessing the usefulness or success of courses. But there is much more agreement about the forces which help curriculum development to flourish or to go forward only slowly. The good influences and unwanted constraints are, in the English picture, easy to spot.

VI

The resister, the phoney, the man with but a single idea, the excessive cynic, the proceduralist, the universalist – each of these acts in constraint on development. Those things which amount to blank resistance or well-mannered apathy, fake enthusiasm, obsessiveness or continuously corrosive lack of belief in the *possibility* of benefit in the process of development, each of these most obviously checks improvement at the level of the individual school.

Outside the school and within the local education authority what used principally to impede development was an unwillingness to take a chance in helping groups of teachers or individual schools to venture on experimental work. If additional money was needed for materials or for visiting, for an extra part-time teacher or for access to other schools, even a rich Authority found it difficult to find the right rules within which to give the type of encouragement that was needed.

Gradually, new rules have been made. Most local education authorities now set aside funds specifically for the purpose of fostering curriculum improvement. Advisers have been appointed whose job this is; teachers' centres and their wardens have come into being.

Had new rules not been made then aids to development would not have been forthcoming. The desire to stick to old procedures would have held things up – as indeed they still do in certain areas of England. At national level, a comparable alteration in procedures has allowed for a great growth in government-sponsored in-service training and, in particular, in the development of continued in-service training schemes between the Department of Education and Science and universities. Money, expertise, repute and good sense can come together – and exercise a demanding but benign influence on development work at large.

The good influences are as easy to identify, then, as the bad. They have their points of origin in many places. Changing approaches to the initial training of teachers, different modes of handling teaching practice and the induction of new teachers into their first full job, changes in the methods by which curriculum and teaching are organised within schools as well as changes in the outward organisation of schools (by introducing nursery education or by setting up middle schools or comprehensive secondary schools), all these make it easier for the review and renewal of what is offered to and learned by the child.

A more detailed picture of the checks and spurs on curriculum development has been drawn elsewhere – and has already been drawn many times and in different ways. Because there is already a comparatively large literature about curriculum development in England – when it had barely begun in 1964 – there is the risk that those who are responsible for development may become too self-regarding. This, in turn, can lead to complacency, to fatigue through the over-use of particular ideas or to the kind of nausea which descends on one when the repetition of ideas reveals only their pallor and inadequacy.

But while the history of curriculum development is still young it is perhaps easier to pick out the good and the bad. It is easy, still, to look back to the originators of reform — to Brian Young and Tony Becher at the Nuffield Foundation and Derek Morrell, Philip Taylor, John Banks and Jack Wrigley at The Schools Council. It is remarkable to see, too, how quickly the cast-list grew and changed in the early years, to trace the influences which people have carried with them into the basic fabric of English education after some direct (and usually national) involvement in curriculum reform.

Constraint on improvement always has to be regarded as something to be rid of: occasionally, while curriculum development moves fast and far in its early years in England, it is possible to sense that mere fashionableness and the vogue for change may do more harm than good.

But behind this fear there is considerable achievement too in an education system which had been largely static in terms of curriculum change for many years. That achievement lies in the creation of a climate of thought which is interested in but not bemused by novelty. This in turn has made government, at both central and local level, more ready to find those resources which planned changes need. From this practitioners have been given the confidence of seeing curriculum development taken seriously. And given that confidence, the major influence of benefit in implementing reform is the readiness of teachers to devote time and energy to the job of professional improvement.

[Sections VII and VIII have been omitted]

IX

Curriculum development is meant to produce change. It can be planned and some of its outcomes can be foreseen. But it differs from other kinds of development in rather obvious ways. Changes on the whole are not a matter of design, are not activities to which a known end can be hoped for, nor are they matters of startling and radical discovery which are likely to change men's view of the world at large.

Education changes slowly, shapelessly and in a way which is more or less uncontrolled. The management of it is not a matter of dealing with hard fact, clear aim, established policies, brilliant scientific rivalry, nor is it something which often receives acclamation within the public domain at large.

If education in England improves, develops, changes or differs in any way from decade to decade, it is because particular people in particular fields have had the patience, good fortune, insight and good experience which is necessary to make them credible when they wish to commend something new to other people.

The Education Acts which govern England and Wales affect the curriculum of children from below the age of five to young people of about the age of eighteen. There are definable segments within this age range and teachers have loyalties, experiences and preferred ideas in each sub-division.

Curriculum development at its most practical is concerned with an education service which offers schooling to a carefully defined range of pupils. The definition of the age and type of student makes things workable. It also means that when those who manage curriculum development wish to appeal to teachers who are responsible for providing education in its most direct form in classrooms, they have to be aware of the particular audience to whom they speak. Teachers are part of a publicly controlled system: their loyalty, when change is mooted, is to principles of professionalism rather than simply to ideals of better learning.

Thus, in the context of England's statutory service the development of curriculum is a matter of manageable and definable things or persons. The persons are parents, teachers and children. Curriculum development will not work unless those who are parents of children in schools present sufficient support and understanding at home for the work of schools to have some bite. Curriculum development will not work if teachers are not trained to expect that their role will change, that their task will need overhauling every five years or so, or that their outlook on what is meant by professionalism will be subject to both informed and unenlightened influences during the entire period of their working life.

Children matter because curriculum in the end is intended to ensure that they become better people than those who were educated before them. If curriculum is simply meant to provide a repetition, generation by generation, of comparable attitudes, similar expectations and identical capacities to fulfil roles within the industrial or social world, then the idea of development need not be raised in any way. But the larger system of social and economic expectation in which the education service is placed is further away from the teacher in the classroom. His relationship to the bigger system is indirect.

Apart from people, the manageable parts of the curriculum deals also with resources. Money matters because it can provide better education both initially and in terms of in-service training for teachers. Money matters too, because it can provide better buildings in which children may carry out their learning and, also, that essential part of the process of curriculum development, namely the provision of a physically identifiable teachers' centre. Money also matters because it can buy materials which directly affect children's ways of learning. But the financial system behind education is something to which the teacher is only indirectly connected.

Conclusion

If the future of curriculum development is confined to quite simple definitions of practical matters affecting people and resources, the outlook may appear fairly bleak. People can be changed (even if we could skilfully use the ill-judged idea of social engineering) only slowly. Resources, too, can be increased year by year only in a very marginal way. There is little room for manoeuvre. There is little that can be quickly added to the repertoire of the developer. And there is not much that he can expect by way of greater direct assistance from those who can change the professional preparation of teachers. If, therefore, he is to manage anything it has to be confined to matters of attitude. Yet we know that it is illusory to speak about attitude change as though it were something which in itself was concise, definable, or capable of being planned.

The education service provides the bare bones around which to create the body of curriculum. There is ample room for despair about the speed of change, about the depth of its effect and about the measure to which it is possible to avoid abuse of that which is new. Yet, as in all public activities, it is unreal to expect that things can be neat and tidy. Curriculum is dependent upon so many variable factors and upon so many differences of experience, training and attitude that the process of development faces an almost impossible task.

Those who are responsible for development have to be aware not only of the various ways in which people can do things systematically within their own field but, also, they have to remember the weight of human experience. They have to have sense, maturity, an awareness of the history of educational change, and above all to have patience and a faith in people. They have to know that it is unreal to expect rapid change or to assume that people will take on fresh attitudes of value overnight. And they will also know that to stand back — aghast, apathetic and lethargic — will achieve nothing. They have to balance enthusiasm with common sense, knowledge with zeal, experience with hope.

If local government reorganisation in England places rich and poor local education authorities together, money will have to spent for a decade in reducing disparities and in trying to equalise basic items such as capitation allowances, grants to pupils and expenditure on school apparatus, equipment and books. If the spending of money has to be made consistent in the process of creating uniformity where it previously did not exist, the expansion, improvement and development of education services cannot be afforded.

In the immediate future the system of education in England will, then, not radically change nor is curriculum development likely, in the next ten years, to flourish.

As a background to development we need constantly to be aware that there is no inevitability about the progress of curriculum development. Equally, there is no inevitability about the way in which teachers may be expected to alter what they do. Teaching is a profession in which much depends, as in other professions, on the integrity and energy of the individual member.

If a teacher knows that there are new ideas afoot, if he realises that the method, content, purpose and style of teaching is under review, he will act unprofessionally if he does not take his own steps to find out and think about what is new and then act — and whether he acts in acceptance or rejection matters less than that he should have devoted honest thought to the problem. Hence, the basis of curriculum development has to be trust that the teacher knows where he needs help. He may only need slight stimulus or some added confidence; he may need only a little fresh information before setting off on his own quest.

Curriculum development, educational reform and the overall improvement of schooling can eat up any amount of energy, skill and money. If, however, the *statement of problems* is sufficient, if teachers can be trained and expected to see a continuing responsibility to monitor their professional performance and the efficiency of their professional equipment, they will find their own method of self-renewal. Resources would then cease to go in one direction. And the emphasis on retraining which starts from sources outside the teacher himself would diminish. The traditional resources of education could be used to stimulate and to interest teachers, to provide a variety of non-training aids and to provide a milieu in which the person's own sense of responsibility would be a paramount force. Instead of the continual repetition of one type of answer (that of formalised in-service training) to the question of how best to promote improvements of curriculum, the creation could begin of what has sometimes been called a learning community.

The shape and focus of such a community would change from time to time. The most essential part would shift from being sometimes within a school to a college of education to a teachers' centre, to a research unit, to a library — or to discussion and to private reading on the part of the teacher himself. The provision of money for the organisation of development and training would pay less attention to fixed systems than to the possibility of catching needs, teachers' readiness, inclinations, time and energy at the moment when these could best be directed to one purpose.

If a future pattern of development could reflect more of the sense of change by which we usually learn, review and reform any part of our professional way of life, there would be no need to look ahead to steadily mounting costs and to the steady exhaustion of sources of leadership. Leadership would matter less than stimulus and inspiration — and these could come from a number of different directions.

At the same time curriculum development has to be something which means a great deal to the teacher. It has to offer hope to those who have faith in the total effects of education and it also has to be something which does not pose questions about extremes of unreality. Those who have a responsibility for curriculum development have to know the limits of change. They have to see what it is that change requires of people.

Time may show that curriculum and the extension of reform within it is likely to be a permanent concern for those in English education. At present we can only assume that this will be so. But the assumption is as

J.G. Owen

yet too tenuous to support a heavy structure of planning and rationalisation.

NOTES

I am indebted to the Cambridge University Press for permission to draw extensively on my book *The Management of Curriculum Development* (CUP, 1973).

REFERENCES

Blackwell, F., *Primary Extension Programme*, Council for Educational Technology, London, 1970.
Central Advisory Council (England), *Half Our Future*, HMSO, London, 1963.
Halliday, M.K., *Linguistics and English Teaching*, Nuffield Foundation, London, 1964.
Hirst, P., 'The Contribution of Philosophy to the Study of the Curriculum' in Kerr, J.F. (ed.), *Changing the Curriculum*, University of London Press, London, 1968.
Kerr, J.F., *Changing the Curriculum*, University of London Press, London, 1968.
Mackay, D., Thompson, B. and Schaub, P., *Breakthrough to Literacy*, Longmans, London, 1970.
Musgrove, F., 'The Contribution of Sociology to the Study of Curriculum' in Kerr, J.F. (ed.), op. cit.
Richardson, E., *The Teacher, the School and the Task of Management*, Heinemann, London, 1973.
Schools Council, *Raising the School Leaving Age*, Working Paper no. 2, HMSO, London, 1965.
Schools Council, *Moral Education*, 13-16 Curriculum Development Project, London, 1967.
Stenhouse, L., 'The humanities curriculum project', *J. Curric. Stud.* 1, 1, pp. 26-33 .
Taylor, P.H., 'The Contribution of Psychology to the Study of the Curriculum' in Kerr J.F. (ed.), op. cit.
Taylor, P.H., Reid, W.A. *et al. Purpose, Power and Constraint in the Primary School Curriculum,* Macmillan Schools Council, London, 1974.
Wilson, J., *Reason and Morals*, Cambridge University Press, London 1961.
Wiseman, S. (ed.), *Examinations and English Education;* Manchester University Press, Manchester, 1961.

4 CURRICULUM DEVELOPMENT IN NORTHERN IRELAND

H. F. McMahon

Adapted by the author from an article in the *Journal of the Irish Association for Curriculum Development,* Vol. 3, no. 1, 1974, pp. 3-6.

[McMahon detects a growing sense of personal autonomy among curriculum developers in Northern Ireland — a trend away from dependence on central initiatives, whether by the ministry or by the Schools Council, towards the development of locally-conceived solutions to curriculum problems.]

There are no peaks of Darien in Northern Ireland from which to view 'with eagle eyes' the panorama of curriculum development and change. All I can manage is a view from the lower slopes, from a point of vantage which is perhaps sufficiently high to allow some of the major features of the landscape to be seen, but not high enough, it must be said, to yield an all-embracing vision of the changing scene.

My eye, like that of most observers, is caught by the slight but sudden movement which stands out against the backdrop of the more permanent features of the landscape. One such eye-catching event took place quite recently at a meeting of the Northern Ireland Schools Curriculum Committee. This Committee of the Northern Ireland Ministry of Education has been in existence since February 1969, and had as its terms of reference 'to advise the Ministry on Northern Ireland participation in Schools Council projects and on the dissemination of information about the Council's work'.[1] After four years of existence the Committee recently reviewed its terms of reference and agreed that its revised objectives should be 'to encourage local curriculum development and innovation and to provide a channel for Northern Ireland participation in appropriate Schools Council projects and such other curriculum activities as seem desirable.'[2]

On paper the change is little more than a re-ordering of the functions of the Committee, seemingly a very minor event in the curriculum arena of Northern Ireland, but in my view this simple change draws attention to and symbolises one of the most significant movements in curriculum development in the North, and that is the growing autonomy of the curriculum developers, whoever they may be. Both individually and collectively, the inspectorate, the local authority advisers, the headmasters, the teachers and the academics increasingly assert their independence from the British scene and deploy their skills in the solution of the special problems of Northern Irish education with a new sense of individuality, authority and purpose. There have been many examples of independent action in the past and there will no doubt be instances of blinkered dependence on externally developed curricula in the future, but the trend is undoubtedly from dependence to independence, from following to leading, from accepting the supposed universal panacea to developing the unique prescription.

Traditionally the education system in Northern Ireland, like that of the Republic, has been centrally orientated. Teachers have accepted the existence of a hierarchy of control and authority and have looked upwards for initial specification and subsequent clarification of the curriculum. The vehicles of communication from the centre have been the detailed examination syllabuses, the programmes of study and the examination papers so familiar to us all. Our job as teachers has been to translate the syllabus to the satisfaction of the bureaucracy in the person of the inspector, and to persuade the pupils that the translation was accurate, in both letter and spirit. For the latent curriculum developer looking for a way of accelerating change within this system, or breaking out of it altogether, the arrival on the educational scene of the 1960s of the Nuffield Foundation and the Schools Council seemed almost a new dawn, a promise of liberation beyond one's dreams, and for a time the danger existed of replacing the unquestioned authority of the Ministry of Education syllabus or examination by the equally unquestioned authority of the British curriculum development project.

But special problems require special solutions, and it is not surprising that the first major locally initiated curriculum development project was in the field of community relations, and that in this context there has been a gradual and more recently an accelerating movement in the direction described. The first major 'grass-roots' response to the political and social upheavals of 1969-70 came from the Association of Head Teachers in Secondary Schools and resulted in the setting up of the Northern Ireland Project on Community Relations in the Schools under the direction of Mr J.M. Malone, at that time Headmaster of Orangefield Boys' Secondary School, Belfast, and now at Queen's University, Belfast. The June 1970 issue of the Northern Ireland Schools Curriculum Committee News Bulletin includes an early report of the work of the project, and coincidentally in the same issue are first reports of the participation of Northern Irish schools in no less than six Schools Council projects. Seen in juxtaposition the significance of contrasting approach is evident. All six Schools Council projects are directed from outside Northern Ireland with limited Northern Irish participation in their control through membership of co-ordinating and consultative committees. In contrast the Northern Ireland Project on Community Relations in Schools, while basing much of its work on existing Schools Council projects such as the York General Studies Project, the Keele Integration of the Humanities Project and the Project on Moral Education, nevertheless relies exclusively for direction and control on locally based educators and reflects this in its energetic approach to the unique and pressing problems facing teachers in the schools of Northern Ireland. Since 1970 there has developed an increased commitment to research and development in this area of the curriculum, with no fewer than five projects in operation at the time of writing. The most recent to be established is the Schools Cultural Studies Project, based on the Education Centre of the New University of Ulster and directed by Professor M. Skilbeck. This project[3] has been funded by the Rowntree Charitable Trust and the Northern Ireland Community Relations Commission, and for this area of the curriculum its establishment represents the final stage in the weaning of Northern Irish curriculum development from the tenuous and remote, but nevertheless ultimate controlling influence of the Schools Council.

But clearly I have chosen as an example of this trend from dependence to autonomy an area of the curriculum where the Northern Irish situation is very special, if not unique, and where locally initiated curriculum change would be almost inevitable. What of areas of the curriculum where one's expectation might be the opposite, where the renewal of the school curriculum is a response to the development of a discipline, and where in the eyes of the teacher the rapid changes in the social and cultural environment of the pupils are of much less immediate relevance? In such cases one might expect that local teachers would be content to follow the lead of the prestigious Schools Council and Nuffield projects as they tended to do in the past. This has certainly not been the case as, for example, can be construed from Dr M. Brown's report on curriculum development in physics in Northern Ireland.[4] Here, the practising teachers of a subject relatively insulated from the rapid social change of the country have, with the help of the staff of the universities, carried the development at school level of at least one element of their subject beyond the stage reached by the corresponding Nuffield project.

I have mentioned so far only two areas of the curriculum where the trend towards autonomy exists, but a reading of the more recent issues of the Northern Ireland Schools Curriculum Committee News Bulletin shows that the movement is more broadly based than may be implied by the limited number of examples touched upon. Reports on several locally initiated, school-based projects, a Community Service Project, a Resources for Learning Project, a Nursery Project, a Six Schools Project, are presented, and a special issue is devoted to the widespread development of teachers' centres.

The last five years have seen the creation of the infra-structure of teachers' centres and personal communication networks which are so essential in the support of an interactive style of curriculum development. Increasingly decision-taking is being shared by a wide group of educators at all levels and in all sections of the educational system. The traditional authority figures have begun to share responsibility, to advise and support small groups of teachers as they carry out the difficult tasks of analysing their existing curricula, developing new materials and assessing their effectiveness. The focus is moving to the school,[5] and teachers are being confronted by the challenge of change towards a more complex role arising from a re-definition of the educational function of the school. This in turn demands an analysis of contemporary culture in Northern Ireland and of its future development, so that the criteria for the selection of the aims of the school can be the more firmly based. Indeed the challenge is even greater in that the teachers are being asked to become the agents of change, to assume an active role in the transformation of society and the construction of a just and creative culture in Northern Ireland.

P. McConnellogue's research on curriculum influences on Northern Ireland primary schools [6] concludes that the majority of teachers still look towards the central authorities for control in the curriculum. Perhaps they would welcome firmer direction from above, but the difference between the 1950s and the 1970s is that those to whom they look are no longer prepared to direct and control from afar. They and many others throughout the system have cut their curriculum development teeth on Nuffield and Schools Council projects and are now weaned and ready to assert their recently won autonomy, not in the exercise of central power through hierarchies of remote control, but in the hurly-burly of interactive decision-taking in the teachers' centres, schools and classrooms of the country.

Recent studies have shown that life in Northern Ireland schools over the last five years has thrown up new and pressing problems and crystallised and exposed to view the problems that have always been with us. [7] The existence of a caucus of experienced curriculum developers at all levels and in all sectors of the system and their growing commitment to an interactive style of curriculum change suggests that the grassroots movement fostered by the Association of Head Teachers in Secondary Schools back in 1969 will continue to gather strength and to permeate the system as a whole.

The one major danger that remains is that energy will be dissipated through piecemeal adjustments of particular elements within the curriculum and unco-ordinated change throughout the country. The integration of change into some form of meaningful whole will involve the co-operation of institutions supporting curriculum development at both provincial and local level. The former exists in the form of the Northern Ireland Schools Curriculum Committee, but in the still early days in the lives of the Area Boards it is in the development of these local curriculum development units that we have yet to see what support structures will emerge at local level. Perhaps we in Northern Ireland have something to learn from experience in the Republic of Ireland. For example, the work of the Dublin Vocational Education Committee's Curriculum Development Unit could prove to be of major interest in this respect. [8]

NOTES

1. Northern Ireland Schools Curriculum Committee, News Bulletin, No. 1, May 1969.
2. Ibid., No. 14, June 1973.
3. *The Education Times,* Vol. 1, no. 4, 17, May 1973.
4. M. Brown, 'Towards a New GCE Physics Syllabus', *The Education Times,* Vol. 1, no. 18, 20, September 1973.
5. M. Skilbeck, 'The School and Cultural Development', *The Northern Teacher,* Winter, 1973.
6. P. McConnellogue, 'Curriculum influences on Northern Ireland Primary Schools', *Journal of the Irish Association for Curriculum Development,* Vol. 3, no. 1, 1974, pp. 7-10.
7. H.A. Lyons, 'The Psychological Effects of the Civil Disturbances on Children', *The Northern Teacher,* Winter, 1973; J.M. Bill, 'Environmental Stress and Educational Outcomes', op. cit.
8. A. Trant, 'Educational Innovation in the Irish Republic', paper presented at the OECD/CERI Seminar on School-based Curriculum Development, New University of Ulster, Coleraine, 1974.

5 CURRICULUM DEVELOPMENT IN SCOTLAND

John Nisbet

From *Journal of Curriculum Studies,* Vol. 2, no. 1, 1970, pp. 5-10.

[Nisbet describes the work of the Consultative Committee on the Curriculum — the Scottish equivalent of the Schools Council. The use of small working parties and curriculum committees has been generally preferred to the more elaborate procedures favoured by the Schools Council. The manner of working may be seen as peculiarly well suited to the Scottish situation.]

The danger of making comparisons is that one easily falls into the trap of exaggerating differences. Examiners, with their fondness for the 'compare and contrast' type of question, know only too well what ingenuity can be used in discovering distinctions where none exist. Similarities can be over-looked because they are too obvious . . . The temptation is not merely to describe the differences which exist but to try to explain them.'[1] The pattern of curriculum development in Scotland is certainly different from that in England, and it is tempting to explain the contrast in terms of differences, in both size and character, between the educational systems of the two countries. Scotland is a small country, with only some 3,180 schools supported wholly or partly by public funds. Its educational system is more tightly knit: over 98 per cent of children attend the public schools (in the literal and Scottish use of the term). The smaller unit can function on a less formal basis, for consultation takes place between people who know each other and meet together frequently. In consequence, some changes can be introduced quickly and easily. Revision of the secondary school mathematics curriculum in Scotland began in 1963; in 1969 over 70 per cent of schools are being examined on the new syllabus, and in 1970 the figure will be 98 per cent.[2] Another consequence is that the process of change is seldom adequately documented, so that it is difficult for those outside the system to know precisely what has happened. Two recent publications have helped to fill in the details of recent developments. In *Scottish Education Looks Ahead,*[3] the Senior Chief Inspector has outlined the machinery of change in Scottish education, and two members of the inspectorate have described the changes in English and mathematics. The *First Report* 1965-8 of the Consultative Committee on the Curriculum gives a comprehensive review of the whole range of curriculum development in Scotland,[4] and provides an opportunity to make comparisons with the Schools Council report, *The First Three Years.*[5]

The Consultative Committee on the Curriculum is the Scottish equivalent of the Schools Council. In both Scotland and England, a considerable amount of work on curriculum development was under way before any formal national co-ordinating body was set up. But whereas the Schools Council was established with a large measure of financial and administrative independence, the Scottish Consultative Committee is a Committee of the Scottish Education Department, with the Secretary of the Department as its chairman.

The Consultative Committee, as an advisory body with no executive functions, has no staff of its own and secretarial services are provided by officers of the Scottish Education Department. The work of enquiry and curriculum development has been carried out 'almost wholly by HM Inspectors and teachers in schools, colleges of education and universities.'[6] Perhaps appropriately, the Scottish arrangement would appear to be economic of funds. Costs are absorbed by other parts of the educational system, but if they could be separately accounted, it seems likely that the total cost of curriculum development in Scotland would fall well below the traditional eleven-eighteiths, which used to serve as a basis for the ratio of Scottish to English expenditure on education. Whereas the report of the Schools Council lists research projects costing a total of over two million pounds, the report of the Consultative Committee does not mention money at all.

The twenty-four members of the Scottish Consultative Committee on the Curriculum are 'appointed as individuals – for their personal knowledge and experience – rather than as representatives of particular organisations'.[7] However, it is not by chance that nine of the members are teachers in schools, together with one from a technical college and one from an art college, while four are from the inspectorate and two are officers of the Scottish Education Department (the Secretary and one under-secretary). The Principals of three of the ten Scottish colleges of education are members; in Scotland, the colleges of education are financed directly by the Scottish Education Department. The other four members are: a director of education, a professor of chemistry, a professor of French and a banker. The Committee is thus very much an organ of the central authority in partnership with the teachers. At least the teaching profession cannot complain of over-representation of outside interests or of domination by the universities. For its independence and freedom of action, the Committee must rely on the independence of mind of its members, and on the frequent and consistent disclaimers by the Scottish Education Department of any wish to encroach on the teachers' freedom in curricular matters.

The Committee's terms of reference require it to maintain a general oversight over the school curriculum, both primary and secondary; (and) to draw attention of the Secretary of State to any aspect of the curriculum, whether general or particular, which seems to call for consideration by specialist bodies . . . Neither the Secretary of State nor the Scottish Education Department has any direct responsibility for the school curriculum. Education authorities . . . acting with the advice of the heads of their schools and their teachers, decide what shall, or shall not, be taught in their schools . . . and it is for them to decide whether or not to accept any advice which is offered to them.[8]

But the essential guarantee against interference by the central authority is the method of working which the Committee has adopted — the small working party, comprising a majority of practising teachers and inspectors, with college of education lecturers and occasionally a university teacher or other adviser. In 1955 the first working party on this model was set up to review the curriculum of the senior secondary school. The recommendations of their report in 1959 led to the introduction of the Ordinary grade in the Scottish Certificate of Education in 1962. Previously, memoranda of advice on the curriculum had been drafted by the inspectorate — for example, *The Primary School in Scotland* (1950), *Junior Secondary Education* (1955) and a series of papers on individual secondary school subjects issued between 1950 and 1961. This was the basis also of the memorandum, *Primary Education in Scotland,* which was published in 1965. Increasingly, however, the working party structure has been favoured, and more than twenty such groups have been formed in the past ten years.

A description of the work of one such group is given by A.G. Robertson,[9] formerly HMI and chairman of the Mathematics Syllabus Committee from 1963 to 1968. The appointment of the Mathematics Syllabus Committee followed from a report by a previous Departmental committee on mathematics, which had reviewed recent changes in university honours courses in mathematics. The new committee was given both a broad remit and a precise task: 'to review the school mathematics syllabus and to initiate in a number of schools experimental work on the introduction of certain aspects of modern mathematics.' The committee comprised fifteen teachers of mathematics in secondary schools, two principal lecturers in mathematics from colleges of education and four inspectors; later, three university lecturers were added to the membership. In April 1964, twelve months after its formation, the committee published draft syllabuses for the O grade in mathematics of the Scottish Certificate of Education. An experimental text with teachers' notes began its trials in fifteen pilot schools in session 1963-4, and the following session forty-five other schools joined in the experiment, thus involving a total of some seven thousand pupils. Seven books were planned to cover the three and a half years of study to O grade. Book I was written in the spring of 1964, printed in the summer and used in the experimental schools in the autumn. The remaining books were written in quick succession, two more being added eventually to take the course up to Higher grade (Scottish

fifth year of secondary school). In-service courses and the supply of appropriate equipment to schools were also organised. Robertson[10] describes
the task involved:

> At any one time from 1964 to 1968 then, the committee was re-
> vising one book, testing the subsequent book in the series, and
> writing the one to follow that. Most chapters for the experimental
> book went through three or four draft stages before being accepted
> by the group as a whole. The committee met about six times each
> year, held several two-day conferences, and worked through sub-
> committees from time to time. Debate and discussion were often
> strenuous, sometimes heated, but rarely acrimonious; the endpoints
> in the syllabus construction and associated writing were invariably
> compromises between the various extremes and shades of opinion.
> A reasonably close liaison between the Syllabus Committee and the
> sixty schools was maintained over the years by means of visits, con-
> ferences, questionnaires, newsletters and correspondence.

The resulting series has had international success,[11] special editions being
prepared for Australia, South Africa, Holland, Germany, Sweden and
Norway.

A number of working parties on this pattern had been set up before the
appointment of the Consultative Committee; others have been appointed
since. Some deal with subjects in breadth, English, science, classics, art,
physical education; others with specific aspects, decimal currency and the
metric system, computers and the school; others again with the specific
applications, modern studies for non-certificate classes, and integrated
science syllabus as a common course in the first two years of secondary
education.

In the field of English, a more extensive network of activities has been
established. The co-ordinating body is the Central Committee on English,
appointed in 1966 with eleven members (four school teachers, two university professors, two college lecturers, two local authority advisers and
an inspector as chairman). Their remit is to 'promote research and development in the teaching of English at all levels'. The Central Committee has
seventeen local development committees, which in turn have set up study
groups to deal with particular aspects. To improve communication and act
as a clearing house and resource centre, the Centre of Information on the
Teaching of English has been established in Moray House College of Education, Edinburgh, with college staff serving on a part-time basis. This Centre
issues regular newsletters one of which provides a detailed description of
the Central Committee's activities.[12]

It will be clear from this account that the various working parties and
committees differ among themselves in their organisation and procedure,
so that it is difficult to write in general terms about curriculum develop-

ment in Scotland. In some subjects, physics, chemistry and mathematics, for example, syllabuses have changed substantially — and, most would agree, for the better. Curricula in other subjects, such as geography, have been changing without the aid of any formal curriculum development organisation. New ideas have been put forward in classics and English: whether these will affect the content of teaching in schools seems to depend on the content of future SCE examination papers more than on the persuasion of teachers. In other subjects, working parties have not yet had time to produce reports. But the production of reports is only the first step in the process of curricular change, as the *First Report*[13] recognises. 'There must be some follow-up locally and nationally, if in the end the work of teachers in all parts of the country is to be influenced and, the Committee hopes, improved, by the changes and developments proposed.'

Curriculum development, however, is slow in arousing genuine involvement of teachers, though Scotland is not unique in this problem. Perhaps the Scottish educational pattern is too authoritarian at heart, so that it is unrealistic to expect teachers to show initiative or to do anything other than wait for a strong lead from the centre. With the concentration of effort in the hands of small working parties, one looks in vain for growth at the grass roots. Provision for discussion and development of the reports issued — through local groups in teachers' centres and through in-service training — is still far from adequate. Also, some of the reports are of a kind which is hardly likely to stimulate discussion. Built up from the experience and considered opinion of practising teachers, they can readily encourage the best of current practice. They can also too easily slip into the hortatory style of *Suggestions for Teachers,* or lay themselves open to criticism that they are just the old 'projects and activity' in a new glossy wrapping. The experimental sequence of defining objectives, designing appropriate materials and method, trials in schools, evaluation and feedback, has not been widely applied in Scotland. The Schools Council type of project has been adopted by the English Committee, but not the others. The working party procedure keeps our feet firmly on the ground, and there are few in Scotland who would object. Nevertheless, there is a danger that a group of busy practical people may be too unreceptive of unconventional ideas which, though unpractical, are often a stimulus to re-thinking about important fundamental issues and are effective at least in provoking controversies and starting discussion.

The major achievement of the Scottish Education Department so far in this area has been its success in starting up the process of curriculum development, without arousing uneasiness or discontent among the teachers. In so far as teachers are aware at all of what is going on, they seem to welcome their new role of partnership with the inspectors and the colleges of education in this task. Some of the criticisms which have been made above must ring a familiar note to English readers. But those who know the Scottish system will recognise that the procedure which has evolved is peculiarly well suited to the Scottish situation. Educational problems know no frontiers, but educational institutions are not exportable. The Schools Council structure is probably too cumbersome for a country with one-tenth the population of England; and one cannot imagine the Scottish working party of twelve to fourteen members (the average size) being acceptable as a nationally representative group in England. Curriculum development in Scotland is practical and down-to-earth; its reports are economical of words; and the provision is relatively inexpensive – three characteristically Scottish virtues, or faults?

NOTES

1. G.S. Osborne, Scottish and English Schools (Longmans, London, 1966), p. 307.
2. J. Nisbet (ed.), Scottish Education Looks Ahead (Chambers, Edinburgh, 1969), p. 87.
3. Op. cit., pp. 1-10, 59-73, 74-90.
4. Scottish Education Department, *Consultative Committee on the Curriculum: First Report* 1965-8 (HMSO, Edinburgh, 1969).
5. Schools Council, *The First Three Years* (HMSO, London, 1968).
6. *First Report 1965-8,* p.6.
7. Ibid., p.5.
8. Ibid.
9. J. Nisbet, op. cit., Ch. 6.
10. Ibid., pp. 80-1.
11. *Modern Mathematics in Schools* (Chambers, Edinburgh).
12. W.A. Gatherer, 'The Central Committee on English: a report', CITE Newsletter, Vol. 1, no. 2, May 1968, pp. 3-5.
13. *First Report 1965-8,* loc. cit.

Part II

CURRICULUM DEVELOPMENT AT NATIONAL LEVEL

6. DES, MINISTERS AND THE CURRICULUM

Gerry Fowler

From R. Bell and W. Prescott, *The Schools Council: a second look* (Ward Lock Educational, London, 1975).

[Fowler argues that the doctrine that the curriculum is for the professional teacher alone to determine, free from direct intervention by politicians or central government, is not an accurate account of what happens, nor in the broad context of educational policy-making, logically coherent. He examines the extent of government intervention, particularly in the field of further education, and concludes that the present system is not necessarily the best even from the standpoint of the teacher.]

In his memoirs R.A. Butler gives an account of his interview with the Prime Minister, Winston Churchill, when he was appointed to the Presidency of the old Board of Education in 1941:[1]

> (Churchill) went on: 'I am too old now to think you can improve people's natures. Everyone has to learn to defend himself. I should not object if you could introduce a note of patriotism into the schools.' And then, with a grin . . ., 'Tell the children that Wolfe won Quebec.' I said that I would like to influence what was taught in schools but that this was always frowned upon. Here he looked very earnest and commented, 'Of course not by instruction or order but by suggestion.'

Butler's reluctance to interfere in the curriculum of the schools, despite his desire to influence it, has characterised Education Ministers of all major parties in Britain in this century. C.A.R. Crosland says of the Secretary of State's impact on the internal organisation of schools and the curriculum:[2]

> . . . the only influence is the indirect one that is exercised through HMIS, through DES participation in the Schools Council and through government-sponsored research projects like the one on comprehensive education. The nearer one comes to the *professional* content of education, the more indirect the Minister's influence is. And I am sure this is right.

We may note at once the notion that the content of education is a matter for the professional, that is to say, for the teacher. It is a universal belief in the teachers' organisations, and explains teacher dominance in the Schools Council and its committees;[3] it is however a tenet of faith among politicians too. Yet, as Crosland's words reveal, the external organisation of the schools – the choice for example between selective and nonselective secondary schools – is deemed a perfectly proper matter for politicians to decide, albeit after consultation with parents and of course teachers. This is however inextricably interwoven with the internal organisation of schools and what teaching and learning goes on within them. A 'comprehensive' school with rigid streaming of children from the first year, and a curriculum equally rigidly differentiated according to measured ability upon entry, is arguably a comprehensive in name only.[4] Decisions upon the organisation and upon the content of education cannot be totally separated.

Secondly, both Churchill and Crosland recognise that a Minister can if he wishes influence the curriculum by what the former calls 'suggestion'. Whatever Churchill meant by the word, Crosland spells out some of the vehicles through which suggestions may be conveyed to those teaching in the schools, from direct ministerial choice of research projects, which may have detailed objectives, to the advice offered by HMIS in the schools. It may well be that Ministers never instruct HMIS as to what advice they should tender. But a powerful Minister, who knows his own mind, is able substantially to alter the climate of opinion within the Department. It is unlikely that a member of the Inspectorate will express positive opinions about early streaming, with its curricular implications, if he knows that it is anathema to his political masters. Ministers may rarely express views about what is taught (in the schools at least), and hardly ever about the way it is taught; but they do sometimes hold strong opinions on matters which affect both.

Thirdly, Churchill's dicta reveal that the content of education *is* political, in some subject areas at least. He need scarcely have bothered to suggest that a note of patriotism be introduced into the schools. Those at school then, and later, will always remember Empire Day parades. Nor need he have worried that children might never learn that Wolfe won Quebec, or even that Gray's *Elegy* would not be mentioned in that context. To some it may have seemed of greater concern that they knew nothing of Montcalm save his defects, and but little of the rectitude, or otherwise, of French claims in the Seven Year War. Much teaching of British history, through the medieval and early modern periods has tended to the denigration or the ridicule of the ancestors of our Common Market partners.

This is not meant as a criticism of British teaching or teachers. The same happens in every country, and in many the bias in the teaching of highly political subjects has been much more marked than in our own. But it does serve to point up a crucial difficulty with the thesis that the content of education is for the professionals alone to determine. Some would maintain that no discipline is value-free. Be that as it may, it is certain that there can (logically) be no approach to the arts and the social sciences which does not embody somewhere social value judgments, which may also be dubbed 'political' in a broad sense of the word (i.e. concerned with the polity, or organised society).

Although Labour Ministers have no more sought to interfere directly with the school curriculum than Conservative, there were during the First World War and between the wars protests within the Labour Party at militarist or imperialist overtones detected by some in the school curriculum, and suggestions that only governmental action could eradicate them.[5] A recurrent theme has been that the organisation *and* the content of education tend to the conservation of a hierarchical and stratified society, for his allotted place in which each is educated. Thus Jack Straw, once President of the National Union of Students and Labour's Deputy Leader on the ILEA, wrote in 1972:[6]

> If people do decide to question their lot I suggest that generally it is in spite of their education, not because of it. What cannot be avoided by teachers and politicians is that an antiseptic attitude towards the teaching of government, or indeed any subject, inevitably assists the preservation of the *status quo*.
> (He concluded) . . . the only way to achieve radical change in education — including an extension of the real freedoms which teachers cherish — is at a political level: and that can only come about if discussion of the curriculum is made a respectable and accepted topic for political debate.

Straw himself recognised that '. . . there exists in this country a powerful convention that the politician — be he Education Minister or school governor — has no business to interfere in what goes on in the classroom. It is a convention which forms part of what Michael Young has described as "the politics of nondecision making".' Yet there is one sector of British public education where that formulation could not be accepted without qualification: it is to further education that we now turn. Examination of it may give new insights into the operation of the convention elsewhere.

The DES knows no inhibitions about direct involvement in the formulation of the syllabus for specific courses (a more detailed involvement than in shaping the broad curriculum) — not of course for the GCE, but for National Certificate and Diplomas. Entry requirements and syllabuses for each course are approved by a Joint Committee, on which sit nominees of the appropriate professional institution (e.g. the Institution of Mechanical Engineers) together with those of organisations representing the colleges, their principals and their teachers (late entrants to the committees), and those of the DES and sometimes of the Scottish Education Department too. The DES provides the secretariat too for some Joint Committees. While colleges may set and mark their own examinations, they are subject to external moderation by assessors appointed by the Committees. Yet the Ordinary National Certificate or Diploma is normally accounted as of about the same standard as GCE A Level, and the Higher National Certificate and Diploma are some way along the road to a degree, some HNDs, it is often argued, reaching a level scarcely short of that of an ordinary degree (or degree without honours).

Of further education as a whole, and especially of the colleges, including polytechnics, offering advanced courses, the Director of North-East London Polytechnic, as written:[7]

> The staff in the colleges, with a great deal of enthusiasm and effi-
> ciency, *operate a system that has been designed by some outside*
> *body.* That is, the great majority of teachers in the public sector of
> further and higher education are compelled, despite their abilities,
> to perform the function of technicians.

This sounds a far cry from the doctrine that the content of education is purely a matter for the professional educators, the teachers, especially when one of the outside bodies with its finger stuck directly and firmly into the pie is the DES itself. Of course, the Secretary of State does not sit on the Joint Committees personally, but his nominees, normally HMIS do. Some may say that engineering or physics or building or hotel management — subjects of national certificate and diploma courses — have no 'political' content, so that all is well. We would disagree, but that is beside the point, since few are likely to assert that business studies are necessarily devoid of political content.

The story does not end there. The Department has been known to insist on the inclusion of certain studies in the college curriculum. Lest it be thought that these were *merely* technical, and that the DES asserted itself in order to secure an adequate flow of qualified manpower into industry, let us consider the spread of liberal or general studies as a course component in the years after 1956. That was the date of the DES Circular 323, *Liberal Education in Technical Colleges,* which suggested that their purpose was the development of 'habits of reflection and free enquiry which are the marks of an educated and liberal mind. All members of the teaching staff should therefore cultivate wide interests and a broad outlook.' There was resistance from more than one source, but Liberal Studies spread rapidly. In a book written for the DES and published as an official guide to further education for the uninitiated, Adrian Bristow, himself a principal, describes the process as follows:[8]

That we overcame is due mainly to the hard line taken by the HMIS.

They put the squeeze on in various subtle and not so subtle ways. Their normal role is to advise, persuade and suggest but, when occasion demands, they are adept at putting on a hammer lock and forcing a submission. This they did with Liberal Studies. It was not only the employers who were awkward. Many of our technical teachers, especially the die-hards in building and engineering were unconvinced of the need for Liberal Studies and contemptuous of their role.

Our own sympathies are entirely with the DES in what it was seeking to achieve, but that does not affect the principle of teacher freedom to determine the curriculum, here clearly breached. Of course many of the 'die-hards' were lecturers who had come into further education with both practical experience and qualifications in their specialism, but without having undergone teacher education. Oddly, many members of GCE subject panels, university dons or the senior staff of grammar schools, were similar in this respect, but no 'hammerlock' has been put on them. This cannot therefore be offered as a full explanation of the attitudes of HMIS, unless we are prepared to devise a very sophisticated answer to the question, when is a professional not a professional?

It is worth quoting one other phrase from Bristow's book which is symptomatic of an attitude in FE to intervention by the DES different from that commonly found in the schools. In describing the changes in some FE courses imposed by the Industrial Training Boards, he says: '. . . the impetus for revision is coming not from educational sources – the colleges, the DES, and the examining bodies – but from the boards.' Here then the Department is deemed 'an educational source', and not merely the organ of central government responsible for the *administration* of public education.

Part of the explanation undoubtedly lies in the regularity of contact between the colleges and their staff and HMIS who are generally seen as helpful counsellors. Their visits are, however, feared if they are concerned with the approval of a new course, especially an advanced course. Before a college can submit its syllabus to the appropriate validating or examining body, it needs the approval of the Regional Advisory Council for Further Education (RAC) and the sanction of the Secretary of State. The RAC is not an organ of central government, it is composed primarily of college, LEA, and industrial representatives, and its principal function is the coordination of regional provision for further education. Most RACs will however refuse to support a course if it is implacably opposed by the Inspectorate, especially by the Regional Staff Inspector (RSI). The RSI may use the RAC to block a course to which he is opposed on national rather than regional considerations; he will have discussed national demand for such a course, and existing provision, with his colleagues elsewhere. If the RAC does not follow his advice, he has no choice but to issue a letter refusing approval to the course. The letter begins: 'I am directed by the Secretary of State . . .'

Even when a course is approved, the RSI may direct a college to cease running it, if it does not recruit the required number of students (normally twenty-four). If it is thought that decisions by a member of the Inspectorate cannot be held to be political involvement in the curriculum, it must be remembered that colleges or LEAs may protest to the Secretary of State, and even ask for an interview with a Minister. Discretion in favour of a course with inadequate recruitment may be exercised at any stage. That Ministers will normally follow the official advice tendered to them is not of constitutional significance. Acts done in the name of supine Ministers are still their responsibility, and they are answerable to Parliament for them.

The Inspectorate is proud of its status as a body appointed in theory directly by the Sovereign; HMIS are not civil servants in the usual sense of that term. Here, however, the RSI acts as an administrative arm of the Secretary of State, like any other DES official. Subject specialist HMIS are involved in the process of course approval too. On this advice many proposals are never submitted by colleges to the RAC or the RSI. More positively they may help a college to improve its submission, or even generate new proposals, suggesting to colleges that they have a strong chance of approval.

The view of HMIS may also be crucial to DES approval for the purchase of large items of equipment which do not fall within the local authority's allocation for locally determined schemes. Such equipment may be essential if a course is to run; here, then, is an indirect means of controlling some elements in the curriculum. For some studies — in science, engineering, catering, music, or art — approval for new buildings or extensions to old may similarly determine what can be taught and learnt, and how. While financial and economic considerations are central to the choice of projects for approval, it is also another lever used by the Department to determine the educational character of colleges.

The formal controls exercised by the Department over the curriculum of FE colleges are of course negative. Nothing can force an LEA or a college to offer what it does not want to offer. Yet the spread of Liberal Studies shows how negative controls can be used to positive effect. HMIS could get a 'hammerlock' on recalcitrant colleges or teachers because of their power to ensure refusal of permission to start a new course or to continue an old, or to replace equipment or extend buildings.

All of this is part of the 'social control' over further education to which the then Secretary of State, C.A.R. Crosland, referred in his speech at Woolwich Polytechnic in 1965, when he first outlined what became the policy of designating thirty 'state universities', to be called polytechnics. Unless such control extended to the curriculum, it would not be possible to ensure that these institutions were 'directly responsive to social needs'.

(For our present purpose we may leave aside the questions of what constitutes a 'social need' and who is the ideal perceiver of it.) Ministers have not subsequently hesitated to pronounce repeatedly and at length on the desired educational character, and curriculum of the polytechnics: for example, part-time courses should be developed alongside full-time, and subdegree alongside degree courses in the same subjects, and there should be an emphasis on 'applied' or 'vocational' studies. No one thinks this odd, though if Ministers had adopted the same prescriptive tone when discussing the curriculum of the universities or even the schools there might have been raised eyebrows. It is what is expected in FE. The 1961 White Paper *Better Opportunities in Technical Education* heralded a restructuring of national certificate and diploma and City and Guilds technician courses.[9] The Secretary of State's acceptance in 1972 of the recommendation of the Haslegrave Committee that a Technician and a Business Education Council be established, must be the precursor to a yet more radical restructuring of technician courses, since otherwise it would have little point.

In general, ministerial control over recurrent expenditure on FE, which may also help to determine the curriculum, has been no tighter than it has on the schools. In Advanced FE it is arguably much looser, since the system of 'pooling' expenditure among all LEAs means that everyone spends what everyone else pays, scarcely a sound principle of financial control. Yet in both 1968 and in 1970 Ministers were quite specific that fees for certain FE courses (primarily but not solely adult 'recreational' courses) should be increased.[10] Since central government grant would be reduced to take account of the suggested increase, LEAs had little choice but to increase fees or to reduce the number of courses offered. An increase in fees is itself tantamount to closing some courses, since they will cease to recruit student numbers. Although couched purely in financial terms, ministerial policy here expressed a clear view that some elements in the FE curriculum should be jettisoned if they could not be made self-financing.[11]

In FE we have identified as means by which central government, ministers and officials, influence the curriculum, the approval of courses, direct representation on some committees responsible for syllabuses and for monitoring examinations, the control of expenditure on large items of equipment, the building programme, financial intervention through the grant to LEAs, formal and informal announcements of new government policies, and of course advice and suggestion, most often through the Inspectorate. This formidable array of weapons is not precisely paralleled in the school sector. Even here, however, the influence of central government on the curriculum is greater than is commonly acknowledged. It is one explanation of a phenomenon to which W.O. Lester Smith draws attention:[12] 'Visitors from overseas, when they notice several schools of the same type with much the same timetable, often express surprise and

65

even doubt whether our teachers are as free in this respect as they are reputed to be.'

Advice and suggestions through the Inspectorate, and in written bulletins and official magazines,[13] again play a major role. While Ministers may or may not take much interest in this, it is they who are responsible for the activities of the Department and we have seen that they can help to create or alter the climate of thinking within it. When there is a major change in the legal recruitment for education, as when the school-leaving age is raised, they may themselves tender advice, albeit couched in broad terms, to the schools, by circular or in speeches. The use to which the 'extra year' given by ROSLA is put affects the whole of the secondary curriculum; Ministers have pronounced upon it.[14]

Provided that LEAs observe the law and the regulations governing schools and their premises, financial aid to them through the Rate Support Grant may be regarded as having no strings attached. At the end of 1973, however, central government tendered advice on how the reductions in local authority expenditure it required should be implemented (Department of the Environment Circular 157/73). There should be no reductions in teaching staff or in expenditure on books, but 10 per cent must come off the total of planned expenditure or procurement for education. LEAs must inevitably cut sharply spending not only on maintenance and repair of premises and equipment — but also on school supplies. That may seem irrelevant to the curriculum until it is remembered that, as one new teacher said, when asked what was the curriculum in her first school, 'the curriculum is the contents of the store-cupboard'. Here then central government, while abstaining from any direct interference in the details of the curriculum, indirectly influences by its advice what can be taught, and how.

The DES must approve all major projects for inclusion in the school-building programme, and the detailed plans for their implementation. It is this which has turned the Architects and Building Branch of the Department into a major force in educational reform. Its influence in securing the acceptance of new school designs is hard to estimate with precision, but has undoubtedly been considerable. Yet what can be and is done within school buildings is materially affected by their shape. 'Open-plan' primary schools lend themselves to the integrated day, team teaching, and learning by discovery; they are quite unsuitable to formal instruction in narrowly defined 'subjects' at fixed hours. Here again the educational thinking of HMIS may be discerned, influencing the work of the Branch,[15] which nevertheless remains the responsibility of the Secretary of State.

None of this would normally be accounted 'political' involvement in the curriculum. The point, however, is that it is impossible to draw a sharp line between activities which affect the curriculum and those which do not, and that many activities for which the Secretary of State is accountable to Parliament clearly do. It seems then illogical to suggest that he should neither express a view on their curriculum implications, nor consider them when formulating policy. Nor have those outside the Department the slightest hope of knowing what Ministers do and say within it. There is thus an illogicality at the heart of the doctrine that politicians should be rigidly excluded from the secret garden of the curriculum.

The more overt intervention of the DES in the FE curriculum than in that of the schools is explicable primarily by the nonstatutory, and therefore entrepreneurial, character of FE. Were there not tight control on the courses offered by the colleges, there might be cut-throat competition for students between the colleges with multiplication of poorly patronised courses, and unnecessary expenditure on equipment. The DES nomination to Joint Committees for national certificates and diplomas arose from the need to establish qualifications nationally recognised by the professions and by industry, and of a guaranteed educational standard — and, most of all, in technical studies in which few in the universities had an interest. The multiplicity of FE courses means that the Department must constantly monitor developments, and sometimes seek rationalisation. By contrast the schools taught for only one type of qualification, the GCE or its precursor, and more recently for two, with the addition in 1965 of the Certificate of Secondary Education. The universities, through their examining boards, maintained an interest in the former, not least as a university qualifying examination. The latter, originating in part from pressure by teachers, could be left to regional boards controlled by the profession.[16] And in the school sector, there is no competition between schools for pupils.

The CSE was in part a response to the growing practice in secondary modern schools of entering pupils for a wide range of external examinations other than those for the GCE, such as the examinations of the Royal Society of Arts. In discouraging such practice, and if there had been resistance to the rationalisation effected by the introduction of CSE, the Minister in the end had the whip hand. The School Regulations do set out the conditions under which pupils may be entered for external examinations, in respect of age or length and type of study.[17] The Regulations were made under the Local Government Act 1958 which empowered the appropriate Minister to make regulations and impose general requirements in respect of the performance of any function by a local authority.[18] The Act was concerned with the system whereby central government pays a grant to local authorities — that is to say, its power to impose conditions on local authorities stems essentially from holding the strings to the biggest purse on which they draw.

Ministers have not been averse to general pronouncements about the curriculum in official policy documents. Thus, the 1958 White Paper *Secondary Education for All — a New Drive* contained the statement:[19] 'Secondary modern schools may each be encouraged to develop a wide variety of courses or the necessary variety may be achieved by encouraging each to develop its own speciality appealing to different aims and interests – technical apprenticeships, careers in commerce, nursing, and so on.' Since the White Paper was chiefly about the external organisation of secondary education, it reveals again how difficult it is to separate this from curricular questions.

The Schools Council's functions in relations to examinations are '... to assist the Secretary of State to carry out his responsibility for the direction of policy and the general arrangements for secondary school examinations, and to discharge on his behalf the functions of a central coordinating authority (DES Circular 13/64). That the word 'assist' is not used loosely, was clearly revealed when in January 1972 the Secretary of State told the Schools Council that she would not endorse their recommendation for a twenty-point grading of GCE A Levels until she had held more consultations. The proposal was in effect dead from that moment, although the Council itself had approved it six months before.

The intimate connection between examinations, the curriculum, and what would generally be accounted 'political' questions is clear. Professor S.J. Eggleston, writing in the *Times Educational Supplement* in 1970, said:[20] 'What then is wrong with the examination system? Fundamentally, there are two problems. One is the disruptive effect it has on the curriculum; the other the disruptive effect it has on the social structure of the schools.' Few would deny to politicians a proper interest in the latter. Yet any attempt by Ministers to effect reform by the exercise of their responsibility for school examinations must entail consideration of its curricular effects.

We may note in passing that the doctrine that politicians and their appointees should leave curricular matters to the professionals has no legal sanction. On the contrary, the principles underlying the powers of secondary school governors in respect of the curriculum, embodied in most Articles of Government, were stated in the 1944 White Paper as follows:[21]

> The local education authority would have the right ... to settle the general educational character of the school and its place in the local system. Subject to this general responsibility, the governors would have general direction of the conduct and curriculum of the school. The headmaster or headmistress would control the internal organisation, management and discipline of the school ...

In many areas the majority of governors are local politicians, or their appointees, chosen for their political reliability or long party service. The potential conflict of function embodied in these principles (where exactly are the boundaries between 'general educational character', 'curriculum' and 'internal organisation'?) has been avoided only by their general abrogation of responsibility in deference to the professional judgment of the head teacher.

At national level, one other factor has strengthened ministerial or governmental influence on the school curriculum, the surveillance exercised by the Department over teacher education. The terms of reference given in 1970 to the James Committee on Teacher Education and Training included an enquiry into 'what should be the content and organisation of courses to be provided'. Its Report covered this topic,[22] and the 1972 White Paper *Education – a Framework for Expansion* ventured some statements not only on the organisation of teacher education courses,[23] but on the desirable character of curricular development in higher education as a whole. It is to be expected that the Inspectorate will exercise great influence over the establishment of a new pattern of teacher education, and over the approval of courses. Yet he who controls teacher education helps to determine what is taught in the schools, and how it is taught. Here then is a further force making towards curricular uniformity within a pluralist system of control.

There is one sector of education we have not discussed – the universities. They are of course 'autonomous', and the University Grants Committee (UGC) protects them from 'political' interference.[24] Yet in 1968 the UGC confessed that as a 'buffer' between the universities and government it was 'by no means wholly passive'. In fixing the quinquennial grant to individual universities it has regard to the broad policies of the government, and there is regular discussion between its officials and those of the DES, and between its Chairman and Ministers. In recent years the government's determination to expand the throughput of scientists and engineers in the universities has bulked large in quinquennial settlements; the 1972 White Paper contained a statement of the desired ratio between science and arts places.[25] It marked in fact some withdrawal from the heavily scientific bias of new provision in the mid and late 1960s, reflecting in part the short-fall in the number of science candidates coming forward from the schools.[26] It is commonplace to argue that the balance of university provision, and the control in theory exercised by the universities over the GCE examining boards, together have a powerful influence on the school curriculum. More recently it has been suggested that lack of active interest among university teachers in the GCE syllabus,[27] and the emphasis of most GCE courses on pure or theoretical study rather than applied, have operated to the detriment of the universities, especially in respect of recruitment to subjects not taught, or little taught, in the schools. Insofar as there is a two-way interaction between school and university curricula, it strengthens the argument that *indirect* influence by the DES on the school curriculum, with direct influence on that of higher education through the allocation of resources, can result in inefficient or wasteful expenditure.

The dilemma which is posed for central government can be illustrated from the letter accompanying the submission (to the Secretary of State for Education and the Minister of Technology)[28] on the Swann Report on the Flow into Employment of Scientists, Engineers, and Technologists. Since

69

it is the educational system which can most readily respond to change, it said, 'it will fall mainly to educationalists . . . to consider what action to take'. Yet it also referred to the guidance which educators, employers and administrators 'are entitled to seek from a national manpower policy'. Even if we assume that the formulation of such a policy is possible, recent evidence does not suggest that educators will observe it without direction firmer than is suggested by the word 'guidance'. Similarly, the Dainton Report[29] which made far-reaching recommendations affecting above all the sixth-form curriculum, was prefaced by the statement: 'we have made some proposals for remedial action affecting the schools, the universities and industry, the implementation of which will largely depend upon the establishment of a consensus of opinion throughout the educational life of the country.' It is not easy to change an existing consensus by suggestion and indirect influence alone, and when it is possible the process may be slow.

Our argument has been that the doctrine that the curriculum is for the professional teacher alone to determine, while the politicians and the organs of central government content themselves with influence by nudge and hint, never seeming to intervene directly, is neither an accurate account of what happens, nor, when set in a broad context of educational policy-making, logically coherent. In further education, the 'forgotten sector', there is naked intervention by central government in curricular questions. Elsewhere, the activities of Ministers and of officials for whose work they are accountable to Parliament affect the curriculum more than is commonly recognised, but they stop short at the point where they would achieve the most efficient utilisation of public resources. There is, however, no clear line between issues deemed to fall within the 'political' sphere and those reserved to the professional. We may dub the doctrine, according to taste, English compromise or English hypocrisy. Either way, there is no evidence that it is the best system even from the standpoint of the teacher. W.O. Lester Smith, a former teacher and Chief Education Officer, has written (1965-1968):[30]

> If administered sympathetically, a system offering more guidance about the curriculum need not detract from the freedom that teachers possess. Nor need it foster an undesirable uniformity: on the contrary, it could help to promote experiment in new directions and lead to more diversity than there is at present.

NOTES

1. R.A.B. Butler, *The Art of the Possible, the Memoirs of Lord Butler* (Hamish Hamilton, London, 1971), p. 90, reprinted in G. Fowler, Morris and Ozga, *Decision-Making in British Education* (Heinemann, London, 1973).

2. C.A.R. Crosland: Edward Boyle and Antony Crosland in conversation in M. Kogan, *The Politics of Education* (Penguin, Harmondsworth, 1971).

3. R.A. Manzer, *Teachers and Politics* (Manchester University Press, Manchester, 1970) reprinted in R. Bell, G. Fowler and A. Little, *Education in Great Britain and Ireland* (Routledge and Kegan Paul, London).

4. For a full account of the variably comprehensive character of 'comprehensive education' see C. Benn and B. Simon, *Half Way There* (Penguin, Harmondsworth, 1972).

5. R. Barker, Education and Politics 1900–51: *A Study of the Labour Party* (Oxford University Press, London, 1972), ch. 8.

6. J. Straw, 'Open up the classroom to straight politics', *Guardian*, 18 March 1972.

7. G. Brosan *et al.*, *Patterns and Politics in Higher Education* (Penguin, Harmondsworth, 1971), p. 125.

8. A. Bristow, *Inside the Colleges of Education* (HMSO, London, 1970). Cf. L.M. Canter and I.F. Roberts, *Further Education in England and Wales* (Routledge and Kegan Paul, London and Boston, Mass., 1972), pp. 75-9.

9. Ministry of Education, *Better Opportunities in Technical Education*, Command 1254 (HMSO, London, 1961).

10. On the 1968 cuts see E. Robinson, 'The cuts and further education', *Higher Education Review*, Summer, 1969, pp. 19-26. For the 1970 policy see *New Policies for Public Spending*, Command 4515 (HMSO, London, October 1970), para. 20, which says, 'The aim will be to save £5 million in a full year.'

11. For FE in general see Bristow, op. cit., note 8 above and G. Fowler, Education in Great Britain and Ireland (Routledge and Kegan Paul, London, 1973), pp. 180-89.

12. W.O. Lester Smith, *Education: An Introductory Survey* (Penguin, Harmondsworth, 1957).

13. For example *Trends in Education*, published for the DES by HMSO. Cf. the series of education pamphlets, e.g. no. 59 *New Thinking in School Geography* (HMSO, London), which discusses among other topics, the purposes of school geography and the methods of the geographer in the classroom.

14. For example DES Circular 8/71. cf. the Rt/Hon. Mrs Margaret Thatcher, in a speech on the subject made on 16 March 1971: '. . . I do not wish to get down too far into what is essentially a professional matter. But the success rate will I believe be higher . . . the more the schools are able to teach these young people things which they positively wish to learn – certainly practical mechanical things about cars and electrical equipment and also practical matters like hire purchase and insurance and buying a house.'

15. For the role of the Inspectorate in spreading 'progressive' methods in primary education see M. Kogan, 'English primary schools, a model of institutional innovation in T. Green (ed.), *Educational Planning Perspective* (IPC, London, 1971), reprinted in G. Fowler *et al.*, *Decision-Making in British Education* (Heinemann, London, 1973).

16. Manzer, *Teacher and Politics*, note 3 above.

17. The School Regulations 1959, no. 364, para. 15, as amended by the Schools (Amending) Regulations 1963, SI 1963, no. 1468.

18. The powers it conferred are now replaced by similar powers under the Local Government Act 1966, section 4(2).

Gerry Fowler

19. Ministry of Education, *Secondary Education for All – A New Drive,* Command 604 (HMSO, London, 1958), para. 20.
20. J.F. Eggleston in *The Times Educational Supplement,* 25 September 1970, p.4.
21. Ministry of Education, *Principles of Government in Maintained Secondary Schools,* Command 6523 (HMSO, London, 1944).
22. DES, *Teacher Education and Training* (The James Report) (HMSO, London, 1972).
23. Id., *Education – A Framework for Expansion,* Command 5174 (HMSO, London, 1972), paras. 73-81, 107-9.
24. University Grants Committee, *University Development 1962-7,* Command, 3820, (HMSO, London, 1968), para.611, reprinted in R. Bell, G. Fowler and A. Little, *Education in Great Britain* (Routledge and Kegan Paul, London).
25. 1972 White Paper, para.136: 'The Government have told the University Grants Committee that they would think it reasonable to plan on the assumption that 47 per cent of the full-time students in 1976-77 will be arts-based and 53 per cent will be science-based.'
26. For a criticism of the policies of the 1960s, and the evidence on which they were based, see K.G. Gannicot and M. Blaug, 'Manpower forecasting since Robbins – a science lobby in action', *Higher Education Review,* autumn 1969, reprinted in G. Fowler, *Decision-Making in British Education* (Heinemann, London, 1973).
27. J. Pearce, *Schools Examination* (Collier-Macmillan, London, 1972) ch. 8, pp. 131-43.
28. *The Flow into Employment of Scientists, Engineers and Technologists,* Report of the Working Group on Manpower for scientific growth, Command 3760 (HMSO, London, 1968), pp. vii, viii.
29. *Enquiry into the Flow of Candidates in Science and Technology into Higher Education,* Command 3541 (HMSO, London, 1968).
30. W.O. Lester Smith, *Government of Education* (Penguin, Harmondsworth, 1965, 1968), p. 108.

7. THE SCHOOLS COUNCIL IN CONTEXT

Geoffrey Caston

From *Journal of Curriculum Studies,* Vol. III, no. 1, May 1971, pp. 50-64.

[The Schools Council's commitment to pluralism, the dispersal of power in education, and professionalism is described. Four characteristics of the Council are discussed: central/local government partnership, professional teacher-control, avoidance of authority, and restriction of its activities to the curriculum. Finally, Caston identifies the enemies of freedom — the lethargic, the complacent and the technocrats.]

Educational Values

In nearly four years of work for the Schools Council I have developed strong personal aspirations for it; I want it to thrive because I believe it embodies certain educational values which I think fundamental to the kind of vigorous and compassionate society of which I want to be a member. I will summarise these values in two concepts — pluralism and professionalism.

First, pluralism. Philosophically, this means a system which acknowledges that there are many good ends, that these ends conflict and no one of them is necessarily overriding. Translated into social and political institutions, it means that there are — and indeed ought to be — many centres of influence and that we should not worry when these conflict.

Briefly then, I use 'pluralism' in this paper to mean 'the dispersal of power in education'. Education is an area of social activity in which the concentration of power can severely damage young people. They are, after all, compulsory inmates of the schools, and thus in a very real sense, their prisoners. This is so even though the purpose of their imprisonment by society is not punitive, but beneficent. It nevertheless involves the exercise of power over them; it is forceful intervention in their personal development. They can be harmed by the *misuse* of this power so as to mould them in the image of the state. Or, to put it in a less sinister way, by treating them as instruments of some national manpower policy rather than as self-determining individuals. That is the obvious danger, but in Britain it would be more probable that concentration of educational power would lead not so much to its damaging *misuse* but to a *disuse* which could be almost as bad. A centralised educational system can be too timid to experiment, too fearful of giving offence ever to allow its professional adventurers a free hand. In such a system change, if it is to happen at all, has to happen everywhere all at once. The consequences of failure are then so awful that no one ever dares to take the risk.

Geoffrey Caston

The second value is professionalism; and here too I must make clear my definition. For educators, the essence of professionalism lies in the exercise by individuals of choice and judgment in the interests, not of ourselves or our employers, but of our clients: in this case our pupils. These choices must be made in terms of a professional ethic which includes an obligation by the educator to provide service in an impartial way to all pupils, regardless of any private preferences between them that he may have. The obligation to the troublemaker, the drug-taker, is equal to the obligation to the academic or athletic star. Professionalism also includes an obligation to provide this service in the light of all the relevant and up to date information which the practitioner can muster. Educators must always be learners, from our own colleagues, from other professions, not least perhaps from our own pupils. Within this double ethic — of impartiality and open-mindedness — the professional can deny any outside authority the right to tell him how to do his job.

Action and reaction

In this country, as in many others, educators have been losing professional self-confidence in the face of rapid social changes that are reflected in the demands not only of governments, but of parents and students. The laymen are asserting themselves; the clients become more insistent. Faced with similar pressures some other professions have retreated into gold and ivory towers, fortified by arcane jargon and high salaries. Educators must not, cannot, respond in this way. What we must do is to keep on the move, constantly demonstrating that we are prepared to deal with young people on the basis of their needs as we, acting professionally and in co-operation with others, perceive them. There will always be legitimate professional differences in these perceptions — no one has a monopoly of educational rightness, and the science which underlies our craft is not a precise one. Nor for that matter is medicine or, still less, law. But these differences between us will remain legitimate only as long as we continue individually to make judgments that are both confident and well-informed. That is to say, as long as we are secure enough in ourselves to have these judgments challenged by our pupils and by society, to defend them rationally, but to be prepared to modify them in the light of new knowledge and new insights. And also as long as we are always seen to be putting in first place the obligation to our clients, the children. On their behalf we can, if necessary, question social norms and governmental expectations. But we cannot do so in our own interests.

It is against the background of these values that I see the present and future role of the Schools Council. It is not just a piece of machinery for spending research funds, or administering examinations. It is a witness to a certain style of running an educational system. And it is in that context that it has attracted very wide attention from educators overseas. Its essential quality lies in its potential to boost professional self-confidence in a pluralistic setting.

The Council is concerned with all those problems which involve the quality of education: what to teach and how. They are problems that loom larger today than ever before. There is world-wide preoccupation with 'curriculum development' – 'the organised improvement of the curriculum.' It is a platitude that the pace of social change is everywhere outrunning the capacity of the school to respond. This change takes many different forms, and I can only hint at a very few examples in this paper. Some are changes in the aspirations and demands of the young people themselves. Pathologically these may be expressed in resort to drugs and violence. Constructively they involve a demand by adolescents for an early and effective assumption of social obligations, an urgent clamour that their schooling be patently relevant; they are impatient with prolonged apprenticeship. The schools – like universities – cannot wishfully pretend that their students are other than they are. They must work with the clients they have.

Other kinds of change are those concerned with knowledge itself, the nature of subjects and disciplines, the traditional 'content of education'. In the natural sciences, for instance, the line between physics and biology is becoming as blurred in the junior school as it is in the realm of Nobel prize-winning research. In the universities the frontiers of academic disciplines are dissolving, and the schools must face this. Nevertheless, the re-grouping of subjects is hard to take. As Musgrove (1968) wrote recently: 'To ask a physics graduate to take general science or an historian to take social studies is not only to expose him as a narrow specialist, it is to threaten his sense of professional identity.' The stress is one that all heads encounter when they try to change the departmental structure of their schools – just as the Schools Council sees it in its sixteen different Subject Committees, each defending its own identity. It has an obvious effect on any development of the whole curriculum, the total range of learning to which a pupil is exposed, and how it is organised.

A third kind of change is in our knowledge of how children learn. A lot of research has since supported William James's assertion in 1892 that learning by discovery, experience, or activity is a principle 'which ought by logical right to dominate the entire conduct of the teacher in the classroom.' But this does not dispose of the professional problem, which is just *where* to strike the balance between open-ended enquiry methods and the inculcation of those skills and knowledge which teachers know that children need to learn? As Bantock (1969) rightly suggested in Black Paper No. 2, it is not a question of structure or no structure, but just how much structure, and this is a matter of delicate professional judgment.

A fourth kind of change is in the skills that society demands of its adults. As the Council Survey of Young School Leavers (Schools Council 1968) showed, pupils want to learn practical things, things that will help

Geoffrey Caston

them to get a good job and then to do it. But the skills that are in the highest demand today — and more so in 1990 — tend to be those that are hardest to teach. The number of jobs involving personal services — waiters, barbers, travel agents, teachers, Schools Council Joint Secretaries — is increasing. Even vocationally, skills in human relations will soon be more relevant than skills in the manipulation of tools. And it is much more difficult to devise a curriculum for them. And even more difficult to examine it.

Style of Response

The Schools Council is a part of the administrative system which helps the educational profession respond to these changes — among other parts are local education authorities and head teachers. But the nature of learning is such that only a certain style of administration *can* help. It has to be supportive, and cannot be hierarchical. Administration can be defined as the arrangement of an environment in which individuals pursue purposes. In the case of education the purpose is learning; the active agent is the pupil. What counts is what happens between learner and teacher. That is where the action is. It is essential that we try to understand the nature of that action — or interaction — if the particular administrative role of the Schools Council is to be intelligible.

As a help to that understanding, I want to quote at some length from a speech made by my predecessor Derek Morrell (1969) not long before he died:

> To understand what is really going on in school, we have to come to grips with extremely complex, constantly changing and immensely particular systems of personal interaction, involving complex relationships between the experience, language and values which the pupils bring into the school from their homes and neighbourhoods, and those which are imported by the teacher. If there is positive reciprocity of feeling and aspiration between teachers and taught, satisfying to both, there is a describable curricular reality . . . If not, if there is a total absence of mutual emotional satisfaction, the curriculum remains simply an idea in the minds of the teachers. It lacks reality, even though the teachers talk and the children go through the motions of scholastic activity . . . In the curriculum we are concerned with human beings whose feelings and aspirations are far more real and immediately important to them than the cognitive development which is the educator's stock-in-trade. Value attaches to cognitive development only because it enables people to organise their feelings in interaction with those of others, to frame realistic aspirations, and to acquire know-how in giving effect to them. It is not an end in itself: it is both a tool and a product of successful

living, a means of maximising the emotional satisfactions of being alive, an aid to coming to terms with the facts of pain, suffering and death.

That statement is, I believe, of fundamental relevance to the process of curriculum development. It means that curriculum development can only be something that essentially happens in a school, and that it is the mutual responsibility of teachers and pupils. The system must be organised to support and reinforce that responsibility, and not to diminish it. The Schools Council does a small, but vital, part of that job — the part which it is sensible and economical to do nationally, on behalf of all pupils, all teachers, all schools and all local authorities.

Research talent is scarce, and should not be dissipated in mini-projects all over the country, though there is a place for these. Perhaps even more important, we cannot afford to squander the creative approaches of the most inventive teachers by leaving them to work unheralded in one locality. Teams must be brought together to develop their ideas and to embody them in descriptions of new methods and in new curriculum materials. These can be tried out by groups of teachers in a variety of different situations, and the results — evidence from the experience of different teachers and different pupils — fed back to the developers for evaluation in the classic model first picked up in this country by the Nuffield Foundation, building on the pioneering work of the Association for Science Education. Then in the light of all this experiment the results must be published so that professionals can choose to use or not to use them, as they wish.

Organised in one way or another, national development work of this kind has been going on in countries all over the world, reflecting the interest of society, as well as that of the profession, in improving the quality of education. But the view of society — expressed through various agencies outside the schools — and those of the profession have naturally not always and everywhere coincided. In the United States, for example, the curriculum development movement started as a move by university scientists to transform science teaching methods. In the early days there was a certain disdain for the school teachers' part in the process, an attempt to produce curriculum materials which were rashly claimed to be teacher-proof. This is now seen to have been a fatal flaw. Whatever instructions are written down in the manual, however carefully structured the pupils' work cards may be, what is learned is inevitably the product of teacher-learner interaction. It is therefore heavily conditioned by the emotional product of that interaction. As Jerome Bruner (1970) said recently: 'The effort to make the curriculum teacher-proof was like trying to make love people-proof.'

In Sweden, on the other hand — and I am greatly oversimplifying — national changes in curriculum have been, for the most part, based on research in which teachers are fully involved. But there they are beginning

Geoffrey Caston

to find that even so, because the resulting national changes were prescribed to teachers, apparent compliance with them has very often masked a stubborn and understandable insistence on the part of individual teachers to go on in the same old way. And the pupils take their cues from the teachers, not from the material.

But the British approach has been different. There has been in the last five years a deliberate resort to democracy, an attempt to secure the commitment of teachers by involving them decisively at every stage in the innovation programme. This includes the making of decisions at national level on policy and on the spending of money, and at local level in the management of teachers' centres and local development groups. Above all there has been a determination that national work in the development of new curriculum should be concerned only to enlarge the freedom of choice of the teacher to determine, in the light of the best available professional knowledge, what is best for his pupils in his school. Somehow we were going to dispel the notion that teachers were being forced to dance to a tune composed and played by people who knew nothing about their problems. This is not just politically convenient, in terms of pressure from teachers' associations. It is an educational necessity, because a teacher who feels professionally coerced is most unlikely to be able to contribute to a productive relationship with his pupils. They cannot learn self-confidence from teachers who have none.

This can be romanticised, of course: everything in the garden is never lovely. Teaching is full of stress, and there are elements in it that support the description of it as 'the paranoid profession – suspicious, conservative, anxious to disclaim responsibility and to find scapegoats for its failures. But the 'we-they' excuse for irresponsibility which is found throughout our society, in labour-management relations, in teacher-local education authority relations and, perhaps consequently, in student-teacher relations must be dispelled. A healthy future for an educational system must lie in constantly asserting and reinforcing the teacher's own responsibility for what he teaches, and with it the pupil's responsibility for what he learns, rather than his subordinate relationship to authority or to an employer. All our educational institutions must be concerned to do this and must be run in ways which foster it. The Schools Council is an institution deliberately constituted for this purpose, and I believe that its success in the future will be judged primarily by its success in this, and only secondarily by the ingenuity of the new physics syllabuses that it may be able to devise.

The Schools Council Analysed

So let me now try, using this criterion, to analyse the nature of the institution, how it seems to me to have worked during the last few years and what might contribute to its success or failure during the next few.

Its first characteristic is the nature of the partnership between central and local government which it represents. From April 1st, 1970, the Council has received half its income in the form of a direct grant from central government through the Department of Education and Science, and the other half from the local education authorities, contributing each according to the number of pupils in its maintained schools. In the Council's early years, these respective contributions, although about equal in amount, had been tied to particular purposes, that from local authorities to research and development grants, that from the Department of Education and Science to payment of overheads, such as staff and accommodation. The Council is now free to dispose of all its income exactly as it wishes. Its independence from central government — which in policy matters was always real — has thus become manifest. This affects its public relations more than its decisions, but by the criterion I am using (getting away from 'we-they') public relations are extremely important.

But the unusual nature of this financial arrangement is not so much the contribution made by central government. The more significant element — and the one which startles overseas observers — is the commitment represented by the investment of local government resources. The local authorities have a statutory responsibility 'to provide education'. They decided, four years ago, to back this by investing their own funds in a national institution concerned with research and development work designed to improve the quality of that education. What they were saying was that the creation of conditions in which the curriculum can be improved is their responsibility locally, but that they recognised that there is a part of this responsibility which could sensibly be carried out nationally. For this purpose they formed a consortium, to be called the Schools Council. It would produce curriculum materials, research working papers, bulletins and other publications which it would be for their teachers in Derbyshire, Cumberland or Exeter to adopt, adapt or discard as they wished. But — and this is even more important — the local education authorities were at the same time committing themselves to making a much larger contribution to a local development effort without which the national investment would be abortive. As local administrators they would provide time, money and other resources for teachers to meet together to discuss, to work, if necessary to reeducate themselves, so as to develop their own ideas about the curriculum and, incidentally, to make use of the material which the Schools Council could produce. Hence the teachers' centre movement, one of the most encouraging and exciting phenomena in British education in the last few years. They flourish in some areas and languish in others, but they are an essential feature of the Schools Council's work. Nothing which is written is real until it is read. If you are trying to communicate something you must pay as much attention to the disposition of the receiver as to the quality of the transmitter. So from the beginning the Council has tried to stimulate local development groups which will provide teachers with a reason for using its stuff, and which will set themselves tasks for which they may find its materials useful. The Council's role here has been to stimulate and encourage. We do not ourselves finance local work, and it cannot and should not be our function to equalise, to put Loamshire's financial contribution to work in Barsetshire because Barsetshire has decided not to make proper provision for its own teachers.

So here is the first characteristic and the first strength of the Council as an institution: local authority commitment to it. My hope, and there are signs of it in the strength of support we get from many chief education officers, is that this will grow. My fear is that in conditions of continued financial stringency it is the facilities for local development work and in-service education which will be the first to be starved. There are signs of this happening too; for example, the reluctance in some areas to provide substitutes for teachers who want to take part in local development work in school time. But in principle the LEAs are fully involved in the Council and for this we are much envied by administrators in other countries who have not succeeded in finding a way of committing local resources to central research and development work and thereby harnessing to it the local enthusiasm without which it cannot be effective.

The second outstanding characteristic of the Council is that public agencies have been prepared to hand over control of these resources to a body which is in theory and in practice controlled by the teaching profession itself. Here I am certain that we underestimate what we have achieved. I know that there are some teachers who are so determined to be victimised that nothing will convince them that the teachers' control of our decision-making is anything but a sham and a facade. Perhaps at the beginning of the Council's life this was understandably felt rather strongly. But I think now that all of those who sit on the Council's committees and cannot always get their own way — and that is every one of us — know that it is not bureaucrats but other teachers who frustrate them. The Schools Council thus provides an opportunity for teachers to see that whatever their different perspectives as individuals or as groups they are all operating within one system which demands compromises if the interests of individual pupils are to be safeguarded. Perhaps 'compromise' is rather a weak word. It is not just that — to use non-Council names — Michael Duane must trade in a bit of his mish philosophy and Tom Howarth a bit of his mash philosophy in order to produce a mish-mash to which each can quarter-heartedly subscribe. What is needed is a recognition that, in a society in which all pupils and parents are increasingly aware of all the opportunities open to all the others, the undiluted pursuit of values which may be appropriate to one group of pupils — say the academically gifted in some special field — may actually damage the educational interest of others.

There are a number of examples of this 'one world' problem; one most in people's minds at the moment is that of the sixth form. The contemporary sixth-form curriculum is very often seen as a set of rules for a national competition for which there are a limited number of prizes, places in universities and elsewhere in higher education. In such a situation it is plain that what suits best the needs of one group of pupils, or group of teachers, may well penalise others. The way you set up the rules determines who will win the prizes. This leads to conflicts of values and interests. One pupil's (and his teachers') freedom to pursue high grades in three highly specialised A level courses limits the freedom of his competitor to do something else which might be of more value to him but which would not qualify him for a prize. The Council – and its relation to higher education – provides for the first time a place in which these conflicts can be mediated and in which representatives of interests can constantly meet each other with a brief to act these collectively.

There is a great opportunity here, but I must confess that there is also great danger. All of us that have watched Council committees and working parties in discussion have been greatly heartened by the visible process of mutual education between individuals starting from quite different viewpoints. I remember with some satisfaction a moment after a recent committee meeting when a newcomer had expressed, very vigorously, views with which I happened to disagree strongly. Someone came to me afterwards and said, 'He must be a National Union of Teachers man.' In fact he was a chief education officer. People's roles get submerged in a new co-operative Council role, and this is very encouraging. I remember also people saying when the Council was set up that nothing could be achieved by a collection of 'interests', teachers' associations, local education authorities and others, all striking required attitudes. In fact, it has not been like that – individuals once appointed have modified their sets of prejudices and opened their minds.

The two sixth form working parties have offered an outstanding example of this. They have worked intensively together over a long period on problems which have baffled the profession for many years. The process of private debate has been a greatly beneficial one, but it is disheartening to see the understandings achieved in face-to-face collaboration melting away in the heat of public controversy. In a small group people have to face up to the consequences for others of what they say: on a public platform, or in a letter to the press, they can get away with almost anything! Our hope for the Council's future must be that in time the quality of the public debate will also improve. One of the Council's functions must be to reduce the name-calling, the stereotyping, the polarisation of attitudes which characterises public debate in the pedagogical profession: Black Papers versus Red Papers, Egalitarianism versus Elitism, Half Our Future versus the Other Half, play-way progressives versus deskbound traditionalists, Pedley versus Pedley.

The Schools Council is a real test of the profession's capacity to take decisions for itself: as an instrument for professional democracy it may

81

Gerffrey Caston

assist the development of rational debate about the curriculum and thus continue to ward off outside intervention. Certainly there has been no warrant so far for the early fears of Government interference in our affairs. But if, in spite of all, in the end it is professional polemic and counter-polemic that prove to be the decisive influence, the way will be left open for others to preempt our decisions for us. We live in a justifiably impatient society.

The first two characteristics then are central/local government partnership and teacher control. The third significant characteristic is that the Council has no authority over teachers. It may — and I hope it does — sometimes carry a certain amount of weight of professional consensus and a great deal of the kind of authority which comes from organised knowledge. But not authority in the Oxford Dictionary definition, 'the right to enforce obedience'. It cannot instruct anyone to do anything. To my mind — though not always to those who command a majority in our ranks — this is a great source of strength. It means that the use of any of the materials or methods which the Council may commend requires a positive act of agreement by the teachers concerned. It is an educational axiom that if individuals do things because they have chosen to do them they do so with infinitely more effect than if they are passively acquiescing in authority. It is true for teachers as for their pupils. 'The right to enforce obedience' has no place in an educational process, either between teachers and organisations, or between teachers and pupils. Once coercion creeps in, education begins to go out.

But to enlarge the range of choice open to teachers is to make their job very much more difficult. Just as for a doctor more research or drugs make possible more accurate diagnosis and more effective therapy but also require a constant refreshment of professional competence. The drug companies, however, sell pretty hard, and there are doctors who see in their brochures the easier way. So with teachers there are many who want instant prescriptions and who insist in spite of all the Council's disclaimers on regarding its words as law. This is something that I am sure we must rebut on every possible occasion. The most effective way of doing so is to issue conflicting recommendations on the same theme, and I am delighted to say that we have several times justifiably been convicted of this. By the same token I hope to see not one Schools Council project in, say, mathematics, but several, offering different schemes but offering each with objective descriptions of what they aim at and what they might achieve. Our job is to offer evidence.

The fourth significant characteristic of the Council is that it operates only in the area of the curriculum, and the organisation of schools insofar as this affects the curriculum. This gives the Council wide scope, but nevertheless sets limits. It sees the curriculum as comprising all those learning experiences which the school intentionally provides, whether this be the fifth-form mathematics syllabus or its prefect system if that is intended to

82

provide opportunities for learning leadership. The Council is concerned with helping teachers take curricular decisions in whatever school situation they find themselves, in special schools, in preschool play groups, in comprehensive schools, in grammar schools, in direct grant schools, in independent schools, in preparatory schools, in middle schools or in sixth form colleges. It is not concerned with arguing which of these forms of organisation is best, but how, given the form of organisation in which he finds himself, the teacher can best do his job. We live in an educational world which is torn by arguments about finance and organisation, and to be free of these is a considerable advantage.

These are the four most important characteristics of the Council as an institution:

1. Central/local government partnership.
2. Professional teacher control.
3. Avoidance of authority.
4. Restriction of activity to the what and how of schooling — the curriculum.

I will now make a few personal predictions about the directions in which the Council will go in the next few years.

The Future

Firstly, I hope it will extend traditional Nuffield-type development work into the more difficult areas of the curriculum. In a way it is no accident that science and mathematics have come first in the United States and here. They are subjects in which teachers are much more ready, perhaps mistakenly, to accept the authority of the expert. What we must look forward to is the far more difficult experimental work in, for example, secondary school history or sixth form social sciences. In a world in which all political debate requires an understanding of sociological and economic evidence this is an essential element in the education of the seventeen year old; the seventeen year olds seem to agree, to judge from the popularity even of the rather dusty syllabuses in sociology and economics which are all we offer them at present. But at the same time the earlier work in other subjects must be reexamined. There must be no new orthodoxy. Tough though it is, the work must constantly be done over and over again, even in science. Perhaps especially in science.

Secondly, I expect the Council to act upon the increasing awareness that teacher skills and attitude count for a great deal more in curriculum renewal than do changes in content and materials. It is not the Council's job to provide in-service education — though it is high time it became a little more clear just whose job it is — but it is our job to ensure that those who do provide it are fully acquainted with up to date information about new approaches and materials. So I foresee perhaps a chain of centres of in-service education and curriculum research, linked in some way with our projects, perhaps partially financed by the Council – on the model of the Modern Languages Teaching Centre at York University, the Centre for Science Education at Chelsea, or the Centre for Education in the Humanities and Social Sciences about to be set up at the University of East Anglia under the direction of Lawrence Stenhouse. Their job will be to train the trainers. The people who do it will be those who are themselves in the front line of new thought and research about teaching methods and content.

Thirdly, I hope – I am not sure that I expect – the Council to be the front runner in research and development work in new techniques of assessment, designed to achieve a situation in which assessment becomes the servant and not the master of the educational process. In this we will work closely with all the examining boards and with the National Foundation for Educational Research. A little is being done already. Much more is needed and it is probably in this respect that the Council has so far most disappointed its founders, its members and its staff.

Fourthly, and here I am quite confident in my prediction, I see increased emphasis on the stimulation and organisation of local curriculum development work, and an expansion of the Council's team of field officers (mostly head teachers on secondment) and communications services. Not only, nor even mainly, communication from the centre to the circumference, but communications between one group, one school, and another. We are already getting geared up for this – though no one yet has found the best means, given the utter inadequacy for this purpose of the written word.

Conclusion

This paper has tried to show the Schools Council as an institution designed to promote the kind of freedom, both responsible and well-informed, which I believe to be essential if the professional clients of educators – the children – are to grow up in the kind of society which I suspect most of us would like to see.

There are three groups of people within the educational profession whom I would characterise – or caricature – as 'the enemy' of this freedom. They are all well-meaning and there is a bit of each of them in everyone.

The first group are the lethargic ones. They do not want their job made any more difficult than it is already. They do not want to choose, and so they do not need to equip themselves to choose by reading or by going on courses. They do not mind change if change is the fashion. They will try to do what they are told, though fundamentally their attitudes will be the ones they inherited from their own schooling. As an American science curriculum developer said to me the other day, 'Teachers teach the way they were taught, not the way they were taught to teach.'

The second group of the enemy are the complacent ones. They know they are doing a good job. They have been doing it for the last twenty years and they are damned if they are going to change it for anybody else. They know there is a lot of talk about change and they have read a few books. But it does not seem to have affected the boys in their school, and those that it has they have rejected. As for research, well they are all ready to repeat the bit about lies, damned lies and statistics.

The third group has a fancier name. The dirigistes or the technocrats. They have worked out just what the needs of the nation are in trained manpower for 1988, and they know that in Sweden research has proved that you can teach an infant Boolean algebra by the time he is three years old. They think that some teachers — not many — are competent technicians and ought to be paid more than others. But the most important thing for them is to set a few really clever people to work compiling programmes and work cards that cannot be fouled up by the teachers who operate them. Even if they do not go to that extreme the one thing they cannot stand is chaos. So let things be arranged so that somebody can sit at the centre and make quite sure that everybody in education does what is best.

In my own career, the temptation has obviously been to fall into the third group of the enemy. But it is a temptation that must be resisted. Education is power over individuals and no one is worthy of enough trust to be given that kind of overall responsibility. So we must disperse power, disperse responsibility, and find ways of providing for all of us, whatever our role in the educational system, alternative means of responding to change. From these we can choose the one that will suit our own personal style and the interests of the pupils or students who are in our care, or the teachers for whom as administrators we provide a supporting environment.

The Schools Council is a most powerful force for decentralisation and pluralism in British education today. It gives power to individuals by organising for them access to research and knowledge which can be made available only centrally. It stimulates, but does not impose the innovation which is the necessary response to change. All this is done under professional control with local sources of finance and with no authority other than that which it derives from its own representative character and the evidence it offers. For that kind of enterprise to be backed with over £1,300,000 of public money is quite a national achievement. Its importance is not just education. It is political, and it is in that context that the work of the Schools Council should be scrutinised.

REFERENCES

Bantock, G.H. (1969), 'Discovery methods' in C.B. Cox and A.E. Dyson (eds.), *Black Paper Two*, Critical Quarterly Society, London.

Geoffrey Caston

Bruner, J. (1970), 'The relevance of skill or the skill of relevance'. Paper presented to Education in the Seventies Conference, Encyclopedia Britannica Limited, London.
James, W. (1921), *Talks to Teachers on Psychology*, Henry Holt, New York.
Morrell, D.H. (1969), Paper read to Educational Associates, London.
Musgrove, F. (1968), 'The contribution of sociology' in J.F. Kerr (ed.), *Changing the Curriculum,* University of London Press, London.
Schools Council (1968), *Enquiry 1 — Young School Leavers,* HMSO, London.

8. TEACHERS AND THE SCHOOLS COUNCIL

Anne Corbett

From R. Bell and W. Prescott (eds.), *The Schools Council: A Second Look* (Ward Lock Educational, London, 1975).

[Anne Corbett considers that the Schools Council as at present constituted is more a forum for teacher politics and professional solidarity than for the general reform of the curriculum. She does not believe that it can promote either genuine innovation or diversity of curriculum practice.]

The Schools Council is [. . .] an immensely influential body in the education world. It is nationally the most weighty source of advice on curriculum and examination matters. It almost monopolises the funds for curriculum development work. It involves hundreds of classroom teachers in developing materials for projects and thousands of teachers in their use.

It is also internationally unique in the curriculum development field in being controlled by teachers. Among the various educational interests represented – universities, local education authorities, teacher training, further education, even parents and employers – the teachers are the largest group. Nearly all are nominated by professional associations. The Schools Council is overwhelmingly a professional body, designed to 'promote education' through encouraging research and keeping under review matters which are seldom ever discussed at any other than school level.

In this chapter I shall be mainly concerned with the teachers' control of the Schools Council. I do so, too, because there is a hypothesis that to my mind needs urgently examining: that the Schools Council, as at present constituted, is more likely to be a forum for teacher politics and professional solidarity than for the general reform of the curriculum. This chapter will see how far that hypothesis is supported; and if it is, ask whether a policy of leaving so much curricular influence in the hands of the teachers is justified, and should continue to attract massive financial support from central and local government. The Schools Council does not, it must be made clear, legally control the curriculum and examinations. The Secretary of State controls policy on examinations while the curriculum is in the hands of school governors and managers and through them the local education authority. But governors and managers and local education authorities seldom exercise their curricular powers, and, in this matter the Secretary of State can do no more than refer frustrated politicians and others wanting to introduce or repress subjects to school governors and managers (Kogan 1971). So teachers in schools largely decide both the curricular aims as well as methods in their school, constrained by external examinations and, for what it is worth, public opinion. This reflects a deeply rooted view, well expressed by a former minister, Anthony Crosland, that the professionals are rather better at controlling the curriculum than either politicians or the public (Kogan 1971).

The Schools Council, in giving teachers an educational rather than a trade union platform, is a national embodiment of the belief that the professionals should, on the whole, be the effective guardians of the curriculum. It underlines also the contention that if classroom teachers are to be presented with new curricular ideas, given access to research and generally aided on curricular matters, a teacher-dominated body should be providing the service. That, after all, is what those represented on the Schools Council agreed when it was set up. Geoffrey Caston, a former joint Secretary of the Schools Council, put that view at its best when he said that the Council was a unique demonstration of pluralism in education or the dispersal of power, allied to a professionalism directed in the interests of the clients rather than the professionals themselves. The Schools Council 'gives power to individuals by organising for them access to research and knowledge . . . it stimulates but does not impose.' [see Caston's article, p. 85.]

So let us have a closer look at the membership of this organisation devoted to professionalism and ostensibly to pluralist views, and see whether the fact that teachers are in the majority means that teachers act mainly as an interest group on their own behalf, or whether they are the source of innovations from which schools in general benefit. On all committees but one, teachers are in the majority. The exception is the committee where the local finance authorities (who with the DES provide the funds) are appropriately in control. Otherwise, from the Governing Council and Programme Committee (which is the Executive Committee), down through steering committees to individual subject committees, teacher majorities are the rule.

The Governing Council has between seventy-five and eighty members (the precise number depends on ex officio appointments) and forty-five of those are members of teachers' associations: seventeen of these come from the NUT, ten from the Joint Four, four from the NAS. On the Programme Committee twelve out of eighteen members are teachers, including ex officio members.

It is some indication of the importance that the teachers' associations accord Schools Council committees that they operate a system of allocating membership of committees according to the size of their associations' membership. Programme Committee members, who make these appointments, may observe that new boys at the NUT soon learn not to demand every seat to which they are entitled. Nevertheless, they have a common view that members ought to have on key committees a recognisable allegiance to a professional association rather than merely to be 'good' people picked by the HMIS. Affiliations do not, in fact, seem to play much part on subject committees (which might explain their low status on the council) but by and large the principle of allegiance is clearly one that most on the Schools Council are concerned to uphold.

As can be seen from these figures, even the NUT (the largest single interest group), cannot expect to carry controversial issues without other support. The figures also show that the teachers' organisations, and outstandingly the NUT, are well organised to exert pressure. Fred Jarvis, the deputy general secretary, describes their approach as being one that takes their responsibilities to their members seriously (Corbett 1973). Much of the NUT's Schools Council policy rests on the union's own advisory committees, and the NUT line is agreed before meetings of the Programmes Committee and the Governing Council meetings. A group like the NUT is therefore well equipped to take on, if necessary, numerical but disorganised majorities — and does not hesitate to do so. (And as Michael Young suggests it is not likely to be opposed by the other large interest group, the LEAs, whose officials would share so many assumptions — see Young 1972).

To take one example, at the Governing Council meeting of July 1971 at which the Butler-Briault proposals for Q and F level examinations were rejected, the NUT was able to carry successfully a union view which committed the Council to work for a new examination at seventeen plus, the Certificate of Extended Education, and a common examination at sixteen plus — in other words, commitments quite beyond the reform of A level intended by the Q and F exercise. The Council is an important political stage for teachers.

Some senior officials with the Council in its early days tend to refute this, saying politics did not play much part in their time. But on the teachers' own admissions, they spent their early life with the Schools Council trying to establish their position in relation to the officials. Sam Fisher and Fred Jarvis of the NUT both talk of teachers 'having to play a straight bat initially' (Corbett 1973). As they themselves describe the Council's history, only in recent years have the teachers been confident enough to take initiatives (as over examinations) instead of merely rejecting the initiatives of others, particularly the officials. It seems clear enough now that ideas cannot make any progress until the teachers' representatives see their relevance.

The history of the Schools Council's attitude towards in-service training is an example of this. As long ago as 1967 officials were urging that projects should be funded to include an element of in-service training. Little action followed until 1972 despite the grumblings of directors of the early projects that their efforts were virtually worthless if teachers and local advisers did not understand the often challenging assumptions on which new materials were based. Then, in 1972, by the time many teachers were confused and council committees worried about the take up of some of the new materials, the Schools Council set up a working party on dissemination. In 1973 it agreed, in line with the working party recommendations, to expand the number of its field officers and that all projects should prepare training materials for use in schools and teacher training.

This time lag points to a peculiarity of the Schools Council. Officials are tactically very weak, committees generally quite expert. This is because senior staff are nearly always seconded or appointed on short-term contracts, allegedly to enable the council to renew itself continuously, tapping current grassroots experience. What is more, committee identity tends to be strengthened by the fact mentioned earlier that many members meet constantly around the tables of other committees like Burnham. It seems clear therefore that the teachers' organisations are sufficiently dominant to be able to take much of the credit for the Schools Council's successes — and at the same time to bear some responsibility for its serious failures.

The Council has some major achievements, the greatest being that its work is accepted as part of the educational scene. That arises largely from the teachers' insistence, backed by the local education authorities, that they, not the government, should direct curriculum development policy. The Schools Council as a committee, composed of nationally known figures, has given curriculum development a respectable currency. Teacher control has also ensured that the Council's early efforts were directed at areas like raising the school leaving age, where teachers were especially keen that something should be done.

A second achievement is to get some sort of involvement from classroom teachers on a scale previously unknown. Projects have been firmly based on the notion that those who have to use the materials should themselves have much to do with their creation — a total contrast with the notion familiar in other countries, of curriculum development by academic experts. Project teams include teachers recruited direct from school. Usually some schools try out pilot materials before publication of projects, and the Council has encouraged local authorities to set up teacher centres for local development work — there are now about 300 of these.

The current trend to even more school-based development could further strengthen teacher involvement. Undoubtedly many other teachers have been stimulated by the Council's existence to independent development work. Objectives, developments, evaluation, dissemination have become part of many a school's conscious vocabulary, and even influenced their work. Teachers can be almost certain that in their area there will be a relevant Schools Council project, which they will want to consult even if they do not want to adopt it. Insofar as raising the school leaving age has been a success, this must often be attributable to projects emanating from the Council.

The scale of development — over £6 million spent on over 100 projects in the nine years of the Council's life — has created some sort of landscape out of what had been a jungle of resistance to curriculum development and change.

One may be fairly sure that little of this would have happened if the teachers' organisations had not been there to underwrite the worthiness of curriculum development. One has only to remember the outcry that greeted the Schools Council's predecessor, the Curriculum Study Group, and the idea that officials might be suggesting to teachers how they should teach. In England, the belief that teachers control the curriculum is so deeply embedded that changes in the curriculum need some sort of teacher sanction.

However, there are less happy features of the Schools Council. In practice, as opposed to theory, it has proved very difficult to get classroom teachers involved in innovation. They take part in a growing amount of development work, or what one might call the extension of good practice, inspired by curriculum projects and also by CSE. But with a few exceptions, like the work of the North West Regional Curriculum Development Project [see Rudd's article, page 127], little of it has broken new ground. It may have been effective in-service training – but scarcely innovation. Few teachers seconded to projects have gone back to schools. Few teachers' centres are more than convenient places for holding meetings. This can, I think, be partly attributed to the failure of teachers' organisations to build up effective grassroots networks to advise them and to use on the Council's subject panels. The machinery for consultation is there (outstandingly in the NUT) the innovation-inclined teachers are not. And at any rate in the NUT, this seems to be because the politically active teachers are preferred.

It also means that the Council is vulnerable to criticism for being out of touch. Many innovatory teachers feel the Council's work is irrelevant to their needs, or that where classroom teachers have taken a major part in development, that the end result is tailor-made for particular schools. Teachers in general may refute their leaders' line. The attempts to reform examinations have been marked by the teacher representatives giving one point of view at the Council, the membership as a whole giving another when asked.

But if that can be read as an attempt to impose an orthodoxy on teachers which they have not always been willing to adopt, there are other examples of the ways in which the Council has pursued a narrowly professional line in which protectionism has been more apparent than progress.

It is instructive to look at the way the Council has reacted to ideas which might threaten teachers. One major challenge came with *Enquiry 1* (Schools Council 1968) the investigation into the attitudes of teachers, parents and pupils towards raising the school leaving age and the school curricula. The abiding message of that research was the gap between the views of teachers on the one hand and parents and pupils on the other. Where parents and their children attached greatest importance to the basic business of acquiring skills, being better equipped to do a job, teachers took a broader view of education's enriching function. And what followed in terms of curriculum projects? Overwhelmingly an enriched approach. Indeed the Schools Council has done very little to sponsor work which might challenge traditional notions of the functions of the school. It has had a number of development proposals for school and community projects. Not one has got through.

But it is not just a question of the Council being challenged from outside. It has been challenged and has resisted assaults on curricular orthodoxy. Art, for example, is an area where it would like to sponsor more work. Yet some of the most potentially innovative proposals have been turned down on the grounds that there is no consensus among art teachers and the Council does not want to support a fringe view. To suggest that there is room at the Council for different philosophies is thought to lay the Council open to charges of associating with extremists. 'We are not a revolutionary body', says the Schools Council chairman, Sir Lincoln Ralphs. 'We cannot go out on either a Black Paper or a progressive line' (Corbett 1973). There is no suggestion here that the diversity to which the Council is supposedly committed could extend to backing projects with competing philosophies.

The implications of school organisation face the Council with another challenge. No one would have suggested in the early days that school organisation should have been much of an issue for the Council. But experience has shown how intimately the content and the context for innovation are linked. That, indeed, is a commonplace of the Council's own literature (Schools Council 1973). How, for example, can an integrated studies project expect to succeed in a school wedded to departmental structure? How can a project which presupposes that the teacher will abandon a didactic role be successful in a school committed to hierarchies of teachers and learners? The issues are manifold. The projects are missing. Elizabeth Richardson's valuable study with Nailsea School is an exception (Richardson 1973) [see the extract in this Reader, p. 170]. But the problem of disseminating her ideas has been sidestepped and there has been almost no other sponsored development in an area which often raises tricky professional questions in threatening existing forms of organisation.

One can take the point by the Council's research director, Professor J. Wrigley (1973) that if the Council had stopped to work out fundamental problems — criteria for development, the role of evaluation and dissemination — it would never have got off the ground. But the Council is now a mature organisation, and there is much expertise on which to draw. However, instead of using it, the Council seems to be even more resistant to research and expertise than it was in the early days. As Ralphs puts it: 'in the past we have accepted ideas from experts. But now we must relate our work more intimately to what is happening in the schools' (Corbett 1973).

Why has the Council taken this course? What is there to show that such expertise cannot be used in the service of classroom teachers? Can it really

be that the Schools Council feels itself a young and amateur organisation, as it likes to suggest? It seems much more likely to me that the
Council is taking the decisions that might be expected from an organisation in the control of the educational politicians and the professional
organisations – and what is more, an organisation in which despite its extensive committee structure, all policy is in the hands of a group whose
primary allegiance will be to their own associations. Even individual project proposals have to get a preliminary vetting from the Programme
Committee before project officers and specialist committees have a chance
of advising. With four-fifths of the applications weeded out at that stage
it is a formidable degree of control.

No case better illustrates the primarily political nature of the Programme Committee than the decision not to sponsor research by the
Humanities Curriculum Project on race. Race is clearly a highly sensitive
political issue, and a project which gives pupils access to extremist racial
statements clearly raises immense problems. Quite possibly the Programme
Committee made the best decision. But it made it in a peculiar way, given
that the Council is the major innovation body in education. None of the
members of the Programme Committee saw the materials in use. Nor have
any of the evaluator's reports on the project been accepted by the Council
for publication.

All this suggests that the Council is far more a forum for teacher politics
than a force for innovation. At its most positive it promotes a professional
consensus – on a larger scale but in a similar way to HMIS. At its most
negative the Council is a defender of professional interests.

But to say that the hypothesis holds is not quite the end of the story.
In the context of English education it is, I believe, necessary that there
should be a consensus body to make teachers more conscious of what they
teach and how. Such a body may well be drawn from the representatives
of the professional associations.

So the Schools Council should be recognised for what it is, instead of
being cloaked as an innovatory body. It might then be asked whether
classroom teachers would benefit more if there were better networks to
the schools, if committees included more serving teachers, and members
had limited terms of office, if chairmen were not almost exclusively retired
headteachers, if officials were appointed for longer. It might also be suggested that the Council would be more effective if it had explicit criteria
for which the Council Chairman and the Programme Committee could be
held accountable. As Professor John Nisbet warns: 'The health of the
Schools Council is linked with the vitality of democracy in teachers'
organisations' (Nisbet, 1973).

Meanwhile no one is particularly helped by believing that the Schools
Council, as it exists, can provide an effective base for innovation and the
propagation of pluralist values. Those who want innovation and diversity
ought, it seems to me, to be putting some of the funds into rival concerns.

Anne Corbett

REFERENCES

Corbett, A. (1973), 'The secret garden of the curriculum', *Times Educational Supplement* 13 July.
Kogan, M. et al. (1971), *The Politics of Education,* Penguin, Harmondsworth.
Nisbet, J. (1973), *Case Studies of Educational Innovation: I At the Central Level Part One,* The Schools Council, United Kingdom, published by CERI/OECD, Paris.
Richardson, E. (1973), *The Teacher, The School and the Task of Management,* Heinemann, London.
Schools Council (1968), *Enquiry 1 – Young School Leavers,* HMSO, London.
Schools Council (1973), *Pattern and Variation in the Curriculum Development Projects,* Macmillan, London.
Young, M.F.D. (1972), 'On the politics of Educational Knowledge', *Economy and Society,* Vol. II, no. 2, pp. 194-215.
Wrigley, J. (1973), in *Dialogue,* autumn.

9. THE SCHOOLS COUNCIL AND EXAMINATIONS

Stuart Maclure

From R. Bell and W. Prescott (eds.), *The Schools Council: a Second Look* (Ward Lock Educational, London, 1975).

[The tensions arising from the Schools Council's responsibilities for curriculum development and examinations are discussed. Examinations are seen as the control mechanism in the English educational system. The Schools Council's cautious approach to examination reform is supported as being necessary in the political and administrative context of English education.]

From the outset the Schools Council has had dual responsibilities for curriculum development and for the supervision of examinations. It is a 'Council for Curriculum and Examinations' and when constituted in 1963, it brought together the ongoing functions of the old Secondary Schools Examinations Council and the new ambitions which had begun to form in the Department of Education's infant Curriculum Study Group.

More than forty years before, the SSEC had been set up on the recommendation of the Consultative Committee of the Board of Education to supervise external examinations for secondary schools. It was this body, with Sir Cyril Norwood at its head for twenty-five years, which presided over the old School and Higher Certificates and initiated the General Certificate of Education at ordinary and advanced level after the Second World War.

The link between curriculum and examinations was, of course, obvious enough — witness the terms of reference of the Norwood Committee in 1941: 'to consider suggested changes in the secondary school curriculum and the question of school examinations in relation thereto'. The Beloe Report, which extended the range of school examinations by introducing the Certificate of Secondary Education network, was the work of a subcommittee of the SSEC. And to complete the circle, it was the desire to break new ground in combining experimental curriculum development with the design of the new CSE examinations which persuaded the DES to set up the CSG on the analogy of the Department's architect's development group which had shown in another context how creative and regulatory functions could usefully be combined.

The tensions which arise from these dual responsibilities are at the centre of the life and work of the Schools Council. It is important therefore to start with the relationship between the examination system and the curriculum at the secondary school level. The apparatus of examinations is one of the principal means by which guidelines are laid down for what Lawrence Stenhouse calls 'the public curriculum'. It is the curriculum control mechanism in our system, different from but performing the same function as, curriculum control mechanisms in other, more centralised educational systems.

Continental education ministers, as every schoolboy knows, commonly lay down the numbers of hours which should be devoted to each subject in a centrally-prescribed curriculum. In some countries, as for example Norway and Sweden, the official document which incorporates these curricular instructions goes into detail about aims and objectives, methods and materials and activities. The governmental communications – in the preparation of which teachers and exteachers contribute extensively – contain subtle variations; different sections carry more or less authority from the mandatory through the hortatory to the purely advisory. All are treated with more or less respect by the recipients in the schools, who naturally pay more regard to those sections which they agree with than those they don't. [For a more detailed discussion of approaches to the curriculum in Norway, Sweden and elsewhere, see the article by Becher and Maclure, p. 15 in this reader.]

The English way of curriculum control is less formal and less authoritarian than elsewhere in Europe. The examination syllabuses of the GCE and CSE boards are much less detailed and less carefully integrated with general educational aims than the study plans prepared for some more centrally-controlled education systems. There is no centrally-determined allocation of time or prescription of subjects. The examination system is run by people who include many teachers. Examination syllabuses are often extremely sketchy and in no sense represent the teaching syllabus which the teacher has to prepare for himself. On the other hand, time-tables bear a fairly strong resemblance to one another for pupils pursuing similar courses in different schools. But whether the system of curriculum control is formal and legal as in France or Germany, or is informal and relies on the examination system as in this country, curriculum developers have to concern themselves *both* with the public curriculum as it is laid down by formal or informal methods *and* with the crucial gap between this and classroom reality. It is not sufficient to confine attention to the public curriculum, nor yet to concentrate exclusively on the teaching and learning situation. It is necessary to work in both areas to bring about qualitative improvements in secondary education.

When the Schools Council got down to business, however, it found that the legal position was far from clear. In important matters the locus of responsibility and decision-making was obscure or, at any rate, many people besides the Schools Council were confused about it. Appropriately enough, perhaps, seeing the extent to which the English system of curricular control is built on myths, nobody has shown any eagerness to spell out exactly where the legal power to decide lies.

Partly this is because the situation has been evolving over many years and the strictly legal definitions may not accurately describe what actually happens. It is fairly clear, for instance, that curriculum is legally the responsibility of the LEAs and the voluntary authorities. But they have allowed it to pass by default to the head teachers and their staff — a fact which has now been recognised in revised instruments of government for secondary schools in several areas. Examinations, on the other hand, though nowhere mentioned in the Education Act, and in many cases administered by Chartered bodies, come within the general jurisdiction of the Secretary of State. This is made explicit in respect of the Certificate of Secondary Education (because CSE boards are set up under DES regulations) and is regarded as implicit in respect of GCE (because the signature of an undersecretary of the DES appears on every certificate). It is reinforced with regard to the A level GCE by the precise importance attached to two A levels as a condition of a mandatory student grant for someone accepted by a university for undergraduate studies.

The real if indirect powers over the examination system which the DES retains are almost all that remains of the 'public' aspect of the public curriculum. It is therefore entirely natural that the Secretary of State should insist that the Schools Council only acts as an advisory body — both on curriculum and examinations. It is part of the conventional wisdom that in curricular matters the Schools Council should not have the executive authority to enforce the innovations which it sponsors. It would, in all conscience, be odd if, that being the case, it had been given executive authority over the examination system, the key control mechanism by which changes in the public curriculum can be brought about.

The episode which brought this home forcefully to the Schools Council occurred when, in 1972, Mrs Margaret Thatcher rejected the Council's scheme for a twenty-point system for grading GCE A levels. After the Schools Council had discussed the matter at length and had argued and compromised to reach its own decision, the Secretary of State took her own canvass of opinion among the relevant interests in the schools, examining boards and universities and refused to accept the Council's formal advice. This caused considerable anguish and undermined the Council's attempt to achieve by prestige what was denied by legal right. The Secretary of State had deliberately checked the Council's endeavour to move in on the 'public curriculum' — something which it had to do if it were to promote the reform of the sixth form to which it had already begun to address itself — and the far-reaching consequences were immediately recognised by the largest group of teacher politicians on the Council, those nominated by the National Union of Teachers. But the logic of the Secretary of State's intervention was sound enough. She was determined to prove that the Council is an advisory body and that 'advisory' means 'advisory' not executive. The political composition of the Council and its carefully balanced constitution [see Anne Corbett's article, p.87] is intended to give the teachers the predominant voice. But this is balanced, too, by the limitations on the Schools Council's power. It is not designed to be an instrument of control but of innovation and renewal.

The main question which arises, then, is not whether the tension between examinations and curriculum reform could be avoided, but whether the Schools Council should not have sought to make it more acute — to assert more positively, as some would say, the supremacy of education over examination. Certainly there has often been a somewhat cosy approach punctuated from time to time (as in the Q and F debates) by occasional flashes of drama. The SSEC had monitored GCE syllabuses and claimed the right without any statutory authority to consider, approve or modify what was set before them. When the Schools Council appeared on the scene the situation was altered by the decision to set up CSE boards and allow them to spawn new generations of examinations on a variety of models. The grip on GCEs was relaxed and the Council was content with a gentleman's agreement that new syllabuses in new subjects at O level are shown to the Council 'for comment', and new syllabuses in existing subjects may be sent to the Council at the examination board's discretion. All new or substantially revised A level syllabuses have to be 'approved' by the Council.

The Council has continued to take a close interest in the work of the fourteen CSE boards but the sheer volume of work has forced aside any ideas which might have been entertained for detailed control. (A single CSE Board may have approved over 1,000 Mode 3 syllabuses which cannot be considered in any detail by the Council.) Cooperation and friendly compromise have been the keynote, with generous representation of the examining boards on Council committees and a determined effort to avoid confrontations unless these are inescapable. In practice, of course, many of the Schools Council members are also examiners with years of experience and the community of ideas is greater than might be suggested by a superficial study of committee constitutions.

It would be correct to deduce from this that the Schools Council has not set out from the start to bring the examination system to heel. Council members pay lip-service to the cliché that 'the curriculum must come first'; so too, of course, do the examination boards [see the article by Wyatt, p.104]. But if the examination system occupies the commanding heights of English secondary education, the Schools Council has been extremely chary of trying to storm them. For most of the time it has been content to perform routine review functions which, over large areas of the curriculum, have not been backed up by any of the solid-development work which might have made a more robust attitude towards the examination system and its role in the formulation of the secondary school curriculum possible.

This is not a very heroic approach to the routine functions inherited from the SSEC but a heroic approach would most likely have failed and led to profitless wrangling. In many respects the Schools Council is a reflection of the peculiar power structure of English education. This is its strength. This, if nothing else, made it highly probable that it would prefer discretion to valour; it is unreasonable to set up a body with one set of characteristics and then ask it to act out of character on some matter of central importance. The first task of the Council was to get itself established, to acquire some of the mossy respectability from which future initiatives could be launched, to take things a step at a time and build up confidence in the power groups whose association in the work of the Council was vital to success. A first class row with the examination boards − even if Council members wanted it, which by and large they didn't − would have destroyed confidence rather than have built it up and, the legal ambiguity of the Council's examination responsibilities being finally exposed, would simply have consolidated in the Secretary of State's hands powers which, de facto at least, are in uneasy commission.

Curriculum development, however, has given rise to particular projects where a direct approach to the examining bodies has been necessary: and here, the good relations cultivated in day-to-day dealings have come into play. The obvious examples of Nuffield Science and SMP maths date from before the Schools Council was set up, but the routine has worked smoothly. The drill is that a project team engaged in the design of a new curriculum which is likely to impinge on the examination apparatus, consults the boards and in time one, or more, boards agrees to take part in a pilot scheme to produce exams suitable for the revised curriculum content. In theory, at least, no major difficulty need arise but there are obvious advantages in the interchangeability of the two roles which the Schools Council fulfils.

Gentlemanly tensions there have certainly been but these have been well concealed. Generally speaking the new curricula have so far been susceptible to examination methods acceptable to the GCE boards and the ground rules remain unchanged. It is equally true, however, that the aims of some projects have been heavily influenced by difficulties encountered or anticipated in negotiating with the boards, and in some of these cases − the Modern Languages Project is one − the result has inhibited the innovation process. That project teams should be required to face the discipline of convincing others − in this case an examination board − of the soundness of their ideas is a safeguard for sanity and common sense, but it may well be that the constitution of the Council's governing committees is not calculated to provide all the support which may be needed at critical times.

Certainly this system doesn't encourage fundamental argument about exams and their function, nor yet a rigorous audit of the educational efficiency of the examination boards themselves. Nor does the devising of an exam for a new curriculum ensure that a school will not contrive, say, to teach new maths by old methods and miss the point of the exercise. If, as is suggested, the emphasis within the Schools Council is to shift away from large-scale national curriculum projects to smaller, more local development exercises involving individual schools or groups of schools, the Council will be required to fulfil a different role — that of supporting and underwriting the efforts of innovating teachers who lack the apparatus of a full-time project team with the time and the muscle needed to negotiate successfully with the boards. This will certainly impose new stresses on the Schools Council and upset the cosiness which now prevails. But it may still be better, as the officers of the Council have always argued, to work in close cooperation with the boards — sharing stage armies with them — towards the solution of specific problems, than to court some general and ill-defined confrontation.

These matters are the important small change of an organisation which has been pragmatically feeling its way through the twin minefields of curriculum and examinations with a good deal of episodic success and no more than an acceptable level of fairly discreet failure. The big issue which threatens this 'softly, softly' approach, is the attempt which has been going on since the middle sixties to get to grips with the reform of the sixth form. What is beyond any doubt is that there can be no major reform of the sixth form without a review of the breadth and depth of the subject structure which forms the basis of the advanced level examinations and to which in turn the universities and the rest of higher education are geared. This means attempting to alter the 'public curriculum' with a vengeance and in so doing opening up a general debate which illustrates most of the issues of control, development, examination and selection which invariably complicate large-scale innovation in English education. Various points stand out and transcend the blow by blow record of events in the Schools Council, in the two working parties on the 'old' and the 'new' sixth form, and in the Standing Conference on University Entrance.

First of all there is the division of opinion among those connected with the schools on the question of early specialisation and the desirability of taking steps through the examination system to broaden the range of studies for the pupil who goes through the routine of what might once have been called grammar school education (in whatever type of school). A strong and influential old guard remains unconvinced of the need to change the examination system, arguing that breadth can adequately be ensured by good teaching and a judicious use of minority time. Among those who accept the need for a modification of the normal pattern of studies — the public curriculum again — by a change in A levels and university entrance requirements, there has been a division between the moderates who have thought in terms of some combination of five major and minor studies, and the radicals who preferred a requirement of five subjects of equal weight, with or without insistence on an approved mix of arts and sciences. The argument has been endless and the differences of opinion are, in themselves, deep enough to make it extremely unlikely that a body composed of representatives of many different schools of thought can come to any clearcut conclusions. Similar divisions of opinion exist at the university level, where the complexity is magnified by the irresponsibility of most contributors to the debate who can argue for liberal general principles while still tending to choose candidates for their own departments by criteria which encourage premature specialisation.

What the Schools Council has been unable to do — and may be open to criticism for not trying to do — is to find an approach to curriculum reform in the sixth form which is genuinely experimental and developmental. It cannot be disputed that the technical difficulty of devising a curriculum and a set of examinations which can cope within existing resources with the diverse and diversifying needs of the full range of pupils at the upper end of the secondary schools system — without at the same time erecting new selective tools to exclude people from future opportunities — are very great indeed. The prolonged deliberation of the various working parties and the lengthy consultations about their reports did no more than recognise this. The Council has been no better than anybody else at trying simultaneously to ride half a dozen horses galloping in different directions.

The kind of general speculation about curriculum and content which the working parties have indulged in is a throwback to earlier, less sophisticated forms of curriculum development — a rerun as it were of the Norwood Committee, charged with far more difficult terms of reference — but still largely a matter of taking thought and soundings, not curriculum 'development' in any special sense. The outcome could at best be a brief which then has to be studied by examiners on the one hand and curriculum developers on the other.

The Schools Council's dilemma is the same as it was over the twenty-point A level: the compromises and the decisions demanded of the members of the Council wearing their Schools Council hats are agonisingly difficult to reach. But it is even more difficult to be sure that the bodies they represent will give the same answer when asked for their comments on the Council's decision. This is not because these same bodies will disown their representatives deliberately but that, when consulted directly, wearing the hats of their special interest, they are immune from the persuasive, compromising influence of collective responsibility.

However the Schools Council resolves its difficulties in the short-term — and however succeeding Secretaries of State judge the situation — the underlying questions about the limitations of the Council's role in relation to the public curriculum remain. In this connection Secretaries of State will tend to listen to the Council as one voice among many, not as some latterday music hall impressionist, 'the voice of them all'.

As I have indicated I think the cautious approach by the Schools Council to the challenge of examinations has been the only possible one for a serious body to adopt in the political and administrative context of English education. But the justification of building up confidence by avoiding unnecessary confrontations in the early stages depends on a willingness at the critical moment to put this confidence to the test later on. Both the sixth form controversy and the question of 16+ examinations look like bringing the Council to just such a moment of crisis. It is certainly not easy to forgive the way the Council decided to plump for a unified 16+ examination on the rebound, when the Q and F proposals were thrown out, or the way in which the ensuing scope of the feasibility studies has been limited so as to minimise the developmental element.

The A level committees represent old-style pre-Sputnik-type curriculum planning — civilised discourse among men of good will, well informed speculation, the sensible expression of *a priori* principles laced with the distillation of practical experience within the present system: the same process which produced the complacent paragraphs on the sixth form in the Crowther Report, but at a somewhat greater level of intensity. Quite deliberately the Schools Council and SCUE have chosen to approach the subject in this way because it is less disconcerting than rigorous and experimental development which might actually lead to the accumulation of empirical evidence about sixth form possibilities and the examination requirements which might flow from the curriculum itself.

If the Schools Council is to be true to its responsibilities, this kind of development still needs to be done, even if the cart has been put before the horse. If it cannot be done sooner it will have to be done later and that's all there is to it. Otherwise the most likely outcome seems to be a new generation of reach-me-down examinations for all which perform certain evaluative tricks reasonably satisfactorily but have a generally rigidifying effect on the school curriculum, thereby actually setting back the cause of curriculum development which it is a prime duty of the Schools Council to advance.

The final conclusion must be that the first ten years of the Schools Council have done nothing to diminish the ultimate responsibility which the Secretary of State and no one else can exercise with regard to public examinations. Successive ministers have backed away from this responsibility till, in the matter of A level reform, it has been forced back to Elizabeth House. Because of the reluctance of any minister to be seen as intervening in a critical curriculum question, the way the Secretary of State's ultimate responsibility is used tends to be negative — to assume there can be no change without consensus in a situation which is so structured as to give the right of veto to many different interest groups.

A Secretary of State who wished to do so could use the Schools Council to carry out the development work needed to integrate a new curriculum and a new set of examinations for the sixth form. The Council's advice should be powerful and influential and it should provide a valuable forum where the conflicting pressure groups within the several sections of the education system can express their views and seek ways of reconciling them. Though the Secretary of State has an essential part to play in getting a decisive result from the lengthy process of argument and disputation, he or she can only act by consent and therefore depends on the advice which is forthcoming. That this is true in a centrally-controlled system like the French, no less than in the English education system, is shown by the repeated attempts which French ministers have made to overhaul the *baccalaureat* and the explosive consequences which have followed the use of ministerial authority to impose changes bitterly opposed by students, teachers and universities.

But to depend on advice is not the same thing as to submit meekly to the veto of every group of school teachers and every powerful body of opinion in the universities. Before a Secretary of State can adopt a more positive attitude and develop the negotiating skills this demands, there has to be a clearer understanding of where the responsibility lies. The Schools Council is not the body to fill the power vacuum at the centre. If it were to do so it would have to change out of recognition and many of the best things about it would disappear.

10. THE G.C.E. EXAMINING BOARDS AND CURRICULUM DEVELOPMENT

T.S. Wyatt

Paper presented to the Schools Council's Working Party on the Whole Curriculum. Published by the Oxford and Cambridge Examination Board, April 1973.

[Wyatt, a former secretary of a GCE board, considers the ways in which the boards have responded to changes in the curriculum. He considers some of the constraints which limit the boards' initiatives: the nature of the GCE examination itself, the influence of public opinion, the unproven quality of some innovations, and the question of finance. Lastly he considers some possible developments in the field of examinations and in the role of the boards themselves.]

The part which an examining body should play in curriculum development through its syllabuses and methods of assessment has been the subject of lively and at times acrimonious debate ever since school examinations were introduced in England. There is little doubt that in the third quarter of the nineteenth century many schools looked to the examining authorities for guidance as to what subjects and what aspects of them should be taught at a time when, following an unparalleled expansion in the provision for secondary education, teaching was carried out in a wide variety of institutions which were neither standardised nor controlled nor, in the main, connected with each other. At the same time, however, the examining boards recognised almost from the first that schools should be free to organise their own courses and to present them for examination. Some boards have been at pains to declare, as did the Oxford Delegacy at the time of its inception, that it was their business to prescribe examination syllabuses and not teaching syllabuses and all subscribed to the principle enunciated in 1918 that examining should follow the curriculum and not determine it.

It is obvious that an examination syllabus can exercise a powerful effect upon teaching, but it is not always understood that because of this an examination has among its various functions that of an instrument of educational policy. The West African Examinations Council has used its examination to influence teaching by making practical tests compulsory in science subjects and by proposing a compulsory oral test in English Language with the aim of making it essential for schools to give their pupils experience of practical work and of stimulating teachers to devote greater attention to spoken English and to adopt more effective methods of teaching the language. In the same way some twenty years ago the Secondary School Examinations Council insisted that oral tests be made compulsory in the G.C.E. Ordinary level examinations in foreign languages in England and Wales and to-day the organisers of curricular projects request that examinations be set on them; it is recognised that examinations ought to be set on the projects which are taught, but on the other hand the provision of an examination provides an inducement for schools to take up a project.

The examining boards thus have to tread a tenuous tightrope between the risks of being accused of dictating to teachers what should be taught and of divorcing their examinations from educational progress by failing to respond to contemporary developments and to give a lead where a lead is required. The tightrope may be whisked deftly from beneath their feet by the critic who asserts that the drafting of a syllabus is the responsibility of the teacher and on no-one else but that, because a board's syllabus may consist of little more than an outline of what the examination itself will be, responsibility for determining the underlying structure of the syllabus is passed to the teacher and sanctified in the name of giving the schools a great deal of choice. But whatever the rights or wrongs of this particular argument may be it is the fact that in the past, as to-day, all boards have responded to relevant developments in teaching and that some have taken the initiative in introducing new subjects, in reforming existing subjects, or in bringing in new methods of assessment. It is perhaps fair to say that in general the boards and the schools have moved together in educational development with the boards playing a decisive role in implementing and establishing new ideas. In this way, to quote a few examples, the boards adopted the list of geometrical theorems proposed by the Mathematical Association and the Assistant Masters' Association in 1923, the syllabus in Domestic Science prepared by a joint committee of the Headmistresses' and Assistant Mistresses' Associations in 1930, the Report of the Science Masters' Association on General Science in 1938 and the reforms in science teaching put forward in more recent years by the Science Masters' Association and the Association for Science Education. The reforms intended by these associations had not become effective and could not become effective until the corresponding examination syllabuses had been taken up by all the boards, and the same is true of the curricular projects on which examinations are provided at the present time. [. . .]

The thoroughness with which the arrangements for introducing major changes in general syllabuses must be made is essential for the boards, which are conscious of their responsibilities to large numbers of teaching institutions and teachers and to even larger numbers of candidates. It implies, however, that the processes of deliberation, consultation and agreement cannot be rapid. Preparation within the board requires on average up to at least two years, to which is to be added a further year for discussion with the relevant Subject Committees of the Schools Council, whose immediate approval cannot be taken for granted, and for subsequent modification and amendment. Since a minimum of two years notice must then be given to schools, a total of up to five years may elapse from the time when the idea of reform is first mooted to that when the first examination can be held on the new syllabus. It is for this reason that the boards are open to the charge of the proponents of instant reform, who may be ignorant of the circumstances, that they are resistant to change and cling obstinately to outworn tradition.

Applications for examinations on special syllabuses (Mode 2, Mode 3 or mixed mode) permit of more rapid progress since fewer interests are involved. Some Mode 2 proposals involve little more than a substitution of an individual syllabus for a part of the ground covered by the general syllabus, and some mixed mode proposals simply the substitution of internal for external assessment in some portion of the candidates' work. Where more substantial innovations are required the usual procedure is for the school or group of schools concerned to notify to the board proposals setting out the shape, aims and objectives of the course and a description of the desired examination syllabus and scheme of examination. The board takes advice as and where necessary and the proposals are discussed by the teachers with the board's advisers and officers. Following these discussions the proposals may be modified before they are submitted for final approval. Important considerations of which the board must take account when taking decisions on such applications are the criteria laid down by the Schools Council for the acceptability of G.C.E. subjects and the board's own responsibility for maintaining the standard associated with the G.C.E. examination and for preserving comparability with the demands made by other syllabuses in the same subject.

The initiative in proposing syllabus reform and development has come in the past from diverse sources – the boards themselves, the professional and subject associations of teachers, individual schools and teachers – and more recently also from the organisers and sponsors of current curricular projects, including the Schools Council which now undertakes responsibility for the curriculum as well as for examinations. Since the end of the Second World War the pace of development has accelerated at an ever-increasing rate in spite of the simultaneous commitment of the boards to provide equitable and efficient examining for their candidates, whose numbers have grown ninefold during the period. The published general syllabuses of the G.C.E. boards which were in existence in 1951 now number half as many again as at that time and those of one board which was established after 1951 also show a substantial increase. As is instanced in the reports on research and development work which are prepared annually by the boards, existing syllabuses undergo continuous modification or are discarded in favour of newer approaches and new subjects are regularly introduced. In recent years the syllabuses in all the science subjects have been radically revised to take account of new developments, those in Mathematics have been expanded by the provision of alternatives for pupils taught on the 'modern' method, those in Geography have been substantially modified in accordance with new approaches and those in the domestic subjects have been overhauled to provide for scientific and sociological study as it applies to matters affecting the family. At the same time a large variety of new subjects has been brought in to meet the needs of schools, whether for a widening of the cultural background or for greater vocational orientation. A list of new subjects introduced since 1960 or now in prospect, too long to be given in the body of the text, is appended as a note. The boards are co-operating also with the project organisers in mounting examinations in Business Studies, on the Nuffield courses in modern languages. Physics, Chemistry, Biology and Physical Science, the S.M.P. courses in Mathematics, Additional Mathematics and Further Mathematics, the various courses in Mathematics for Education and Industry, the Midlands Mathematics Experiment, the J.A.C.T. course in Ancient History and the Cambridge Classics Project — in all 14 examinations at Ordinary level and 12 at Advanced level and it is expected that additions will be made to these numbers in due course. So long as these curricular projects are in the experimental stage, the boards have agreed that in the interest of efficiency and economy one of them should undertake the examining of each project on behalf of all. Since it is also the practice for entries to be made to, and results and certificates to be issued by the board whose examination is taken by the school in other subjects the administrative complications are not few. At the same time the boards are experimenting with individual schools or groups of schools in the provision of examinations on integrated or inter-disciplinary studies and with the C.S.E. boards, in various combinations, in feasibility and development studies towards a common system of examining at 16+. Additionally they are conducting their own research and experiments in assessment by means of multiple choice and other forms of objective tests, structured questions and multiple marking, and in the assessment of coursework and project work.

By far the greatest part of G.C.E. examining, like the greater part of C.S.E. examining, taking the C.S.E. boards as a whole, is still carried out on general syllabuses under Mode 1. As has been hinted, the general syllabus aims to represent a consensus between the views of as many interested parties as possible and to reflect what is generally taught, or what it is generally considered desirable to teach. This implies that it will not represent the ideals of all individuals or sets of individuals; it will rather be that which is able to command the approval of a number of co-operating parties, all legitimately concerned with it. The procedure is not likely to produce anything which is extravagantly radical because the boards have to consider that the nature of schools and the capacities of their pupils will not rapidly be changed by the announcement of an examination syllabus. The syllabuses do, however, provide a number of options, permit a number of different approaches, or offer the opportunity to concentrate upon certain aspects rather than others, in such a way that it is hoped that most interests will be catered for. Nevertheless it has been fully recognised for over a century that the general syllabuses will not meet all requirements and, as already indicated, provision has been made for schools to offer their own special syllabuses for approval and examination. As early as 1862 the Cambridge Syndicate, whose original Local Examinations were based on general syllabuses intended for individual candidates and not for schools as such, instituted school examinations, sometimes supplemented by inspection, in which the schools provided schedules of their courses upon which papers of questions were set by examiners appointed by the Syndicate, the answers being marked by the teachers and subsequently re-scrutinised by the examiners, who moderated the marking; in addition to the written tests, *viva voce* tests could be conducted by a visiting examiner. A similar system of school examinations was instituted by the Oxford Delegacy in 1876, while the Oxford and Cambridge Schools Examination Board on its foundation in 1873 had made provision for schools to offer their own individual syllabuses. Such 'alternative syllabuses' were also accepted by the ancestor of the present University of London University Entrance and School Examinations Council on its inception in 1902. When the Joint Matriculation Board of the Universities of Manchester, Liverpool, Leeds and Sheffield introduced its examinations for School Certificates and Senior School Certificates a few years later it went so far as to publish no general syllabuses at all with the intention that question papers would be set on syllabuses submitted by the schools themselves. Finally, the option for schools to be examined on their own courses was written into the 1918 scheme for the School Certificate and Higher School Certificates which the then existing examining bodies agreed to conduct and from which it has been carried forward into the G.C.E. examinations.

The examining boards have therefore not attempted to impose general syllabuses on schools, but the excellent intentions of the past have borne singularly little fruit. In 1912, shortly after the establishment of its school examinations, the Joint Matriculation Board published general syllabuses while still expressing the hope that schools would present their own special schemes but this hope was not fulfilled to any extent. The experience of the other boards has been similar and the position, which has varied little over the years, is at present that the Mode 2 syllabuses examined by the G.C.E. boards in England and Wales total only about 85. Even if allowance is made for the fact that some syllabuses are shared by more than one school the proportion of schools which use this Mode is a tiny fraction of the whole. The syllabuses themselves are in a comparatively small number of subjects, mainly on the Arts side and particularly in the English subjects, History and Religious Knowledge. The reasons for this state of affairs are probably diverse and some may not be obvious. A Mode 2 syllabus may perish when the teacher who originated it leaves the school. Some teachers may feel that their candidates may be more equitably assessed if they take common papers on which their performance can be compared with that of other candidates than if they take special tests which make comparison indirect and difficult. It is possible that others find that they have adequate scope within the general syllabus. A syllabus, regarded as an examination syllabus, determines the maximum field in which the examiner can operate; within this there can be for the teacher the possibility of different methods of approach and considerable freedom of treatment. There can also be a surprisingly wide range of choice; it has been calculated, for example, that the Advanced level History syllabus of one board offers 272 possible combinations of papers together with the almost infinite options of individual project work, and that the board's Advanced level English syllabus provides 36 possible combinations of papers and, according to the options chosen, 70 different selections of prescribed texts without having more than one text in common. Another, less apparent, reason is undoubtedly that in some cases after experience has been gained with a Mode 2 syllabus either the general syllabus has been widened so as to incorporate the desirable elements of the former or the Mode 2 syllabus has proved so successful that it has been made available to other schools and eventually has itself become a general alternative open to all schools which wish to take it, with the result that the need for the special syllabus has disappeared. It has also been observed that schools have welcomed the opportunity of working to a common syllabus (as can be instanced by those which work to a common Mode 2 or Mode 3 syllabus), even though this should not be taken to signify that they are necessarily in agreement with all its details. Finally, the desire of teachers to participate more fully in the examination process which has been stimulated in recent years has probably expressed itself rather through Mode 3 and mixed mode examining, than through the traditional Mode 2. For the time being, Mode 3 examining at A level is not undertaken since the Schools Council is considering its policy and criteria in this matter, on which the boards are awaiting guidance. At Ordinary level, however, the boards have been encouraged to adopt Mode 3 and with one exception they have accepted it in principle with the proviso that standards must be maintained. As with Mode 2, demand has been principally in the Arts subjects and several thousands of candidates now take the special English Language examinations of four of the boards. In addition to English Language, about 50 syllabuses in other subjects are currently in use. More important than Mode 3 is the mixed mode examining in which the school controls a part of the syllabus and/or of the assessment, most often in practical work, coursework or project work but also in written tests, while the board controls the rest.

It has to be recognised that the encouragement of curriculum development through examinations is subject to certain limitations, not all of which can be removed by the unaided efforts of the boards. One problem is inherent in the character of the G.C.E. examination itself, which was designed by the Secondary School Examinations Council not as a school examination but as a 'qualifying' examination open to all comers who were to be classified only into the two categories of 'pass' and 'fail'. The G.C.E. was thus not conceived as a genuine achievement examination in which candidates throughout the ability range are graded according to their performance. The situation at Advanced level has subsequently been improved by the introduction of the present grading scheme even though this may not give entire satisfaction, but requests by the boards for the official grading of Ordinary level performances have not been accepted by the Schools Council. The Council itself as the successor of the Secondary School Examinations Council has inherited the responsibility of maintaining the minimum 'qualifying' standard and all new or substantially modified Advanced level subjects and syllabuses have to be judged according to this and the criteria which the Council has laid down; as mentioned above, the same procedure has applied until recently to Ordinary level subjects and syllabuses, and in the exercise of its duties the Council regularly reviews syllabuses, question papers, marking schemes and specimen marked scripts. It cannot be assumed that all syllabuses proposed by the boards, whether originating from schools, the boards themselves, or other sources, will be accepted without modification or a period, long or short, for discussion or experimentation as was instanced by a delicate situation which arose over the approval of 'modern' elements in the reformed science syllabuses presented by certain boards. In such cases both points of view have no doubt their justification but time is required for the resolution of the issue.

There is also the limitation imposed by public opinion and by the interests of users of certificates, since education and examinations do not exist *in vacuo* but are conditioned by environmental circumstances. The G.C.E. examinations are well established and widely familiar, the general public expects the boards to second the Schools Council's efforts to maintain their essential characteristics until or unless these are officially changed, and any apparent aberrations are news for the media. Because of the periodic witch-hunts which are conducted over the comparability of standards between boards and between different subjects of the same board, examining authorities may understandably approach with some caution new techniques of assessment which are urged on them but of which the reliability has not yet been satisfactorily established. The interests of users of certificates require that the title of a subject should give reasonable guidance as to the nature of the course which has been followed. At present the requirements in subjects are reasonably well known, although there are minor variations between the boards, and if not they can for the great majority of candidates, be found in the published regulations and syllabuses. If in the future there is a large growth in the number of individual syllabuses provided for different schools the boards will face the problem of reconciling the need for faithful description of the course with the requests which have been made to them by the Schools

Council and the Standing Conference on University Entrance that subject titles should be standardised so far as possible between the boards and that their number should be reduced if this is practicable.

There is also the fact that not all innovations carry an inbuilt guarantee of success. Over the now long years of its existence General Science has failed to fulfil the aspirations of those pioneers who conceived it. Those boards which took the initiative in launching a subject in the history and philosophy of science, an apparently interesting and rewarding field of study, have been disappointed by the response. An alternative syllabus in English Language prepared by the London Association of Teachers of English and adopted by one board has never attracted more than six schools. In the modern languages at Advanced level opportunity has been given for some 30 years for the study of the recent and contemporary history, life and institutions of the foreign country concerned but very few schools have taken advantage of it. Only a short life was enjoyed by an alternative syllabus in French provided at the time of the First World War for candidates taught by the Direct Method, which did not include translation into French. The investigators appointed by the Secondary School Examinations Council to conduct an inquiry into the examination of 1918 reported that they were not satisfied that any hardship would be inflicted on candidates well taught on the Direct Method if these candidates were required to translate an easy passage of narrative English into French. The syllabus was withdrawn, and some 50 years have been required for an alternative to prose composition to be provided again at what is now the Ordinary level.

Lastly there is the question of staffing and finance. If the boards are to play an effective part in curriculum development they will need to strengthen their staffs by the appointment of more project directors, subject specialists and research officers – which will naturally have financial implications. The Schools Council may have to reinforce its staff and overhaul its committee structure if the present procedure for the approval of Advanced level subjects is maintained. More important, however, is the fact that the conduct of a number of different examinations, each for a small number of candidates, is more expensive than Mode 1 examining, the cost effectiveness of which is high both in manpower and money thanks to the economics of scale. In the past most boards have recognised this to some extent by making a small charge, in some cases nominal and in no case exceeding the extra cost of providing the question papers, for conducting an examination on a special syllabus requested by a school. The higher costs of special syllabus examining arise in fact not only from the additional direct expenses of examining and moderating but also from the increased complications in administrative work. The special syllabus is, in short, tailor-made to individual requirements and for that reason more costly. Some of the special examinations mounted by the boards on the current curricular projects now attract reasonably large numbers of candidates, but only one of them covers even its direct costs (i.e. the payment for examining, moderating and printing). It is possible that one or two others might also reach this position eventually but it is clear that in some an increase in the number of candidates will merely increase the deficit. The boards have themselves borne the major part of the cost of developing these examinations during the experimental stages, since subsidies from project funds have been few and small, but it is questionable how long such support can or should continue if the examinations are to be established as a long-term open-ended commitment. Since by far the largest share of the cost of examining falls on public funds through the fees paid on behalf of candidates it will in the end be for the community to decide how much it is willing to pay for examinations.

While the difficulties outlined above will not be resolved overnight and while it is not easy to foresee what the longer-term future may bring it seems that examining will certainly become more diversified than it has been in the past. In some respects the situation seems likely to resemble that of the mid-nineteenth century in that for some time to come, in place of the fairly homogeneous group of candidates which the boards have served in the relatively recent past there will be a wide variety of teaching institutions resulting from different schemes of re-organisation, that the ability range of their pupils will be wide, and that the task of devising suitable courses and examinations for them will not be light or easy. At the same time the desire of teachers to frame their own courses and to take part in the assessment process will grow. So far as the modes of examining go, it can be guessed that Mode 1 will be required for those teachers who wish to use it and in any case for the external candidates who now take the G.C.E. examination in large numbers. The suitability or otherwise of the general syllabus for a wide ability range poses an interesting question. At first sight it would seem that such a syllabus would be quite unfitted for this use but the close similarity between some G.C.E. and some C.S.E. Mode 1 syllabuses in the same subjects suggests that in fact the crux is to be found in the scheme of examination and the tests set rather than in the syllabus. If past history is a guide, Mode 2 may not grow significantly (though this may be an erroneous estimate) since the general syllabuses may provide an adequate range of choice for those who wish the examining to be carried out by the examiners of the boards. The present examinations on curricular projects will become established alternatives to the general syllabuses or their more successful elements will be taken up into the general 'modern' syllabuses which the boards have been devising before, during and after the existence of the projects. Growth points will be in Mode 3 and, especially, in the mixed modes which while having the disadvantages of all compromises have the corresponding advantage of making something out of all worlds.

Among these likely or possible developments the examining boards can have a central role to play by putting new ideas, whether their own or proposed by others, to the test of practice and, if they stand the test, of assisting them to become established. Amid the conflicting pressures to which they are subjected they have to be realists and, being independent, they can take an impartial view. They are not monopolistic since under the present arrangements a school which is dissatisfied with the services provided by the one board can have recourse to another in whatever subject it chooses. They have considerable resources which can be utilised to bring about development and flexibility in the curriculum by encouraging and stimulating teachers to put forward new courses and new schemes of examination upon them. They might to this end mount regular courses of instruction for teachers on the preparation of syllabuses according to defined aims and objectives based on the work already being done in this field, and on the techniques of test construction including the necessary specifications and the evaluation of content validity, and on methods of assessment. The prototypes of such courses already exist. The boards, which form a natural forum for debate and discussion, could also become the agents for bringing together teachers from different quarters either locally or at the board's office for an encouraging exchange of ideas and experiences; here again the prototypes exist in the committee meetings and conferences which are already held, in the meetings between teachers from different schools which follow a common alternative syllabus and in the consortia of teachers for Mode 3 examinations. For such teachers the meetings or the consortia constitute a regular, almost obligatory, means of contact which brings considerable benefits in the cross-fertilisation of ideas. In a wider field, as has been suggested by H.G. Macintosh ('A Constructive Role for Examining Bodies', *Journal of Curriculum Studies,* Vol. 2, no. 1, May 1970) a significant contribution might be made by the examining boards, through their development and research units, in the evaluation of the effectiveness of curricular projects. Their experience and expertise could play in this way an important part in the dialogue between all the parties engaged in development work. For this, however, it would be necessary that the boards should be involved and called into consultation in the earliest stages of the work and not only, as has happened too frequently in the past, in the last stages when the shape of the project has been decided and it is desired to frame an examination on it.

NOTE

The following list, which is not claimed to be exhaustive, details new subjects introduced by G.C.E. boards since 1960 or now being developed. It does not include Mode 2 or Mode 3 syllabuses or syllabuses in modern foreign languages.

Advanced level: General Studies, Political Studies, Social Studies, Sociology, Economics (as a separate subject), Law, Psychology, History of Art, Statistics, Computations, Physics-and-Mathematics, Physical Science, Applied Chemistry, Social Biology,

Human Biology, Engineering, Engineering Science, Engineering Drawing, Elements of Engineering Design, Technical Drawing, Electronics, Computer Science, Horticultural Science, Home Economics.

Ordinary level (including alternative syllabuses for sixth form candidates): General Studies Spoken English, Ballet, Drama, Drama and Theatre Arts, Sociology, Economic History, American History, World History, Government, Economics and Commerce, Social Economics, Economic and Social History, Classics in Translation, Classical Studies, Latin with Classical Studies, Greek with Classical Studies, Law, General Principles of English Law, History and Appreciation of Music, Statistics, Additional Statistics, Mathematics with Statistics, Mathematics for Biology, Geology, Physical Science, Environmental Science, Rural Environmental Studies, Astronomy, General Engineering Science, Engineering Workshop Theory and Practice, Elements of Engineering Design, Materials Science, Applied Science and Technology, Craftwork (Design and Communication), Design and Technology, Home and Community Studies, Food and Nutrition.

11. THE EXAMINATION SYSTEM AND A FREER CURRICULUM

Henry G. Macintosh and Leslie Smith

From Henry G. Macintosh and Leslie Smith, *Towards A Freer Curriculum* (University of London Press, London, 1974), pp. 20-23, 78-87.

[The importance of CSE examinations is underlined, and the failure of many schools to take advantage of Mode 3 examining is considered. The authors then consider how teachers may move towards a freer curriculum. They envisage a regionally based communications network largely maintained by an examination board. Teachers would be encouraged to come forward at an early stage with their ideas for changing the curriculum, and would be put in touch with others thinking along the same lines.]

In the second half of the 1960s [. . .] the pace of curriculum development in secondary schools not only accelerated but changed direction and took an increasingly integrated and inter-disciplinary form. This was partly the result of developments within primary schools, partly a by-product of the extension of comprehensive education and partly a result of increased staying on at school beyond the statutory leaving age. For those schools which wished to develop integrated curricula the existing examination structure posed, on the face of it, an insuperable problem. What would have happened had it not been for the opportunity presented by the new Certificate of Secondary Education (C.S.E.) for development and innovation within the existing system is a matter for speculation, but one thing is certain, that without C.S.E. more and more teachers would have advocated the abolition of external examinations.

Why was C.S.E., established in 1964 on the recommendation of the Beloe Report, so significant? Why in retrospect may it turn out to have been for Britain one of the most significant educational events of the twentieth century? The reasons for making these rather sweeping statements are four in number:

1. It involved teachers directly for the first time in assessment in nationally recognised external examinations.
2. It took teachers for the first time in substantial numbers into schools other than their own.
3. It stimulated the development and use of a much wider range of techniques of assessment.
4. It introduced the school based or Mode 3 examination.

The fourth point is in reality the culmination of the first point but the two need separate consideration, however artificial at times the distinction between them may become.

C.S.E. thus created an environment for curriculum development and innovation within the national external examination structure.[1] The opportunity was given to teachers to visit other schools to see and criticise constructively what was going on there. Examining boards began to consider in detail the purposes of the assessment they were providing and in consequence to make use of techniques of assessment which they had previously ignored or had decided were only feasible for use with small numbers. In this they were aided by the newly constituted Schools Council. These techniques included amongst others objective testing, projects or individual studies, the use of course work and the continuous assessment of pupil performance. The introduction of such techniques, some of which could only be undertaken if the pupil's own teacher was involved, necessitated the introduction of research and development studies by examining boards and caused them to give thought to the nature and size of their staffs. Teachers became more actively involved in the work of examining boards not only in a representative capacity but in the decision-making process affecting their own pupils. Above all Mode 3 provided a unique opportunity to combine an evaluation of a course of a teacher's own choice, with certification in a nationally recognised external examination. The term Mode 3 was originally introduced with the establishment of C.S.E. in 1964. Although in theory it is available in both C.S.E. and G.C.E. in practice G.C.E. Boards vary very markedly in their attitude to it. In Mode 3 the syllabus and the assessment is proposed by a single school or group of schools who also carry out the grading of the pupils concerned, these grades being moderated by the examining boards. It is necessary to make the point, however, that the term, like so much educational terminology, has become blurred in use. There are, for example, many current Mode 1 or external examinations in which there is a substantial Mode 3 or school-based component.

The opportunity for curriculum development and innovation provided by C.S.E., is obvious, and yet by early 1973 when this book was being written it had been grasped by very few. In 1972, Mode 3 accounted for only 14.8 per cent of all the subject entries in C.S.E; the number of approved Mode 3s in G.C.E. at 'O' level was minimal and at 'A' level non-existent. Possibly even more significant is the fact that many Mode 3s are currently being put forward not for educational reasons but for reasons of administrative convenience. In consequence much of the hard work undertaken has not led to any significant improvement in existing curricula or to new developments. Why is this?

There are a number of reasons. First of all there are the difficulties created by the present examination system. The existence side by side of two examinations of 16+, one graded, the other pass/fail, and of two sets of boards with different syllabuses, one set obliged to accept Mode 3 proposals in principle, the other not, does not encourage schools with pupils entering for both examinations to experiment. Moreover the C.S.E. boards differ very markedly in their attitudes to Mode 3 proposals, despite their constitutional position which gives them in theory comparatively limited powers of rejection. Additionally, the development of interdisciplinary courses for whose assessment Mode 3 is essential has been hindered by the examination pattern adopted in the G.C.E., which reflects the single disciplinary nature of the overwhelming majority of secondary school curricula at the present time. Finally, examining bodies, despite recent changes, are still not able or willing to spend the sums of money necessary to promote research and development into the problems created by school-based assessment and to investigate the range of techniques required. This is particularly true of C.S.E. boards which, in relation to the problems with which they have to deal, are inadequately financed and staffed. Also, it is only fair to make the point that recent developments in methods of examining have led to increased involvement by teachers in both G.C.E. and C.S.E., making the Mode 1 examinations more satisfactory and less open to criticism. It is important too to appreciate that curriculum development ought never to be undertaken at the expense of the pupil. The development of a new course assessed under a Mode 3 arrangement by a single teacher could put pupils seriously at risk if the teacher were to leave in the middle of the course. Heads, rightly concerned to see that this does not happen, may therefore put a brake upon such single-minded developments. This underlines once again the importance of the co-operative group approach to curriculum development.

These are all practical difficulties, and while very real and serious can be solved if the will is there. There are, however, a number of more fundamental issues involved which act as obstacles to curriculum development and innovation through the use of Mode 3. These are much less easy to overcome since their solution requires attitudes to change. There is, first of all, the attitude of teachers to themselves as assessors. Owing to the nature and importance of external examinations in England and Wales a distinction has grown up in the minds of many teachers between assessment as a natural classroom activity and assessment as an external artificial exercise conducted by some outside agency. This distinction is entirely artificial and has caused teachers to neglect assessment as an integral part of their professional work.

This attitude to assessment is reflected in the instruction provided for teachers in this field during their training period. The basic principles of assessment are rarely discussed in any detail, even in 1973, and the opportunities for applying them in practice in pre-service training are almost non-existent. Considerable strides have been made in recent years in relation to in-service training but much remains to be done as the Schools Council have recently publicly recognised in their Examinations Bulletin No. 23. This situation has meant that teachers considering the development of Mode 3 have been held back by their concern over the need to provide appropriate assessment or, even worse, have been providing inappropriate assessment for the courses they have developed.

Secondly, examining boards today, both C.S.E. and G.C.E., still regard themselves in the main, not as educational, but as administrative bodies. They see their role primarily as one of organising to the best of their ability the examinations that they have and of refining the techniques of assessment they use rather than as one of assisting in curriculum development. Their staffing has been organised accordingly. This negative view of their role assumes that examining can be undertaken as an exercise isolated from the rest of the educational process. It also assumes that taking a positive line in relation to curriculum development must, of necessity, interfere with a school's freedom of action, historically a sacred cow. The necessary marriage between curriculum development as it takes place in schools and assessment as an evaluation instrument developed by examining boards in conjunction with schools has thus never been consummated to the great disadvantage of the curriculum.

Such points must be borne in mind lest one presents too rosy a view of the future. It would be unwise to assume that the majority of teachers or examining boards see the present situation in regard to assessment as containing the potential for future curriculum improvement that the authors have suggested. Moreover, the organisational patterns adopted by schools and their physical layout may well discourage or hinder new developments even where these are desired.

[. . .] A teacher in any school or college begins development in any area from his or her existing position. For most this means a subject-based curriculum. Therefore this [. . .] chapter is concerned with finding ways and means for all teachers to move towards a freer curriculum as they see it rather than as others see it for them. One vital ingredient in any joint operation, however large or small, is a first class communications network. In the context of curriculum development in this country such a network does exist, but is remarkably diffuse and informal, involving agencies like the Schools Council, the Inspectorate, Local Education Authorities, Advisers and Teachers' Centres. The varied nature of the sources from which information and advice about educational matters can be obtained has often been regarded as a source of potential strength; the authors strongly disagree with this view. They regard it rather as a source of potential weakness. It results in schools and teachers spending far too much time on the mechanics of communicating and far too little time in discussing the result of the contracts they make through these communications. Not only is valuable information often missed but information which is obtained is often too fragmentary to be of much use. The authors argue that since curriculum development and its evaluation are integral activities, one of the most potent seed-beds for a freer curriculum at the secondary level lies in the interplay between examining board and schools. Therefore the principal agencies in a communications network relating to curriculum and assessment development should be examining boards (at present at the secondary level this means the G.C.E. and C.S.E. boards) with the remaining agencies acting as feeders and providing valuable supporting services upon request. There are two additional practical reasons for this suggestion. First that in embryo such a network already exists within and between examining boards, and secondly that the boards represent the one relatively stable element in the interaction model which this book has put forward. Schools disappear and re-emerge, the curriculum changes and assessment practices vary and develop; the boards, however, remain essentially the same. They ought, therefore, to become the hub of the wheel.

The kind of communications network here would be much wider than that which examining boards or any of the other agencies mentioned possess at present. Unlike those in use now, it would not be concerned exclusively with dealing with problems as they arise. At present communications mean such things as letters, talks, visits and discussions. Instead, the principal concerns would lie with information storage, retrieval, and dissemination. This too would require letters, talks, visits and discussions, but these would be designed for a different and longer term purpose. In summary, the communications network required should not only put like-minded people in touch with each other, but should also give those same people help and advice in developing and extending the contracts which have been made. It should be a clearing house and an advisory centre rolled into one; and, acting as a clearing house, the quality of service it would provide as an advisory centre would improve immensely. There are problems in devising the kind of organisational structure best suited to perform both functions satisfactorily. Certain facets of the work would demand large units with perhaps national[1] coverage, whilst other facets would require smaller units operating on a regular basis with close local links. The answer seems to lie in a regional unit servicing local groups of schools which has access to expensive facilities such as computing, statistical, printing and question banking services provided by a larger body serving several regions. Suggestions of this kind are being put forward at the present time (1973) in relation to a new administrative structure for a common examining system at 16+, so these ideas are not merely a mirage without substance.

The key element in the mix suggested here is the teacher who will supply most of the information. If this information is to be put to the best use, then the time at which it becomes available is almost as important as its nature. The phenomenon which can be called 'teacher modesty' is relevant here. Teachers are rarely willing to submit 'raw' plans of what they are doing, let alone tentative outlines of what they might be doing, and yet these are more important than the polished statements that they prefer to produce.

Although it seems natural to want to give a very polished statement about an idea that has been urging one to action when making it public,

119

this line of approach has two distinct disadvantages for the development of the idea. In the first place, a statement, highly polished in the eyes of the creator, concerning an innovation in curriculum design and classroom practice, has probably been produced with much personal, lonely effort. Hence, the creator is almost bound to feel sensitive about both the statement and the idea it communicates. He or she may well resent criticism of the idea and to some extent will have frozen its immediate potential for further development through failing to work on it with others. The gap between 'raw' and 'highly polished' in terms of one's ability to expose an idea upon which one is working is subject to a large number of variables which are of no concern to us here. The important point is that a teacher's first initiative to an examining board for starting a dialogue will be more effective within the framework of that dialogue if it is written and presented early in the process of his thinking. Under these circumstances, the dialogue (even if restricted to teacher and examining board) is likely to be 'developmental' rather than almost totally 'judgemental'. This is vitally important if teachers are to feel that they really are involved in an equal partnership with an examination board and hence in the external examination system. Teachers are not easily persuaded to seek early help with a line of development they have chosen, but the position is gradually being reached in which 'tentativeness' is regarded as acceptable in our working environment. We would like to encourage teachers to take advantage of this new environment, and to make it an even more powerful ingredient in educational development through being prepared to be 'tentative' in a positive rather than in a negative way.

This phenomenon of teacher modesty has a bearing on the suggestion made earlier that examining boards should communicate 'early' statements of ideas to other interested teachers on a wide scale. As matters stand the teacher who has made a private approach to an examination board with a tentative proposal may well not give the permission needed for such dissemination. A highly polished statement from a teacher is much more likely to be given the 'publish and be damned' green light than one which is perceived as being crude. It is at this point that the examining board staff together with the existing teacher-supporting agencies (for example, inspectors, advisers, colleagues in teachers' centres) should be able to provide the encouragement necessary to make teachers feel that their ideas deserve to be aired. In this way they will not only set in motion a process which might bring them help for their own ideas, but they will also give encouragement to others who have not yet gained even a hazy understanding of their own innovatory work.

This may sound a trifle over-dramatic. The 'new idea' may be a well tried approach to educational practice of which the teacher has only recently become aware. If such is the case he can be encouraged to read about the work already done by others on this particular line of development, although this would not provide the help that association with fellow fumblers might bring. The 'new idea' may also be no more than a slight realignment of the content-matter of a traditional subject, or a relatively small variation in the way orthodox material is presented to students. These are, perhaps, both the most mundane and the most potent 'new ideas'. Tinkering with the orthodox subject syllabus and the class-teaching approach is a commonplace practice upon which much scorn has been poured by the high-priests of radical innovation, but it is the starting place for change for many teachers, and so deserves as much attention within the communications system as other forms of 'innovation'. The 'new idea' may also take on the guise of one of a dozen well-tried techniques of teaching which contain the germ of an enquiry-based approach to learning, and they too should be viewed as 'growth points'. They deserve support and ought to be communicated to others, notwithstanding the likelihood that somewhere along the line they will be called 'old hat'. The point is that nobody is in a strong position to evaluate the growing points of others. We are all 'growing' and are thus open to the critical gaze of those who have already enjoyed the state of growth in which we find ourselves. The authors do not consider it over-dramatic to ask teachers to see themselves as humble learners who are capable of being helped by others, as well as being in a position to help even their 'helpers'! This is what education is about.

Let us make the large assumption that a position has been reached in which teachers are prepared to do two things; first to submit their ideas at an early state to a communications network largely maintained by an examination board, and secondly to allow such submissions to be given an airing within this network. The exercise may well produce a trickle of comments from teachers who, within the supportive environment which it is hoped will have emerged, are eager to share views with a teacher who has aired his ideas in the way described. What happens next depends very much on the nature of the idea that is central to this stage of groping towards a dialogue.

The communications network can perhaps best be illustrated by seeing how it might work in a particular set of circumstances. The illustration chosen is concerned with developments in a single subject, geography. Had the choice been an integrated course or I.D.E. [Inter-disciplinary enquiry. This approach to curriculum design is discussed more fully in the book from which this extract is taken.] What follows would be equally applicable: such courses would, however, throw up one or two additional points to which attention will be drawn later.

The example concerns a teacher who is redesigning a programme in geography so that it involves fourth and fifth year students in studies and practical activities in the fields of urban geography and oceanography, with special reference to the use man makes of sea food, in addition to other, perhaps more general, studies in geography. Slightly expanded, this statement is turned into a 'declaration of intent' which is sent to an examining board. In view of the fact that the two fields referred to in the redesigned programme are capable of being developed and studied in ways which will draw attention to certain pressing matters of public concern, it is likely that other teachers of geography, not to mention teachers of other subjects, are thinking about their school programmes in similar ways. They may not all choose the same list of 'concerns' upon which to base their working schemes, but there may well be a measure of agreement that a geography programme, orientated towards subjects of public concern is likely to be seen as relevant by the students who will be exposed to it.

Without stretching the imagination too far, it seems reasonable to suggest that if an examining board makes known to a large number of teachers the broad outline of such a programme it will receive communications from some of those teachers who are thinking along similar lines. In such circumstances the board can call a meeting of the teachers concerned together with a member or members of its staff either at a central point or in groups in different areas. The initial 'declaration of intent' and the information supplied by other teachers who have reacted to it is made available at these meetings. This perhaps becomes the starting point for a general discussion about the potential of specialised programmes of this type in geography, and about the means of identifying the requirements to be met if such programmes are developed further and presented for assessment and certification. Thus a dialogue is started which might be followed up by various activities. For example, perhaps some teachers see that schemes of work being developed within a number of their schools are now so similar that they can form a consortium, and use a group Mode 2 or Mode 3 to mount an assessment/certification exercise. Other teachers might find that while they agreed on the broad objectives contained within an educational approach to geography to which the various 'declarations of intent' pointed, they cannot find agreement on the areas that 'should be studied'. They might be able to develop a programme similar to the one described for the World History Project, with an agreement on the title of the course and the aims of the educational work it might promote. As with the World History Project, the examining board and the teachers involved could then work towards an agreement whereby each school submits its own interpretation of the title and the aims, and then over a period of time develops an assessment pattern which involves both the teachers and the board. In fact the ideas implicit in the World History Project offer a great deal to such a programme of development in, say, 'Contemporary Geography'. Finally, there might well be teachers at the original meeting whose points of contact with the rest of the group are not sufficient for them to participate in a joint exercise. For such teachers an individual Mode 3 would constitute the best approach if they wish their course to be assessed. Some of these teachers might leave the group, while others might stay in close contact in order to obtain assistance with the development of assessment techniques. Whatever happens, there will be a considerable feed-back to those who are involved with the development of Mode 1 examinations in geography within the examinations board. Moreover, in those areas of the curriculum in which geography plays a part, the development techniques used for assessing students' understanding of geographical concepts and of the skills of the geographer would benefit immensely by such a joint teacher/examining board initiative.

The stimulus for the suggestions originally put forward by the geography teacher might have been provided by the use made of materials produced as part of a curriculum development project, say one of the Schools Council projects. Much project material is produced without formal assessment and certification in mind. A study by L.A. Smith has shown that many teachers have difficulties in developing appropriate assessment techniques for evaluating their success in putting over the educational activities sponsored by such material.[2] This difficulty becomes more acute when teachers wish to have the course externally assessed and certificated. A sharing of experiences in relation to project and other materials, which can be infinitely variable, seems to be another possible use of the communications network. There is no reason at all why a storage and retrieval system for project materials and their use should not be built up as an extension to the network, and be used in association with banks of questions designed to assess the skills and concepts whose mastery and understanding the use of the materials is intended to develop. This would be particularly valuable in relation to a project like the Schools Council Humanities Project where an ounce of practical experience in the use of materials deliberately designed to stimulate discussion is worth a ton of theory. Such material and its use also create particularly acute assessment problems, and practical accounts of ways of tackling issues like the individual's contribution to a group discussion and the whole question of how to assess discussion would be invaluable. Here the communication might consist of tapes as well as of pieces of paper.

Integrated studies programmes present a peculiar problem in relation to communication. Ideas about such programmes are unique in a way which ideas about single subject programmes can never be. This results from the process of integration itself. The preparation of an integrated studies programme by a group of teachers within a school involves them in defining not only the areas of study they wish to promote but also the ways in which they see these areas interrelating. The resulting mixture of content, attitudes and concepts within the chosen subjects is bound to be unique for the group or individual who has proposed the integration. This makes it unlikely that the communication of the full programme will be of great value to other teachers, since the thinking behind it will be peculiar to the programme and not always easy to explain. The value of encouraging teachers to let others do their thinking for them in the preparation of an integrated programme is also questionable. There is no doubt, however, that contact between teachers who are engaged on differing programmes is as valuable when these are integrated as it is when they are not.

The best way to secure this contact, without in any way inhibiting freedom of action and choice, seems to lie in communicating, not the details, but the aims of the programmes and a list of the subjects involved. The detail may have to be provided subsequently, to the board, should the school wish to have its programmes assessed and certified. These statements of aims and lists of subjects would permit interested teachers to follow up on their own any programmes which look like potential allies. The statements of aims would also provide useful information for the board in its consideration of the assessment problems of integrated programmes, and thus in the preparation of appropriate advisory services.

Much of what was said in the preceding paragraphs about integrated programmes applies also to I.D.E. programmes. Here, however, the aims of the programmes should be supplemented not by a list of the subjects involved but by the titles of the chosen themes. Teachers with experience of I.D.E. will be able to recognise the type of enquiry-based work that is likely to be promoted by most of the themes publicised in this way. Almost certainly, while any number of themes will be put forward, they will tend to fall within a few broad categories. Thus a team of teachers in one school may well find that because of the nature of their theme they can, with profit, contact a team working in another school which has decided to work on a different or allied theme. Communications over I.D.E. programmes might thus turn out to be both easier and more fruitful over integrated programmes, although the difficulties of combining within a communications network maximum utility with the absence of any pressure to use what is provided remain formidable. It is hoped, however, that this very brief indication of some of the ways in which such a network could operate will have served to indicate its key position in the successful working of any interaction model designed to promote a freer curriculum. Perhaps its greatest value is that as it expands so do the possibilities for its further expansion, and so too does the quality of assistance that those involved can provide for each other.

In order to achieve a freer curriculum at the secondary level within the framework of externally recognised assessment and certification, we have advocated [. . .] a different role for examining boards. The implementation of such a role will inevitably require different structures from those at present in existence, and will involve re-thinking the relationship that examining boards have with the rest of the education service. Ought they, for example, to continue to charge fees and make token payments to teachers, or ought they instead to be one service amongst many provided by local authorities or area training organisations for a teaching profession whose salaries are adjusted to take account of their involvement as an integral part of their professional work? Such changes will not be easy to introduce. Unless, however, a structure is found which can permit the continuous servicing of local groups of teachers and schools (with the emphasis upon the word 'local') and unless there can be found staff interested and skilled in providing consultancy services on a continuous basis, then a happy marriage between examining boards and schools will not be possible. Only through such a marriage can the potential of both curriculum development and assessment practice be properly exploited.

This changed role does not mean that the supervisory moderating function should cease to be part of the work of future examining boards. If, however, the exercise of this necessary function is not to interfere with curriculum development, then the emphasis at present placed upon comparability between boards and between subjects will have to be abandoned. Instead, moderation in the future will need to be increasingly concerned with the demands that particular curricula and the courses developed from them place upon the group who takes them. In relation to these demands, levels of performance will have to be established. If this is to be done then the first thing that must disappear is our present system of presenting results in the form of global grades. Such grades can be, and are, treated as if they represent comparable levels of performance between boards and subjects and measure in accurate fashion differences in levels of performance within subjects. Different methods of presenting information about performance will have to be introduced, and in particular profile reporting ought to be investigated in detail. If this is not done the curriculum needs of secondary schools will remain constrained by the examining system despite any efforts that examining boards may make in other directions to assist schools to develop and assess their own courses.

We have advocated a different role for teachers in relation to nationally recognised examinations, which many of the profession will neither consider desirable nor wish to undertake. It is also a role for which their present training in large measure does not fit them. Regrettably, considerations of space and the line of argument pursued here do not enable the authors to develop the points made in these last paragraphs in any greater detail. The willingness, however, of both examining boards and teachers to accept these changed roles is vital to the emergence of a freer curriculum at the secondary level as the authors have defined it. It is only if the willingness exists that the necessary support of other agencies within the education service such as the colleges of education and local authorities will be forthcoming. This reference, albeit brief, does, however, serve to underline once again the enormous amount of work required if we are to use the examining system in ways suggested in this book as an aid rather than as a hindrance to curriculum development. Recent developments in public examinations although encouraging have done little more than make examining boards passive partners in the developmental process, and this is not enough. The task may be long and expensive, but the rewards both for students and teachers will be enormous. It must surely be worth trying.

Henry G. Macintosh and Leslie Smith

NOTES

1. The word 'national' has been used advisedly here since the strengths of certain of the local school certificates established in the decade before the coming of C.S.E. are often overlooked, for example, those in Reading and Hertfordshire. Their contribution to curriculum development in a local context was often significant.
2. L.A. Smith, 'New Resources Dialogue', *Ideas,* no. 27, February 1974.

Part III

CURRICULUM DEVELOPMENT AT LOCAL LEVEL

12. LOCAL CURRICULUM DEVELOPMENT

Allan Rudd

From R. Watkins, *In-service Training: structure and content* (Ward Lock Educational London, 1973).

[Rudd considers the James Report proposals for professional centres. He examines some aspects of the North West Regional Curriculum Project in the light of these proposals: the focus on the ROSLA problem, the provision of the resources of manpower, finance and support services, the support of the working groups. Rudd concludes from this examination that the James proposals for a network of professional centres are well conceived.]

An Exercise in Partnership

The James Report envisages local curriculum development and evaluation as one important type of third cycle activity, through which teachers can extend their personal education, develop their professional competence and improve their understanding of educational principles and techniques. Such work (among other types) would go on in a network of professional centres, each under the leadership of a full-time professional warden who enjoyed an independent role. The work of these centres would involve bringing into partnership diverse agencies — schools, universities, polytechnics, colleges of education, advisory services, teachers centres, resource centres and further education institutions — notably in helping to staff the professional centre. The basic principles of this proposal bear a marked resemblance to those on which local teachers centres were established in north-west England during 1967, though the scale of activities now proposed is greatly in excess of that realised to date in teachers centres:

> There are two basic principles in which progress on curriculum development should be built: first, that motive power should come primarily from local groups of teachers accessible to one another, second, that there should be effective and close collaboration between teachers and all those who are able to offer co-operation. There is no hierarchy of initiative or control. The co-operative effort of each interest needs to be involved in equal partnership, and all parties should be ready to give or to seek support.[1]

Allan Rudd

This paper presents a critique of some aspects of the North West Regional Curriculum Development Project, in terms of certain of the James principles. But before doing so I must affirm my own basic belief about teacher education, which shortage of space prevents me from attempting to justify. I believe that teachers learn in fundamentally the same manner as do their pupils. If we really expect them to adopt demonstrably better procedures in the classroom we must set up appropriate conditions for establishing and maintaining the new behaviours. Just as telling pupils how to carry through a task is not a sufficient condition for ensuring pupils mastery of that task, so merely telling teachers how to improve their teaching or presenting them with persuasive propaganda about the merits of particular techniques is unlikely by itself to lead to improved teaching. I regard it as axiomatic that the teacher who learns from his own (appropriate) experience understands in a way which is just not available to persons who merely try to follow the instructions of others or who seek to please their superiors. For experience-based innovation not only promotes increased pedagogical skill; from the manner in which the new skill is accumulated the teacher also learns concurrently the art of mastering new professional skills, and that confidence and sureness of touch which are hallmarks of the full professional. In short, I see the local curriculum development group as a setting within which teachers can become the willing agents of their own continuing professional education.

Task Orientation

The North West Project is a consortium of fifteen teachers centres established and maintained by thirteen LEAs, most centres being supported jointly by two LEAs. The whole enterprise is coordinated through the University of Manchester Area Training Organisation; but except for major committees, all the project's work is carried on in one or other of the teachers centres. When the project was launched early in 1967 few educationists in the region (or elsewhere in the country) had many clearly developed ideas as to how such centres might run, and a good question was (and remains) 'Why should teachers take their professional concerns to local teachers centres?'

The academic answer usually given is that such centres provide like-minded teachers with a local and relatively unstructured setting within which to discuss professional matters, often as a preliminary to proposing innovations within their own school setting. Yet five years later it has to be confessed that most such centres are still bedevilled by the problem of how to entice teachers into the centres for sustained bouts of professional work. Short in-service courses, exhibitions of teaching materials or of pupils' work, a reference library/resource centre, a workshop for making needed apparatus – all are valuable services for a teachers centre to offer. It has been our experience, however, that creative work in curriculum development provides much the strongest stimulus for schools' commitment to the work of teachers centres. In turn such commitment provides the teachers centre with the life-space it needs if it is to function positively in its local area.

From our experience the teachers centre leader who wishes to stimulate creative work in curriculum planning would do well to concentrate attention on the critical areas of teacher concern, *viz* pupil needs and interests and the demand which society makes on its young people. This is where commitment can begin; and it is only by dealing with the significant concerns of teachers that a professional centre can win recognition as a worthwhile focus for local professional effort.

The leader who succeeds in winning such life-space may well find that the issue which a group of teachers brings to his centre seems so vast, so complex and so basic that the working group despairs of its own capacity to contribute anything substantial to the problem's solution. In reply, the leader may argue that by pooling their knowledge, by drawing upon particular individual skills and by extending their thought as they interact with other educationists, the group will achieve much more than could have been obtained by any one member working in isolation. Though teachers may be impressed they will not necessarily be convinced by such arguments; for they are, rightly, jealous of those demands upon professional time which interfere with their primary task, that of planning and guiding their pupils' learning. This implies that any professional centre's first development scheme must be, and be seen to be, successful. The scheme need not be large, but it must deal with a real and urgent issue facing a definable group of teachers in the area, must appear from the outset to be well organised, must achieve its intermediate targets and must yield a product which demonstrates unequivocally the advantages of teachers co-operating for professional purposes.

The North West Project has derived much continued goodwill from teachers and LEAs in the region over a period of several years by focussing its effort on the ROSLA problem, by maintaining several groups working in parallel (so that the anticipated total product would exceed the sum of its parts) and by meeting intermediate targets published before the project began.

There is of course no lack of suitable focal points for professional effort. Local schemes for combining two secondary into one comprehensive school, for preparing pupils for examination under a new syllabus or for introducing counsellors into an Authority's schools are but three examples of situations where innovations initiated outside the school put strong pressure on identifiable groups of teachers to modify traditional practices. Less demanding of change, but no less stimulating towards innovation, are the curriculum products published for the Schools Council or the findings of research carried out by NFER or similar bodies. An alert professional centre leader will seek to grasp such 'teachable moments' and to fan a spark of passing interest into a steadily burning flame of commit-

129

ment to inquiry, one capable of sustaining and directing effort over a period of time.

Provision of Needed Resources

Once the development task has been given and accepted, adequate resources need to be provided for the work. These fall under three main headings: manpower, finance and support services. Only passing reference will be made here to questions of manpower, important as these are. It is a basic principle of local development work that teacher participation be voluntary. Two implications of this principle are: that the dynamics and the climate of a working group must be constructive and satisfying (rather than merely congenial); and that in an extended enterprise, such as the North West Project, regular opportunities have to be provided for group membership to change. Though in theory the latter implication might bring about dissipation of accumulating experience, this circumstance has never arisen in the North West Project.

At no time has the project distinguished among types of teachers when panel members were being recruited. We have sought heterogeneous groups, whose members come from varying professional backgrounds. The enthusiasm and energy of the young have been as valued as the experience and wisdom of more senior teachers; and we have found that groups of such heterogeneity have ensured that a wide range of interest, ideas and suggestions is taken into account in reaching decisions. Now, near the end of the fifth year of development work, about one quarter of current panel membership consists of founder members, with another quarter having joined the project when field trials began, and since remained with us.

Though it is a cardinal principle of the North West Project that all curriculum development work be controlled by teachers, such control could be absolute only were the teachers themselves to underwrite project finances. In the early days the work was substantially, though not entirely, supported by finance from the Schools Council; but collectively the thirteen LEAs concerned have provided more than £200,000 of public money to support the project's work. Thus ways have had to be found to make possible the essential freedoms development panels need, within the normal rules and practices of LEA financial administration.

For accounting purposes each project team (of which there were seven) has been regarded as an educational unit (such as a school), with the panel chairman being cast in the role of headmaster. Estimates of proposed expenditure for the financial year 1969-70 (for example) and forecasts for the year 1970-71, based upon discussions between panel chairman, panel members and project director, were compiled according to the codes of expenditure in normal LEA use. Those familiar with LEA procedures will know that the financial year 1969-70 began in April 1969 and that, if the needed finance were to be available then, estimates would have to be submitted in October 1968 — just one month after the development panel had first met to plan and carry through its 1968-69 year's work. Thus each panel's first major activity involved making detailed predictions as to the form, content and extent of the field studies it was to undertake during the 1969-70 school year, since money for providing teaching kits to be used in these studies had to come from funds then being estimated. Since the writing of a course worthy of field trials and the accumulation of a suitable teaching kit for this course were to be the focus of the year's panel work which was only then beginning, it is not difficult to appreciate the frustration among developers to which this demand might have given rise, however necessary this procedure was in the eyes of administrators.

The source of such possible irritation was removed, however, when the project's finance and general purposes committee agreed to group estimates into a small number of codes, and later to allow virement between codes and between years on each panel's account. These latter two provisions are believed to be outside the strict code of LEA rules, though within the discretionary powers available to administrators. The element of freedom introduced by these changes made it possible for panels at all times to approach their development task without any serious financial constraint on their planning.

This example illustrates beautifully the creative role which a liberal administration can play in local curriculum development work. However, if one is to generalise on the basis of this single example, two additional points need to be stressed. First, that administrative initiatives such as this are likely only when a basis of mutual trust and a sense of common purpose exist between developers and administrators. Second, that an important element in such trust is administrative competence on the part of the project executive (i.e. the professional centre leader); in particular, his ability to persuade panel chairmen to budget prudently and wisely in the first instance, rather than to follow the common practice of submitting estimates greatly in excess of what the panel is likely to need, against the chance of across the board reductions before these estimates are approved.

Teacher control of local development work is a principle to which much thought has been given in the North West Project. Coupled with the need for adequate representation of all other interests involved in a wide-ranging and complex regional experiment, the principle inevitably implies a steering committee, which is more effective as a reaction group than as a discussion group. Yet over the period under review the committee, far from degenerating into a mere 'talking shop' has proved a striking example of the processes of democratic control of a many-sided exercise. The fact is that at most meetings there have been serious matters for consideration, and discussion has never been cut short by the chairman. Papers on a great variety of topics have been presented for consideration, and have received the benefit of close scrutiny by a large number of people from different backgrounds.

Allan Rudd

Committee papers are prepared in the regional study group, an executive body comprising the project director, the deputy director, and leaders of all fifteen teachers centres. Anticipation of close scrutiny in committee, and knowing that the eventual decision will have to be given effect by the executive, ensures careful planning in all matters. This organisation also has the merit of keeping open three channels of communication between teachers and steering committee: via teachers' associations; via LEA administrations; and via teacher centre leaders (who are nonvoting members of steering committee).

Without doubt the most notable feature of the steering committee has been the relationship with its finance and general purposes committee. A school normally functions within a financial framework established by its LEA, one which generally bears little close relationship to the curricula proposed by the teaching staff of that school. In the North West Project, however, the finance and general purposes committee has functioned within a framework of general policy and curriculum proposals decided by a steering committee on which LEAs (even collectively) had only minority representation. The novelty of this relationship, and its success as a working organisation provide striking evidence of the spirit of initiative and co-operation, shown by both elected and professional LEA representatives throughout the life of the project.

Support for Working Groups

An important asset of group work in local curriculum development centres is that each teacher brings to the group his own background of knowledge, skill and ability to think. These qualities offer great scope for studying curriculum problems because, when given the opportunity to think about his work, a teacher has greater potential than an outsider for promoting change, because he knows his own situation, its dynamics and the need for improvement. This problem under review has personal meaning for him. However, this asset may turn into something of a liability, should an emerging identity induce the group to adopt a narrow interpretation of its problem, and to become impervious to suggestions originating outside the group.

One way of avoiding this situation developing is to include among the group teachers crossing traditional lines of association and pockets of thinking. For example, it would have been very stimulating to have had a few primary school teachers among the North West Project's panel membership; but the pattern of release for panel work made this difficult to achieve. Another method, of which some but not enough use was made, is to include in each panel's programme events designed to extend professional insights, e.g. reviews of relevant literature, visits to schools where interesting work is taking place.

A third method, in which the project became very effective, was based on functions in which panel representatives met other teachers from schools in the region. Almost always such meetings were held for specific purposes, e.g. to recruit teachers for panel work or schools for field trials; but this purpose was always set in the general context of reporting back to teachers an outline of current plans, policies and proposed courses of action. Wherever possible these meetings were kept small, were held in teachers centres and were led by members of the development panel concerned. Despite their informality, the challenge of presenting the panel's ideas to an informed and critical audience always put panel members on their mettle. Not every member welcomed the prospect of such meetings, but all prepared thoroughly for them. Afterwards many members reported deriving new insights from the encounter, and in the end felt a thrill in realising their ability to hold and convince such an audience as to the value of the general thrust of their panel's work.

The regional study group has played a crucial role in supporting local development work. In the early days the discrepancy in leadership experience between the project director and the newly-appointed leaders of local centres was vast. The latter had for the most part been recruited straight from the classroom, often on a temporary basis; and they were given the task of establishing and maintaining centres for which few models then existed. At that time, therefore, the regional study group became excessively director-centred, the local centre leaders being both professionally and emotionally overdependent. Within a year, however, the professional confidence of local leaders began visibly to grow, as they realised their ability to describe (and where necessary to defend) the project's ideas to teachers in their areas, and as the centres themselves became increasingly acceptable as focal points for local, as well as regional, initiative. This proved a very difficult time in the regional study group, as each local leader struggled to achieve more autonomy during discussions of both educational and administrative matters. Such struggles generally arose when individuals or subgroups invested great personal and professional capital in ideas which seemed to others unlikely to chime with the wider educational purposes of the project.

At such times it would have been very easy for the project director to have adopted either an excessively dominant or recessive style of leadership. Respectable arguments were not lacking to support either approach, for example:

1. The project had been set up to carry out a specific programme of work within a given period of time, and it was important to work within these terms of reference.
2. The project had been established to study the feasibility of groups of teachers working as curriculum developers. Such groups had first to 'learn the trade'; and the short-term role of leadership was to teach the needed skills. If the project were to fail to demonstrate the

competence of teacher groups for such work, the inhibiting effect of that failure upon curriculum development work within the region (and perhaps also elsewhere) might be very great indeed.

3. Where appointed leaders were unable to convince their groups of the wisdom of proposed courses of action, each group should be allowed to go its own way, and to learn from its own (perhaps bitter) experience.

In the director's view, the project had to concern itself with all three of these major purposes (products, feasibility and training); and the result was that at this time regional study group meetings sometimes became very exhausting encounters indeed. It is therefore appropriate at this point to recognise the high degree of commitment and energy (both intellectual and emotional) which the local leaders brought to this work, from which they learned above all else how to create and maintain a humane yet purposeful climate for local development work.

Perhaps the most lasting problem with which the North West Project has struggled is that of making available to development panels the knowledge, wisdom and skill which specialist educationists are anxious to place at panels' disposal. At an early stage in its life the project drew up and circulated extensive lists of such persons and institutions, leaving to panels themselves the initiative for seeking such support. It must be reported that these services have only very rarely been called for.

For much of its life morale in the panels, as well as among centre leaders, has been dominated by a feeling which might be expressed thus: 'For the first time groups of teachers have been given the opportunity to show what they can do as curriculum developers — and by God, we're going to show them!' Even the project director, when visiting a panel, has occasionally been asked, half-jocularly 'Have you come to tell us what to do?' The tone of voice in which the question is asked may indicate either resentment at the apparent suggestion that in any crisis leadership passes out of teachers' hands, or relief that in an emergency an authority figure is willing to come to the rescue. The question itself epitomises the difficulties inherent in introducing outside consultants into local development panels.

This determination of teachers to throw off the (perceived) weight of imposed authority is one of the most persuasive features of the climate within which the project has operated. The source of perceived authority may vary, embracing, for example, traditional school practices, the pressure of new curriculum orthodoxies, the weight of the standard literature, the thrust of advice given by those in positions of authority in the educational system. The response to the pressure from outside has always been the same; 'Why should we? We want to do it our way. Let us experiment for ourselves.' The parallels between this response and that of any young person discovering some new insight or developing some new skill are striking, and provide (at least for the project director), convincing evidence of the value of local curriculum development work as in-service education. Once more it is necessary to affirm a belief (for which the project now has a good deal of supporting evidence) that teachers who learn by discovery and learn to discover are more likely to establish subsequently in their classrooms conditions in which their pupils can do likewise.

Nevertheless, a curriculum development project is concerned with products as well as with processes; and it would be a sign of increasing professional maturity when a panel felt sufficiently confident in itself to state in effect: 'As a panel we do not know enough about the problem with which we are trying to cope. Please come and give us your advice as to how we might best proceed.' It is encouraging to be able to report that in general panels in the North West Project have for the past year or so felt sufficiently mature to seek such support informally through their acquaintances, if not yet formally from available professional sources.

A Humane Working Climate

Any professional centre leader finding himself in this position will give a great deal of his attention to creating in his centre circumstances likely to foster such emerging professional maturity. Experience in the North West Project suggests the importance for such outcomes of a humane working climate.

A humane working climate stems from many little actions and influences, too numerous to mention in detail. In the context of this paper, however, these may be summarised as follows:

1. Willingness on the part of 'the authorities' to allow panels to work on problems which panel members and other teachers perceive as real and worthy of attention.
2. Presence within the panel of able personnel in sufficient numbers to accomplish worthwhile tasks.
3. Freedom for panel members to express dissatisfaction with the current state of those affairs in schools, in LEAs, in the project or within the panel in which they have a legitimate interest.
4. Willingness on the part of all panel members to work together to achieve common ends through agreed means.
5. Recognition that many kinds of educationist can contribute to curriculum improvement.
6. An attitude of openmindedness and healthy scepticism about both what is traditional and what is new.
7. Absence of undue pressure by those in authority (whether within or outside the project) about matters which properly fall within the panel's decision.

Allan Rudd

The Professional Centre Leader

It will be apparent that if local curriculum development is to be successful, the centre must enjoy thoroughly competent professional leadership. In an age of specialists the centre leader needs to be a high-level general practitioner, able to understand and appreciate the concerns of class teacher, headteacher, LEA administrator, resource specialist, teacher trainer and higher education exponent. At the same time he needs to be good at establishing and maintaining productive and satisfying work relationships among persons drawn from several of these backgrounds but functioning as partners in a common task. To do this effectively he also needs a reasonable grounding in the several areas of academic study with which the centre's work is concerned.

Merely to list these attributes is to invite two questions: where are such masters of all the arts to be found? Why should such persons go into, and remain in, professional centre leadership? In the author's view the answer to the first question is that since few such persons are currently available we must set up leadership training programmes. It is, of course, true that if the James proposals for professional centre leaders are to be adopted courses need to be established through which potentially suitable applicants can accumulate the basic knowledge and rudiments of the skills they need for their work. Essentially, however, it is in the field that the professional centre leader, as general practitioner, accumulates wisdom, finesse, judgment, sensitivity and imaginative flair. So what is deceptive about the proposals for leadership training programmes is that real, worthwhile and acceptable projects have to be maintained so that such journeymen can learn the arts and can experience the humane working environment they must later seek to create elsewhere. And who is to lead *these* projects? Experience in the North West Project has shown the feasibility of university and LEA personnel working together on such a task. Once again, perhaps our most important finding has been that the centre leader who is a creative and enthusiastic member of a regional development panel is the one who induces in his centre a climate within which the teachers working there can also catch the spirit of creative endeavour.

Finally, why should so well qualified an exponent remain in professional centre work? It is obviously important to the education system that he do so; for in sociological terms he is a change agent, aiming to release more potential for innovation by promoting creative encounters among people interacting in flexible partnership.

But he is also a person, often with a family and always with career prospects, living in a society which tends to promote specialists to high-status posts, even where the work done in those posts approximates more to general than to specialist practice. That the James Committee has considered this point is obvious from its recommendations that the leader be called a warden, that he be given an independent role and that he enjoy at

136

least senior lecturer status. These may well be necessary conditions for the post: but in the experience of the North West Project they are not sufficient conditions. Sufficient conditions are that the leader's work be emotionally and professionally satisfying, offering him also the experience of personal development and some evidence of the impact of his efforts upon schools. Because most of the project's centre leaders have experienced these rewards from their work I make bold to claim that were the James proposals accepted there would never be found lacking able teachers who were eager to make careers as professional centre leaders. Accordingly, I conclude that the James proposals for a network of professional centres, each under the leadership of a full-time professional warden are well-conceived, and merit the support of all proposed partners in third cycle teacher education.

NOTES

1. Schools Council, *Curriculum Development Teachers' Groups and Centres*, Working paper 10 (HMSO, London, 1967).

13. THE MALMÖ REGION

From *Case Studies of Educational Innovation: IV. Strategies for Innovation in Education* (CERI/OECD, Paris, 1973).

[The work of the Malmö Educational Development Centre is described. The overall objectives of the curriculum in Sweden are determined at the level of central government, but the regions are empowered to explore new and better ways of meeting these overall objectives.]

The reforms of Swedish education were prepared by several commissions and also by experimental work in several regions throughout the whole country. Much of this experimental work was not systematically organised, though most of it was initiated by the National Board of Education. In 1958 however the NBE selected seven special experimental schools to develop particular carefully evaluated innovations, one of which was a municipal high school for girls in Malmö. This school initiated a number of experiments, such as flexible groupings, inter-subject instruction, team teaching and individualisation.

In 1962, when the headmistress of the Experimental School was appointed Assistant Director of Education in the School Office for Malmö she brought with her the idea of creating a development centre for the whole Malmö region. With such an expansion it would be possible to give equal consideration to all levels and types of school, secure the co-operation and involvement of many teachers in different schools, and ensure that the results of examination would not depend entirely on teachers in highly selected experimental settings. In 1964 the NBE, in a board decision on State financial support, finally recognised the Malmö educational development centre: its main objectives were[1]

[to find] practicable ways of giving effect to the intentions of the educational reforms proposed or already decided, also at the levels higher than the compulsory school, [and] to facilitate the progressive revision of the curriculum.

Sweden is divided into 24 counties, of which Malmöhus, situated in the extreme south-west of the country, is by far the most densely populated, with the largest absolute population. Malmö, the biggest city in Malmohus, is the third largest city in Sweden.

Each of the 24 counties has its own County School Board. The boards appoint teachers on the recommendation of individual municipalities and are also responsible for the in-service training of teachers in the county.

The county is responsible for the implementation of the 'teaching plans' laid down by the central government (through NBE). Compared with an English local authority, a Swedish county has less authority and freedom of manoeuvre, in particular concerning the main points of the curriculum which is decided by the central authorities.

In the city of Malmö the Malmö City Board of Education, which comprises 11 politicians elected for a term of four years, is the responsible body for all schools in the city. The City Board has a school office in Malmö headed by a Director of Education and three assistant directors who are all appointed directly by the Government in Stockholm, on the recommendation of the Malmö Board of Education in consultation with the country school board and the NBE. The Educational Development Centre, therefore, was organised directly under the City School Office.

Since 1962 there has been an Institute for Educational Research at the School of Education in Malmö — now the biggest educational research unit in Sweden — which plays an important role in the research and development work in Malmö. Research in the School of Education is predominantly funded by the Research and Development Department in NBE.[2]

The body responsible for the work of the Malmö Educational Development Centre is the Planning Group, which is appointed by the NBE on the recommendation of the City Board of Education. It is composed of the Director of Education from Malmö (Chairman), the rector of the Malmo School of Education, one scientific expert of the Department of Educational and Psychological Research of the School of Education, one representative of the county board, an experimental leader and an assistant director of education.

The Planning Group appoints an Experiment Committee whose members are chosen to represent the most important on-going projects. This group prepares a programme of experiments in co-operation with city schools participating in experimentation. The Planning Group examines this programme, gives its approval and submits it to NBE through the City Board of Education. The NBE examines the programme and determines the State contribution to the activities.

The School of Education is therefore through the Planning Group directly involved in the experiments in the City of Malmö. In addition, this School of Education has an on-going research and development programme which to a large extent is based on school experiments in the Malmö region.

Type of Innovations

A number of innovations have been introduced since 1962. Most of them are in the curriculum area [. . .] such as training in study techniques, team teaching and work with variable pupil groups, and the development of learning materials and curriculum revision. They are either planned out-side Malmö (and adapted for testing by the Development Centre), initiated by the Centre itself, or originate from the School of Education on the basis of experiments initiated in Malmö. Examples of such projects are: individualised mathematics teaching (IMU), teaching methods for German (UMT), learning studio, closed circuit television projects, an experiment in flexible pupil grouping, flexible timing and team teaching (PEDO), new forms of practical vocational orientation, compulsory music teaching, in-struction by tape in typing instruction, remedial teaching, expanded pupil co-operation in the planning of the curriculum, and co-operation between pre-school and lower level of the comprehensive school.

In the Institute of Education Research there are at present 19 exclu-sively school-related projects which include material-oriented projects, teacher-oriented projects, pupil-oriented projects and projects mainly con-cerned with the working environment and organisation. In many cases they are evaluation projects of the experiments initiated by the Develop-ment Centre, but independent projects are also organised in the schools as direct research projects.

The Process of Innovation in Malmö

An important characteristic of initiative in innovation in Malmö is that teachers take part, to a large extent, in the discussion of priorities and in the creation of projects. However, the persons who played the key roles in establishing the Development Centre have probably also been most instru-mental in the creation of projects. In Malmö there are 200 teachers and head teachers who are members of so-called subject-groups with the specific task of analysing problems relating to instruction in their subject in the region and of proposing innovations within the framework of the curriculum guidelines. This is probably the most important source of information for problem identification in the region. Until recently no other formal systematic problem identification has existed. Another im-portant characteristic of the planning is that all innovations are related to the overall objectives of the curriculum. The new curriculum of 1969 for compulsory schools was to a large degree influenced by regional develop-ments. There seems to be agreement in Sweden at the regional level that the objectives of the innovation process are to find new and better means to meet the objectives of the stated curriculum which is decided at the central level.

The planning of innovation in Malmö is done by the planning group and the experiment committee. It would be noted, however, that Malmö has a network of international contacts which helps the innovation pro-cess — in particular, contacts with the USA and Britain have had influence, as well as contacts with other Nordic countries.

The model for experiments in the Malmö region has a number of similarities with our planning-research- and development model and with the general problem-solving approach, and is illustrated in the figure following:[3]

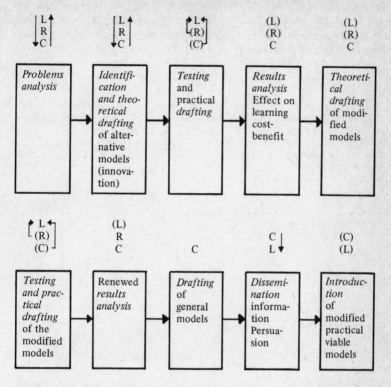

The diagram shows experimentally for the various phases of development a possible sharing of work by the central school authorities (C), the research institutions (R) and the local school authorities (L).

If one looks at the rather systematic process outlined in the diagram, including the evaluation and revision, one would think that this has a thorough, systematic, scientific basis. From the discussion of Malmö, one observes that the researchers at the School of Education have difficulty in evaluating the experiment with traditional tests and evaluation procedures. To a large extent the researchers have not been able to influence the planning as they would like to have done and have too often readily accepted the auxiliary role assigned to them. The experiments by their very nature cover a number of variables and in many cases the researchers find it difficult to establish sensible evaluation procedures which cover all the relevant variables. In spite of this, a number of important evaluations and recommendations have come out of the experiments in Malmö.

The dissemination of regional experiments in a country with central administration of educational planning gives rise to some specific problems. A region is responsible for the dissemination of results from experimental settings to other schools in its own region if the innovations can be interpreted inside the framework of the curriculum. Innovations which do not fall into this framework, however, cannot be implemented without a policy decision by the central government. [. . .]

NOTES

1. W.P. Teschner, 'Malmö, Sweden' in *Case Studies of Educational Innovation: II, At the Regional Level* (CERI/OECD, Paris, 1973), p.346.
2. O. Vovmeland, 'The National Board of Education (NBE), Sweden' in *Case Studies of Educational Innovation: I – At the Central Level* (CERI/OECD, Paris, 1973).
3. Teschner, op. cit., p.341.

14. STAFF DEVELOPMENT: THE LEAGUE MODEL

John I. Goodlad

From *Theory into Practice*, Vol. xi, no. 4, 1972, pp.207–14.

[This paper has four foci. First, it presents a model designed to identify factors to be taken into account in effecting educational improvement within the context of schooling. Second, it describes a strategy for change based on elements in this model. Third, the paper discusses aspects of staff development inherent in this strategy. Finally, it presents some ideas for further development of the strategy and some attendant problems.]

Goals for education and schooling tend to be stated in the form of some desired changes or accomplishments for students: citizenship, work habits, understanding selected concepts, and the like. Consequently, efforts to improve tend to focus on specific pedagogical procedures and the measurement of pupil outcomes, with some accompanying feedback designed to provide information for revision. This effort to refine ends and means and the relationship between them is exceedingly important but insufficient. It fails to account for other factors which may be of considerable importance. For example, attempts to improve reading performance through alternative methodologies alone seem to account for relatively small deviations in pupil attainment. Clearly, factors in addition to pedagogy are at work.[1]

The ultimate criterion for judging school programs is, indeed, what happens to students in them. Unfortunately, however, exclusive preoccupation with this criterion often has led to short-term experiments and premature rejection or endorsement of this or that technique. Meanwhile, the general context of schooling within which the experiments are conducted, which probably has a great deal to do with what is happening to the students, remains unchanged. We often merely tinker when more fundamental examination and rehabilitation of the organism is called for.

Current concern and a growing body of evidence regarding the functioning of schools suggest that, in addition to precise ends-means relationships of goals and industrial procedures, we must devote attention to the major variables making up the character of schools. Two such variables are the culture of the school as a whole and its relationship to the larger context, particularly the formal educational system of which it is a part. Focus on these variables leads one to think about what constitutes a healthy, productive school-culture and about the effect of conditions in the larger system on that culture. The adjective 'healthy' rather than 'healthful' is used here deliberately. To a degree and for some considerable

143

time, we propose that major attention be given to the health of the school, not only to its healthful properties for students in it.

Goals for schooling can now be stated in the form of some desired conditions in and for the school itself: decision-making authority and responsibility, relations between principal and teachers and between teachers and children, processes of human interaction and the like. It is appropriate, for example, to talk about humane and inhumane environments on the basis of criteria going back to our conceptions of man and the good life, quite apart from specific behavioral objectives for pupils. Consideration of means focuses on what adds to or detracts from these environments. In the process of seeking these environments, it is important, of course, to engage in formative evaluation with respect to what is happening to students. But critical judgments of the effect of these environments on pupil behavior must await assurance that the environments sought have, indeed, been created — a development too frequently not awaited in much conventional summative evaluation.

The research and development paradigm resulting from this kind of thinking adds considerably to the well known and much used paradigm involving pupil outcomes and immediately prior instructional interactions. In the latter, pupil outcomes constitute the dependent variables — that is, outcomes presumed to be affected by these interactions which are, in turn, the independent variables. Figure 1 portrays this well-known paradigm, D.V. standing for dependent variables and I.V. for independent variables.

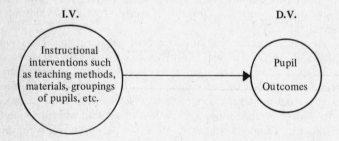

Figure 1. The conventional model for studying ends — means relationships when improving the achievement of pupils is the goal.

Carroll has developed a convenient model for examining the full range of independent variables to be reckoned with at the instructional level in seeking to improve pupil outcomes.[2]

When we consider the culture of the school as the dependent variable, however a new paradigm emerges. In Figure 2, the culture of the school becomes the dependent variable and factors to be considered in seeking to change this culture become the independent variables. It is now possible to develop a model for examining the range of independent variables at the institutional level to be reckoned with in seeking to improve or strengthen the culture of the school.[3]

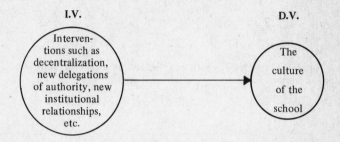

I.V.

Interventions such as decentralization, new delegations of authority, new institutional relationships, etc.

D.V.

The culture of the school

Figure 2. A paradigm for studying ends-means relationships when improving the health of the school becomes the goal.

By combining Figures 1 and 2, a more comprehensive set of relationships emerges, suggesting what must be taken into account in seeking to improve the health of both school and pupil. (Figure 3). We now see the school, first, as a variable dependent on conditions (independent variables) which are subject to adjustments of various kinds. But we see it, second, as a composite set of conditions (independent variables) which can be arranged to affect students who are at least partially dependent on it. It becomes apparent that teaching methodology, for example, is only part of what goes on in school and that changing pedagogical procedures alone is not likely to produce pupil outcomes as great as those that occur when a more comprehensive array of variables is attended to.

Of course, this model for understanding or effecting educational change is incomplete, since the school is only one of several major institutions impinging upon the student and affecting his learning. But it does provide a reasonably comprehensive picture of what should be examined and reconstructed in making the school more effective. Also, it can serve to broaden our perspective from myopic preoccupation with individual teachers to groups of teachers and the culture of the school as a whole. When one keeps this more comprehensive model in view, the limitations of focusing on only one element – even one as powerful as the individual teacher – become apparent, as revealed in Figure 4. The teacher and attendant methodologies are, indeed, important but it is clear that the teacher cannot screen out the impact of the total school culture on the student.

John L. Goodlad

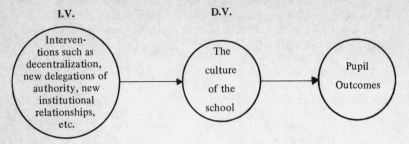

Figure 3. A paradigm for studying ends-means relationships and for improving schooling and learning.

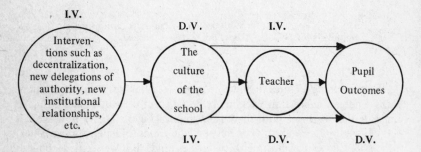

Figure 4. A paradigm for studying ends-means relationships and for improving schooling and learning with the teach extracted from the school as a whole but influenced by it.

We shall now turn to a strategy of improvement which takes the culture of the school as basic and central to the processes of educational change.

II

In 1966, the Research Division of the Institute for Development of Educational Activities, Inc., (IDEA), an affiliate of the Charles F. Kettering Foundation, organised the League of Co-operating Schools for purposes of improving our insights into processes of educational change. In addition to studying what happens to principals and teachers when they try to improve their schools, IDEA and the 18 schools in the League sought also to test and refine a strategy for continuous school improvement. A major part of this strategy focused on the inservice growth of teachers, individually and as total faculties.

In retrospect, it is difficult to sort out the assumptions underlying the initial creation of the League and those that emerged as the project progressed. It is easier, therefore, to collapse time and summarise these assumptions and the structure of the League as they existed around 1972.[4]

The initial assumption was that the individual school, with its principal, teachers, pupils, and, less intimately, parents and citizens, is the largest organic unit for educational change.[5] There needs to be a critical number of 'responsible parties', to use Joyce's phrase,[6] at work on the problems of the school.[7] By collective action these parties, of which the principal and teachers constitute the group most naturally accountable, must define the school's mission. There is a school culture which emerges, for better or worse, whether or not such processes occur — a culture which can be molded to a set of beliefs: a culture which deeply affects and should be shaped by all who are included in it.[8] To be healthy, this culture must be sensitive to those within it and attuned to the conditions and events surrounding it.

Realising the centrality of the school, we sought at the outset to secure from the larger context, through the superintendent and the board, a certain recognition of local school sovereignty. The agreement signed by IDEA and the participating school districts sought more for the spirit than the specifics. Nonetheless, a minimal flexibility, at least, with respect to principals being permitted to attend monthly meetings and faculties being free to utilise minimum school days (established by law yet frequently discouraged in practice) was established. (It sometimes proved not to be assured, however, in the face of critical tests). The principle of increased decentralisation and increased authority for the local school was introduced at the outset and became more firmly established during the five years of the project.

The second assumption was that the individual school is not sufficiently strong, within existing constraints, to overcome the prevailing and in large measure, necessary conservative (in the classic sense of preserving or conserving) characteristics of the surrounding school district. There is a set of expectancies for individual schools that is set by the district as a whole. Principals are appointed in anticipation of their establishing and maintaining these expectations, not of challenging them. They may innovate (innovation is good by definition!) 'around the edges' but should not change anything basic. For a local school, principal, or group of teachers to deviate markedly from the established expectations, more often than not unwritten, is to become very lonely and to risk censure.

In recognition of the conservative restraints built into the school system, expectations for supporting rather than deviating from established procedures, the ever-present shortage of bold leadership, and the loneliness of being just one agent for change, we sought to create a new social system of the 18 schools and to concentrate on the strengthening of this social system. Each school was in a different district; consequently, two schools experienced the same set of restraints. Early meetings of the 18 principals concentrated on what it means to lead; later meetings sought to develop leadership skills. Gradually, membership in the League resulted in both moral and advisory support from colleagues as individual schools, principals, and teachers began to effect changes. In other words, the new and somewhat countervailing social system began to take hold.

A third assumption was that persons about to take risks are more willing to do so when some elements of success already are built into the structure. We may support the underdog in a game or when little of a personal nature is involved, but when our work or life style is at stake, we prefer to be associated with a winner. And so the relationship with UCLA, IDEA, and the Kettering Foundation loomed large at the outset, but became less important and less visible as the League itself and individual schools achieved increased feelings of potency.

A fourth assumption was that some screening, legitimising, and communicating of ideas, beyond what individual schools might do informally, must be built into the new social system. A consortium of schools is, at best, a loosely defined entity. It needs a central point, a hub. The offices of the Research Division of IDEA in West Los Angeles which happened to be centrally located, served this need. Early in the life of the project, this hub provided limited consultant help, bibliographies of selected readings, a newsletter, a meeting place, a small library, etc. As the project progressed, these services were provided less and less through IDEA and more and more by the co-operating schools. But the hub, whether in spite of or because of its changing character, always constituted a major part of the strategy.

At the present time, IDEA is no longer involved, the League has grown to 22 schools, and the education of teachers has become a major function. This brings us to some assumptions about staff development and some accompanying realities.

The preceding list of guiding assumptions regarding the League is incomplete but is sufficient, probably, for the purposes of this paper. Assumptions pertaining to the research effort have been omitted, since this is not a research paper.

III

The project sought to focus on the culture of the school as central to both understanding and effecting educational change. The individual school was assumed to be the organic unit for change and a network of cooperating schools was created to provide a new social system committed to change. This social system legitimised and created a press for change, with all that this implies in new expectations, roles, activities, relationships, and rewards. The inherent significance of normal staff development becomes apparent.

What perhaps is not quite so apparent is that both new demands and new resources for staff development were created. What was sought by the League was that each school should become self-improving — diagnosing its problems, formulating solutions, taking action on recommended solutions, and then trying to get evidence about the effects of such action. For research purposes, a process termed DDAE (dialogue, decisions, actions, and evaluation) became the dependent variable. The overall strategy for change, as partially described in part II, became the independent variable. (These research concepts are used somewhat loosely here since part of the research design was to get insights which, in turn, could be used to modify the strategy). Clearly, then, the initial goal of staff development was refinement of DDAE in each school.

This is distinctly different from the expectations for and activities of most inservice education. Traditionally, staff development has meant inservice education for the individual teacher. The teacher has been regarded as important to the virtual exclusion of other factors, the prime independent variable in the conventional ends-means model of educational improvement. (See Figure 1). Consequently, teachers have been expected to engage in so many units of inservice education per year and have been rewarded in salary for so doing, often *whether or not the activity pertained to their teaching*. Many teachers have been rewarded on the *teaching* salary schedule for preparing to be school principals. Most inservice education activities approved by school districts take the teachers away from the problems of their schools.[9] Griffin's study, for example, suggests that curriculum planning is more neglected at the level of the local school than at the societal and instructional levels of decision-making.[10] The strategy described here turns teacher attention to the school and its problems.

A prime task undertaken by principals and teachers in the League was the preparation of a set of guidelines and criteria for promoting, monitoring and evaluating DDAE in the schools. The criteria involved such elements of school planning as processes of group interaction, use of the literature for ideas and research evidence, pre- and post-planning of faculty meetings, and conducting faculty and small-group meetings. The principals imposed training sessions upon themselves to prepare for their new leadership roles. And total school faculties and sub-groups more and more imposed upon themselves the processes implied by their own criteria. School improvement and staff development became virtually synonymous. Interestingly, research showed that as teachers became more involved in DDAE, they also placed staff development high among areas of needed self-improvement.

After the first two years, the League as a resource for staff development became increasingly powerful with each passing year. The hub, through the newsletter, contributed significantly to the mutual support and assistance roles envisioned early in the project. Each school appointed a reporter who submitted brief 'League reports', recounting successes and difficulties. A classified ad section ultimately appeared, in which schools advertised if they had assistance they could offer to other schools, or if they wanted help with a problem. Sometimes, communication occurred directly from school to school: sometimes it was facilitated by the hub. The result usually was a short training session between interested parties. These became commonplace during the fourth and fifth years of the project.

Three patterns of help to schools or groups of teachers emerged. Quite early in the League's history, teachers from schools which had forged ahead quickly were in demand as group leaders for workshops and staff institutes in neighbouring school districts (rarely in their own, at first). Likewise, a few of the principals were called upon relatively early for leadership roles in summer conferences and institutes. Somewhat later both principals and teachers served in such capacities in their own school districts observing that it is easier to become an expert in a neighbouring school system than at home. Paralleling these developments, teachers in the League visited each other and engaged in mutual assistance.

Some enlarging and restructuring of the League, with termination of the initial project in 1971, brought new elements into staff development. Paradoxically, schools that want to change turn to the colleges and universities, seeking a mythical teacher-innovator, while teacher-preparing institutions look to the schools to provide observable examples of largely non-existent innovative practices. The lamentable fact is that teachers continue to be prepared for the *status quo*.

UCLA, one of the initial partners in the League, had been effecting certain structural changes in its teacher education programs while the project was taking shape. These were joined with substantive changes in 1971-72, when the clinical component and some of the campus classes were moved out into League schools. Teacher-students suddenly had access to changing school environments. Teachers in the schools suddenly had access to courses taught to university students but open also to working teachers. Student teachers were assigned to schools for a broad array of teaching experiences, instead of to individual supervising teachers. They, like the experienced teachers, had access to ongoing programs of staff development in their schools. Much of the distinction between preservice and inservice education disappeared. There simply were teachers with more and less experience in the schools.

IV

The collaborative effort in staff development described here, with the resulting blending or merging of preservice and inservice education, is still in embryonic form. The League was created as much to study what happens when school personnel attempt to change themselves and their schools as to effect educational improvement. Already, some coming steps and their attendant problems can be foreseen.

First, the concept of teachers helping each other in individual and staff development has scarcely been exploited. Teachers learn a great deal from the demands of teaching each other and take readily to instruction by peers, with whose experience they readily identify. It seems reasonable to assume that cooperating school districts through a mechanism such as the League might provide a series of 'pedagogical service stations', temporary inservice institutes staffed by teachers released from teaching duty and attended by teachers currently involved in their own schools with problems related to offerings of the service stations. Both groups would receive inservice education credit; most teachers would serve at some time in their career as staff members. The costs need not exceed current expenditures for inservice education.

Second, much remains to be done in working out the appropriate contributing roles of universities and school systems in the approach to teacher education beginning to emerge in the League and at UCLA. Experienced teachers in the schools might take over some of the 'preservice' functions now assumed by the university. In return, university personnel could contribute much more than they currently do to inservice staff development and school improvement. In the process, the universities would be presented, as never before, with an array of phenomena and problems calling for research. The kind of sharing suggested appears to be very appropriate, given the declining need for new teachers and the growing need for continuous self-improvement of schools and their personnel. One begins to see the possibility for a relationship not unlike that of schools of medicine to their teaching hospitals. When one envisions the prospect of some of these teaching centres being in the inner city, simultaneous school improvement and teacher education look particularly promising and timely. Merely assigning student teachers to inner city schools accomplishes little and sometimes leads to increased disillusionment on the part of both schools and teacher training institutions, to say nothing of the tender student teacher.

Some major hurdles remain to be overcome. The kind of collaboration suggested here calls for a balance of power between schools and colleges or universities. Is an intermediate, third party called for? If so, what would be its relationship to both parties and to the state's teacher certification structure?

How does all this relate to the growing interest in performance criteria for evaluating and perhaps even certifying teachers? And is teacher performance to be judged on the basis of pupil achievement, demonstrated ability to use a variety of pedagogical procedures, contributions to the improved health of the school's culture, or some combination of these?

Looking only to the immediate future and the problems arising out of our first five years with the league, it is apparent that staff development and school improvement of the kind described here must be legitimised by the school district as an approved and rewarded inservice activity.

John I. Goodlad

Otherwise, the questionable practice of adding 'brownie points' for more and more courses and more and more lectures on teacher institute days, whether related or not to teachers' problems and growth, will not be broken.

There are implications too, for the all-year school. Simultaneously keeping school and changing the schools is a task of Gargantuan proportions. The schools appear to grow less and less responsive to rapid social change and new demands. Increasingly, it becomes apparent that schools need more than a few hours each month for the processes of DDAE required for continuing improvement. At least a core of career staff members should have weeks of time in any given year for the necessary processes of curriculum development, school reorganisation, and institutional 're-treading'. Such a core should be employed for an eleven month year, with up to two months for planning. It follows that the students should attend for only nine or ten months or, if longer, that they be under the supervision of other teachers. Perhaps, if they are to have more instruction each year than they have now, it should be in careers and community services, taught by persons not in 'schools' who probably are better prepared to provide it. At any rate, there is little point in students spending still more time in schools already judged inadequate.

Focusing on the individual school as the organic unit for educational improvement departs more abruptly from conventional approaches than is at first apparent. The most difficult aspect of this departure is that it calls for us to lift our eyes and efforts temporarily from customary practices which focus only on pupils and individual teachers. It is the school as a social institution that is ailing. Let us concentrate for a time on what is required not only for it to become healthy but also for it to become capable of sustaining itself in a healthy state. Once the condition is established, it will be interesting to see what happens to boys and girls over a period of years spent in healthful school environments.

NOTES

1.   See for example, James S. Coleman, *Equality of Educational Opportunity* (Office of Education, Department of Health, Education and Welfare, Washington, D.C., (1966); Philip W. Jackson, *Life in Classrooms* (Holt, Rinehart, and Winston, New York, 1968); Charles E. Silberman, *Crisis in the Classroom* (Random House, New York, 1970); L.M. Smith and W. Geoffrey, *The Complexities of an Urban Classroom* (Holt, Rinehart, and Winston, New York, 1968).

2.   John R. Carroll, 'A Model of School Learning', *Teachers College Record*, 64, 1963, pp. 723-33.

3.   Goodlad has developed a conceptual scheme for separating decisions affecting pupil learning into societal, institutional and instructional. See John I. Goodlad (with Maurice N. Richter, Jr.). *The Development of a Conceptual System for Dealing with Problems of Curriculum and Instruction*, HEW Contract No. SAE-8024, Project No. 454 (University of California and Institute for Develop-

ment of Educational Activities, Los Angeles, 1966). (Temporarily out of print while being revised).

4. A number of books and monographs describing the change strategy and its effects are being prepared. A documentary film entitled 'The League' is available from IDEA, P.O. Box 628, Far Hills Branch, Dayton, Ohio 45419.

5. For this and other assumptions, see John I. Goodlad, 'Educational Change: A Strategy for Study and Action', *National Elementary Principal,* 48, 1969, pp. 6-13.

6. Bruce R. Joyce, *Alternative Models of Elementary Education* (Ginn, Waltham, Massachusetts, 1969).

7. Related research reveals that few school faculties are so engaged. See John I. Goodlad, M. Frances Klein and Associates, *Behind the Classroom Door* (Charles A. Jones, Worthington, Ohio, 1970).

8. Seymour B. Sarason, *The Culture of the School and the Problem of Change* (Allyn and Bacon, Boston, 1971).

9. Goodlad, Klein, and Associates, op. cit., p. 108.

10. Gary A. Griffin, 'Curricular Decision-Making in Selected School Systems.' Unpublished doctoral dissertation, Graduate School of Education; University of California, Los Angeles, 1970.

Part IV
INNOVATION AND THE SCHOOL

15. OPEN SCHOOLS, OPEN SOCIETY
Basil Bernstein

From *New Society*, 14 September 1967, pp. 351–3.

[Bernstein applies the concepts 'mechanical' and 'organic solidarity' to contemporary developments in British education. The movement from 'closed' to 'open' schools implies a shift in emphasis in some of the main features of the school; the forms of social control, the division of labour among the staff, the curriculum (and especially the view of subjects), the pedagogy and the organisation of teaching groups. These changes may have profound effects for the role of the teacher and the pupil.]

There has been much talk among sociologists concerned with education about the possibilities of analysing the school as a complex organisation. The approach to current changes in the structure of the contemporary school system, which I attempt in this article, was initially set out by Durkheim over seventy years ago in his book, *The Division of Labour in Society*. I shall interpret the changes in terms of a shift of emphasis in the principles of social integration from 'mechanical' to 'organic' solidarity. Such changes in social integration within schools are linked to fundamental changes in the character of the British educational system: a change from education in depth to education in breadth. I shall raise throughout this article the question of the relationship between the belief and moral order of the school, its social organisation and its forms of social integration.

The concepts, mechanical and organic solidarity, can be used to indicate the emphasis within a society of one form of social integration rather than another. Organic solidarity is emphasised wherever individuals relate to each other through a complex interdependence of specialised social functions. Therefore organic solidarity presupposes a society whose social integration arises out of *differences* between individuals. These differences between individuals find expression which became crystallised into *achieved* roles. Mechanical solidarity is emphasised wherever individuals share a common system of belief and common sentiments which produce a detailed regulation of conduct. If social roles are achieved under organic solidarity, they are *assigned* or 'ascribed' under mechanical solidarity.

Wherever we have mechanical solidarity, according to Durkheim, punishment is necessary in order to revivify shared values and sentiments; i.e. punishment takes on a symbolic value over and beyond its specific utilitarian function. The belief system is made palpable in the symbolisation of punishment. Durkheim took what he called repressive (criminal) law as an index of mechanical solidarity.

Under conditions of organic solidarity, the concern is less to punish but more to reconcile conflicting claims. Social control, in conditions of organic solidarity, is concerned with the relationships between *individuals* which have in some way been damaged. Durkheim took what he called restitutive law (civil) as his index of organic solidarity. Here the system of social control becomes restitutive or reparative in function. Whereas under mechanical solidarity individuals confront one another indirectly — their confrontation being mediated by the belief system — under organic solidarity, in situations of social control, the belief system recedes into the background and the individuals confront one another directly.

Mechanical solidarity, according to Durkheim, arises in what he called a segmental society. He meant by this a type of society which could lose much of its personnel without damage to its continuity. Organic solidarity would correspond to the differentiated society, with diverse specialisation of social roles; consequently the loss of a particular group of specialists might seriously impair the society. One can infer that segmental societies would make clear distinctions between inside and outside, whereas in differentiated societies the boundaries, as all symbolic boundaries, between inside and outside would become blurred.

Durkheim argued that a secondary cause of the division of labour arose out of the growing indeterminacy of the collective conscience (the value system). He said that sentiments would be aroused only by the infringement of highly general values, rather than by the minutiae of social actions. This, he said, would give rise to wider choice and so would facilitate individualism.

Organic solidarity refers to social integration at the level of individualised, specialised interdependent social roles, whereas mechanical solidarity refers to social integration at the level of shared beliefs. Under mechanical solidarity, there would be little tension between private beliefs and role obligations. In organic solidarity, the tensions between private belief and role obligations could be severe. This tension might be felt particularly by those individuals in socialising roles — for example, parents, teachers, probation officers, psychiatrists.

This is the shift of emphasis in the principles of social integration in schools — from mechanical to organic solidarity — that I shall be talking about. I am not concerned whether all the relationships I refer to are factually present in all schools. Clearly, some schools will have shifted not at all, others more: the shift may be more pronounced in the education of special groups of pupils or within different subjects. I am interested only in the general movement which at the moment may exist at the ideological rather than the substantive level. However, the list of shifts in emphasis may form a measure or scale of the change in the principles of social integration.

Consider, first, the forms of social control. In secondary schools there has been a move away from the transmission of common values through a ritual order and control based upon position or status, to more personalised forms of control where teachers and taught confront each other as individuals. The forms of social control appeal less to shared values, group loyalties and involvements; they are based rather upon the recognition of differences between individuals. And with this there has been a weakening of the symbolic significance and ritualisation of punishment.

Look now at the division of labour of the school staff. Irrespective of the pupil/teacher ratios, the staff is now much larger. The division of labour is more complex from the point of view of the range of subjects taught. Within the main subjects, the hierarchy of responsibility has become more differentiated. The teacher's role itself has fragmented to form a series of specialised roles (vocational, counselling, housemaster, social worker and so on). Still within the broad category of the division of labour consider very briefly, for the moment — the organisation of pupils. The pupils' position in the new schools in 'principle' is less likely to be fixed in terms of sex, age or IQ, for ideally their position, within limits, is achieved in terms of their individual qualities.

Thus we find (a) a movement towards a more complex division of labour among the staff and a greater differentiation of the teacher's role: and (b) at the same time, the pupils' relationships with other pupils in principle arise from their expression of their education differences. This is good evidence of a shift towards organic solidarity.

Let us turn, next, to shifts in emphasis in the curriculum, pedagogy, the organisation of teaching groups and teaching and pupil roles. Here we are at the heart of the instrumental order of the school: the transmission of skills and sensitivities.

Take the organisation of teaching groups first. Here we can begin to see a shift from a situation where the teaching group is a fixed structural unit of the school's organisation (the form or class), to secondary schools where the teaching group is a flexible or variable unit of the social organisation. The teaching group can consist of one, five, twenty, forty or even a hundred pupils and this number can vary from subject to subject. At the same time there has been an increase in the number of different teaching groups a pupil of a given age is in. The form or class tends to be weakened as a basis for relation and organisation.

One can raise the level of abstraction and point out that space and time in the new schools, relative to the old, have (again within limits) ceased to have fixed references. Social spaces can be used for a variety of purposes and filled in a number of different ways. This potential is built into the very architecture.

Now for the changes in pedagogy. There is a shift — from a pedagogy which, for the majority of secondary school pupils, was concerned with the learning of standard operations tied to specific contexts — to a pedagogy which emphasises the exploration of principles; from schools which emphasised the teacher as a solution-giver to schools which emphasise the teacher as a problem-poser or creator. Such a change in pedagogy (itself perhaps a response to changed concepts of skill in industry) alters the authority relationships between teacher and taught, and possibly changes the nature of the authority inherent in the subject. The pedagogy now emphasises the *means* whereby knowledge is created and principles established, in a context of self-discovery by the pupils. The act of learning itself celebrates choice.

But what about the curriculum? I mean by curriculum the principles governing the selection of, and relation between, subjects. We are witnessing a shift in emphasis away from schools where the subject is a clear-cut definable unit of the curriculum, to schools where the unit of the curriculum is not so much a subject as an *idea* — say, topic-centred inter-disciplinary inquiry. Such a shift is already under way at the university level.

Now, when the basis of the curriculum is an idea which is supra subject, and which governs the relationship between subjects, a number of consequences may follow. The subject is no longer dominant, but subordinate to the idea which governs a particular form of integration. If the subject is no longer dominant, then this could affect the position of teacher as specialist. His reference point may no longer be his subject or discipline. His allegiance, his social point of gravity, may tend to switch from his commitment to his subject to the bearing his subject has upon the *idea* which is relating him to other teachers.

In the older schools, integration between subjects, when it existed, was determined by the public examination system and this is one of the brakes on the shift I am describing. In the new schools, integration at the level of idea involves a new principle of social integration of staff: that of organic solidarity. This shift in the basis of the curriculum from subject to idea may point towards a fundamental change in the character of British education: a change from education in depth to education in breadth.

As a corollary of this, we are moving from secondary schools where the teaching roles were insulated from each other, where the teacher had an assigned area of authority and autonomy, to secondary schools where the teaching role is less autonomous and where it is a shared or co-operative role. There has been a shift from a teaching role which is, so to speak, 'given' (in the sense that one steps into assigned duties), to a role which has to be *achieved* in relation with other teachers. It is a role which is no longer made but *has to be made*. The teacher is no longer isolated from other teachers, as where the principle of integration is the relation of his subject to a public examination. The teacher is now in a complementary relation with other teachers at the level of his day-by-day teaching.

Under these conditions of co-operative, shared teaching roles, the loss of a teacher can be most damaging to the staff because of the inter-dependence of roles. Here we can begin to see the essence of organic solidarity as it affects the crucial role of teacher. The act of teaching itself expresses the organic articulation between subjects, teachers and taught. The form of social integration, in the central area of the school's function, is organic rather than mechanical.

How is the role of pupil affected? I said that, under mechanical solidarity, social roles were likely to be fixed and ascribed, aspirations would be limited, and individuals would relate to each other through common beliefs and shared sentiments. These beliefs and sentiments would regulate the details of social action. In the older secondary schools, individual choice was severely curtailed, aspirations were controlled through careful streaming, and streaming itself produced homogeneous groups according to an imputed similarity in ability. The learning process emphasised the teacher as solution-giver rather than problem-poser. The role of pupil was circumscribed and well defined.

Now there has been a move towards giving the pupil greater choice. Aspirations are likely to be raised in the new schools, partly because of changes in their social organisation. The learning process creates greater autonomy for the pupil. The teaching group may be either a heterogeneous unit (unstreamed class) or a series of different homogeneous units (sets) or even both. The pupil's role is less clearly defined. Of equal significance, his role conception evolves out of a series of diverse contexts and relation-ships. The enacting of the role of pupil reveals less his similarity to others, but rather his difference from others.

I suggested earlier that, where the form of social integration was mechanical, the community would tend to become sealed off, self-enclosed and its boundary relationship would be sharply defined. Inside and outside would be clearly differentiated. These notions can apply to changes both within the school and to its relation to the outside.

Schools' boundary relations, both within and without, are now more open. This can be seen at many levels. First of all, the very architecture of the new schools points up their openness compared with the old schools. The inside of the institution has become visible. Of more significance, the boundary relation between the home and school has changed, and parents (their beliefs and socialising styles) are incorporated within the school in a way unheard of in the older schools. The range and number of non-school adults who visit the school and talk to the pupils have increased. The barrier between the informal teenage subcultures and the culture of the school has weakened: often the non-school age-group subculture becomes a content of a syllabus. The outside penetrates the new schools in other fundamental ways. The careful editing, specially for schools, of books, papers, films, is being replaced by a diverse representation of the outside both within the library and through films shown to the pupils.

Within the school as we have seen, the insulation between forms and between teaching roles has weakened, and authority relationships are less formal. The diminishing of a one-to-one relation between a given activity, a given space and a given time − i.e. flexibility − must reduce the symbolic significance of particular spaces and particular times. The controls over flow in the new schools carry a different symbolic significance from the controls over flow in the old schools.

Let me summarise at a more general level the significance of these shifts of emphasis. There has been a shift from secondary schools whose symbolic orders point up or celebrate the idea of purity of categories − whether these categories be values, subjects in a curriculum, teaching groups or teachers − to secondary schools whose symbolic orders point up or celebrate the idea of mixture or diversity of categories. (These concepts have been developed by Mary Douglas in her book, *Purity and Danger*). For example:

1. The mixing of categories at the level of values. Changes in the boundary relationships between the inside and the outside of the school lead to a value system which is more ambiguous and more open to the influence of diverse values from outside.

2. The mixing of categories at the level of curriculum. The move away from a curriculum where subjects are insulated and autonomous, to a curriculum which involves the subordination of subjects and their integration.

3. The mixing of categories at the level of the teaching group. Heterogeneous rather than homogeneous teaching groups and differentiated sets of pupils rather than fixed forms or classes.

The secondary schools celebrate diversity, not purity. This may be symptomatic of basic changes in the culture of our society, particularly changes in the principles of special control. Until recently the British educational system epitomised the concept of purity of categories. At the apex of the system sat the lonely, specialised figure of the arts PhD; a dodo in terms of our current needs.

There are also the separation of the arts and the sciences, and within each the careful insulation between the 'pure' and the 'applied'. (Contrast all this with the United States.)

The concept of knowledge was one that partook of the 'sacred': its organisation and dissemination was intimately related to the principles of social control. Knowledge (on this view) is dangerous, it cannot be exchanged like money, it must be confined to special well-chosen persons and even divorced from practical concerns. The forms of knowledge must always be bounded and well insulated from each other; there must be no sparking across the forms with unpredictable outcomes. Specialisation makes knowledge safe and protects the vital principles of social order.

Preferably knowledge should be transmitted in a context where the teacher has maximum control or surveillance, as in hierarchical school relationships or the university tutorial relation. Knowledge and the principles of social order are made safe if knowledge is subdivived, well insulated and transmitted by authorities who themselves view their own knowledge or disciplines with the jealous eye of a threatened priesthood. (This applies much more to the arts than to the sciences.)

Education in breadth, with its implications of mixture of categories, arouses in educational guardians an abhorrence and disgust like the sentiments aroused by incest. This is understandable because education in breadth arouses fears of the dissolution of the principles of social order. Education in depth, the palpable expression of purity of categories, creates monolithic authority systems serving elitist functions; education in breadth weakens authority systems or renders them pluralistic, and it is apparently consensual in function. One origin of the purity and mixing of categories may be in the general social principles regulating the mixing of diverse groups in society. But monolithic societies are unlikely to develop education in breadth, in school systems with pronounced principles of organic solidarity. Such forms of social integration are inadequate to transmit collective beliefs and values.

It might now be helpful to drop the terms mechanical and organic solidarity and refer instead to 'closed' and 'open' schools.

Individuals, be they teachers or taught, may be able (under certain conditions) to make their own roles in a way never experienced before in the public sector of secondary education. But staff and students are likely to experience a sense of loss of structure and, with this, problems of boundary, continuity, order and ambivalence are likely to arise. This problem of the relationship between the transmission of belief and social organisation is likely to be acute in large-scale 'open' church schools. It may be that the open school with its organic modes of social integration, its personalised forms of social control, the indeterminacy of its belief and moral order (except at the level of very general values) will strengthen the adherence of the pupils to their age group as a major source of belief, relation and identity. Thus, is it possible that, as the open school moves further towards organic solidarity as its major principle of social integration, so the pupils may move further towards the 'closed' society of the age group? Are the educational dropouts of the fifties to be replaced by the moral dropouts of the seventies?

None of this should be taken in the spirit that yesterday there was order; today there is only flux. Neither should it be taken as a long sigh over the weakening of authority and its social basis. Rather we should be eager to explore changes in the forms of social integration in order to re-examine the basis for social control. This, as Durkheim pointed out decades ago, is a central concern of a sociology of education.

16. OPEN SPACE – OPEN CLASSROOM

Clem Adelman and Rob Walker

From *Education,* November 1974.

[The relationship between open space and open education is explored. The surface features of open classrooms are too often exaggerated while the importance of the quality of the interaction is neglected. The authors see the nature of 'talk' rather than structural arrangements as the crucial indicator of openness.]

Many educationists support the development of 'the open classroom' in primary schools, and its transfer to the secondary sector. But although there is some consensus about what open space classroom designs look like, there has been very inadequate investigation of the links between the size and shape of school spaces, the arrangement of objects within them, *and* the human qualities involved in initiating and sustaining open classroom situations. For example, the recent DES Education Survey 16, *Open plan primary schools,* hardly mentions these human and social qualities, but considers only architecture, planning and organisation. It thus leaves the assumption 'open plan – open classroom' uninspected.

Many teachers are interested in the possibilities inherent in open space designs, because they prefer the kind of teaching such settings allow and because they feel children learn more or better than they do in traditional settings. But as decisions about designs are rarely in the hands of teachers, and more often the responsibility of architects and administrators, it is quite common to find enthusiastic teachers developing 'open' education within traditional classrooms, and to find open space designs where un-committed teachers are wrestling with problems arising from a clash be-tween their own educational assumptions and those imposed upon them by their immediate environment.

It follows that research has to be concerned, not only with distinctions between 'open' and 'traditional' conceptions of education and their rela-tion to different architectural spaces, but also with educationally signifi-cant differences *within* overall concepts like 'open' and 'traditional'. Educational research (like much else in education) has an unfortunate habit of presenting all real situations in terms of dichotomies.

Indications of Openness

The surface appearance of an open classroom is of a large area where pupils work alone or in groups, where the furniture is adaptable to several different kinds of activity. The teacher usually walks around the space, monitoring progress and dealing with difficulties as they occur, but is not highly visible or a central focus of attention. There is often a variety of different tasks being carried out by different groups of children at any one time, and the overall climate is usually one of informality and a lack of obvious restraint.

Although the general impression is one of 'freedom' it is also true that the situation is subject to a series of constraints, deriving not only from the architecture, but from the teacher's ideas and actions, and so ultimately from wider influences in the community, society and culture. When we talk of the open classroom as 'free', we should always mean 'relatively free', and even 'free in a different sense'.

In an open space design classroom the teacher talks to more pupils, and more pupils talk to each other, compared to the kinds of social situations that usually evolve when the desks are in rows. But it is *what* is said, to *whom*, and the range and kinds of *interpretation* allowed the children, that reveals whether the classroom is educationally open or not.

In changing from traditional to open space classrooms the teacher might find that he seems to be 'repeating himself' when each child has a worksheet, and finds himself 'hurrying along' pupils to ensure that they are working in step. In discussion it is *he*, or *she*, who directs the changes in topic, does most talking and summarises each section. This is perhaps the situation best described by the phrase 'innovation without change'.

If 'openness' in education is ultimately a quality found in the knowledge, beliefs and values that people hold, then it will be recognised in particular educational settings by the extent and varieties of legitimate experiences and the expression of those experiences. Surface features like furniture arrangements, use of space, timetabling, allocation and storage are tools that can be used by teachers to create settings for social action. As tools they may *facilitate* an open pedagogy, but in themselves they cannot constitute openness.

In some of the schools we have studied we have seen the surface features of openness, but often a failure to *use* these to create educationally open settings. Often systems of work cards or a proliferation of resources are used by teachers as a way of shifting authority from themselves on to materials. They are able to ease themselves from out of what they perceive as an undesirable, and difficult role, that of the 'traditional teacher', without fundamentally changing the nature of the classroom. Instead of authority residing in the teacher, it resides in the materials. So in one case a card index system became a source of 'right' answers, allowing the teacher to become 'informal', neutral, seeming not to be constantly evaluating children's actions.

If we rule out surface features as sole indicators of openness then what should we look for in classrooms as indicating openness? We consider that the nature of talk is the crucial feature, for talk is the only readily available manifestation of the extent and process by which mutual understandings of what counts as knowledge in any context are transacted. Within the concept of 'talk' we include aspects of the 'non-verbal' which accompany and emphasise what is said, but in themselves such signals seem to be limited as a mode for the expression and communication of concepts.

All the openness of talk is related to the social relationships, within which shared meanings evolve over time; no single transcript is a fully adequate illustration of what we mean by openness within the classroom. Thus it is not possible to present model examples of types of talk. However here are two extracts from different classes which clarify the distinction we perceive in talk and which may also elucidate what we mean by negotiation of realities (but see also the Bernstein quote).

Extract A

Ps Do you want our fish? Do you want our fish? Oh we'll have your fish.

T Well look Gillian, stop being so silly about this. If you won't take any notice of these — find out about those.

P Oh we will have these.
 — we will. We — can we cut off its head?

T No, not at the moment. I want you to find out what you can see now. How many fins has it got? Where are they? Where is the eye? What shape are the gills? Look there are the gills. What are they like inside?

P Oh aren't they funny.

T See?

P Miss, can we get dissecting needles? we went to the zoo —

T Record what you've got on the outside first.

P — Miss we went to a fish shop Miss — Miss do they have hearts?

T Yes they do.

P Is that it that's there?

T No, that's its bones inside — its rib cage.

P Ooh isn't that —

T I think its heart's been taken out.

P Ooh! Miss!

T I know it's a bit unpleasant but don't start getting silly about it. It's only its inside (pause). Come on what else can you see about it?

P 'Ere Miss, if you pull this off you'd rip off its head.

T Do you know what — this is where it breathes. All those little —

P Yeah.

T — things there. Water —

P Where is what?

T Breathes. It pulls in the water and takes oxygen out —

P   Miss, it . . . in and out. It comes out its gills.
T   No. No it draws it in its gills and pushes it out its mouth.
P   Yes, it goes right through, doesn't it?
T   Yes. Now how are you going to re —

Extract B

T   Have you ever seen a glass paperweight the shape of an egg?
P   Yes.
T   Well that's because it's supposed to sit on the paper and also go round like that in preference to rolling. Anyway do you think it's a good idea to have this hard outside bit here?
Ps Yes, yes.
P   So it protects the chick.
P   And it throws the beak into its . . .
T   Now if the chick's inside . . . All right, do you think this must be completely sealed up?
Ps Yes.
P   Does it . . .?
P   Some people say that birds eat milk . . . eats these little stones.
T   Oh I know what you are talking about, we'll talk about that in a minute. Now I'm thinking about if there's a chick living inside here . . .
Ps Yeah.
T   . . . do you think that chick wants to be surrounded by a very, very tough . . . where there's not a single hole?
P   Yeah for anything to get through.
P   No it's living yeah, because it might be eating.
T   Does that chick want anything in there, what sort of thing does he want in there?
P   Yellow yolk.
T   He wants food, yes, but what else does he want?
P   Air.
T   Air, air, yes, only a little bit. Doesn't need too much air but he wants air through doesn't he?
P   Got to have some.
P   Where do you get air from?
T   Ah well, if you were to magnify this you would find that there's some little gaps going through, but just by looking at it, just like this, the gaps are so small we can't see them.
P   Oh I get you, get it.
T   All right, so air can get through. Anyway let's have a crack inside.
P   Oh no, we want to see exactly what's happening on the inside. (She breaks the egg.)
Ps Oh it's broke, yolk, yolk, yolk. You've got the yolk.
T   Oh, I have the yolk.

P	The yolk's broke.
T	I need tweezers . . . there we are (pupils laugh) . . . now somebody said that the yolk wasn't the chick.
P	It is.
P1	That's why . . . he causes that.
P2	Well it can't be yolk because that's what it eats.
P3	. . . little bit formed . . .
P	Might be a cannibal . . . might eat the yolk . . . cannibal ate it.
P	When we collect these . . .
T	Let's see if I can pull the shell off and get a sort of white thing. Do you know when you pull the egg sometimes . . .
Ps	Yes.
T	. . . there's like a skin . . . you see that bit of skin there . . .?
Ps	Yes.
T	. . . flapping around in here so it looks as if there's a shell and inside the shell there's a sort of skin.
P	Polythene bag.
T	Yes, polythene bag. What do you think it wants a sort of polythene bag for?
P	So if he gets any bangs.
P	He wouldn't be able to breathe if it were a polythene bag.
T	Now that's a point so the polythene bag must . . .
Ps	Have holes in . . .
T	. . . still have holes in so that, um, what do you get in . . .?
Ps	Air.
T	. . . what's the special part of air?
Ps	Oxygen.
P	Have you heard of oxygen before?
T	I said that.

We are using 'openness' not to distinguish a type of classroom but as a quality of action within the classroom. The partial manifestation of the nature of these actions in talk is not a continuous phenomenon. Only sometimes does the collection of perception, interpretation and communication of ideas, objects of social context provide the sensitised teacher with the opportunity to engage in 'openness'. We consider that one of these transcripts is more illustrative than the other. However, the differences we perceive in transcript arise from contextual aspects rather than individual qualities of the teacher. In fact one transcript comes from the beginning of the lesson, the other from way into the lesson.

Problems with Tasks

To reason the child must have access to information in a way that generates problems and enables constructive work to continue. Occasions continually arise where the child requires information which is in fact inaccessible through direct experience within the immediate resources. The teacher is continually faced with the problem of when to 'tell' the child something, and how to tell him. It is not necessarily a feature of open classrooms that all that the children are learning is through direct experience. In fact such classrooms would be quite limiting in terms of the knowledge and experiences they would make available to the child. For this reason we see the nature of questioning between teacher and children as quite critical. This means that the fundamental problems of 'openness' revolve around the difficulties of asking and answering questions. In particular the problem of when to tell and when not to tell in order to try and encourage reasoning often leads teachers into a double bind where they are trying to communicate ideas whilst withholding information. In such circumstances they can easily find themselves so absorbed with intricacies of their own logical consistency that they fail to see the problem from the child's point of view. Even 'simple' problems can become tortuous logical knots which end up confusing and mystifying to both teacher and children.

In part this happens because of the sheer pressure of work on teachers – in the moment of attempting communication he may be hurried and faced with other immediate problems or imminent crises, nevertheless he has to decide:

1. What he *considers* might be reason by the children. This may be based on the teacher's understanding of Piagetian developmental psychology, communication code, social class, I.Q., as well as judgments about attitudes and personality.
2. What must be told to enable the child to continue to reason for himself. (Does this raise the question as to whether the teacher is a reasonable person?)

One and two involve internal acts, they exist in the mind of the teacher. Bernstein says 'If the culture of the teacher is to become part of the consciousness of the child, then the culture of the child must first be in the consciousness of the teacher. We should start knowing that the social experience the child already possesses is valid and significant, and that this social experience should be reflected back to him as being valid and significant. It can only be reflected back to him if it is part of the texture of the learning experience we create.[1]

This comes closer to explicating what we mean by negotiation of realities. This does not mean that 'anything goes' as has been the interpretation and practice of many American, and to a lesser extent British primary (and some secondary) schools. Nor does it mean that only teaching 'pure' subjects' is worthwhile and a good 'training for mind'. It does mean (and teachers will confirm this in conversation) that the amount of thought, sensitivity and empathy that the teacher has to mobilise to accomplish 'openness' makes his task more challenging, vulnerable and exhausting than in a 'closed' classroom where the 'rules' for access to knowledge are set rather than negotiated.

Exploring Alternatives

What we want to suggest is that the 'openness' of a classroom is basically related to the sort of talk and associated relationships that go on in it. The principle of enabling free movement in space is only a preliminary, which itself may be variously interpreted by each teacher. As E.T. Hall says, 'space talks' differently in each culture (and we include all the varieties within the culture 'the classroom').[2]

Talk itself is a resource and how it is used distinguishes classroom from classroom, school from school. It is a more reliable index than furniture arrangements or seating patterns. If the teacher faces rows of desks, the thirty or so participants find it hard to monitor each other's responses, so that it demands exceptional co-operation and empathy from the whole class and the teacher to have a real discussion. However, in principle, if a continuous negotiation through talk was sustained, where no one's attempt to talk was impeded, ignored or sanctioned, then this situation (in spite of the rows of desks) would be 'open' in the sense that we have been using the word.

Large group discussion is probably the most difficult kind of situation for most teachers and children to manage. A more common means of attaining 'open' relationships is through individual and small group exchanges. In secondary and middle schools, art, craft and science have for some years operated in this way for practical reasons. But looking at the development of innovatory programmes in these areas we have often found more 'openness' in the non-innovatory than in the new curricula. Using our interpretation of the word 'open' it seems that the labels of innovation have no necessary implication of change.

Similarly, a new open plan school containing adaptable furniture and flexible services, small groups, individualised curricula, resource areas and community services, does not equal open education in action. Open education is found in the people and the relationships between them, not in objects themselves. Plans for change should start with the human, first of all giving teachers real autonomy to experiment and modify those aspects of teaching that involve the interrelation of ideas and the apparent constraints of situations. In the way we have described the problems this means finding ways for teachers to explore alternative ways of talking and interacting with children in the context of the classroom. Then, the children, to whom everyone's efforts are avowedly directed, may benefit.

NOTES

1. B. Bernstein, 'A critique of compensatory education', in Rubenstein and Stoneman (eds.), *Education for Democracy* (Penguin, Harmondsworth, 1970).

2. E.T. Hall, *The Silent Language* (Doubleday, 1959).

17. THE EVOLUTION OF THE CONTINUOUS STAFF CONFERENCE

Elizabeth Richardson

From Elizabeth Richardson, *The Teacher, the School and the Task of Management* *(Heinemann, London, 1973), pp. 312–33.*

[The importance of the social system of the school is emphasised in this extract, from a management study by Elizabeth Richardson, which is concerned with the struggle of the staff to define their roles and relationships. This struggle is treated within the following perspectives: staff relationships and institutional growth; professional advancement; staff experience; consultation and decision-making; the discussions among the staff.]

Staff Relationships and Institutional Growth

It has been my thesis [. . .] that the process of learning about the changing demands of the schools, if it is to be effective in the long run, must be strengthened by the examination of relationships within the staff group itself. We cannot learn about the effects of streaming, setting and banding without examining our own fears that we are somehow grading and assessing one another as 'A', 'B' or 'C' teachers. We cannot learn about curriculum development and the organisation of knowledge without examining the double pull within ourselves from the attraction of a subject area to which we have become committed and from the claims upon us of children or students who may not share our commitment to that subject. We cannot learn to understand the problems of deviant, delinquent or emotionally disturbed children without recognising the elements of deviance, delinquency and emotional disturbance in ourselves as staff members.

We tend to assume that the best way to offer able teachers the opportunity to study all these problems in greater depth is to take them out of the schools and away from the distractions of the day-to-day work in the classroom. Conversely, many people feel that initial training should be far more school-based than it is at present. There is much to be said for both these arguments. But the danger is that we may find ourselves recreating in a somewhat new form the old practice-theory dichotomy by saying that we give training for practical competence in the classroom at the early stage and a theory-based process of re-education at the later stage. Such a dichotomy implies that a kind of distancing or removal from the practical distractions of the school institution is a necessary condition for theoretical study of the fundamental problems of education. Yet throughout the lifetime of teachers now approaching retirement the most crucial problem of all has been one of communication between people who are teaching together in the same school about the principles upon which they base their work. And I do not believe that these problems of communication occur only between the long-established members of the profession and those who are just entering it. Much of this polarisation of attitudes between the veterans and the novices results from an unconscious wish to simplify relationships, and thus to falsify them, by introducing sharp dichotomies between extreme purposes and views, thus masking the much more comfortable truths about ambivalence and uncertainty.

A good deal of the current public discussion about school management, both at the level of talk and at the level of print, turns on the question of a headmaster's authority to make decisions about how his school should be operated. This question is frequently seen as an all-or-nothing matter. It is implied that either the head makes all the decisions or the staff make all the decisions. One headmaster, much quoted, is alleged to deny that he is the leader of the staff group, although he does not deny his obligation to represent the school (and therefore the staff) in all dealings with governors, local authorities and the outside world in general. Yet offering leadership to the staff group within the school and being its voice outside the school are really two aspects of the same task of headship. Furthermore, since over-all leadership implies the necessity to delegate authority, the same kind of dual responsibility is essentially present in all leadership roles within the staff group, on the boundaries of the various sub-task systems within the organisation.

Yet the act of delegation always arouses, on both sides, strongly ambivalent feelings. A head both wants and does not want to pass on part of the burden of his task; his colleagues both want and do not want to accept full responsibility for their share of this burden. When a headmaster delegates to a member of his staff the authority to carry out a particular task and therefore to make decisions relating to that task, this delegation may be felt by the teacher concerned to be real, or it may be experienced as hollow. Similarly, the notion of 'consultation' within a staff group as a whole can imply for one group of teachers a genuine expectation that they will become personally and professionally involved in the struggle of policy-making, or for another group an empty assurance (which they cannot believe) that their opinions will count for something. The problem is not simply that different schools experience 'consultation' in these contrasted ways, but that different sub-groups in the same school can experience it differently and even that the same staff member may have to cope with disturbing oscillations between his belief in the reality of the consultative processes and his suspicion that they are hollow and false.

Consultation is in reality something far more complex than 'having a say in decision making', although of course it includes this. Essentially, it is a kind of self-education. It therefore involves a commitment to learning that is bound to entail pain, struggle and risk. For learning, if it reaches any depth, exposes one's own inconsistencies, anxieties and double feelings. We talk easily enough about the need for 'good' relationships between pupils and teachers, between students in training and the teachers who supervise their work, between probationary staff and established staff, between staff and parents, between the school and its governing body, and of course between the headmaster and all these people. But what exactly do we mean by 'good' relationships in any of these contexts? Do we mean that they should be unfailingly harmonious? Or do we mean that they are always honest? Or should we really be talking about the problem of exploring reality — a reality that will inevitably contain both harmony and disharmony, both cooperativeness and competitiveness, both the sharing of truth and the withholding of truth, and indeed ignorance of what the truth is? On the whole, schools prefer to preserve the illusion that unruffled happiness — or apparent happiness — in the staff means that everything is well in the best of all possible worlds. To ask probing questions of oneself and one's colleagues is to expose the underlying uncertainties that have been there all the time, to discover the mixture of good and bad that every school has to contain, and to face the necessity of trying to understand the bad as well as appreciate the good.

The effort to identify what is inadequate in the system and to replace it or augment it with something new inevitably brings conflict in its wake. For innovation — be it undertaken by an individual teacher working in isolation, by a group of teachers working together in one school or in a number of different schools, or by the whole staff group in a particular school — is likely to result in some sacrifice of personal security, since to turn from known policies to untried ones demands an act of faith and offers no guarantee of successful outcomes. Consultation about what shall be changed and what shall be preserved unchanged is thus inseparable from the continuous process of re-education within the staff group. And it is in this sense that I am using the concept of 'in-service education' in this final section, not as a substitute for the evolving pattern of college and university education of teachers but as an indispensable part of that pattern.

Every staff group has within it the ingredients of a kind of continuous educational workshop. For it is in the staff group itself that meeting points can be found between student and practitioner, between the young and the middle-aged, between the inexperienced and the experienced, between the enthusiasts and the cynics, the optimists and the pessimists, between the so-called 'pupil-orientated' and the so-called 'subject-orientated' teachers. Some of the paired, yet mutually contradictory, terms I have just used may appear to imply an acceptance of the very dichotomies I have been trying to reconcile in this book. Are these sub-groups in the staff room imaginary? Or do they really exist? Is the polarisation to which I am drawing attention inevitable? Or can teachers, by recognising some of the unconscious mechanisms that create them, take steps to remove them, so that individual members of a staff group can escape from the kind of trap they are put into by their colleagues? Does it lie within the professional competence of teachers to reduce the element of polarisation in their own working groups?

What we really mean by 'polarisation' is an unconscious mutual agreement to take up entrenched positions at opposite ends of an argument, a hardening of apparently irreconcilable attitudes, springing from a profound human reluctance to acknowledge the co-existence of conflicting views about important issues, and arising most sharply in times of crisis. During the Suez crisis friends became unsure how to talk to each other, and the persons who probably suffered most acutely were those one-time aliens who had taken British citizenship and no longer understood what they had embraced in their country of adoption. The deeply divisive effects of a student sit-in, as experienced by the members of a university, cannot really be understood by those outside it. In the educational world the repercussions of a controversial book or film are felt very differently by those who view the controversy from outside and by those who, because they belong to the institution held responsible, have to contain conflicting feelings of anger, guilt, pain and bewilderment.

Personal Maturing and Professional Advancement

To many people outside the world of school, teaching implies restriction to the society of the immature. The teacher can thus be parodied as a man among boys and a boy among men — as someone who can exercise authority only over children. Joseph Wicksteed, in comparing the roles of teachers and parents, once described this state in a more idealistic way, using an appealing image, by saying that it was the teacher's privilege to 'dwell at the headwaters of the fountain of youth' while the parent travels 'down the watercourse'.[1] In fact many teachers also travel 'down the watercourse', and few of those who make a career in education remain throughout their working lives with the same age group or operate as leaders only in relation to their pupils. With the growing complexity of the educational system, a teacher may find himself, within the compass of forty years, working successively with pupils in pre-adolescence, early adolescence and late adolescence, with young adults in student roles in colleges or departments of education, with experienced teachers in their late twenties and early thirties, with middle-aged teachers in senior staff roles, even with head teachers in charge of large schools who are studying the tasks of management.

It is a rather remarkable fact that a secondary school may contain within its total age span of pupils and staff nearly all ages between ten and sixty. Thus for the oldest members of a staff group — those approaching their sixties — some of these colleagues already in senior roles as heads of sections or departments could, symbolically speaking, be their sons and daughters, while pupils entering the first year could, symbolically speaking, be their grandchildren. This experience of watching pupils and young colleagues growing and acquiring new skills, and the experience of influencing this growth, is part of the satisfaction of teaching; and for a whole generation of childless women, during the middle part of this century when marriageable women greatly outnumbered marriageable men in the population, it must have been providing at least vicariously some of the pleasures and the pains of emotional investment in a future generation. Teachers, like parents, have to learn to help the young to attain the independence they seek and thus to be prepared to lose them, and this means that they themselves have to come to terms with their ageing processes, accepting the growing burdens of responsibility in middle age and the relinquishing of those burdens in old age. We talk comparatively easily about 'educating our masters'; it is more painful to think, and talk, about educating our successors.

I believe that there is, for most teachers, a natural progression from an initial interest that is centred on the younger pupils in a school, through a later interest in those in their late teens, to an ultimate concern about how to help colleagues to develop their potential by providing a better management structure in which the skills and expertise of one's successors can be nurtured in the interest of the next generation of children. An increased interest in working with sixth-form pupils does not therefore necessarily imply an absence of concern about pupils as persons or an overriding concern about an academic subject. There are, as we have seen, powerful pressures within the staff group to push sixth-form tutors into this role — pressures emanating from those who seek to build up and maintain the old grammar-school 'standards' without much regard to the changing nature of the sixth-form intake. Within the sub-group of sixth-form tutors there will be a need to respond to these pressures from other colleagues in order to preserve what is known and, by comparison with its alternative, predictable. But the persons who make up this sub-group, within the boundary of the sixth form or upper school for which they have responsibility, are persons who have caring concerns for young people, and — however alien some of those young people may sometimes appear to be — can see in them parts of their own earlier selves with which they can sympathetically identify, even perhaps in moments of anger and bewilderment. The difficulty of handling these complex feelings about young people then reproduces within the sub-group of tutors the same kind of polarisation that exists in the staff group as a whole, with the result that a strong dichotomy between 'pupil-centred' and 'subject-centred' attitudes is set up in that part of the system. It then becomes a vital part of the task of leadership in that sub-section of the staff group to work towards some understanding of these processes and thus to reduce the dichotomy. For it is through working on the meaning of the polarisation that people become able to reduce its effects upon their own personal and professional relationships with pupils.

Examination of Experience in the Staff Group

It must by now be apparent that the Nailsea staff, in working with me in the way they did, had to examine the effects of polarisation and the real meaning of ambivalence at many different levels in the system. With the growing sanction to bring out in staff meetings feelings that might formerly have been suppressed, the real educational problems with which people were having to grapple came more clearly into focus. To their own surprise, perhaps, the increasing freedom to acknowledge weakness, uncertainty and bewilderment created a climate in which leadership skills could grow and flourish. For in these situations it became more and more clear that leadership was not being exercised only by the designated leader or chairman in a particular meeting.

Many members of the staff from the most junior to the most senior offered leadership to their colleagues by opening up for investigation important areas of feeling and thought, often at considerable risk to themselves as persons. Nor was it only I, in my role as consultant, who made interpretative comments during staff meetings. The members of the standing committee in particular became increasingly able to do this, not because they arrived at staff meetings armed with prepared comments but because the work they did together during their weekly meetings made them more sensitive to the feelings of their colleagues and to the ideas with which those colleagues were struggling in the larger meetings. It seemed that as the most senior people learned to listen more attentively, they found themselves both intellectually and emotionally in touch with the deeper undercurrents in the staff discussions. Certain people – both in this top-management group and in the rest of the staff group – became less competitive in discussion than they had formerly been; and as the style and content of their contributions changed, quieter and more reserved colleagues found voices where before they had remained silent.

When I look back over the events of the spring and summer of 1970 certain meetings stand out as turning points in the development of a kind of joint capability within the staff group of relating questions about the inner feelings of persons in the sentient system to questions about the outward behaviour, in professional roles, of those same persons as colleagues in the task system. Three meetings in particular during that year appear to me in retrospect to have been crucial: the standing committee meeting of 30 January, the senior staff meeting of 19 May and the full staff meeting of 18 June. Each of these marked a new stage in the progress towards making available for public discussion matters which would, at an earlier stage in the school's history, have been considered private and therefore accessible only to personal friends.

Scrutinising more closely the three occasions I have selected, I find that they show a gradual enlarging of the areas of human concern that can be encompassed in this way. The first of those three meetings, within the small-group boundary of the standing committee, marked a turning point, or sudden development, of a new kind of awareness in the area of inter-personal relationships; the second, within the wider boundary of the fairly large senior staff meeting, marked a turning point in the examination of inter-group relationships; and the third, in the very large group to which all the teaching staff belonged, and at least two of the non-teaching staff as well, marked a new stage of understanding in the area of the relationships between the institution and the outside world.

Significantly, I believe, each of these meetings took place soon after a full staff meeting devoted to open discussion of some aspect of my own gradual move towards the writing and publication of this report. The earliest of these was the meeting of January 1970, at which my internal report to the staff, distributed just before Christmas, was discussed. During that meeting the problem of differentiating between the role and the person was somewhat dramatically highlighted, when I was suddenly taken to task by a part-time teacher in the modern-languages department for allowing my feelings to show in meetings. She told me, with a directness and severity that I found unnerving, yet at the same time strangely re-assuring, that she did not think I behaved as a consultant should, that I did not maintain the calmness she felt ought to be part of consultant be-haviour, and that in getting 'worked up' (as indeed I had done earlier in that meeting when I felt that people were trying to evade the real task we were there to tackle) I stirred up too much emotional heat in the group. Following this confrontation, the staff began to recognise that I, like any of them, had to come to terms with the person I was, and use, as best I could, my own feelings about a situation as indicators that might help me to understand it better. Thus their struggle to relate themselves to me in my role as consultant could not be separated from the problem of relating themselves to me as a person, any more than their pupils could entirely separate them as the persons *they* were from them in their roles as teachers in that school. Both the staff and I had to acknowledge that another con-sultant, even if he or she had striven to behave consistently within the same role as I had tried to take, would have brought different personal characteristics to bear on the task. This problem of distinguishing between the role and the person without denying the effect of each upon the other was to recur in many ways during the coming months, when roles in the staff group and the characteristics of different persons in the same roles came under scrutiny.

It was less than a week after that meeting that the first significant turning point was reached in the standing committee of 30 January, when the members of the committee found themselves recognising, with a con-siderable sense of shock, that their deliberations with colleagues over curricular matters were making unexpected demands on their capacity to work with the strong feelings exposed by those colleagues, as persons under stress in maintaining their roles in a difficult task. This recognition produced a sudden and dramatic fusion of the thinking and feeling sides of the task of consultation, which must, later, have influenced the way in which the members of the committee were able to help their colleagues to examine more critically the extent to which the staff structure was still forcing a separation between the handling of children as persons and the recognition of those children as learners.

In the senior staff meeting of 19 May there was a second turning point when the place of the house system in the total organisation was discussed. The actual question before the senior staff at that time was not whether houses should continue to be part of the middle-school structure but only whether they should continue to be linked with the lower-school tutorial system. The surprise was that it became possible, even in that early meeting, for questions to be raised about the justification of the house system itself, and that although the house heads were anxious to defend the system, they did not appear to be as threatened in their own roles as might have been expected. This preliminary exploration of some of the issues paved the way for the subsequent discussions, first between the lower-school and middle-school tutorial staff groups later in that same term, then, many months later, between the standing committee and the house heads, and later still in the summer of 1971 in the senior staff group in the context of future reorganisation and of the allocation of posts of special responsibility. These developments made it clear that already by the spring of 1970 the senior staff meeting had begun to provide a framework within which those in middle-management roles, whether technically in the curricular system or technically in the pastoral system, could share with each other and with the top-management group the responsibility for projecting their thinking forward into the future, recognising that their own roles, if they remained in the school, might change radically as a result of this forward thinking, since it concerned broad questions of policy as distinct from immediate questions of implementation.

In the full staff meeting of 18 June 1970, which I now identify as a third turning point, the problem of determining how much of what had hitherto been private could increasingly be made public was explored in another context — that of assessment. In this context 'public' began to mean something more than in the earlier discussion about the house system and the still earlier encounters between the standing committee and certain individual colleagues: for it now involved the boundary between staff and parents, where before it had involved only the internal boundaries between staff groups and between individual staff members.

This was the meeting on assessment, in which problems of trust and distrust between parents and teachers were opened up, along with acknowledgements that the difficulty about arriving at acceptable assessment scales that could be used generally throughout the school and by all staff was closely linked with the wish to preserve the good aspects of a teacher's relationship with pupils by claiming for it a kind of privacy that might be at variance with the teacher's responsibility towards the parents of those pupils.

This progression corresponded with the gradual shift in the staff group's thinking about my written accounts, real or projected, of the Nailsea experience. In the January meeting, preceding the standing committee's first painful awakening to the stresses of top-management responsibility, the shift was towards an examination of their reactions to my first written communication to themselves as a staff group. In the May meeting, preceding the senior-staff group's discussion about role relationships between the lower and middle-school tutorial staff groups, the shift was towards consideration of the possibility that I might publish two articles about the implications for other schools of this school's experience. And in the June meetings, preceding the full staff meeting on the subject of assessment and the communication of information to parents, the shift was towards consideration of the more alarming, because less controllable, presentation of a course of six lectures to Bristol students, each lecture to be followed by a forty-five-minute discussion period.

In fact, in that year, I neither wrote the articles nor gave the lectures. But the opening up of discussion with the staff group about the two possibilities released them, it appeared, to open up new areas of difficult, even painful discussion among themselves. For it was around this time that the house heads were publicly challenged about the nature of their authority in the middle school, that Mike Burnham was publicly challenged about the nature of his authority in the upper school and that Denys John was publicly challenged about the nature of his authority in the school as a whole. And it was during this period that Denys John began to change the style of documentation for staff meetings and to develop a programme of phased discussions that were to lead up to known dates on which decisions about major policy matters would have to be made.

Consultation, Documentation and Decision-making

Readers of this book may from time to time have wondered whether the reorganisation of the management structure at Nailsea was in the direction of a strengthening or of a weakening of the 'hierarchy'. Now the word 'hierarchy' is very often used as though it were a descriptive term applicable only to those at the 'top'. But in fact the word means a 'graded organisation'. We can therefore speak of a hierarchy of responsibilities that includes every single person in a school staff group; and we must recognise that every sub-section itself implies some hierarchical ordering of responsibilities. Even within the standing committee there were three identifiable orders of responsibility: namely the first-order responsibility of the headmaster, who was ultimately answerable to the outside world for what happened in his institution, the second-order responsibility of the deputy head and the senior mistress, who — notwithstanding all the uncertainties about their respective roles — could and did exercise authority on behalf of the headmaster over the school as a whole, and the third-order responsibilities of the heads of the three main sections of the school, who between them had authority over the lower, middle and upper schools but not over the whole school.

Part of the problem of growth for a large institution is that people are reluctant to acknowledge that such hierarchical divisions are present, or if not present, are needed, in every important sub-section as well as in the management system as a whole. The difficulty seems to arise from the error of perceiving each identifiable sub-group as separate from the rest rather than as interrelated with the rest. The standing committee's separateness from the rest, as a bounded group with the responsibilities of top management, had to be reconciled with its inclusion in the larger 'senior-staff group' that also included within *its* boundary the two dozen or so colleagues in middle management roles. And the senior-staff group in its turn had to be recognised as both a separate consultative body within the organisation and as an integral part of the full staff group (see Figure 1).

The strength of the resistance to the notion of 'hierarchy' as a necessary aspect of efficient organisation was illustrated by Denys John himself on the occasion [. . .] when, in introducing Dawn Castell into the already established Fourth Year Curriculum study group in the autumn of 1968, he assured her that there was 'no hierarchy' in that group. It was illustrated in my hearing again about a year later, in a meeting of the house heads with Clive Vanloo, when consideration was being given to a suggestion that had come from one of the house tutors, that they might learn more about what went on in one another's house groups if they instituted a practice of inter-house visiting, perhaps by rotating tutors between the houses in some assemblies or on some lunch occasions. Peter Chapman remarked that it was difficult to find times when tutors could talk about educational matters, adding rather sadly and also with a touch of exasperation that on those occasions when 'the hierarchy' came to have lunch in one of the houses the conversation, inevitably perhaps, was just social. Later in this discussion Clive Vanloo was assured categorically by Graeme Osborn that he was 'not in the hierarchy'. It was clear from the discussion that all four house heads were thinking of the hierarchy as including Denys John, Robin Thomas and John Bradbury, as probably not including the three section heads, and as almost certainly excluding themselves. What was not clear was whether Graeme Osborn, in telling Clive Vanloo that he was not part of it, was offering him a friendly gesture implying solidarity between him and the house heads or a hurtful rebuff implying their rejection of him in his leadership role.

Consultation, participation, discussions about educational matters: all these imply situations in which some people talk and others listen, in which some ask questions and others attempt to answer them (or are expected to do so), in which some throw out challenges or appeals and others respond

179

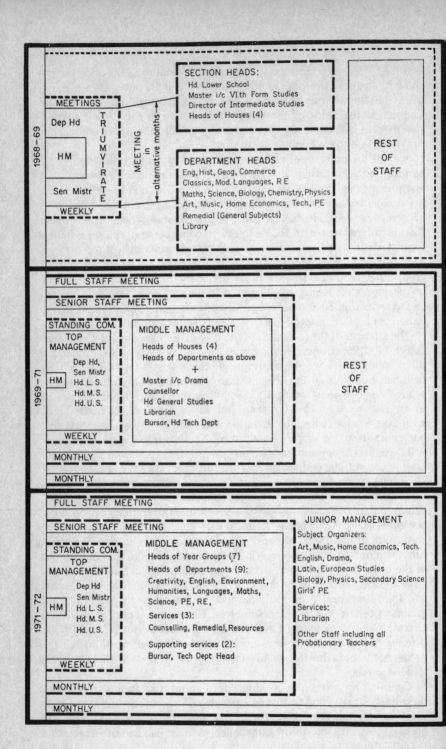

FIG. 1 Successive modifications of management and consultative structure

or fail to respond, in which some offer leads and others follow or turn the other way. Many people assume that ideas are unlikely to be generated during a large meeting unless someone writes a paper as a focus for discussion. Others believe that the important writing is done after a meeting when the ideas that have been generated are recorded, analysed and interpreted. In the earlier months of this three-year study the staff, more often than not, were provided either with a speculative or theoretical paper written by Denys John or with tabulated proposals, very often concerned with curriculum organisation or time-tabling, drawn up sometimes by himself and sometimes by Robin Thomas and Joan Bradbury. In the later months, the staff were more likely to find themselves offered the more challenging task of responding to a broad theme, such as 'the tutorial function' or 'the role of the school counsellor' or 'lower-school organisation' or 'assessment and relations with parents'. The effect of introducing this more open kind of discussion was that the old style of pre-meeting manifesto based on the head's ideas gave way to a new style of post-meeting summary, based on the verbal contributions of the staff during their meetings.

The staff experienced this change on one occasion quite suddenly and, perhaps for many of them, unexpectedly. In March 1970, following the January and February meetings on curriculum development when twenty-eight people had talked with the standing committee. Denys John issued to all his colleagues a document that must have been perceived by them to be radically different in tone and content from those he had circulated from time to time in the past. This document took the form of a collated summary of the suggestions yielded by those meetings, each item linked with the initials of the staff member who had been responsible for it, some being accompanied by the head's own comment or interpretation. To the seventeen separate items drawn from the meetings of the standing committee, he added two that were based on discussions he had had, outside the standing-committee meetings, with Tina Bateman and Margaret Fisher, who had put before him some of the problems of leadership and teamwork that they predicted might arise for them in the complex overlapping areas of humanities, religious education and counselling. The inclusion of these two additional items must have implied, both to the two persons concerned and to the rest of the staff that although Denys John as headmaster could not (and would not wish to) refuse to be accessible to individual staff members who were anxious about any particular aspect of a developing situation, he could not, as chairman of the standing committee, go into collusion with attempts to create 'private' conversations about staff-wide problems unless it was understood that the content of such conversations must be part of the available data for the public discussions in the senior-staff and full-staff meetings during the period of consultation.

The sequel to this new way of following up staff discussions was the evolution of a new way of preparing for them. In the summer term of that year the staff were given a framework in which the phases of consultation were clearly related, first to specific problems that need to be examined by all staff, secondly to the differentiation between the standing-committee, senior-staff and full-staff meetings, and thirdly to the dates upon which any particular decisions would have to be made. The phasing of discussion on three different problems – namely, 'lower-school organisation', 'third-year curriculum and time allocation', and 'assessments and objectives' – over the fifteen weeks of that summer term is shown in Figure 2, which has been reproduced from Denys John's own circular distributed to all staff at the beginning of the term. The special full staff meeting of 1 June, arranged unexpectedly to discuss my proposed lecture course, has been added to the diagram, but no other alteration has been made.

Did this schedule of phased discussions turn out to be an answer to all the problems of consultation? By no means. The special meeting to discuss the third-year curriculum, which took place on 7 July, affords an illustration of the inevitable gap between intention and actuality – a meeting that I described in the previous chapter as being focused on a curious 'exchange of boasts and confessions' about the use of time. In fact the standing committee, despite the forecast that decisions would be reached by 25 June, were still trying to find some way of providing an additional five hours for the options that were to start in Year III instead of in Year IV as they had formerly done; and when Denys John postponed his decisions he posted a notice in the staff common-room to make this known. A schedule, clearly, is not infallible. It is at best a forecast of the kind of sequence that may prove helpful in controlling the boundaries of debate and in regulating the relations between the sentient and task systems so that the need to preserve known advantages or comfortable situations does not militate against necessary change. The schedule does not protect the headmaster, or any of his colleagues, from the unpredictable difficulties that may interfere with the process. Nor should it insulate the staff group against unexpected creative ideas that may necessitate a modification of the schedule.

Sub-group Discussion and Plenary Discussion in General Staff Meetings

One of the constraints upon creativeness in the general staff discussions was the sheer size of the full staff group, which, by 1970, numbered seventy-five, including the ten part-time staff who were, of course, entitled to attend staff meetings. The discussions about the possible substitution of sectional staff meetings, based on the tutorial teams in the lower, middle and upper schools, had exposed the fears of being over-identified with one particular age group of pupils in the school, and this particular solution to the problem of size was not reconsidered. But the need to find ways of tackling the difficulties of exchanging useful information and ideas in the large group was now being openly acknowledged. Sometimes this acknowledgement would take the form of accusatory remarks – surprise that

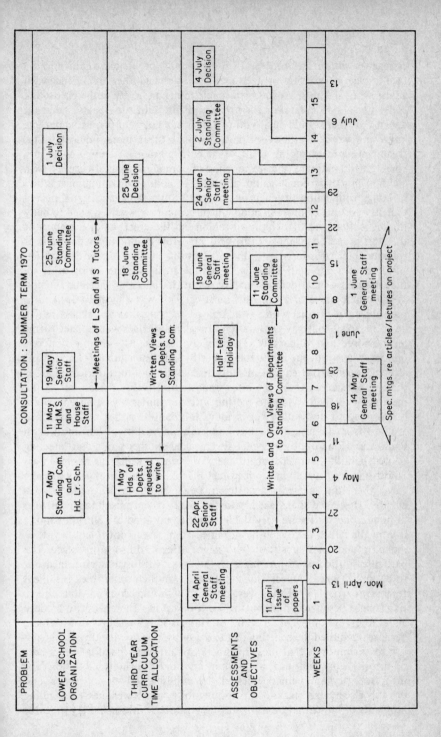

FIG. 2. Schedule of staff meetings in relation to consultation and decision making

colleagues within the same staff group should be unable to enter into a face-to-face relationship or deal openly with one another, impatience with adults who, although accustomed to exercising authority in the classroom, could be so inarticulate, or even totally silent, with their peers, indignant denial that there could be anything to fear in a group of people whom one knew and worked with every day. At other times there would be a far greater acceptance of the reality that even a group of known colleagues could be intimidating, that experience of communicating effectively with children in a classroom was no guarantee of ability to communicate, in a meeting, with fellow teachers in the staff room. Sometimes it appeared that it was some of those in middle-management roles who wished to deny the difficulties and that the most senior and the most junior members of the staff group could most easily find a meeting ground in a willingness to tolerate their own insecurity and inadequacy in face of the difficulties.

There was one staff meeting in particular, during the spring of 1970, that revealed a great deal of anxiety about risking experience and opinion in the public arena of a full staff meeting. This was a meeting devoted to the subject of tutorial work – an area of teaching that was clearly felt to be so personal that any exploration of real experiences would make tutors feel exposed and vulnerable. The anxiety showed itself in the first few minutes when someone broke the silence by announcing that John Phillips, although unable to attend the meeting, had left a list of the tutorial functions that he considered to be the most important. This list – read out to the meeting – recalled vividly to me the written manifesto which Denys John had offered to the section heads about ten months earlier, and which had aroused from them a veiled but unmistakable hostility. The use of John Phillips as a kind of absent leader also recalled another senior staff meeting of that period – the department heads' meeting at which the absent Lewis Smith had been used, and indeed had offered himself, in much the same way, when 'the role of a department head' had been the theme for discussion. It seemed that, faced with the need to scrutinise their own roles in public, the staff were very liable to resist any kind of laying down of a law by the head: yet, when he refrained from laying down any law, they looked round for a substitute who might offer to do so in his place. The particular difficulty of probing into the area of tutorial work turned out to be linked with fears lest some colleagues, in their other roles as subject teachers, particularly if they were involved with English or religious education, might be encroaching on the work of tutors. There was also anxiety about the developing programme of Human Relationships work, which, because it required the splitting of tutor groups, was proving divisive, giving rise to assumptions that most members of staff were 'good' at one aspect of tutorial work and 'bad' at another, and that the Human Relationships tutor was perhaps being perceived, by children and by colleagues, and possibly also by parents, as compensating for a tutor's weakness in handling problems of human relationships as they might be arising in his own tutor group.

Eventually, out of the exploration of these problems, a creative idea emerged. In the autumn of 1970, one of the new members of staff suggested to Denys John a new form of staff meeting [. . .] which came into effect almost immediately. The proposal was that the first hour or so of the full staff meeting should be spent in small groups which would contain members from a cross-section of departments and sections and from all levels of responsibility, and that the groups should then come together into a plenary session for the last half-hour of the meeting and work as a total group. This suggestion provided a much more acceptable alternative to the earlier notion of having separate meetings of the lower, middle and upper-school tutorial staff groups, since it did not threaten people with loss of the already tenuous sense of belonging to the whole school and therefore to a corporate body of staff.

The staff now had the opportunity, in its monthly general meetings, to explore important problems of policy, as well as immediate problems of implementing agreed policies, in groups that were small enough to offer support so that people felt more prepared to risk exposing their ideas and sharing bad experiences as well as good ones. But the new-style staff meeting went further than this. It also provided a work pattern in which the problems of bringing back, not the content necessarily, but the resultant learning into the large and increasingly complex staff group, including both its full-time and its part-time members, could really be examined. For people could now test out their ideas both in the intimate setting of a small but diverse group of colleagues and in the public arena of the full staff group, when 'colleagues' had so often appeared to be 'strangers'. It also raised a number of questions about role definition, group cohesion and commitment to a new set of relationships, questions that could be used as pointers to comparable problems arising every day in the management of learning situations in classroom, laboratory, workshop and gymnasium.

Unexpectedly the standing committee found themselves having to examine again in this new context how the role of the head differed from and related to the roles of his five most senior colleagues, for it was these five who had to take on the responsibility for accepting in the small groups a role that was consistent with their task as members of top management. And immediately new questions presented themselves. Were the members of the committee to be 'leaders', 'consultants' or just 'ordinary members' of the groups? Should there be six groups or only five? If the headmaster did not actually take a group himself, should he move around from one to another to 'get a feel of the discussions'? And if he did this what effect would his presence or absence have on the groups and on the members of the standing committee as they tried to work out their own roles in relation to the task of the groups? Should each standing-committee member remain with the same group throughout the school year, or should they rotate? Ought the groups themselves to be reshuffled at intervals or perhaps for every meeting in the interest of variety of experience, or ought they to persist with the same membership so that some identity could be established that would assist their work at the task?

Surprisingly, yet in another way predictably, there was pressure from the staff for movement, variety and impermanence. This pressure was surprising because so many had experienced the difficulties of communicating effectively with colleagues who were not well known to them; it was, nevertheless, predictable in face of the evidence (shared by many members) that commitment to task-centred working groups over a long period could prove exacting and even painful. The standing committee — again surprisingly at one level and predictably at another — found themselves very ready at first to collude with those who wanted to keep the groups fluid, thus both depriving themselves of the opportunity to work through authority problems with comparable cross-sections of the staff group, and protecting themselves from the need to test their own leadership skills beyond the known limits of their competence.

Even Denys John with the experience of the Human Relationships staff study group behind him and knowing that his role as headmaster would inevitably affect his leadership of any one small group in the situation, nevertheless chose to take one of the groups himself in the first meeting. In the later meetings, when he relinquished this role, he decided to go in and out of his colleagues' groups rather than accept the much greater strain of staying out of them during the first hour. Yet had he stayed out — as on an earlier occasion he had been able to stay out of the special meeting of the lower and middle-school tutorial teams chaired by Robin Thomas — he would probably have freed himself to work more creatively in the follow-up session with the whole staff group, and would have freed the other five members of the top-management group to carry a greater authority in working with the sub-groups during the preceding hour.

Again, my own experience in this situation, as in so many others, illuminated for me the nature of a headmaster's dilemma in making these decisions. For when I attended one of these new-style staff meetings I too found myself uncertain what I ought to do during that first hour when the staff were dispersed and working in five different places with five different leaders or co-ordinators. Like Denys John, I decided to 'visit' groups. In the time available I visited three, the third for only the last few minutes of its time. I scarcely knew whether it was joining a group or leaving it that made me more anxious, since the first felt like intruding on privacy and the second felt like expressing rejection or boredom, however much I really wanted to remain.

Examining the situation in the standing committee the following week, we learned that the arrival of either Denys John or myself in a group produced an immediately inhibiting effect upon the members, as sensed by the five standing-committee members who had been leading or interpreting the discussions. Yet neither of us had been aware of any particular change in the atmosphere as we moved in on a group and sat down to listen to its deliberations. Nor had we any means of knowing, except at second hand through the reports of the standing-committee members, how the quality or content of the discussion before the entrance of either of us had differed from what happened while either of us was present. As for any discomfiture, nervousness or sense of being intruders that he or I might have felt, this had evidently passed unnoticed by the members, just as their sudden inhibitedness had passed unnoticed by us. There was a further problem for Denys John in deciding whether or not he would continue the 'visiting' or 'sitting-in' pattern in later meetings. For a decision to visit groups could be interpreted either as 'the head taking an interest' or 'the head keeping tabs on us', even perhaps as 'the head interfering'; conversely, however, a decision *not* to visit them could be interpreted either as indifference or as trust.

Having decided to delegate responsibility for the small-group sessions entirely to the other five members of the standing committee, Denys John then had to face the assembled staff group without any knowledge of what had been going on during the previous hour and a quarter. The natural defence against the discomfort of this situation, for himself and for the large staff group, was to build in a reporting session, which in fact he did, at the urgent written request of one of the younger men on the staff. But the reporting back – undertaken, appropriately, by the standing committee members – quickly reduced the time available for discussion from forty-five minutes to about twenty-five, since it was difficult in practice for anyone to give a coherent account in less than four minutes of a discussion that had only just ended, leaving no time for any considered preparation of a more condensed report. Thus the standing-committee found themselves forced into a sort of collective monologue, which was time-consuming and repetitive, however competent the individual reporting might be, and which forced the rest of the staff into the roles of audience, with consequent frustration on all sides.

The removal of this defence in the meeting of November 1971, a meeting devoted to problems of staff-pupil relationships within the school, left the staff feeling exposed and unprotected. The standing-committee was taken to task for having 'abdicated' from the responsibility of reporting back to the meeting; some argument followed about the value or futility of such reporting; and again, as on the two earlier occasions to which I referred above, there was resort to an absent leader, this time Pip Ridgwell, who had been unable to attend the meeting but had furnished his group with a written statement giving his views about the present troubles the school was experiencing. Nevertheless, it required only a quiet but provocative question from Denys John – 'Are we evading the real topic?' and an acknowledgement from Pat Richardson (who had initiated the protest at

Elizabeth Richardson

the beginning) that they had now wasted ten minutes, for the real discussion to get under way. As it turned out, the removal of the ritual reporting did, after the initial resistance, free the staff to open up some of their real anxieties about how they were operating as the adults responsible for the work and general climate of feeling in the school. Repeatedly it seemed that these anxieties were focused on the fear that they could not match their concern for the children and young people in their care with the skill needed to stimulate them to effective work and learning.

It was hard for Denys John to close a meeting in which so much frustration and inadequacy was being expressed. And in fact there was a burst of discussion at the very end of the time available which made it very difficult for him to close it, as he suddenly found himself under attack for interpreting the questions about 'sanctions' as references to the need to punish children. Yet to close it on all this uncertainty − knowing that it would be another month before he could hold another full staff meeting − must itself have been an indication to the staff of his own belief that the staff had strengths as well as the weaknesses they had been acknowledging, and that there was leadership available to them in the intervening days and weeks if they could find ways of mobilising it, not only in the section heads and in the year-group and department heads, but within teaching and tutorial teams. For the evidence that even some of the youngest members of staff could offer such leadership had been there in the meeting for all to see.

The Oldness and Newness of a School

Sometimes one hears in one context the formulation of an idea that quite suddenly illuminates another. A few months ago, by chance, listening to a radio talk by Hans Keller about the music of Beethoven, I heard him say: 'We cannot understand the newness of Beethoven's mind except in the context of the oldness of his creative memory'. A week or so later, in another radio talk, he illustrated over and over again his belief that at the very moment when Beethoven was exhibiting one characteristic he was also exhibiting the opposite. If we transfer these insights to the field of education, we find they are just as applicable in helping us to understand schools as in helping us to listen more sensitively to music. For a school, too, must reconcile creatively its newness and its oldness, and its staff have to learn to recognise in one another not only the obvious and familiar behaviour that everyone has learned to expect but also the less obvious, often unseen or unheard dual of that behaviour. We have to try to acknowledge the latent radicalism of the 'conservative' teacher and the latent conservatism of the 'radical' teacher, and so avoid the mutual stereotyping that is so destructive of personality and therefore so impoverishing to the work of the institution.

The tension between nostalgia for the past and hope for the future could at times produce an effect almost like a collision. For the wish to return to a past that had been, in fantasy, trouble-free, was inevitably accompanied by a scarcely acknowledged wish to punish those who offended against that image — a wish that might express itself in a rather desperate search for certainty about what 'sanctions' were available to staff when they found themselves baffled by the defiant or merely casual attitudes of pupils, or in futile longings for assurance that seventy-five colleagues working in the same school could be relied on to agree about standards and to be entirely consistent in the demands they made on pupils. But almost in the same breath could come a challenge that they ought rather to be examining self-critically their own deficiencies in setting up learning situations for these bored, indifferent or rebellious pupils and that they should be devising ways of engaging these pupils in work that they might find satisfying.

There was some evidence that at least one member of the staff, apart from Denys John himself, feared that the reorganisation of the departments might prove to be only 'another aspirin', and that fundamental rethinking had yet to be started in the area of curriculum change. Yet this same member of the staff, despite the at times despairing talk about declining standards of behaviour, felt that real progress in understanding had been made on the caring side of the school's work, if only, perhaps, because far more attention was being given to the personal needs of those very pupils who gave the staff most trouble.

Because the sharing of a caring concern for children and young people brings into play the parent or potential parent in every man or woman, the members of a staff group can risk more exposure to one another in the pursuit of a more effective organisation for caring. But the professional training in a subject or group of subjects that every student has to undergo before he can take on the role of a teacher, places him in a situation of rivalry with many of his colleagues and is thus a divisive agent in the staff group. Real exposure of 'teaching' problems is therefore more difficult to tolerate than exposure of problems that can be described as 'tutorial'. Paradoxically, the area in which both the teacher and the pupil are presumed to perceive one another most clearly as persons, may after all prove less difficult to talk about in public than the area in which those same persons as learners and as promoters of learning have to confront and evaluate one another. For the ability to handle in one's own classes the day-to-day consequences of curriculum development is still perceived as the real test of professional competence, as though it were not indissolubly bound up with the other, more elusive, kind of tutorial competence, where personal awareness of children as children is more easily acknowledged to be of primary importance.

Experienced teachers are being judged in both roles by their pupils, by the students who come into the school for limited periods to carry out their assigned school practice, by young probationary teachers who join their departments or houses or year groups, by parents who build up images of them from the slender evidence of children's conversations about what goes on in their classes and tutor groups and from the other kind of evidence afforded by their own discussions with them during parents' evening or in special interviews at times of crucial decision-making or at times of crisis. The school is constantly under pressure, from outside as well as from inside, to review its own methods of evaluating its own work.

The stability of a staff group is never certain. Every school of any size or importance experiences annually the fluctuating intake and output of students in training, the inward flow of new colleagues and the inevitable loss of old colleagues. In addition there may be the temporary withdrawal of experienced staff on secondment to the universities to pursue further studies in education, and the consequent necessity to assimilate their new ideas, often critical of school values and practices formerly taken for granted. Every school must therefore accept a three-fold responsibility to work at the task of reconciling the old and the new, first in its own internal arrangements for the planning and implementation of policy (which has really been the main theme of this book), secondly in its relations with the colleges and departments of education that carry responsibility for the initial training of teachers, and thirdly in its relations with other educational institutions through the experienced teachers it exports, either to pursue advanced studies or to take up responsible posts in other parts of the educational system (see Figure 3).

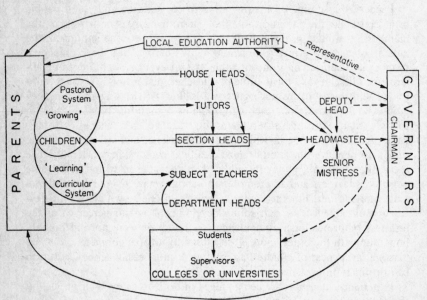

FIG. 3 Patterns of accountability.

NOTES

1. J.H. Wicksteed, The Challenge of Childhood (Chapman and Hall, 1936), p.25.

18. PLANNED CHANGE AND ORGANISATIONAL HEALTH: FIGURE AND GROUND

Matthew B. Miles

From Richard O. Carlson (ed.), *Change Processes in the Public Schools* (Centre for the Advanced Study of Educational Administration, University of Oregon Press, 1965).

[The health of the school organisation will affect its ability to operate efficiently and to develop. Miles offers ten dimensions in a checklist of organisational health. Some approaches to achieving this condition are also propounded. Miles concludes that the organisational health of the school must be the real target of change, not short-term innovations.]

Organisational Health

Our present thinking about organisation health is that it can be seen as a set of fairly durable *second-order* system properties, which tend to transcend short-run effectiveness. A healthy organisation in this sense not only survives in its environment, but continues to cope adequately over the long haul, and continuously develops and extends its surviving and coping abilities. Short-run operations on any particular day may be effective or ineffective, but continued survival, adequate coping, and growth are taking place.

A *steadily* ineffective organisation would presumably not be healthy; on balance, 'health' implies a summation of effective short-run coping. But notice that an organisation *may* cope effectively in the short run (as for example by a speed-up or a harsh cost-cutting drive), but at the cost of longer-run variables, such as those noted below. The classic example, of course, is an efficiency drive which cuts short-run costs and results in long-run labour dissatisfaction and high turnover.

To illustrate in more detail what is meant by 'second-order property', here is a list of ten dimensions of organisation health that seem plausible to me. Many of them are drawn by heuristic analogy from the behaviour of persons or small groups; this does *not* mean, of course, that organisations necessarily are precisely homologous to persons or groups — only that thinking in this way may get us somewhere on what, it must be admitted, is a very complex problem indeed. Here then are ten dimensions. They are not, of course mutually exclusive, and interact with each other vigorously within any particular organisation. Both Jahoda (1958) and Argyris (1964) have commented on the importance of a multiple-criterion approach to the assessment of health, given the present state of our knowledge and the fact that, as a college roommate of mine once remarked

192

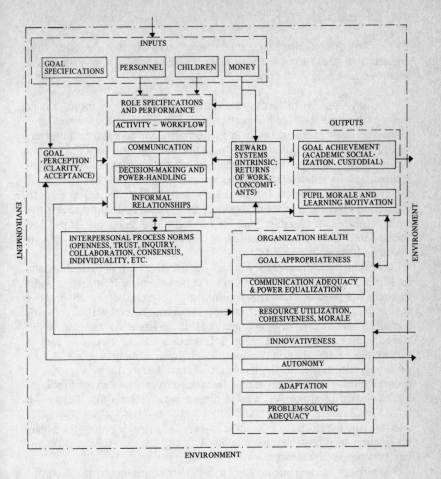

Figure 1. Schematic model of organization functioning and change environment

Carlson, Richard O. (Ed.) 1965, *Change Processes in the Public Schools*, Centre for the Advanced Study of Educational Administration, University of Oregon Press.

with blinding insight, 'You know, everything is really connected to everything else.'

The first three dimensions are relatively 'tasky', in that they deal with organisation goals, the transmission of messages, and the way in which decisions are made.

1. *Goal focus.* In a healthy organisation, the goal (or more usually goals) of the system would be reasonably clear to the system members, and reasonably well accepted by them.[1] This clarity and acceptance, however, should be seen as a necessary but insufficient condition for organisation health. The goals must also be *achievable* with existing or available resources, and be *appropriate* — more or less congruent with the demands of the environment. The last feature may be most critical. Switching back to the person level for a moment, consider the obsessive patient who sets the clear, accepted, achievable goal for himself of washing his hands 250 times a day. The question remains: is this an appropriate goal in light of what else there is to do in life?

2. *Communication adequacy.* Since organisations are not simultaneous face-to-face systems like small groups, the movement of information within them becomes crucial. This dimension of organisation health implies that there is relatively distortion-free communication 'vertically , horizontally', and across the boundary of the system to and from the surrounding environment. That is, information travels reasonably well — just as the healthy person 'knows himself' with a minimum level of repression, distortion, etc. In the healthy organisation, there is good and prompt sensing of internal strains; there are enough data about problems of the system to insure that a good diagnosis of system difficulties can be made. People have the information they need, and have gotten it without exerting undue efforts, such as those involved in moseying up to the superintendent's secretary, reading the local newspaper, or calling excessive numbers of special meetings.

3. *Optimal power equalisation.* In a healthy organisation the distribution of influence is relatively equitable. Subordinates (if there is a formal authority chart) can influence upward, and even more important — as Likert (1961) has demonstrated — they perceive that their boss can do likewise with *his* boss. In such an organisation, inter-group struggles for power would not be bitter, though inter-group conflict, (as in every human system known to man) would undoubtedly be present. The basic stance of persons in such an organisation, as they look up, sideways and down, is that of collaboration rather than explicit or implicit coercion. The units of the organisation (persons in roles, work groups, etc.) would stand in an interdependent relationship to each other, with rather less emphasis on the ability of a 'master' part to control the entire operation. The exertion of influence in a healthy organisation would presumably rest on the competence of the influence *vis-à-vis* the issue at hand, his stake in the outcome,

and the amount of knowledge or data he has — rather than on his organisational position, personal charisma, or other factors with little direct relevance to the problem.

These then are three 'task-centred' dimensions of organisation health. A second group of three dimensions deals essentially with the internal state of the system, and its inhabitants' 'maintenance' needs. These are resource utilisation, cohesiveness, and morale.

4. *Resource utilisation.* We say of a healthy person, such as a second-grader, that he is 'working up to his potential'. To put this another way, the classroom system is evoking a contribution from him at an appropriate and goal-directed level of tension. At the organisation level, 'health' would imply that the system's inputs, particularly the personnel, are used effectively. The overall coordination is such that people are neither overloaded nor idling. There is a minimal sense of strain, generally speaking (in the sense that trying to do something with a weak or inappropriate structure puts strain on that structure). In the healthy organisation, people may be working very hard indeed, but they feel that they are not working against themselves, or against the organisation. The fit between people's own dispositions and the role demands of the system is good. Beyond this, people feel reasonably 'self-actualised'; they not only 'feel good' in their jobs, but they have a genuine sense of learning, growing, and developing as persons in the process of making their organisational contribution.

5. *Cohesiveness.* We think of a healthy person as one who has a clear sense of identity; he knows who he is, underneath all the specific goals he sets for himself. Beyond this, he *likes himself;* his stance toward life does not require self-derogation, even when there are aspects of his behaviour which are unlovely or ineffective. By analogy at the organisation level, system health would imply that the organisation knows 'who it is'. Its members feel attracted to membership in the organisation. They want to stay with it, be influenced by it, and exert their own influence in the collaborative style suggested above.

6. *Morale.* The history of this concept in the social-psychological literature is so appalling that I hesitate to introduce it at all. The implied notion is one of well-being or satisfaction. Satisfaction is not enough for health, of course; a person may report feelings of well-being and satisfaction in his life, while successfully denying deep-lying hostilities, anxieties, and conflicts. Yet it still seems useful to evoke, at the organisation level, the idea of morale: a summated set of individual sentiments, centering around feelings of well-being, satisfaction, and pleasure, as opposed to feelings of discomfort, unwished-for strain and dissatisfaction. In an *un*healthy system, life might be perceived rosily as 'good', or as unabashedly bad; in a healthy organisation it is hard to entertain the idea that the dominant personal response of organisation members would be anything else than one of

well-being.

Finally, there are four more dimensions of organisation health, which deal with growth and changefulness: the notions of innovativeness, autonomy, adaptation *vis-à-vis* the environment, and problem-solving adequacy.

7. *Innovativeness.* A healthy system would tend to invent new procedures, move toward new goals, produce new kinds of products, diversify itself, and become more rather than less differentiated over time. In a sense, such a system could be said to grow, develop, and change, rather than remaining routinised, and standard. The analogue here is to the self-renewing properties of a Picasso; or to Schachtel's (1959) 'activity' orientation (curious, exploring) as contrasted with 'embeddedness' orientation (tension-reducing, protective) in persons.[2]

8. *Autonomy.* The healthy person acts 'from his own center outward'. Seen in a training or therapy group, for example, such a person appears nearly free of the need to submit dependently to authority figures, *and* from the need to rebel and destroy symbolic fathers of any kind. A healthy organisation, similarly, would not respond passively to demands from the outside, feeling itself the tool of the environment, and it would not respond destructively or rebelliously to perceived demands either. It would tend to have a kind of independence from the environment, in the same sense that the healthy person, while he has transactions with others, does not treat their responses as *determinative* of his own behaviour.

9. *Adaptation.* The notions of autonomy and innovativeness are both connected with the idea that a healthy person, group, or organisation is in realistic, effective contact with the surroundings. When environmental demands and organisation resources do not match, a problem-solving, restructuring approach evolves in which *both* the environment and the organisation become different in some respect. More adequate, continued coping of the organisation, as a result of changes in the local system, the relevant portions of the environment, or more usually both, occurs. And such a system has sufficient stability and stress tolerance to manage the difficulties which occur during the adaptation process. Perhaps inherent in this notion is that the system's ability to bring about corrective change in itself is faster than the change cycle in the surrounding environment. Explanations for the disappearance of dinosaurs vary, but it is quite clear that in some way this criterion was not met.

10. *Problem-solving adequacy.* Finally, any healthy organism — even one as theoretically impervious to fallibility as a computer — *always* has problems, strains, difficulties, and instances of ineffective coping. The issue is not the presence or absence of problems, therefore, but the *manner* in which the person, group, or organisation copes with problems. Argyris (1964) has suggested that in an effective system, problems are solved with minimal energy; they stay solved; and the problem-solving mechanisms

used are not weakened, but maintained or strengthened. An adequate organisation, then, has well-developed structures and procedures for sensing the existence of problems, for inventing possible solutions, for deciding on the solutions, for implementing them, and for evaluating their effectiveness. Such an organisation would conceive of its own operations (whether directed outward to goal achievement, inward to maintenance, or inward-outward to problems of adaptation) as being *controllable*. We would see active coping with problems, rather than passive withdrawing, compulsive responses, scapegoating, or denial.

Here then are ten dimensions of a healthy organisation, stated abstractly — even vaguely in many instances. They must, of course, be operationalised into meaningful indicators of organisation functioning; the staff of our project is currently into this with more than a little trepidation, but with keen interest to see whether these ways of viewing the health of a system prove to have a reasonable amount of empirical steam behind them. [. . .] [3]

The Induction of Organisation Health

The particular degree of health of any local school system, given a multiple-criterion approach such as that suggested here, undoubtedly varies from time to time. A question of considerable interest is: what can be done to induce a greater degree of organisation health in any particular system? By now a fair amount of experience exists, drawn from the interesting blend of consultation and research in which an increasing number of behavioural scientists now find themselves involved, primarily with industrial organisations. These methods can perhaps most usefully be considered as *interventions* in the on-going life of a system; this term implies an action which interferes with or reorients processes — either pathological or normal — ordinarily occurring in the system. A teacher's intervention in a child's problem-solving serves to reorient his thinking; perhaps more importantly, it can aid the child to mobilise his own energies more effectively. Thus the usual aim of an intervention is to start internal change processes going in the system at hand, rather than only causing an immediate change.

Below are described six interventions aimed at improving organisation health.[4] In some cases, plausible statements can be made about which dimensions of health are most typically influenced by a particular intervention. For the most part, however, we do not really know; it is exactly the function of our research project to discover how these are likely to work in educational organisations. In conclusion, some common principles underlying the six interventions are discussed.

1. *Team training.* In this approach, the members of an intact work group (for example, the superintendent and his central office personnel) meet for a period of several days away from their offices, with consultant

help. They examine their own effectiveness as a problem solving team, the role of each member in the group and how it affects the group and the person himself, and the operations of the group in relation to its organisational environment. This problem-solving may be based on fairly careful prior data collection from individuals as to their views on the current problems of the system; these data are summarised and form the beginning of the group's agenda. Occasionally, exercises and theoretical material on group and organisation functioning may be supplied by the outside consultant.

Under these circumstances, the members of the group usually improve in their abilities to express feelings directly, and to listen to – and understand – each other. Communication adequacy is thus considerably increased. The members also deal with internal conflicts in the team, and learn to solve problems more effectively as a unit, thus presumably increasing their ability to meet the demands placed upon them by other parts of the system. Over a period of time, beginning with the top decision-making group of the system, this intervention may be repeated with other groups as well. Industrial programs of this sort have been described by Argyris (1962) and Blake and Mouton (1962).

2. *Survey feedback.* In this approach, data bearing on attitudes, opinions, and beliefs of members of a system are collected via questionnaire. An external researcher summarises the data for the organisation as a whole, and for each of a number of relevant work groups. Each work group, under the guidance of its own superior, and perhaps with consultant help, examines its own summarised data, in comparison with those for the organisation as a whole. The group makes plans for change stemming from these discussions and carries them out. The focus of this intervention is on many or all of the work groups within a total setting. The aim is to free up communication, leading to goal clarification and problem-solving work. The relative objectification involved in looking at data helps to reduce feelings of being misunderstood and isolated, and makes problems more susceptible to solution, rather than retaining them as a focus for blaming, scapegoating, griping and so on. For an account of survey feedback procedure, see Mann (1961); Gage (1963a) has tried a similar approach effectively with student-to-teacher feedback, and is now studying teacher-to-principal feedback.

3. *Role workshop.* Sometimes called the 'horizontal slice' meeting, this intervention involves all the people in a particular role (for example, elementary principal). They fill out research instruments dealing with role expectations which various others hold for them, the fit between their own wishes and these expectations, their actual role performance, etc. These data are summarised, and form the vehicle for a series of activities (discussion, role practice, decision-making exercises, problem-solving and so on) at a workshop attended by all the people in the role. The main focus here is on role clarity, effectiveness, and improved fit between the person and the role. By sharing common role problems, people occupying the

role may develop alternative solutions which result in better performance of that role and more 'self-actualised' operation in general.

4. *'Target setting' and supporting activities.* In this approach, periodic meetings are held between a superior and each of his subordinates, separately. In a school system, this might involve the superintendent and his staff members, or a principal and his teachers. The work of each subordinate is reviewed in relation to organisational and personal goals, and the superior and subordinate agree collaboratively on new targets for the subordinate's work and personal development. These 'targets' are in turn reviewed after some work time (usually six months or so) has elapsed. During that period, other activities such as role meetings, consultation, self-operated data collection, academic courses, and workshops, may be engaged in by the subordinate to develop needed skills and understandings as he works toward the collaboratively-set goals. The focus of attention here is the working relationship between superior and subordinate, and the degree to which they are together able to help the subordinate grow and develop on the job. Improved trust, feelings of support, better and more satisfying role performance, and more open communication usually result. Zander (1963) has reviewed thoroughly the problems and values of performance appraisal, including commentary on the target-setting approach.

5. *Organisational diagnosis and problem-solving.* This intervention involves a residential meeting of members of an intact work group, usually at the top of the organisation (or in small organisations, up to size 40-50, the entire work force). They meet for several days to identify problems facing the system, and the reasons for the existence of these; to invent possible solutions; to decide on needed system changes; and to plan implementation of these through regular channels and newly-constructed ones. It differs from team training as described above in that relatively less attention is given to team relationships and interpersonal effectiveness as such, and more to system problems in the large. The main focus of attention is on the organisation and its current functioning. The improvement of problem-solving activity and communication adequacy are typical results. For an account of two such meetings conducted with an industrial organisation, see Zand, Miles, and Lytle (forthcoming)

6. *Organisational experiment.* In this approach, a major organisational variable of interest is changed *directly,*[5] by agreement of the responsible administrators, and needed implementation efforts. One such approach is described vividly by Morse and Reimer (1956): in several divisions of a large organisation, the level of decision-making was moved radically downward, thus giving more autonomy to subordinates; in several other divisions the level of decision-making was moved up; and in several divisions no change was made. Such an approach requires the careful collection of pre-post data, and the use of control groups in order to test the consequences of the change. The halo of 'experiment' is an aid to acceptance, since the arrangement is seen as not only temporary, but scientific, and

199

responsibly managed. Such an approach ordinarily includes a feedback stage, in which the results are examined carefully and implications for the continuing functioning of the organisation drawn.

These, then, are six possible approaches to the induction of organisation health. Certain common threads appear to flow through all of them.

1. *Self-study.* These approaches reject the 'technocratic' change model involving the recommendations of a detached expert, and actively involve the system itself in what might be called organisational introspection. The same holds true for approaches involving group self-study for various teams in the organisation, and personal introspection and re-examination by role occupants.

In common with the action research movement in education, these approaches also carry the assumption that an operant stance on the part of the organisation is both theoretically and practically preferable to the problems involved in dependence on outsiders for system change.

2. *Relational emphasis.* These approaches do not conceive of the organisation as a collection of jobs with isolated persons in them, but as a network of groups and role relationships; it is the functioning of these groups and relationships, as such, which requires examination and self-operated, experimental alteration. The aim is not to ferret out and 'change the attitude' of old-fogey Principal A, but to focus on the relationships and group settings in which Principal A's attitudes are evoked.

3. *Increased data flow.* These approaches all involve the heightening or intensification of communication, especially vertically, but also diagonally and horizontally. New feedback loops are often built in to the existing system. The use of status-equalising devices such as intensive residential meetings also encourages fuller and freer flow of information through channels which may have been blocked or have always carried distorted messages.

4. *Norms as a change target.* By focusing on groups and relationships, and increasing data flow, these approaches have the effect of altering existing norms which regulate interpersonal transactions in the organisation. If, for example, a work group where the norms are 'play it close to the vest, and don't disagree with the boss' engages in a team training session, it is quite likely — since all group members have participated in the experience — that norms such as 'be open about your feelings whether or not they tally with the boss's wishes' will develop. These approaches thus have a strong culture-changing component, based on intensive, data-based interaction with others.[6]

5. *Temporary-system approach.* But norm-changing is by definition very difficult under the usual pressures of day-to-day operation in the organisation. 'Business as usual' has to prevail. Most of the interventions described involve the use of residential meetings, which constitute a de-

tached, 'cultural island' approach to organisational introspection and self-correction. They are in effect temporary systems,[7] where new norms can develop, and where, given the suspension of the usual pressures, meaningful changes can be made in the structure and functioning of the permanent system.

6. *Expert facilitation.* All of these interventions also include the presence of a semi-detached consultant figure, whose main functions are to facilitate, provoke, and support the efforts of the system to understand itself, free up communication and engage in more adequate problem-solving behaviour. The outsider role, however, is seen as impermanent; it is only associated with the system during the actual period of the intervention itself. If the intervention is successful, the organisation itself continues the self-corrective processes which have been begun by the intervention.

Whether or not these interventions drawn from work with thing-producing organisations, can be used plausibly with people-processing organisations such as school is an interesting question, to which my colleagues and I are beginning to gather some answers. Our impulse at the moment is to believe that the answer will be affirmative. With the assistance of two or three school systems, we expect to have some empirical data on intervention results in about two years, an eventuality to which we look forward with a good deal of pleasure.

In Conclusion

It might be useful to point out in conclusion that the position taken in this paper is *not* that an organisation must necessarily be brought to a state of perfect health before it can engage in any meaningful short-run innovative projects at all. Rather, we feel it is quite likely that the very act of carrying out small scale projects in planned change can undoubtedly strengthen the health of an educational organisation — but only if *direct attention is paid concurrently to the state of the organisation.* The basic innovative project, we believe, must be one of organisation development itself.

NOTES

1. Note that the question of actual goal achievement as such is here conceived of as separate, analytically speaking, from the question of organisation health. Argyris has suggested that organisation effectiveness, a concept resembling the health notion, resides in the organisation's ability to (1) achieve goals, (2) maintain itself internally, (3) engage in adaptation processes with the environment — and to accomplish these three 'core activities' at a constant or increasing level of effectiveness, given the same or decreasing increments in energy input (Argyris 1964, p. 123). This three-way scheme is also used in the present discussion.

2. Clark (1962) has suggested that organisation health resides primarily in the

continuous possibility of *both* kinds of orientation: toward change and development, and for stability and maintenance. This dual possibility should be realised, he suggests, at the personal, group, inter-group, and total organisational
levels.

3. Little has been said here about the actual form of the organisation which is
    most likely to meet these criteria of organisational health at some optimal level.
    Some applied work in organisation change (Argyris 1964; Bennis 1962) suggests
    that strongly pyramidal organisations designed around strict division of labour,
    accountability, limited span of control, etc., are uniquely *ill*-fitted to the demands
    of survival in today's world. Argyris (1964) has suggested a number of alterna-
    tives to the pyramidal model (such as the use of temporary 'product teams').
4. See Bennis (1963, 1964) for a thorough review of alternative approaches being
    used.
5. I am reminded of Hollis Caswell's classic remark when asked in 1943 how the
    newly-formed Horace Mann-Lincoln Institute would proceed in its program of
    school experimentation: 'We'll change the curriculum by changing it.'
6. In retrospect, the crucial role of norms in the maintenance of organisational
    health has probably been underplayed in this paper. In our research, we are
    planning to collect data on norms such as those regulating interpersonal authen-
    ticity and awareness, trust, objectivity, collaboration, altruistic concern, con-
    sensual decision-making, innovativeness, and creativity. Most of these are directly
    co-ordinated to the dimensions of organisational health reviewed above.
7. See Miles (1964) for an analysis of the special properties of temporary systems
    for change-inducing purposes.

REFERENCES

ARGYRIS, C. (1964), *Integrating the Individual and the Organisation;* Wiley, New
York,
        (1962), *Interpersonal Competence and Organisational Effectiveness,* Dorsey
Press, Homewood, Ill.
BENNIS, W.G. (1962), 'Towards a "Truly" Scientific Management: The Concept of
Organisation Health', in A. Rapaport (ed.), *General Systems* (Yearbook of the
Society for the Advancement of General Systems Theory), Ann Arbor, Michigan.
        (1963), 'A New Role for the Behavioural Sciences: Effecting Organisational
Change', *Administrative Science Quarterly, Vol. 8, no. 2, pp. 125–65.*
        (1964), 'Theory and Method in Applying Behavioural Science to Planned
Organisational Change', Alfred P. Sloan School of Management, M.I.T., Cambridge,
Mimeographed.
BLAKE, R.R., BLANSFIELD, M.G., and MOUTON, J.S. (1962), 'How Executive
Team Training Can Help You', *Journal American Society of Training Directors,*
Vol. 16, no. 1, pp. 3–11.
CLARK, J.V. (1962), 'A Healthy Organisation', Institute of Industrial Relations,
University of California, Los Angeles.
GAGE, N.L. (1963), 'A Method for "Improving" Teacher Behaviour', *Journal of
Teacher Education,* Vol. 14, no. 3, pp. 261–6.
JAHODA, M. (1958), *Current Concepts of Positive Mental Health,* Basic Books, New
York.
LIKERT, R. (1961), *New Patterns of Management,* McGraw-Hill, New York.
MANN, F.C. (1961), 'Studying and Creating Change' in W.G. Bennis, K.D. Benne,
and R. Chin, *The Planning of Change: Readings in the Applied Behavioural
Sciences,* Holt, Rinehart and Winston, New York, pp. 605–15.
MILES, M.B. (1964a), *Innovation in Education,* Bureau of Publications, Teachers
College, Columbia University, New York.

(1964b), 'On Temporary Systems', in M.B. Miles (ed.), *Innovation in Education,* Bureau of Publications, Teachers College, Columbia University, New York, pp. 437–92.

MORSE, N. and REIMER, E. (1956), 'The Experimental Change of a Major Organisational Variable', *Journal of Abnormal and Social Psychology,* Vol. 52, pp. 120–9.

SCHACHTEL, E.G. (1959), *Metamorphosis,* Basic Books, New York.

ZAND, D., MILES, M.B. and LYTLE, W.O. Jr, 'Organisational Improvement Through Use of a Temporary Problem-Solving System', in D.E. Zand and P.C. Buhanan, (eds.), *Organisation Development: Theory and Practice.* Forthcoming.

ZANDER, A. (ed.), (1963), *Performance Appraisals: Effects on Employees and Their Performance;* Foundation for Research on Human Behaviour, Ann Arbor, Michigan.

Part V

INNOVATION AND THE TEACHER

19. UNDERSTANDING LIFE IN CLASSROOMS

Philip W. Jackson

From *Life in Classrooms* (Holt, Rinehart and Winston, New York), pp. 143–55.

[Every strategy for change must take into account the views of the participants. How the teacher sees his or her role, with all its ambiguities and
responsibilities, is the concern of Jackson. The teacher's preoccupation
with the immediacy of the classroom rather than educational research or
professional collaboration seems to be evident from this survey.]

Having identified the broad themes around which the talks with teachers
seemed to revolve, there remains the task of considering the general relevance of the interview material for an understanding of life in classrooms.
In doing so it will be necessary to touch upon aspects of the interviews
that have only been briefly mentioned as well as those about which there
has already been extensive discussion. The conversations of the teachers
bear broadly on two topics: the conditions of teaching, and the general
psychology of those adults who choose to work in elementary schools.
These two topics are related, in turn, to the general question of how individuals, adults and children alike, come to grips with the demands of institutional life.

   One of the most notable features of teacher talk is the absence of a
technical vocabulary. Unlike professional encounters between doctors,
lawyers, garage mechanics, and astrophysicists, when teachers talk together
almost any reasonably intelligent adult can listen in and comprehend what
is being said. Occasionally familiar words are used in a specialised sense,
and the uninitiated listener may be momentarily puzzled by the mention of
'units', or 'projects', or 'curriculum guides', or 'word attack skills', but it is
unlikely he will encounter many words that he has never heard before or
even those with a specialised meaning.[1]

   Not only is there an absence of a technical vocabulary unique to
teaching, but also little use is made of jargon from related fields. A few
psychological expressions are used from time to time (IQ is doubtlessly the
most popular), but technical terms from the literature of psychopathology,
group dynamics, learning theory, social organisation, and developmental
psychology — to name only the more obvious supporting disciplines — are

noticeably absent. Teachers rarely talk about defense mechanisms, group cohesiveness, reinforcement schedules, role expectations, and sociocentric stages, even when it might be appropriate for them to do so.

The absence of technical terms is related to another characteristic of teachers' talk: its conceptual simplicity. Not only do teachers avoid elaborate words, they also seem to shun elaborate ideas. Obviously, this characteristic is not unique to teachers. Complicated thought is difficult and most people avoid it when they can, but such an avoidance (if that is what it should be called) does take on a special significance when we consider the importance of the teacher's work. Superficially at least, it would seem as if the thinking of teachers ought to be as complex as they can make it, as they set about the serious business of helping students to learn. Unnecessary simplicity, therefore, when revealed in the language of a teacher, would be interpreted by many as a cause for alarm. Whether or not that alarm is justified is a question to which we shall return.

Four aspects of the conceptual simplicity revealed in teachers' language are worthy of comment. These are: (1) an uncomplicated view of causality; (2) an intuitive, rather than rational approach to classroom events; (3) an opinionated, as opposed to an open-minded, stance when confronted with alternative teaching practices; and (4) a narrowness in the working definitions assigned to abstract terms.

When discussing the events with which they are confronted daily, teachers often talk as if theirs was a world in which single causes typically produced single effects. As they struggle to explain a puzzling classroom episode they commonly settle on what they consider to be *the* explanation. Why is Billy doing so well in school? Because he has a high IQ. Why is Fred such a trouble-maker? Because he comes from a broken family. Why are the children so noisy today? Because it's getting near the Christmas holiday. Even their own behaviour as teachers is approached as if there were some kind of a one-to-one correspondence between cause and effect. Why, for example, did they choose to become teachers in the first place? The answer is obvious. Because they like children. Why else?

It is easy, of course, to make fun of these oversimplifications, but the complexity underlying most classroom events is so great that the teacher's search for a quick resolution of this complexity is understandable, perhaps even forgivable. Were she seriously to try untangling the web of forces that combine to produce reality as she knows it, there would be no time for anything else. Moreover, when all is said and done, who does know for certain why Billy performs so well in school or why Miss Jones has elected to spend her life in a kindergarten? The assignment of single causes to these events is short-sighted, to be sure, but it does bring some semblance of order to an otherwise confusing and often chaotic environment.

Their willingness to accept simple explanations for complex events does not mean that teachers commonly insist on explanations for everything they witness. On the contrary, they are unusually willing to accept things as they are without probing too deeply into the whys and wherefores. Indeed, many classroom phenomena are so unexpected and their causes so hidden from sight that teachers tend to treat them as minor miracles. This attitude is particularly evident when the event in question is pedagogically desirable. When a student makes a sudden leap of progress or when an apathetic youngster undergoes a dramatic reversal of attitude, the teacher's response, quite naturally, is apt to be one of delight and thankfulness. But this response is unlikely to be followed by an analytic scrutiny of what has taken place. When good fortune strikes, the teachers seem to be saying, it is best not to ask too many questions.

The unquestioning acceptance of classroom miracles is part of a broader tendency that reveals itself in several ways in the talk of teachers. This is the tendency to approach educational affairs intuitively rather than rationally. When called on to justify their professional decisions, for example, my informants often declared that their classroom behaviour was based more on impulse and feeling than on reflection and thought. In other words, they were more likely to defend themselves by pointing out that a particular course of action *felt* like the right thing to do, rather than by claiming that they *knew* it to be right. As the structure of a teaching session or of a class day unfolds, the teacher frequently behaves like a musician without a score. He ad-libs.

It must be remembered, of course, that the impulses and intuitive hunches of most of these teachers had been tempered by years of practical experience. Thus, the basis of their action might be much more rational than their self-reports would lead us to believe. In their daily doings they may, in effect, be rendering 'by heart' a type of performance that would have to be carefully reasoned and rehearsed by a group of novices. But whether they advanced to this intuitive level late in their careers or whether they performed this way from the beginning is less important within the present context than is the fact that now, as seasoned teachers, they often reported themselves to be playing the melody by ear.

The alert critic will be quick to point out that almost all of the interviewees were women, thus intimating that the so-called intuitive quality revealed in the interviews is nothing more than interviewees exercising their feminine birthright. 'After all,' he might argue, 'women are supposed to be intuitive. Why should we be surprised to find female teachers behaving like other women?' But the important question is not whether the teachers are more intuitive than their non-teaching sisters. Rather, it is whether they are necessarily intuitive when their actions might better be guided by reason. We must ask, in other words, about the overall propriety of intuition in the classroom. No one objects if a cook adds an extra pinch of salt just because she feels like it. But the same behaviour on the part of a pharmacist is quite another matter.

One might expect people who do not inquire into the reasons for things and who tend to act impulsively to be indecisive when expressing their own tastes. But, judging from the interviews, classroom teachers could hardly be so described. Despite the weakness of their intellectual tenacity and the softness of their talk, they commonly expressed strong opinions concerning their ways of teaching. Moreover, the strength of their opinions did not seem to be affected by the fact that they were often unable to defend their choices. Like amateur art-lovers they knew what they liked, even if they did not always know why they liked it. When pressed for a rationalisation of their pedagogical tastes they not infrequently became impatient or hid behind the defense of *de gustibus non est disputandum*. Rarely, if ever, did they turn to evidence beyond their own personal experience to justify their professional preferences.

A fourth indicator of the conceptual simplicity contained in the teachers' language is reflected in the narrowness of the working definitions they assign to common terms. Although teachers often use words and phrases denoting global aspects of human behaviour (such as *motivation, social relations,* and *intellectual development*) the referents of these terms, on close inspection, are usually found to contain only pale reflections of the rich concepts from which they are derived. *Motivation,* in pedagogical shop-talk, typically refers to a student's zest for undertaking school assignments, and little else. *Social relations* commonly has as its sole referent the quality of the student's interaction with his classmates and his teacher, and the complexity of that definition is often further reduced to a crude estimate of the student's popularity with his peers. When intellectual development is discussed by teachers, that development is described almost exclusively in terms of the student's mastery of curricular objectives, or a summary statistic depicting his performance on a test of general ability. As might be expected, these conceptual curtailments correspond roughly to the limits of the teacher's experience in the classroom. Teachers do not usually have occasion to probe the unconscious motives of their students or sketch the contours of their social life space or examine the depths of their intellectual powers. Perhaps it is not surprising, therefore, to find that profound words, in the teacher's lexicon, have a distinctly parochial cast.

The narrowness of the definitions assigned to global terms not only provides further evidence of conceptual simplicity, it also serves to introduce another major characteristic of teachers' language. Even though she may attach abstract labels to what she observes, the focus of the teacher's concern is on her concrete experience with a particular group of students. In brief, she lives in a world of *sharp existential boundaries* and those boundaries evince themselves in the way she talks.

There is a striking immediacy about the things that concerned the teachers — a here-and-nowness about their talk that becomes compellingly evident after prolonged listening. Perhaps this quality should not surprise us. After all, during every working day the teacher is immersed in an environment of real people and things whose demands upon her are continuous and insistent. Moreover, many of the unique features of her world become so well known to the teacher that it becomes difficult for her mentally to erase their identity and think of them as merely concrete manifestations of more abstract phenomena. Consequently, generalisations about the characteristics of children or about the merits of an educational theory are continually being tested, as the teacher considers them, against the qualities of the particular students with whom she is working and the specific constraints of her classroom. As might be expected, this degree of specificity greatly inhibits the easy translation of theory into practice and serves to increase the difficulty of communications between the teacher and others with more abstract interests.

The teacher's focus on the physical and social reality of her classroom — her embeddedness, so to speak, in the here-and-now — is not the only indicator of existential boundaries defining the limits of her concern. In addition, there are signs of emotional ties to her students and to other aspects of her environment, ties binding her even more securely than does mere familiarity to the setting in which she works. Of course everyone cares to some extent about what he is doing and about his daily associates. To that extent, then, teachers are no different from anyone else. But the intensity of the teacher's emotional investment in her work, if we can believe the way she talks about it, often exceeds this common concern. In this respect, teachers resemble clergymen, therapists, physicians, and others whose duties link them intimately to the personal well-being of their clientele. Yet the teacher's clientele, it must be remembered, are children and her contact with them is much more intensive in most cases than is true for those who perform these other professional services.

The teacher's concern with the here-and-now and her emotional attachment to her world was often accompanied in her conversations by an accepting attitude toward educational conditions as they presently exist. Interest in educational change was usually mild and typically was restricted to ideas about how to rearrange her room or how to regroup her students — how to work better with the educational "givens," in other words. Rarely, if ever, was there talk of the need for broad or dramatic educational reforms, even though the interviews provided ample opportunity to discuss these matters. This acceptance of the status quo, which might be described as a kind of pedagogical conservatism, appeared to be part of the general myopia typifying the classroom teacher's intellectual vision.

From one point of view, the features of teacher's language that have been described here are anything but flattering. Lacking a technical vocabulary, skimming the intellectual surface of the problems they encounter, fenced in, as it were, by the walls of their concrete experience, these teachers hardly look like the type of people who should be allowed to supervise the intellectual development of young children. Yet it must be remembered that most of the teachers from whose conversations these generalisations were derived were themselves highly respected practitioners of the teaching craft. Three possible explanations of this apparent paradox deserve brief comment.

First, it is possible that the evidence was badly misread. Perhaps someone else listening to the same set of interviews would come up with impressions quite different from those presented here. Second, it is possible that these teachers were not as highly gifted as their administrators and colleagues thought they were. Perhaps they more closely resemble the average, or even below-average, practitioner than they do the masters of their craft. Third, it is possible that the seemingly undesirable aspects of teachers' language are not so undesirable after all. Perhaps those qualities that might be a hindrance in many other settings do not adversely affect the teacher's functioning in the classroom. Indeed, it may even be that what looks like a general weakness in the quality of the teacher's thought processes is actually a strength when seen within the context of her life in the classroom.[2]

The possibility of having grossly misread the data or of having inadvertently chosen an inappropriate sample cannot be effectively dismissed. Consequently, it is necessary to remain skeptical while considering the third and far more intriguing possibility: namely, that what seems to be a human failing on the part of the teachers may be, at least in part, a pedagogical virtue.

The job of managing the activities of 25 or 30 children for 5 or 6 hours a day, 5 days a week, 40 weeks a year, is quite a bit different from what an abstract consideration of the learning process might lead us to believe. In the small but crowded world of the classroom, events come and go with astonishing rapidity. There is evidence, as we have seen, to show that the elementary school teacher typically engages in 200 or 300 interpersonal interchanges every hour of her working day. Moreover, although that number may remain fairly stable from hour to hour, the content and sequence of those interchanges cannot be predicted or preplanned with any exactitude. In short, classrooms are not neat and orderly places even though some educational theories make them sound as if they are or should be. This does not mean that there is no order in educational affairs (indeed, some teachers strive so hard to maintain some semblance of order that they lose sight of everything else), but the structure underlying these kaleidoscopic events is not easily discerned, nor is it, except superficially, under the control of the teacher.

The personal qualities enabling teaching to withstand the demands of classroom life have never been adequately described. But among those qualities is surely the ability to tolerate the enormous amount of ambiguity, unpredictability, and occasional chaos created each hour by 25 or 30 not-so-willing learners. What is here called the conceptual simplicity evident in teachers' language may be related to that ability. If teachers sought a more thorough understanding of their world, insisted on greater rationality in their actions, were completely open-minded in their consideration of pedagogical choices, and profound in their view of the human condition, they might well receive greater applause from intellectuals, but it is doubtful that they would perform with greater efficiency in the classroom. On the contrary, it is quite possible that such paragons of virtue, if they could be found to exist, would actually have a deuce of a time coping in any sustained way with a class of third graders or a play-yard full of nursery school tots.

The existential boundaries said to be revealed in the talk of teachers may also have adaptive significance when considered in the context of the demands of classroom life. There is a certain appropriateness, even charm perhaps, in the image of the absentminded professor. If he is to do his work well he must be able, at least figuratively, to free himself for long periods of time from his physical and social surroundings. But the image of an absent-minded elementary school teacher is not nearly so appealing. Indeed, such a combination of qualities might prove to be quite disastrous. People who work with groups of children cannot afford to be absent, in either mind or body, for any extended period of time. Moreover, even after the pupils leave for home they are gone but not forgotten in the mind of their teacher. The slightest mention of an abstract concept having educational overtones is enough to stir up a vision of Carl, the red-headed boy in the third row.

There is, of course, something romantic, even sentimental perhaps, about the image of teachers being presented here. But that romanticism is itself consonant with the qualities being described. Although they might never verbalise it in these terms, the interviewees, as a group, did seem to lean toward a tender-minded world view. Despite their immersion in the here-and-now, their view of children was definitely idealised and was tinged with a quasi-mystical faith in human perfectability. These signs of romantic idealism and mystical optimism may be disturbing to many people, especially to researchers and others who believe their mission in life is to dispel such old-fashioned views. But the persistence of this tender-mindedness in generations of teachers is surely no accident. Like conceptual simplicity and sharp existential boundaries, it too may have its adaptive significance. As Broudy and Palmer remind us in their informative book, *Exemplars of Teaching Method:*

> Modern psychology has given a solid and nonsentimental basis for mental hygiene and careful attention to child development, but unless a culture is entranced by the potentiality of childhood and passionately devoted to its realisation, the commitment to the long nurture of the young would be prudential at best. Once the 'cosmic' dimension of childhood is dropped, the life and activities of the child degenerate either into means to be manipulated for the benefit of adults or into a necessary but unfortunate marking of time.[3]

211

Philip W. Jackson

The teachers with whom I have spoken would probably agree with this statement, at least intuitively.

Here, then, are a few impressions stimulated by the talk of teachers. From one point of view, that talk does indeed leave much to be desired. It might even be described as dull much of the time. Yet, if listened to carefully and if considered in the light of what we know about classroom life, it does begin to make a lot of sense.

VI

Sometimes teaching is described as a highly rational affair. Such descriptions often emphasise the decision-making function of the teacher, or liken his task to that of a problem-solver or hypothesis-tester. Yet the interviews with elementary teachers raise serious doubts about these ways of looking at the teaching process. The immediacy of classroom life, the fleeting and sometimes cryptic signs on which the teacher relies for determining his pedagogical moves and for evaluating the effectiveness of his actions call into question the appropriateness of using conventional models of rationality to depict the teacher's classroom behaviour.

This questioning of the usefulness of rational models is not intended to imply that teaching is totally irrational or that the customary laws of cause and effect somehow fail to operate in the classroom. Obviously events are as lawful there as they are in any other sphere of human endeavour. But the activities assumed to accompany rational thought processes — activities such as the identification of alternative courses of action, the conscious deliberation over choice, the weighing of evidence, the evaluation of outcomes — these and other manifestations of orderly cognition are not very salient in the teacher's behaviour as he flits back and forth from one student to another and from one activity to the next.

The fact that the teacher does not appear to be very analytic or deliberative in his moment-to-moment dealings with students should not obscure the fact that there *are* times when this is not true. During periods of solitude, in particular, before and after his face-to-face encounter with students, the teacher often seems to be engaged in a type of intellectual activity that has many of the formal properties of a problem-solving procedure. At such moments the teacher's work does look highly rational.

This brief mention of the teacher's behaviour during moments when he is not actively engaged with students calls attention to an important division in the total set of teaching responsibilities. There is a crucial difference it would seem between what the teacher does when he is alone at his desk and what he does when his room fills up with students. Although this difference was not explicitly mentioned in the interviews with the elementary teachers it was implicit in their discussion of such matters as the relationship between lesson plans and their daily work. In the classroom, as elsewhere, the best laid schemes suffer their usual fate.

212

The distinction being made here between two aspects of the teacher's work is so fundamental and has so many implications for educational matters that it deserves some kind of official recognition in the language used to describe the teaching process. The terms 'interactive' and 'preactive' might serve this purpose. What the teacher does *vis-à-vis* students could be called 'interactive teaching' and what he does at other times – in an empty classroom, so to speak – could be called 'preactive teaching'. These terms help us keep in mind a qualitative difference that is often overlooked in educational discussions.

There is something special, in a cognitive sense, about interactive teaching, about what goes on when a teacher is standing before his students. At such times the spontaneity and immediacy and irrationality of the teacher's behaviour seem to be its most salient characteristics. At such times there appears to be a high degree of uncertainty, unpredictability, and even confusion about the events in the classroom.

At first glance the teacher's intuition, his delight over the mystery of human change, and his buoyant optimism appear strangely out of keeping with the highly organised setting in which he works. Such qualities might even be expected to be dysfunctional when they occur in a person who must perform within the confines of a formal institution. Highly rational and reality-oriented persons – tough-minded realists – might seem much better suited to the demands of the teaching task than are the tender-minded romantics who currently do the job. Yet this judgment of fit is not as easy to make as it first appears. As we look more closely at what goes on in an institution we begin to see how our present cadre of elementary school teachers, with all of their intellectual fuzziness and sticky sentimentality, may be doing the job better than would an army of human engineers.

One way in which the world view that has been discussed may be educationally beneficial is by prompting actions that serve as antidotes to the toxic qualities of institutional life. By being less than completely rational and methodical in his dealings with students the teacher may help to soften the impact of the impersonal institution. In a world of time schedules and objectives and tests and routines, the teacher's humanness, which includes his feelings of uncertainty and his Boy Scout idealism, stands out in bold relief.

Ideally, teachers might help to protect students in several ways from the anonymity and isolation implicit in institutional living. First, and most important, they come to know their students and to be known by them. Much of the teacher's effective knowledge as he goes about his work consists of idiosyncratic information about the particular set of students with whom he deals. Thus, the teacher may help to preserve the student's sense of personal identity by responding to him as a person, not just as a role incumbent.

Second, in some classrooms the teacher not only knows his students as persons, he also *cares* about them. He takes delight in their progress and is disappointed by their failure. This empathic response to a student's progress, or lack of it, may of course be feigned rather than genuine. But even when students come to realise that teachers, like other adults, are sometimes merely being polite in their praise and sanctimonious in their reproof, it is doubtful that these actions lose all of their effect. As we all know, a favourite device of young children when dealing with competitive claims or threats from their peers is to respond with the query: 'Who cares?' The answer to that question, when it refers to matters dealing with school and school work, is usually: 'The Teacher'.

Another aspect of the teacher's caring about his students involves his missing them when they are not there. The individual student is much less indispensable to the operation of a classroom than is his teacher. Witness the practice of hiring substitutes for teachers but not for students; it is almost as if a student's presence in a room does not really matter except to the student himself. Teachers, however, frequently note absences and often comment on them. As a result students are encouraged to feel that their own presence or absence might make a difference after all.

A third, and for our purposes, final, way in which the teacher might help to dull the sharp edges of classroom life is by presenting his students with a model of human fallibility. Unlike the computer in the records office and the electrical system that regulates the bells and buzzers, classroom teachers sometimes get angry or laugh or make mistakes or look confused. Unlike televised instructors or teaching machines or textbooks, real live teachers must often confess (if they are honest) that they do not know something or that they have made an error. Thus teachers are able to personify the virtue of possessing knowledge while at the same time demonstrating the limits of that virtue. In this way the abstract goals of learning are given a human referent. Students cannot aspire to become a computer or a teaching machine or a textbook but they can aspire to become a teacher.

At this point some readers, searching their memories of past and present dealings with elementary school teachers, may complain that the image presented here is too idealised and partakes too much of the teacher's own tendency to romanticise his work. Many teachers, it might be argued, do not really care about their students, except in the most superficial way; many do not really miss their students when they are absent, except perhaps when the absentees are teacher's pets. Moreover, the fallibility of many teachers may be so great that rather than serving as a model of the attainable they personify instead the comic and the undesirable. Add to this the fact that many teachers act like obsequious handmaidens of school administrators and their function as human antidotes to institutional constraints begins to look like a sentimental pipe-dream.

Yet reality surely lies somewhere between the ideal and the cynical views of the teacher's function. What is more, each extreme can probably be found to exist in some classrooms. The important point is that the teacher has it within his power to dull some of the abrasive aspects of school life *if he so desires.* Moreover, certain qualities of the teacher's general outlook, his world view as it has been called here, seem like natural prerequisites for his serving to make classroom life more tolerable for students.

Clearly the teacher is not the only agent who might make the institutional aspect of school life easier to take. In most classrooms, particularly in the upper grades, there is also a well-established peer culture which is connected to activities outside the school and which operates internally to reduce discomfort, or to strengthen the student's resistance by sharing criticism, subverting regulations, ridiculing authority, and in other ways providing defenses against the more unpleasant aspects of institutional living. The student who suffers an injustice in the hands of his teacher or who chafes under the constraint of an unyielding rule can usually find solace among his peers.

But whether he gets it from his teacher or from his peers or elsewhere, the individual student often stands in need of protection, of a sort, from those qualities of classroom life that threaten his sense of uniqueness and personal worth. It is also likely that he needs this protection while he is physically present in the institution and that compensatory experiences at home or at play will not be adequate substitutes for a humane classroom environment. School comprises too large a segment of a child's life to have its effect completely neutralised by what happens after the dismissal bell rings.

Finally, this discussion reveals a fundamental ambiguity in the teacher's role. In a sense he is working for the school and against it at the same time. He has a dual allegiance — to the preservation of both the institution and the individuals who inhabit it. This double concern and the teacher's way of dealing with it imbues his work with a special quality. The social theorist Charles Horton Cooley once pointed out that,

> An institution is a mature, specialised and comparatively rigid part of the social structure. It is made up of persons, but not of whole persons, each one enters into it with a trained and specialised part of himself . . . in antithesis to the institution, therefore, the person represents the wholeness and humanness of life . . . A man is no man at all if he is merely a piece of an institution, he must stand also for human nature, for the instinctive, the plastic and the ideal.[4]

Paraphrasing Cooley, we might conclude that a teacher is not a teacher at all if he is merely a piece of an institution. He too must stand for qualities extending beyond the official boundaries of his task. Some teachers (no one seems to know how many) recognise this fact and act accordingly.

Philip W. Jackson

NOTES

1. This quality of teacher language has also been noted by my colleague Professor Dan Lortie. See, for example, his article 'Teacher socialisation: the Robinson Crusoe model', in *The Real World of the Beginning Teacher* (National Education Association, Washington, D.C.; 1966), pp. 54–66.
2. The possibility of socially undesirable traits having adaptive significance for the teacher has also been suggested by J.M. Stephens in his fascinating article, 'Spontaneous schooling and success in teaching', *School Review*, 68; Summer 1960, pp. 152–63. This argument is more fully elaborated in his recent book, *The Process of Schooling: A Psychological Examination* (Holt, Rinehart and Winston, New York, 1967).
3. Harry Broudy and John Palmer, *Exemplars of Teaching Method* (Rand McNally, Skokie, Ill., 1965), p. 129.
4. Charles Horton Cooley, 'Institutions and The Person', in E. Borgatta and Henry J. Meyer (eds.), *Sociological Theory* (Knopf, New York, 1956), p. 254.

20. THE TEACHER IN THE AUTHORITY SYSTEM OF THE PUBLIC SCHOOL[1]

Howard S. Becker

Dr Becker is in the department of Sociology at the University of Chicago. This paper is based on research done under a grant from the Committee on Education, Training and Research in Race Relations of the University of Chicago.

From Journal of Educational Sociology, Vol. 26, 1953, pp. 128–41.

[Becker considers the manner in which the teacher maintains her authority. He considers the teacher's relationships with parents, principals and other teachers. The teacher is presented as a person who is concerned with maintaining what she considers to be her legitimate authority over pupils and parents. The principal and fellow teachers help to organise a system of defences and secrecy to prevent the intrusion of parents and children into the authority system.]

Institutions can be thought of as forms of collective action which are somewhat firmly established.[1] These forms consist of the organised and related activities of several socially defined categories of people. In service institutions (like the school) the major categories of people so defined are those who do the work of the institution, its functionaries, and those for whom the work is done, its clients. These categories are often subdivided, so that there may be several categories of functionaries and several varieties of client.

One aspect of the institutional organisation of activity is a division of authority, a set of shared understandings specifying the amount and kind of control each kind of person involved in the institution is to have over others: who is allowed to do what, and who may give orders to whom. This authority is subject to stresses and possible change to the degree that participants ignore the shared understandings and refuse to operate in terms of them. A chronic feature of service institutions is the indifference or ignorance of the client with regard to the authority system set up by institutional functionaries; this stems from the fact that he looks at the institution's operation from other perspectives and with other interests.[2] In addition to the problems of authority which arise in the internal life of any organisation, the service institution's functionaries must deal with such problems in the client relationship as well. One of their preoccupations tends to be the maintenance of their authority definitions over those of clients, in order to assure a stable and congenial work setting.

This paper deals with the authority problems of the metropolitan public school teacher. I have elsewhere described the problems of the teacher in her relations with her pupils,[3] and will here continue that discussion to include the teacher's relations with parents, principals, and other teachers. The following points will be considered in connection with each of these relationships: the teacher's conception of her rights and prerogatives, her problems in getting and maintaining acceptance of this conception on the part of others, and the methods used to handle such problems. The picture one should get is that of the teacher striving to maintain what she regards as her legitimate sphere of authority in the face of possible challenge by others. This analysis of the working authority system of the public school is followed by a discussion which attempts to point up its more general relevance. The description presented here is based on sixty long and detailed interviews with teachers in the Chicago public schools.[4]

Teacher and Parent

The teacher conceives of herself as a professional with specialised training and knowledge in the field of her school activity: teaching and taking care of children. To her, the parent is a person who lacks such background and is therefore unable to understand her problems properly. Such a person, as the following quotation shows, is considered to have no legitimate right to interfere with the work of the school in any way:

> One thing, I don't think a parent should try and tell you what to do in your classroom, or interfere in any way with your teaching. I don't think that's right and I would never permit it. After all, I've a special education fit me to do what I'm doing, and a great many of them have never had any education at all, to speak of, and even if they did, they certainly haven't had my experience. So I would never let a parent interfere with my teaching.

Hers is the legitimate authority in the classroom and the parent should not interfere with it.

Problems of authority appear whenever parents challenge this conception, and are potentially present whenever parents become involved in the school's operation. They become so involved because the teacher attempts to make use of them to bolster her authority over the child, or because they become aware of some event about which they wish to complain. In either case the teacher fears a possible challenge of her basic assumption that the parent has no legitimate voice with regard to what is done to her child in school.

In the first instance, the teacher may send for the parent to secure her help in dealing with a 'problem child'. But this is always done with an eye to possible consequences for her authority. Thus, this expedient is avoided with parents of higher social-class position, who may not only fail to help solve the problem but may actually accuse the teacher of being the source of the problem and defend the child, thus materially weakening the teacher's power over her children:

> You've got these parents who, you know, they don't think that their child could do anything wrong, can't conceive of it. If a teacher has to reprimand their child for something they're up in arms right away, it couldn't be that the child did anything wrong, it must be the teacher. So it's a lot of bother. And the children come from those kind of homes, so you can imagine that they're the same way.

The teacher feels more secure with lower-class parents, whom she considers less likely challengers. But they fail to help solve the problem, either ignoring the teacher's requests or responding in a way that increases the problem or is personally distasteful to the teacher.

> [They] have a problem child, but you can't get them to school for love or money. You can send notes home, you can write letters, you can call up, but they just won't come.
> If you send for [the child's] parents, they're liable to beat the child or something. I've seen a mother bring an ironing cord to school and beat her child with it, right in front of me. And, of course, that's not what you want at all.

This tactic, then, is ordinarily dangerous in the sense that the teacher's authority may be undermined by its consequences. Where it is not dangerous, it tends to be useless for strengthening authority over the child. This reinforces the notion that the parent has no place in the school.

Parents may also become involved in the school's operation on their own initiative, when they come to complain about some action of the school's functionaries. Teachers recognise that there are kinds of activity about which they may legitimately be held responsible, although the consequences of the exercise of this right are greatly feared. They recognise, that is, that the community in giving them a mandate to teach, reserves the right to interfere when that mandate is not acted on in the 'proper' manner. As Cooley put it:

> The rule of public opinion, then, means for the most part a latent authority which the public will exercise when sufficiently dissatisfied with the specialist who is in charge of a particular function.[5]

Teachers fear that the exercise of this latent authority by parents will be dangerous to them.

One form of this fear is a fear that one will be held responsible for any physical harm that befalls the child:

As far as the worst thing that could happen to me here in school, I'd say it would be if something awful happened someplace where I was supposed to be and wasn't. That would be terrible.

This, it is obvious, is more than a concern for the child's welfare. It is also a concern that the teacher not be held responsible for that welfare in such a way as to give the parents cause for complaint, as the following incident makes clear:

I've never had any trouble like that when the children were in my care. Of course, if it happens on the playground or someplace where I'm not there to watch, then it's not my responsibility, you see . . . My children have had accidents. Last year two of the little boys got into a fight. They were out on the playground and Ronald gave Nick a little push, you know, and one thing led to another and pretty soon Nick threw a big stone at Ronald and cut the back of his head open. It was terrible to happen, but it wasn't my fault, I wasn't out there when it happened and wasn't supposed to be . . . Now if it had happened in my room when I was in there or should have been in there, that's different, then I would be responsible and I'd have had something to worry about. That's why I'm always careful when there's something like that might happen. For instance, when we have work with scissors I always am on my toes and keep looking over the whole room in case anything should happen like that.

Another area in which a similar fear that the parents will exercise their legitimate latent authority arises is that of teaching competence; the following incident is the kind that provokes such fears:

There was a French teacher — well, there's no question about it, the old man was senile. He was getting near retirement; I think he was sixty-four and had one year to go to retire. The parents began to complain that he couldn't teach. That was true, of course, he couldn't teach any more. He'd just get up in front of his classes and sort of mumble along. Well, the parents came to school and put so much pressure on that they had to get rid of him.

The teachers' fear in these and similar situations is that intrusion by the parents, even on legitimate grounds, will damage their authority position and make them subject to forms of control that are, for them, illegitimate — control by outsiders. This fear is greatest with higher class groups, who are considered quick to complain and challenge the school's authority. Such parents are regarded as organised and militant and, consequently, dangerous. In the lower-class school, on the other hand:

We don't have any PTA at all. You see, most of the parents work; in most families it's both parents who work. So that there can't be much of a PTA.

These parents are not likely to interfere.

To illustrate this point, one teacher told a story of one of her pupils stabbing another with a scissors, and contrasted the reaction of the lower-class mother with that to be expected from the parents of higher status whose children she now taught:

I sure expected the Momma to show up, but she never showed. I guess the Negroes are so used to being squelched that they just take it as a matter of course, you know, and never complain about anything. Momma never showed up at all. You take a neighbourhood like the one I'm teaching in now, why, my God, they'd be suing the Board of Education and me, and there'd be a court trial and everything.

It is because of dangers like this that movement to a school in such a neighbourhood, desirable as it might be for other reasons, is feared.[6]

The school is for the teacher, then, a place in which the entrance of the parent on the scene is always potentially dangerous. People faced with chronic potential danger ordinarily develop some means of handling it should it become 'real' rather than 'potential', some kind of defense. The more elaborate defenses will be considered below. Here I want to point to the existence of devices which teachers develop or grow into which allow them some means of defense in face-to-face interaction with the parent.

These devices operate by building up in the parent's mind an image of herself and of her relation to the teacher which leads her to respect the teacher's authority and subordinate herself to it:

Quite often the offense is a matter of sassiness or backtalk . . . So I'll explain to the parent, and tell him that the child has been sassy and disrespectful. And I ask them if they would like to be treated like that if they came to a group of children . . . I say, 'Now I can tell just by looking at you, though I've never met you before, that you're not the kind of a person who wants this child to grow up to be disrespectful like that. You want that child to grow up mannerly and polite'. Well, when I put it to them that way, there's never any argument about it . . . Of course, I don't mean that I'm not sincere when I say those things, because I most certainly am. But still, they have that effect on those people.

The danger may also be reduced when the teacher, over a period of years, grows into a kind of relationship with the parents of the community

Howard S. Becker

which minimises the possibilities of conflict and challenge:

> If you have a teacher who's been in a school twenty years, say, why she's known in that community. Like as not she's had some of the parents as pupils. They know her and they are more willing to help her in handling the children than if they didn't know who she was.

If the teacher works in the same neighbourhood that she lives in she may acquire a similar advantage, although there is some evidence that the degree of advantage is a function of the teacher's age. Where she is a middle-aged woman whose neighbourhood social life is carried on with those women of similar age who are the parents of her pupils, the relationship gives her a distinct advantage in dealing with those same women in the school situation. If, however, she is a younger woman, parents are likely to regard her as 'a kid from the neighbourhood' and treat her accordingly, and the danger of her authority being successfully challenged is that much greater.

In short, the teacher wishes to avoid any dispute over her authority with parents and feels that this can be accomplished best when the parent does not get involved in the school's operation any more than absolutely necessary. The devices described are used to handle the 'parent problem' when it arises, but none of them are foolproof and every teacher is aware of the ever-present possibility of a parent intruding and endangering her authority. This constant danger creates a need for defenses and the relations of teacher and principal and of teachers to one another are shaped by this need. The internal organisation of the school may be seen as a system of defenses against parental intrusion.

Teacher and Principal

The principal is accepted as the supreme authority in the school:

> After all, he's the principal, he is the boss, what he says should go, you know what I mean . . . He's the principal and he's the authority, and you have to follow his orders. That's all there is to it.

This is true no matter how poorly he fills the position. The office contains the authority, which is legitimated in terms of the same principles of professional education and experience which the teacher uses to legitimate her authority over parents.

But this acceptance of superiority has limits. Teachers have a well-developed conception of just how and toward what ends the principal's authority should be used, and conflict arises when it is used without regard for the teachers' expectations. These expectations are especially clear with regard to the teacher's relationships with parents and pupils, where the principal is expected to act to uphold the teacher's authority regardless of

222

circumstances. Failure to do this produces dissatisfaction and conflict, for such action by the principal is considered one of the most efficient defenses against attack on authority, whether from parents or pupils.

The principal is expected to 'back the teacher up' — support her authority — in all cases of parental 'interference'. This is, for teachers, one of the major criteria of a 'good' principal. In this next quotation the teacher reacts to the failure of a principal to provide this:

> That's another thing the teachers have against her. She really can't be counted on to back you up against a child or a parent. She got one of our teachers most irate with her, and I can't say I blame her. The child was being very difficult and it ended up with a conference with the parent, principal, and teacher. And the principal had the nerve to say to the parent that she couldn't understand the difficulty, none of the other teachers who had the child had ever had any trouble. Well, that was nothing but a damn lie, if you'll excuse me. . . . And everybody knew it was a lie . . . And the principal knew it too, she must have. And yet she had the nerve to stand there and say that in front of the teacher and the parent. She should never have done that at all, even if it was true she shouldn't have said it. [Interviewer: What was the right thing to do?] Well, naturally, what she should have done is to stand behind the teacher all the way. Otherwise, the teacher loses face with the kids and with the parents and that makes it harder for her to keep order or anything from then on.

This necessity for support is independent of the legitimacy of the teacher's action; she can be punished later, but without parents knowing about it. And the principal should use any means necessary to preserve authority, lying himself or supporting the teacher's lies:

> You could always count on him to back you up. If a parent came to school hollering that a teacher had struck her child, Mr. D— would handle it. He'd say, 'Why, Mrs. So-an-So, I'm sure you must be mistaken. I can't believe that any of our teachers would do a thing like that. Of course, I'll look into the matter and do what's necessary but I'm sure you've made a mistake. You know how children are.' And he'd go on like that until he had talked them out of the whole thing.'
>
> Of course the teacher would certainly catch it later. He'd call them down to the office and really give them a tongue lashing that they wouldn't forget. But he never failed them when it came to parents.

Not all principals live up to this expectation. Their failure to support the teacher is attributed to cowardice, 'liberalism', or an unfortunate ability to see both sides of a question. The withholding of support may also, however, be a deliberate gesture of disapproval and punishment. This undermining of the teacher's authority is one of the most extreme and effective sanctions at the principal's command:

> [The teacher had started a class project in which the class, boys and girls, made towels to be given to the parents as Christmas presents.] We were quite well along in our project when in walked this principal one day. And did she give it to me! Boy! She wanted to know what the idea was. I told her it was our Christmas project and that I didn't see anything the matter with it. Well, she fussed and fumed. Finally, she said, 'Alright, you may continue. But I warn you if there are any complaints by fathers to the Board downtown about one of our teachers making sissies out of their boys you will have to take full responsibility for it. I'm not going to take any responsibility for this kind of thing.' And out she marched.

Teachers expect the same kind of support and defense in their dealings with pupils, again without regard for the justice of any particular student complaint. If the students find the principal a friendly court of appeal it is much harder for the teacher to maintain control over them.[7]

The amount of threat to authority, in the form of challenges to classroom control, appears to teachers to be directly related to the principal's strictness. Where he fails to act impressively 'tough' the school has a restless atmosphere and control over pupils is difficult to attain. The opposite is true where the children know that the principal will support any action of a teacher.

> The children are scared to death of her [the principal]. All she has to do is walk down the hall and let the children hear her footsteps and right away the children would perk up and get very attentive. They're really afraid of her. But it's better that way than the other.

Such a principal can materially minimise the discipline problem, and is especially prized in the lower-class school, where this problem is greatest.

The principal provides this solid underpinning for the teachers' authority over pupils by daily acts of 'toughness', daily reaffirmations of his intention to keep the children 'in line'. The following quotation contrasts successful and unsuccessful principal activity in this area:

> For instance, let's take a case where a teacher sends a pupil down to the office . . . When you send a child down to this new principal, he goes down there and he sits on the bench there . . . Pretty soon, the clerk needs a messenger and she sees this boy sitting there. Well, she

sends him running all over the school. That's no punishment as far as he's concerned. Not at all.

The old principal didn't do things that way. If a child was sent down to the office he knew he was in for a tough time and he didn't like it much. Mr. G— would walk out of his office and look over the children sitting on the bench and I mean he'd look right through them, each one of them. You could just see them shiver when he looked at them. Then he'd walk back in the office and they could see him going over papers, writing. Then, he'd send for them, one at a time. And he'd give them a lecture, a real lecture. Then he'd give them some punishment, like writing an essay on good manners and memorising it so they could come and recite it to him the next day by heart. Well, that was effective. They didn't like being sent to Mr. G—. When you sent someone there that was the end of it. They didn't relish the idea of going there another time. That's the kind of backing up a teacher likes to feel she can count on.

The principal is expected to support all teachers in this way, even the chronic complainers who do not deserve it:

If the principal's any good he knows that the complaints of a woman like that don't mean anything but he's got to back her just the same. But he knows that when a teacher is down complaining about students twice a week that there's nothing the matter with the students, there's something the matter with her. And he knows that if a teacher comes down once a semester with a student that the kid has probably committed a real crime, really done something bad. And his punishments will vary accordingly.

The teacher's authority, then, is subject to attack by pupils and may be strengthened or weakened depending on which way the principal throws the weight of his authority. Teachers expect the principal to throw it their way, and provide them with a needed defense.

The need for recognition of their independent professional authority informs teachers' conceptions of the principal's supervisory role. It is legitimate for him to give professional criticism, but only in a way that preserves this professional authority. He should give 'constructive' rather than 'arbitrary' orders, 'ask' rather than 'snoop'. It is the infringement of authority that is the real distinction in these pairs of terms. For example:

You see, a principal ought to give you good supervision. He ought to go around and visit his teachers and see how they're doing – come and sit in the room awhile and then if he has any constructive criticism to make, speak to the teacher about it privately later. Not this nagging bitching that some of them go in for, you know what I mean, but real constructive criticism.

But I've seen some of those bastards that would go so far as to really bawl someone out in public. Now that's a terrible thing to do. They don't care who it's in front of, either. It might be a parent, or it might be other teachers, or it might even be the kids. That's terrible, but they actually do it.

Conflict arises when the principal ignores his teachers' need for professional independence and defense against attacks on authority. Both principal and teachers command sanctions which may be used to win such a conflict and establish their definition of the situation: i.e., they have available means for controlling each other's behaviour. The principal has, as noted above, the powerful weapon of refusing to support the teacher in crucial situations; but this has the drawback of antagonising other teachers and, also, is not available to a principal whose trouble with teachers stems from his initial failure to do this.

The principal's administrative functions provide him with his most commonly used sanctions. As administrator he allocates extra work of various kinds, equipment, rooms, and (in the elementary school) pupils to his teachers. In each category, some things are desired by teachers while others are disliked — some rooms are better than others, some equipment newer, etc. By distributing the desired things to a given teacher's disadvantage, the principal can effectively discipline her. A subtle use of such sanctions is seen in this statement:

Teacher: That woman really used to run the school, too. You had to do just what she said.
Interviewer: What did she do if you 'disobeyed?'
Teacher: There were lots of things she could do. She had charge of assigning children to their new rooms when they passed. If she didn't like you she could really make it tough for you. You'd get all the slow children and all the behaviour problems, the dregs of the school. After six months of that you'd really know what work meant. She had methods like that.

Such sanctions are ineffective against those few teachers who are either eccentric or determined enough to ignore them. They may also fail in lower-class schools where the teacher does not intend to stay.[8]

The sanctions teachers can apply to a principal who fails to respect or protect their authority are somewhat less direct. They may just ignore him. 'After all if the principal gets to be too big a bother, all you have to do is walk in your room and shut the door, and he can't bother you.' Another weapon is hardly a weapon at all — making use of the power to request transfer to another school in the system. It achieves its force when many teachers use it, presumably causing higher authorities to question the principal's ability:

> I know of one instance, a principal of that type, practically every teacher in her school asked to leave. Well, you might think that was because of a group that just didn't get along with the new principal. But when three or four sets of teachers go through a school like that, then you know something's wrong.

Finally, the teachers may collectively agree on a line of passive resistance, and just do things their way, without any reference to the principal's desires.

In some cases of extreme conflict, the teachers (some of whom may have been located in the school for a longer period than the principal) may use their connections in the community to create sentiment against the principal. Cooperative action of parents and teachers directed toward the principal's superiors is the teachers' ultimate sanction.

The principal, then, is expected to provide a defense against parental interference and student revolt, by supporting and protecting the teacher whenever her authority is challenged. He is expected, in his supervisory role, to respect the teacher's independence. When he does not do these things a conflict may arise. Both parties to the conflict have at their disposal effective means of controlling the other's behaviour, so that the ordinary situation is one of compromise (if there is a dispute at all), with sanctions being used only when the agreed-on boundaries are overstepped.

Colleague Relations

It is considered that teachers ought to cooperate to defend themselves against authority attacks and to refrain from directly endangering the authority of another teacher. Teachers, like other work groups, develop a sense that they share a similar position and common dangers, and this provides them with a feeling of colleagueship that makes them amenable to influence in these directions by fellow teachers.

Challenging of another teacher so as to diminish her authority is the basic crime:

> For one thing, you must never question another teacher's grade, no matter if you know it's unjustified. That just wouldn't do. There are some teachers that mark unfairly. A girl, or say a boy, will have a four 'S' report book and this woman will mark it a 'G' . . . Well, I hate to see them get a deal like that, but there's nothing you can do.

Another teacher put it more generally: 'For one thing, no teacher should ever disagree with another teacher or contradict her, in front of a pupil.' The result in terms of authority *vis-à-vis* students is feared: 'just let another teacher raise her eyebrow funny, just so they [the children] know and they don't miss a thing, and their respect for you goes down right away.' With regard to authority threats by parents it is felt that teachers should not try to cast responsibility for actions which may provoke parental interference on another teacher.

Since teachers work in separate rooms and deal with their own groups of parents and pupils, it is hard for another teacher to get the opportunity to break these rules, even if she were so inclined. This difficulty is increased by an informal rule against entering another teacher's room while she is teaching. Breaches of these rules are rare and, when do they occur, are usually a kind of punishment aimed at a colleague disliked for exceeding the group work quotas or for more personal reasons. However, the danger inherent in such an action — that it may affect your own authority in some way or be employed against you — is so feared that it is seldom used.

In short, teachers can depend on each other to 'act right' in authority situations, because of colleague feeling, lack of opportunity to act 'wrong', and fear of the consequences of such action.

Discussion

I have presented the teacher as a person who is concerned (among other things) with maintaining what she considers to be her legitimate authority over pupils and parents, with avoiding and defending against challenges from these sources. In her view, the principal and other teachers should help her in building a system of defenses against such challenges. Through feelings of colleagueship and the use of various kinds of sanctions, a system of defenses and secrecy (oriented toward preventing the intrusion of parents and children into the authority system) is organised.

This picture discloses certain points of general relevance for the study of institutional authority systems. In the first place, an institution like the school can be seen as a small, self-contained system of social control. Its functionaries (principal and teachers) are able to control one another; each has some power to influence the others' conduct. This creates a stable and predictable work setting, in which the limits of behaviour for every individual are known, and in which one can build a satisfactory authority position of which he can be sure, knowing that he has certain methods of controlling those who ignore his authority.

In contrast the activities of those who are outside the professional group are not involved in such a network of mutual understanding and control. Parents do not necessarily share the values by which the teacher legitimates her authority. And while parents can apply sanctions to the teacher, the teacher has no means of control which she can use in return, in direct retaliation.

To the teacher, then, the parent appears as an unpredictable and uncontrollable element, as a force which endangers and may even destroy the existing authority system over which she has some measure of control. For this reason, teachers (and principals who abide by their expectations) carry on an essentially secretive relationship *vis-à-vis* parents and the community, trying to prevent any event which will give these groups a permanent place of authority in the school situation. The emphasis on never admitting mistakes of school personnel to parents is an attempt to prevent these outsiders (who would not be subject to teacher control) from getting any excuse which might justify their intrusion into and possible destruction of the existing authority system.

This suggests the general proposition that the relations of institutional functionaries to one another are relations of mutual influence and control, and that outsiders are systematically prevented from exerting any authority over the institution's operations because they are not involved in this web of control and would literally be uncontrollable, and destructive of the institutional organisation, as the functionaries desire it to be preserved, if they were allowed such authority.[9]

NOTES

1. Cf. E.C. Hughes, 'The Study of Institutions', *Social Forces, XX*, March 1942, pp. 307–10.
2. See my earlier statement in 'The Professional Dance Musician and His Audience', *American Journal of Sociology*, LVII, Sept., 1951, pp. 136–44.
3. Howard S. Becker, 'Social-Class Variations in the Teacher-Pupil Relationship', *Journal of Educational Sociology*, XXV, April 1952, pp. 451–65.
4. Details of method are reported in Howard S. Becker, 'Role and Career Problems of the Chicago Public School Teacher' (unpublished PhD dissertation, University of Chicago, 1951).
5. Charles Horton Cooley, *Social Organisation* (Charles Scribner's Sons, New York 1927), p. 131.
6. See Howard S. Becker, 'The Career of the Chicago Public School Teacher', *American Journal of Sociology*, LVII, March 1952, p. 475.
7. Cf. *The Sociology of Georg Simmel*, trans. Kurt Wolff (Free Press, Glencoe, 1950), p. 235: 'The position of the subordinate in regard to his super-ordinate is favourable if the latter, in his turn, is subordinate to a still higher authority in which the former finds support.'
8. See Becker, 'The Career of the Chicago Public School Teacher', op. cit., pp. 472-3.
9. Cf. Max Weber: 'Bureaucratic administration always tends to be an administration of 'secret sessions': in so far as it can, it hides its knowledge and action from criticism . . . the tendency toward secrecy in certain administrative fields follows their material nature: everywhere that the power interests of the domination structure toward *the outside* are at stake . . . we find secrecy.' In H.H. Gerth and C. Wright Mills, *From Max Weber: Essays in Sociology* (Oxford University Press, New York, 1946), p. 233.

21. INNOVATION AND THE AUTHORITY STRUCTURE OF THE SCHOOL

Dan Lortie

From Dan Lortie, 'The Teacher and Team Teaching: Suggestions for Long Range Research', in T.F. Shaplin and H.T. Olds (eds.), Team Teaching (Harper and Row, New York, 1965), pp. 279–86, 289–96.

[Innovatory changes in the school often involve changes in the working relationships between teachers. Lortie takes one such innovation, team teaching, and identifies two possible changes to the authority structure of the school — the vertical-bureaucratic outcome and the horizontal-collegial outcome — and the problems attached to each.]

Before we speculate on how team teaching might influence the teaching craft by changing the authority structure, we must consider the alternative forms that authority might take under team teaching. The writer believes that two polar possibilities exist. Team teaching might strengthen the formal authority structure so greatly that schools will become essentially *vertical-bureaucratic* in their authority arrangements. It is also possible that team teaching will diffuse authority into the hands of small colleague groups and take the *horizontal-collegial* form. Since both alternatives are possible from the essential characteristics of team teaching, emphasis on one set of characteristics rather than another would be the determining factor.

There are two features of most team teaching projects that are of enormous sociological importance. First, team teaching insists that teachers work closely together, and it suggests that teachers will often work simultaneously with the same group of students. Thus, the isolation found under autonomy-equality disappears. Secondly, teaching teams frequently contain a hierarchy of authority positions, formally designated by such titles as team leader, senior teacher, and so forth (earlier in this book it is suggested that such a hierarchy is virtually essential for the effective functioning of a teaching team). Thus, the norm of teacher equality is displaced. Two difficult questions arise. Since team teaching seeks to combine elements which, according to our previous discussion, seem to be unstable in mixture (close working relationships and hierarchical rank), which of the two elements is likely to dominate? And, where one rather than another dominates, what are the likely effects on teaching and learning?

What is certainly clear is that the widespread adoption of team teaching will bring about significant changes in the status of the American public school teacher. Individualism, previously supported by the autonomy-equality pattern, will be weakened by pressures either from administrative officials or close colleagues, and teachers who rejoice in their working autonomy must face difficult, important questions in taking their stand on the issue of team teaching. Perhaps the most important query they must answer is whether they can find other sources of autonomy once the isolation of autonomy-equality is gone. It is possible that they might find a more powerful type of protection than the tentative and uncertain power based on informal understandings which they now possess.

Authority: The Vertical-Bureaucratic Outcome

In conventional school situations, administrators find it impossible to supervise teachers closely. The span of control is generally too broad and their tasks too numerous to allow full-time involvement in supervisory duties. Team teaching, however, offers a solution to the problem of control by segmenting faculties into small units. Even the largest school, with teams each under a leader, could be brought under effective administrative control. It is conceivable that under some circumstances this possibility for holding a tight rein on the teacher's activities would be seized and used. The structure of the school could feature a lengthened line of authority stretching from the top administration, through principals and team leaders, to classroom teachers. Where team leaders identify themselves with management, they might see themselves not as spokesmen for a group of teachers but as local administrators responsible for implementing school and school system policies. If there were a system where the team leaders generally did assume this stance, few classroom teachers could escape the minute control found in tight administrative structures.

It is difficult to predict the circumstances under which this extreme type of vertical authority would emerge, for it would call for considerable change in the work values of public school personnel. There are some school boards, one suspects, which would welcome the change to run the show, but how many superintendents would go along with that ambition? Would administrators emerge who see themselves as strong line officers eager and ready to issue multiple orders over detailed matters? One also notes that the possibilities for gaps in the line of authority are numerous and that these gaps are accompanied by the likelihood of role conflicts at several levels in the hierarchy. (Even where the concept of line authority is strong, as in industry, foremen are men in the middle and must choose between identifying up with management or identifying down with the workers.) One can also visualise several variations from the extreme case of clear-cut line authority, and research must be planned to study these varieties when and if they emerge. It is distinctly possible that teaching and learning will differ according to the dominant mode of authority distribution and organisation.

Dan Lortie

The consequences of this type of authority system are manifold, and discussion of them would take more space than is available here. As far as the classroom teacher is concerned, however, it probably would result in routinisation of task and subordination of status, especially where team leaders were closely coordinated throughout the school system. Levels of output could be more closely controlled than under current arrangements since the amount of effort expended by individual teachers would be readily apparent and would influence administrators' attitudes and actions toward them. Teaching style and content could come under the control of a dominant leader since he would possess powerful sanctions. Educational objectives would become more specific and standard throughout the system, whether explicitly stated or not. Team leaders would serve as the focal point in the teacher-class relationship, for it is likely that where vertical authority is paramount, students would recognise the higher status and greater authority of the team leader. The range of choices made by the classroom teacher would contract, and the locus of professional decision would be concentrated above him in a formal structure. The possibilities for close coordination of system activities make it likely that a greater degree of curriculum specification would be found throughout all grades and schools. The position of the nonleader teacher would call for less personal initiative and require fewer complex decisions because decisions of any difficulty would, presumably, be made at the team leader level or above. The process involved would be one which industrial sociologists call 'de-skilling' in the working ranks.

To examine the desirability or undesirability of the close supervision of teachers could involve us in exceedingly long, complicated, and even heated deliberations, but research can, we believe, be planned to resolve some of the issues. One argument for increased centralisation is that it brings about greater standarisation among different teachers and schools, and that standardisation, paced by better qualified teachers, will result in a higher level of student learning. The implicit assumption is, of course, that the quality of teaching varies directly with the amount of supervision. Providing a clear-cut definition of student learning is accepted, such an assumption is testable by standard research techniques, and the variety of outcomes likely with team teaching means that comparative situations will be available for study. Another argument for centralised control rests in the success of the armed services in teaching certain specific skills (e.g. jet plane flying) and communicating set bodies of information (the navigation taught novice naval officers). Research could, using a variety of educational outcomes with relevant tests, inquire into whether the vertical authority system results in more effective teaching in some specific areas. Conversely, it might be found that such a structure is less effective in teaching nonmilitary types of capacity such as initiative, a questioning attitude, and respect for equalitarian values. Sociologists would be interested to see if vertical-authority school systems tend toward a single set of values in all classrooms and thus act to counter pluralism in our society. Close observation of the content and values expressed in the classroom could permit analysis based on firsthand data. The argument that centralisation means quicker adoption of innovations can also be tested by comparing the receptivity to change of vertical-bureaucratic systems with that of other authority distributions.

The lines of inquiry suggested, then, are several. Observations should begin on the organisation realities that occur with team teaching, and close attention should be paid to the degree to which school boards eager for close control are able to attain it. The role of the classroom teacher should be watched carefully to see whether it comes to require less personal ability and imagination, and the stances taken by team leaders toward their superordinates and subordinates should be the subject of intense research effort. The mechanisms of supervision should be studied closely, and the levels of effort, styles, emphases, and techniques of teachers should be recorded in a variety of situations. Instructional outcomes should be examined and data gathered in terms of a wide range of things learned, from mechanical skills to abstract values. The task of those who will assess team teaching in the future will require great philosophical insight. It should not be hampered by ignorance of what vertical-bureaucratic authority means for teaching and learning but should begin with results and assess those results in terms of several value positions. With knowledge, there is a much greater likelihood that the debate and discussion that takes place will reach rational levels of discourse.

Authority: The Horizontal-Collegial Outcome

By initiating close working relationships among small groups of teachers, team teaching might result in a form of authority now rare in public schools — the 'collegium', where equals rule their affairs by internal democratic procedures.[1] Although such structures are not common in our society, we do find them in some universities, churches, and artistic groups. The sociological theory devoted to this form of authority is less well developed than that dealing with bureaucratic organisation. We should expect, however, that where there is a strong emphasis on internal equality and close, harmonious relationships, such groups will tend to resist formal and lasting status differences. The members will have an interest in granting leadership according to the needs of the immediate group. Leadership in a collegial team will reflect the sentiments and norms of the small group. As noted previously in this book, even the most informal of groups will feature leadership of some kind. However, attempts by outsiders, such as bureaucratic superiors, to impose a rigid hierarchy are likely to encounter resistance.

Small groups having stability through time tend to develop common ways and common expectations which bind members into a miniature society.[2] The group, in short, develops a culture which may encompass a wide variety of concerns. In work groups it may define the nature of high performance, the amount of effort involved in a fair day's work, and the appropriate relationships that should obtain among members and between members and outsiders.

Our analysis of the conventional school situation suggests that teachers in teams will confront many problems requiring solution in the group context. Who will handle discipline when several teachers observe an infraction? How will teachers cope with students who show deference to one team member and none to another? Will team members display disagreements over facts or interpretations in front of their students, or will they stoutly maintain a united front? These questions can, of course, be answered in several ways. But we cannot predict *a priori* how a given team will answer the questions or whether a group of teams will select similar answers. Our knowledge of small groups and the processes whereby they build cultures permits us to say only that they will come up with collective answers to many of these questions. We cannot say which will be dealt with by the group and which will be left to individual choice, and we cannot predict the specific solutions which will be selected in those areas where collective rules are developed. It seems likely, however, that teams will develop norms to cover both the appropriate level of effort and the style and content of member teaching, and that teacher-student relationships will be a critical area for team concern. We can illustrate the complications by considering the question of effort levels.

It is reasonable to predict that teams will define a normal amount of effort, and that they will develop techniques for controlling both the slacker and the eager beaver. But what will that level of effort be? Will joint teaching, with its attendant visibility of individual work, result in higher standards of presentation and preparation? (We do know that the best law, medicine, and architecture is practiced where professionals face the criticism of colleagues and get assistance as well.) Will teams enforce effort levels equal to those of the dedicated teacher today or less demanding levels? If they choose the latter, how will the average effort of teachers compare with the average found in conventional situations? It is obvious that only carefully conducted research can answer a question such as this.

What of the teacher's craft and instructional outcomes, where teams bring about horizontal, collegial authority? Would a tendency toward conformity in presentation of materials, for example, reduce teacher satisfactions or lower student interest and achievement? Or would emulation of the best teacher raise performance levels and student effectiveness? Would content become more exciting when team members chose to argue in front of students, or would students find themselves unable to cope with the intellectual and emotional complexities introduced by open disagreement among people they consider to be authorities? Or will team members, necessarily concerned with maintaining smooth relationships within their group, choose to avoid open disagreement and thereby present students with less variety of thought than they would find in going from one teacher to another in conventional schools?

Should the team come to play a central part in the teacher's work orientation, problems of integration would assuredly arise within schools and school systems. Perhaps one development would be competition between teams, and, if this occurred, researchers would have to watch, most specifically, what rules were used to judge winning or losing in such rivalries. Where winning is defined in ways consistent with system objectives, such competition could enhance the achievement of organisational goals. Where the rules are selected for institutionally irrelevant purposes (e.g. ease of measuring output and victory), such competition could, however, retard achievement of the system's aims.

One possible outcome from collegial teams could have important repercussions for the 'art of teaching'. Under autonomy-equality individual teachers can work at their own teaching and develop highly effective techniques which are not communicated to others. Under vertical-bureaucratic structures, teaching is likely to become formalised into organisation procedures, and, where lay control is heavy, the craft may tend to be ignored or lost if the distinction between teachers and nonteachers is weakened. Collegial teams call for close cooperation, and this may, initially, inhibit the spontaneous improvisation of the isolated teacher and require 'scripts' for the teachers. In time, however, this could move teaching into a more recorded form, and improvements might accumulate in a context of conscious choice and refinement. This could lead to a greater emphasis on scientific values (communicability, accumulative experience) coupled with clinical practice, and such an outcome could do much to advance the state of the art.

The hypotheses put forth point to a variety of research possibilities and suggest a variety of techniques. It is clear that we shall need detailed observational reports which cover the subtle interactions involved in the development of team cultures. Close watch should be kept on how each team defines its norms and how individual members react to those norms. Records of conferences will necessarily be supplemented by observations of classroom behaviour and running accounts of the attitudes of teachers as individuals. Not to begin early would be serious since turnover among teams may be highly significant. It may represent, for example, the screening out of particular personality types and the selection of others. Such researches can profit from the experience of social scientists in a variety of settings, particularly the studies of industrial work groups. It is clear that research cannot be of the hit-and-run variety, but that research personnel will have to be in steady, regular contact with teams as this new organisation of teaching develops. [. . .]

Dan Lortie

Rewards: The Vertical-Bureaucratic Outcome

Where team teaching takes a vertical emphasis, the position of team leader will provide an important amount of differentiation in extrinsic rewards. Presumably pay, authority, and prestige gains will be greatest for team leaders where hierarchical facets receive the greatest encouragement. Schools, as organisations, will augment their resources of incentives with this position and will have more leeway in rewarding those whose services are found to be most valuable. This aspect of team teaching has already received considerable attention, and so it need not delay us here. There is, however, a possible side effect of this new step which is of interest to those who would augment the total extrinsic rewards available to teachers.

It is quite possible that the prestige gains made by team leaders will result in prestige losses for teachers who do not occupy that role. One is tempted, in seeking to label these teachers, to call them ordinary teachers to differentiate them from their senior colleagues. We encounter here a somewhat mysterious property of prestige systems – they are at times quite finite in that deference paid to some results in deference lost to others. Where the status 'teacher' is undifferentiated, the status of an individual teacher stems primarily from the status of the group. Where some teachers are accorded special recognition, however, the position of those who do not receive such recognition is weakened, for other teachers may ask, overtly or covertly, why they have not attained the more honored post. Should students consider the difference between leaders and nonleaders important, the authority of nonleaders might well wane, and this could lead to an increase in disciplinary problems. In short, two types of extrinsic rewards – prestige and authority – could show a net decrease when we consider *all* teachers under vertically oriented team teaching. Such an outcome is potentially one of enormous gravity, for few persons today wish to reduce the status of the teaching profession. Research should be conducted to examine such changes and to watch for any countervailing trends such as the possibility that vertical team teaching, by establishing higher standards of performance, could raise public evaluation of teachers generally.

It appears certain that intrinsic rewards will change when team teaching results in a heavy emphasis on vertical-bureaucratic authority. Team leaders, where the extreme vertical form prevails, are not likely to gain much over the teacher working under autonomy-equality today. For if team teaching is used as a vehicle for increasing the rigidity of line authority, team leaders may find themselves unable to exercise free choices. When team leaders exercise authority over their subordinates but are not in turn regulated closely by their superiors, they will, of course, obtain whatever gratifications are associated with leading a group of subordinates.

The majority of classroom teachers, however, will have to shift the loci of their intrinsic rewards. For example, close supervision will make it difficult for a teacher to feel that any given outcome is clearly his own achievement. All achievements, and possible failures, must be shared with the supervisor. Here again, personality differences must clearly be taken into account, for some teachers, more passive or dependent than others, may feel pleasure in meeting the expectations of an immediate superior. On the other hand, the more independent and aggressive teachers would undoubtedly find their satisfactions decreased. The psychic income obtained from student responses would undergo similar changes in situations where teachers of unequal rank worked with the same students. We would expect that where ranking is taken seriously by teachers, students will also be expected to respect it (students who failed to support the status distinctions would, after all, create tensions among faculty members adjusted to these distinctions). But developing such mechanisms will not be easy, and some junior teachers may compensate by identifying closely with students and thereby challenging faculty solidarity. This problem of aligning student response with faculty hierarchy may prove too difficult, and it would be a strong pressure countering rank and favouring collegial equality. But even if successful mechanisms can be developed, most teachers will still have to accept a lower level of effective response from students than occurs with autonomy-equality.

Emphasis on rank differences would decrease the pure sociability possible among teachers, at least in the presence of superordinates possessing genuine authority. The tendency for persons in stratified groups to choose equals for social purposes is well known and can be seen in the army's provisions for recreational facilities that are separated according to rank. The net cost of this change, however, may not be high if team relationships are internally cordial or if teachers find close, relaxed associations outside their work. But where ordinary teachers fear their superiors' judgments in class, it is unlikely that they will find it easy to mix with them outside. Research observers should watch these phenomena very carefully. Specifically, free period and lunch groups should be observed for tendencies toward grouping according to rank. In larger schools leaders may sort themselves out socially while nonleaders may similarly prefer the company of others of like status, but awkward situations may arise where the school staff is too small to support separate sociability groupings.

It is difficult to foresee the effect of vertical orientation on the opportunities for variety among teachers. Certainly the freedom to follow one's own mood will be lost where group planning replaces individual planning. but the leader's attitude toward specialisation is probably more crucial. Leaders favoring regular assignments and specialisation may inhibit opportunities for change while those who prefer rotation and generality may enhance it. The team situation opens up, in theory, a larger number of potential roles and activities for the individual teacher.

Despite the lack of data we have on current teacher gratifications and the speculative nature of this discussion, future research might hypothesise that there will be a net decrease in rewards of both types for *most* teachers if team teaching follows the vertical-bureaucratic line of development (the comparatively few teachers who have special status in the teams will, of course, receive increased extrinsic rewards). If the findings surprised the researchers, they would be forced to discover whether substitute gratifications have arisen; or they might find that teachers develop ways to guarantee the persistence of prized rewards by developing new and subtle informal arrangements within the changed formal organisation.

Rewards: The Horizontal-Collegial Outcome

Predicting the effect of collegially oriented teams on the system of extrinsic rewards (money income, prestige, and authority) available to teachers is almost impossible at the present time. First, the ways in which these rewards are distributed will have enormous effect on their legitimacy and psychological meaning as far as teachers are concerned. They could become empty formalities in the eyes of both those who do and those who do not receive them as currently occurs in some schools where the rank of department head is almost meaningless. Secondly, collegial teams which persist will develop a stake in the extrinsic reward system, for they will want to align rewards with their own norms and judgments in the interests of team cohesiveness. Yet central administration will also care about such distributions of rewards since they mobilise efforts to achieve system-wide goals and interests. One would expect, therefore, that there will be a significant and continuing struggle between teams and the central administration for control over the allocation of meaningful rewards. When teams do not subscribe to the means used by top administrators or the specific decisions they make, they will probably depreciate formal differentiation and supplement it with a prestige and authority system of their own. They may never be able to control money rewards (unless teams are given the right to elect leaders), but they could weaken the significance of money differentials for team members.

One situation which would augment the total extrinsic rewards available for all team teachers would be where there is close agreement between administrative and peer judgments on the proper allocation of differential income, prestige, and authority, for in this instance team leaders would receive increments which do not detract from the rewards of other teachers. Other teachers would probably regard such additional rewards as just payment for valuable services rendered. To bring about this high level of consensus will not be easy, and, where it is lacking, it is doubtful that team teaching will add any appreciable set of extrinsic rewards to the total currently available to public school teachers. Those who see the addition of rewards as a basic feature of team teaching should concern themselves, if this reasoning be accurate, with finding ways to ensure consensus among team members and administrative officers. Research efforts could assist in discovering what situations enhance such consensus and what situations militate against it.

The question of what will happen to intrinsic rewards under collegially-oriented team teaching is fascinating. As noted before, the type of craft pride found among teachers working under autonomy-equality is essentially individualistic with delight accompanying recognition of one's personal effectiveness with students. But can this type of craft pride be replaced by one which is collective in form? Can teachers come to feel equal pride in the accomplishment of their teams? Commentators have felt for years that the division of labour found in factories results in the alienation of the worker from his product. Dublin, however, in a most suggestive article, points to the possibility that workers obtain alternative forms of gratification from participation in a complex system of specialisation.[3] We know little of this phenomenon and are therefore ill equipped to predict under what conditions team identifications can replace individualistic ones. This issue is central, however, if team teaching is to give its participants a sense of pride and accomplishment linked to work effort. It is here that the personality psychologist's researches will be especially valuable, for it seems most likely that some teachers will find team-centred achievement gratifying while others will not. For team teaching to succeed, it will be necessary to identify such personality differences and to recruit those who obtain personal gratification in small-group settings. Without a predisposition of this type of reward, it seems unlikely that team members will put forth their best energies.

The role of effective response from students is also a crucial question when we anticipate collegial teams working with a common group of students. Differential student response could, after all, threaten the solidarity of the team, and members would eventually have to resolve emotionally complex issues of jealousy and pride. One solution lies in heavy controls on competition (professional ethics) which specify just how the individual practitioner may seek to obtain clients, or more appropriately in this case, impress them. If teams find it necessary to employ such controls, teachers will be less free to seek popularity with students and to win their cooperation. This could result in less affective response and a consequent deprivation for team teachers generally. However, an alternative source of gratification, which will probably become a prized reward, will be found in the approbation of colleagues. The instructional consequences of this change could be most interesting since it raises age-old issues of pedagogy. Who teaches most and best, the teacher who seeks to win students to his side or the teacher who lays down rigorous demands? Freed from the quest for popularity, will teachers increase the work loads they give students, and will this result in an increase or decrease in total learning? It is possible that team teachers may select other ways of coping with differences in student response and may reinforce team members who manage to receive it. If so, what alternative gratifications will occur for those sterner teachers who are either unable or unwilling to win student approval? The questions here are important ones, and working on them as they arise in team teaching should prove informative to educational knowledge and practice in general.

The gratifications associated with colleague interactions are likely to take a different form in collegial-team situations, for close working relationships, long hours at a time, will probably make spontaneous, nonwork intercourse less frequent. Teammates will find it harder in outside interaction to avoid work content and the inevitable tensions associated with it. For some teachers (notably those with rich social lives outside of school), this will probably be a minimal loss since the dangers of infantilisation are reduced where adults work together. But the problem of finding free and uncontrolled interactions will be aggravated for some teachers, and this may prove fateful for those whose nonwork lives are lonely. Perhaps such needs will impel teachers to find associations among members of other teams and will thereby act to reduce competition between teams. But researchers observing team teaching would be wise to consider the total needs of people at work, for we have considerable evidence that work interactions fulfill many general needs for people.

Depending on the specific handling of task assignments, horizontally organised team teaching could increase or decrease possibilities for variety. If some team members are highly motivated and prepare carefully, the remaining members of the team may find the intellectual content of their day more interesting and variegated. If assignments are rotated, the individual teacher's work round may be more varied than where autonomy-equality makes repetitive demands. On the other hand, decisions by teams to move toward separate classes and fixed, specialised assignments could result in less variety for individual teachers. For under autonomy-equality a teacher can make changes from one presentation to the next without worrying much about the reactions of other teachers or about an over-all plan. It will be interesting to see whether teams opt for the more flexible or more rigid handling of assignments and to discover the circumstances which affect the choice.

It seems likely that team teaching with a horizontal-collegial emphasis will introduce considerable change in the intrinsic reward received by teachers. If this be so, the consequences are of great importance for a change in these selective mechanisms which attract people to and keep people in teaching will ultimately produce a change in the composition of the teaching force. And this could easily set off a chain reaction of further changes. If we are to understand what direction such change is likely to take, we shall need a constant inventory on the make-up of teachers as team-teaching spreads. Close co-operation is indicated, then, between psychologists interested in personality and sociologists interested in the group phenomena involved in team teaching. [. . .]

NOTES

1. Everett C. Hughes, 'Institutions', in A.M. Lee (ed.), *Principles of Sociology* (Barnes and Noble, New York, 1957).
2. George Homans, *The Human Group* (Harcourt, Brace, New York, 1950).
3. Robert Dubin, 'Industrial Workers' Worlds: A Study of the "Central Life Interests" of Industrial Workers', *Social Problems,* Vol. IV, 1956, pp. 131–42.

22. HOW CAN THE TEACHING PROFESSION BE IMPROVED?

R.G. Corwin

From R.G. Corwin, *Reform and Organisational Survival: the Teacher Corps as an instrument of educational change* (John Wiley and Sons, New York, 1973),pp. 373–81.

[The Teacher-Corps' experiment in the United States was a programme of teacher education directed towards the education of low-income children. One of the concerns of the project was the problem of changing a conservative profession towards new goals. Its conclusions affect all aspects of professionalism and are discussed under the following areas: (1) Ideologies (2) Knowledge (3) Collaboration (4) New Teaching Institutions (5) Specialized Roles.]

Ideologies

Perhaps the main contributions of this program to the teaching profession were: (1) to provide a channel to attract reform-minded young people into education, (2) to provide a vehicle available to educators who wish to experiment, and (3) to publicise and perpetuate the general *philosophy* that teachers in low-income schools ought to become more sensitive to the special problems of their pupils. Its effectiveness, however, was contingent on the kind of ideologies that it supported and the competencies for which it provided.

The program succeeded in attracting a few new teachers who were more open to new ideas and who advocated a more humane and liberal philosophy of teaching than prevailed in the schools. Their compassionate social consciousness, their support for innovation and structural change, and their dedication to, respect for, and rapport with low-income children served as reminders of the need to find alternatives to better serve these youngsters. By insisting on more egalitarian and personal relationships with children, the interns challenged the traditional assumption held by university professors that cognitive knowledge is the basis of good classroom teaching, and they challenged the assumption held by teachers that 'experience' and maintenance of discipline in the classroom are the critical ingredients of good teaching.

However, the humane and liberal ideologies were introduced at the expense of other scholarly and academic values. Thus the interns who were the most self-consciously personable, warm, and compassionate in their relationships with students also appeared to be the most hostile to scholarship; they not only discounted the importance of cognitive achievement in their own pupils but often regarded university course work as meaningless and irrelevant for themselves. Similarly, the interns who were the most dedicated to the need for educational reform often espoused a radical political dogma that undermined their ability either to present a balanced view of society in the classroom or to work toward reform effectively within the existing system. Perhaps the interns' marginal relationship to the society and to the profession accounts for their humane and liberal posture toward the teaching profession and also for their inability to fully accept the academic principles of reasoned scholarship and detached fairness. This does not imply that scholarship is inherently incompatible with compassion and liberal dogma; there are other traditions within academia that provide for a workable combination of these characteristics, but the interns were not committed to them, either. In light of this marginal relationship to both academe and the profession of teaching, their actions were largely influenced by their own personal predispositions, especially when their inclinations were reinforced by the peer-group climate.

But regardless of the reasons for the interns' radical and dogmatic approach to political and social problems, the interns posed a dilemma for the liberal professors and teachers in the study who were committed to social reform. On the one hand, the radicals alienated so many people that they were relatively ineffective; indeed, many of them dropped out of the program or withdrew entirely. On the other hand, the radicals upheld challenging standards for what could be done. Although doomed to frustration, they provided a thrust for change. But these questions arise: Is it possible to train people who are passionately committed to the need for reform *and* who are calculating and patient enough to work effectively within the system? Can they become *sophisticated* about the system without losing their zest for change? Can they learn to temper their *romanticism* without losing their *compassion* for and *optimism* concerning the children? In many instances these ingredients did not mix.

Nor was the interns' compassion for the children necessarily an unmixed blessing. The interns were discounting the importance of cognitive achievement for precisely the group of youngsters who most needed to improve their academic skills.

New Bodies of Knowledge

The program was probably more successful in supporting a philosophy in favour of improving teaching in low-income schools than in developing or applying the essential techniques. Although the professors seemed to be more cognisant of the problems and were reading more widely as a result of the program, the interns continued to complain that professors did not systematically incorporate the available information about the effects of ethnicity, class, race, and minority group problems into their courses. This explains why the majority of interns, team leaders, and classroom teachers identified course work as the least relevant aspect of the program, and only a negligible number rated university-conducted preservice experiences as excellent. For example, where there was a serious language problem connected with the disadvantaged group, universities seldom provided courses in the second language that would have helped the teachers work more effectively with the students. Moreover, even when professors tried to employ special information, they tended to present it at such an abstract level that its relevance for the practical problems of teaching was seldom immediately apparent to the interns. This is one of the reasons why the interns were only slightly more satisfied with social science courses than with their other courses.

In addition to the tendency to ignore minority-group problems, little attention was given to the principles of innovation as intellectual subject matter. Thus, while the interns advocated change, they seldom were encouraged to read the literature on change or to consider the effects of alternative strategies for implementing it. As a result, even promising projects were often resisted because of the manner in which they were introduced. These inadequacies can be traced to a number of problems.

1. There was no consensus in the program and, indeed, in the teaching professions, as to whether specialised knowledge is required to teach in low-income schools. And, if so, what should the content of that knowledge be? To a certain extent, this reflects a level of primitiveness in the state of the art, which was further compounded by the goal conflicts and role confusion within the program. But the program failed to resolve the question of what kind of knowledge a special training program such as this one must develop and disseminate. In fact, it failed to take notice of the question, despite the rationale used to justify the program to Congress, that the problems of teaching in low-income schools were so unique that they required a special training program.

2. Most of the professors themselves had very little of the formal training or practical experience in low-income schools that might have equipped them for this program. The majority of the interns rated 'almost none' of their professors as superior teachers on these counts, and over four out of five rated less than half of their instructors as superior. On the other hand, one of the most important factors accounting for the changes that did occur in the colleges pertained to characteristics of the faculty, including their competence and their political liberalism. Probably the major obstacle here was the failure of the program to overcome the social isolation between schools and universities, that is, the failure to develop new forms of collaboration.

3. The tendency of interns to disparage the importance of cog-

nitive knowledge, in favour of developing affective rapport with children as a basis for teaching, accounted for some of their negativism toward the professors and also discouraged the interns from seeking out other sources of information.

4. Vested interest groups within the universities often refused to make room for new courses in the college curriculum. The fact that it was necessary to *add on* changes to existing requirements without a change in priorities or redistribution of resources imposed unreasonable demands on personnel in the program. When changes did occur, they amounted to little more than superficial alterations of what already existed.

But, no matter what the reasons were, *the program produced very little codified knowledge related to teaching in low-income schools, as distinct from other types of schools,* that could be disseminated to new generations of teachers. This might signify that there are neither unique learning principles nor special skills required; that the same skills can be applied to any setting; and that the teachers who are effective with bright middle-class children will be as effective as possible with academically retarded lower-class children. If that were true, it would indicate that the problems in low-income schools cannot be rectified by training better teachers or through a special teacher-training program.

Nevertheless, I am reluctant to reach this conclusion. *Although the learning principles may not differ, certainly the settings to which the principles were being applied did.* In the schools I visited there were severe language problems, even between teachers and students of the same ethnic background, and there were differences in values and in subcultures. The teachers often appeared to be almost oblivious or apathetic to many of the differences that separated them from their children. I observed cases of insensitive white, middle-class teachers in Indian schools who had never visited an Indian home and could not speak the language. I observed cases of equally insensitive middle-class black and white teachers in the large cities who punished lower-class children for fighting on the playground or running in the halls while winking at middle-class children who sought to destroy one another in intense status competition and through slanderous gossip. Although the special training did not deal with these problems either, it seems that the kind of detailed information needed to understand a particular subculture can be conveyed only by a special training program.

In retrospect, it appears that the political dimensions of the program were quite large, precisely because the program did not produce a clear consensus on what skills a technically competent teacher would need for teaching in low-income schools. Since individuals in the program could not readily establish their authority on the basis of their *specialised technical competence,* they turned for authority to their *positions* in the official structure of the schools and colleges. But because this basis of authority presumed a degree of commitment to the present system that the interns could not accept, they tended to discount it. This left teachers and professors without legitimacy in the eyes of many of the interns, which forced the teachers and professors to fall back on their *personal influence* and *power*.

Similarly, the interns failed to develop a specialised set of skills that they could use to justify their authority as leaders of educational reform, but they did not occupy positions of authority that would have permitted them to carry out their aspirations for leadership. Therefore, they, too, turned to power tactics. But they did not have sufficient power in most cases to have a real effect. In short, if there had been a special body of knowledge that people in the program could have pointed to as a basis of their authority, there might have been fewer problems and more change. Lacking this sense of technical competence, participants in the program were forced to rely on their official positions and 'experience' or to use power; and the forces for change were not as strong as the sources of resistance.

New Forms of Collaboration and New Activities

Although, logically, the university and the school district had a common interest in educational reform, each institution had its own vested interests, clientele, and independent resources, and it was subject to different incentives. The university was oriented to the academic-prestige system, and the schools were plagued with day-to-day problems. A negative relationship between innovation in the schools and the quality of the university signifies the marked remoteness of the most prestigious institutions from the local schools. The social distance was reinforced by the fact that most of the local program headquarters were located on university campuses away from school districts. A plan by the universities and the schools to have courses jointly taught at the schools seldom materialised because of different hiring and evaluation practices and different schedules used by the two institutions. The hoped-for 'hybrid' professional, trained in the social sciences but concerned with the application of knowledge to educational practice, seldom appeared. This was largely because the social scientists were primarily oriented to the academic system and were not provided with sufficient inducements to turn their attention to other matters.

The presence of very liberal interns seemed to have an adverse effect on the relationship between schools and colleges and seemed to reduce their willingness to cooperate with one another. Conversely, cooperation was better where interns endorsed an ideology of close control over the pupils and rejected 'permissiveness'. The competence of the university faculty members, as rated by the interns, and the liberalism of the team leaders also had an important positive influence on the extent of cooperation.

The program tried to promote new relationships among schools, the community, and the home. But since community activities were not part of the daily routine, they were the first to be slighted under the pressure of time, even though they were less bound by established routines and offered more latitude for experimentation. Teachers preferred to have the interns help them in the classroom, and principals were concerned about the tendency of some interns to engage in 'social action' in the community (as opposed to social service). The interns tended to define their community-activity responsibilities more broadly than did the teachers. The teachers considered community activities to be of value only when the activities had an immediate bearing on their own classrooms.

New Teaching Institutions

The program introduced an internship in the schools that, generally, was very useful, in principle, for both the interns and classroom teachers. It provided for direct experience with children in actual school settings, facilitated their understanding of disadvantaged children and the communities in which they live, and taught the interns about the 'political realities' of school. But the apprenticeship enabled the school to control a large portion of the training experience. The fact that the classrooms had not been selected for their known innovative qualities implied that the internship was designed to teach the interns to adapt to typical classrooms rather than to depart from tradition. Few interns had learned to become more 'innovative' by virtue of their apprenticeship. The teachers, of course, complained of the opposite kind of problems: interns did not spend enough time in the classroom; interns did not provide teachers with enough assistance; interns were too 'permissive'; they were unrealistic about the changes that could be accomplished within the school system; and they were so protected by the contrived team situations that they were not really prepared to assume responsibilities for large, unruly, self-contained classrooms.

Specialized Roles

The special roles in the program were not well integrated into the status structure and did not carry sufficient authority to support the interns, team leaders, and other people in the program against traditional role obligations. Consequently there were numerous role conflicts. Over one half of the principals and interns and one fourth of the cooperating teachers reported disagreements, usually with team leaders, about the amount of time interns should spend in the schools, the appropriate degree of permissiveness in the classroom and the amount of control that should be exercised over the children, who should supervise the interns, and the resistance of team leaders to trying out interns' proposals.

Each member of the program advocated the role definition that would reinforce his own status. Professors emphasised the intellectual foundations of teaching, that is, the importance of their subject matter and of cognitive skills, while classroom teachers regarded their practical experience as the critical ingredient for leadership in education. The interns, wanting to 'humanise' teaching, regarded their own ability to establish rapport with the children as the critical factor. When the interns tried to encourage 'permissive' classrooms in schools that were experiencing a high incidence of assault, extortion, drug use, and sexual attacks, the veteran teachers became more convinced that interns were naive and poorly informed.

Although the team structure provided some protection for the interns' nebulous status, it contributed to the role conflict. The teams, after all, had been assigned contradictory objectives. There was not a clear-cut division of labor among the members nor a consensus within the school about the team's function; this undermined the authority of members of the program to act as change agents. Teams seldom operated as viable social groups in the classrooms largely because veteran teachers were in full control of the self-contained units. The only exceptions occurred where teams were given complete responsibility for a classroom or for implementing a program and, in some cases, where they could work together on a community project after school hours without being constrained by the school schedule. In these cases the teams seemed to work cooperatively and were able to institute new programs.

Full-Time Statuses and Units Responsible for Implementing Innovation

A major obstacle to the success of this program was that there had been no provision for a special organisational unit in the universities and schools that would be explicitly responsible for implementing it. If special departments had been created that were directly responsible to the chief administrator of the university and of the school system, they might have provided better protection from local pressures. There were, of course, some 'full time' positions assigned responsibility for implementing the program, but a high rate of rotation among program directors, team leaders, and coordinators reduced their effectiveness. Mobile teachers and administrators used these positions as stepping-stones into school or university administration.

Team leaders could have provided stable leadership because they supervised the day-to-day operations, but federal guidelines prohibited them from serving more than two years in their positions; and, as employees of the local schools who served subject to the principal's discretion, they had little reason to be committed to the success of the *program*. Because they were dependent on the cooperation of other teachers and were assigned largely administrative responsibilities, they seldom functioned as master classroom teachers who provided role models for the interns. Even so, the team leaders were more sympathetic to the interns' objectives than were most other classroom teachers; this put the team leaders in a position to mediate conflicting pressures on the team. [. . .]

23. FULL—TIME PEOPLE WORKERS AND CONCEPTIONS OF THE 'PROFESSIONAL'

William S. Bennett Jr. and Merl C. Hokenstad Jr.

*Work for this paper on the part of the senior author was begun under a faculty research grant from Western Michigan University in the summer of 1971.

From: P. Halmos (ed.), *Professionalisation and Social Change* (Sociological Review Monograph 20, University of Keele), pp. 21—45.

[An exploratory analysis of the concept 'professional' is made here by Bennett and Hokenstad. Using the main organizing concepts of Knowledge, Autonomy and Service Goals, a distinction is made between 'people working' professions and the traditional professions — socially and historically.]

The concept of 'professional' has been well worked over by sociologists. This includes specific attention to the most visible people working professions of education, social work and the mental health fields. These latter occupations have been variously referred to as 'semi-professions' (Etzioni, 1966); 'personal service professions' (Halmos, 1970); 'new professions' (Marshall, 1965); 'aspiring' professions (Goode, 1969); the 'human services' (Riessman and Pearl, 1965); and many others. Typically, the people working professions have been treated as generically related to the 'traditional' professions, and the sociology of these fields as modes of work has had a close affinity to that of the older professions. The present paper, however, wishes to raise some serious questions about this approach, and by implication the way in which the concept of 'professional' has been used to evaluate all forms of work in modern society. It will be suggested that the ideal type of professional will *not* do for a sociological analysis of the world of full-time people workers.

With a few exceptions, the sociological (and quasi-sociological) literature on professions can be said to assert two major theses concerning professions. First, as best illustrated in a recent book by Moore (1970), it is held that the professional role can be conceptualized by a series of traits, each of which is a component of a complete continuum with professionalism at one end and non-professionalism at the other. A second proposition (most clearly expounded by Etzioni, 1966, 1969; and Goode, 1969) is that a variety of occupations, including especially human service jobs like teaching and social work have progressed only so far on one or some of these continua, but will steadily improve their position in the future: that is, they will become professionalized.[1].

250

The main position taken in this paper is that the nature of human service work raises serious questions about both of these established propositions. It is, in fact, distinctly open to debate as to whether the 'professional model' is at all appropriate for describing the major modes of people working. This in turn implies that collective growth or 'progress' in the human services cannot be adequately assessed in terms of a rank on a single continuum of professionalization. Put more positively, this paper will argue that the people working professions must be conceptualized differently from the traditional professions. Current professionalism, of course, derives from attitudes toward the 'classic' professions of medicine, law, the ministry and scholarship; and historically has its origins in the social position of medieval crafts, guilds and clerical orders, especially the latter. The people working professions seem distinguishable both analytically and in terms of historical origin. Nor is the distinctiveness of people working professions just a matter of degree, or points, on a professionalism scale as Moore would imply, but is grounded in fundamental differences of a social and political sort.

Even superficially, the major people working professions share certain obvious social characteristics which distinguish them and their field of work. Their knowledge base is *more methodological* and *less substantive* than most other professions in modern society and their period of formal training emphasizes *methodological skills* rather than substantive knowledge to a greater extent than other professions. A second important difference is the object of the service rendered. In the human services, the object *is* the client himself, his personality, behaviour or relationships, rather than a third party or thing such as a law suit, a viral disease, a set of blueprints, or an engineering proposal. The service focus is often on the total client and his interaction with his environment rather than part of him or some distinctive object from him.

This position is very similar to Halmos' distinction (1970) in which he differentiates 'personal service professions' from other professions which he calls 'impersonal professions'. Halmos defines the personal service professions as concerned with 'bringing about changes in the personality or body of the client'. The authors of this paper have found his distinction very useful, but do differ from Halmos on one potentially critical point. People working professions[2] (as referred to in this paper) are workers who deal with clients' personalities. This definition places those workers who deal exclusively or predominantly with a client's body outside the boundaries of people working professions. Some medical practitioners (e.g. surgeons) often deal with parts of the body in rather impersonal ways. Likewise, parts of the body (the shin bone, for example) do not have a high existential priority for most individuals. This distinction will be elaborated upon later in the article, but at this point let it suffice to say that the authors feel their distinction differs from Halmos' not just analytically, but also in terms of its potential for a theoretical treatment of the professions as a mode to work (e.g. their knowledge base, definitions of clients and professional careers).

Other differences are the type of work done and the meaning of this work. People workers primarily function as catalysts who, through the communication of information and sharing of insights, attempt to help the client help himself. They can be differentiated from those professions who use knowledge to help the client but do not share it with them, e.g., a physician uses his knowledge of the kidney, but does not attempt to explain (at least in any detail) the organ to the patient. Because the people workers are concerned with the client's relationship to his environment and communicate knowledge about this relationship, this type of professional frequently finds his performance related to economic or social goals of clients. Such a situation gives political meaning to his work. The person worker often finds himself acting as a *gate keeper* for some scarce resource in a way that is rarely true of an architect or even a physician. It is not an accident that teachers and social workers are more often viewed as political agents than are doctors (except psychiatrists) or engineers.

A less clearcut, but nevertheless significant, distinction between people workers and other professionals is the auspice under which the service is performed. These total person-focused professions function largely in bureaucratic settings as contrasted to the private or group practice arrangements of law, medicine (at least in the United States) and engineering. They are salaried employees rather than entrepreneurs. Although such an organizational base for their activity limits professional autonomy, it at the same time accentuates the gate keeper role and thus, the political meaning of the work. While some segments of all professions are now functioning in bureaucratic settings, bureaucracy is the standard condition only for full time people workers, again with the exception of many psychiatrists (and a few others) in private practice.

These unique conditions of work seem anything but trivial for understanding the present and future conditions of people working fields, not the least in separating them from other 'professions' to which they are nearly universally linked. In fact, this makes up only a partial list of the more obvious differences characterizing the personal service fields. The latter portion of this paper will try to put their distinctiveness in a more systematic framework. As perhaps the most rapidly growing occupational area it is extremely important that sociologists understand the people working fields *as social forms in their own right.*

The Professional

Their names are legion who (among sociologists) have addressed themselves to the question of what is a professional. Most of their writing, however, is clearly redundant and involves sufficient consensus to justify the assertion that there is an agreed upon ideal type of professionalism, which includes three major criteria: (1) an esoteric knowledge base, (2) a service ideal, and (3) public trust and/or personal autonomy (however one chooses to phrase it).[3] As indicated, Moore has recently presented a six dimension model for defining professionalism; but by comparing several other authors against Moore's description one can see that there is general agreement on only three of Moore's six dimensions. Moore also most clearly states the argument that the components form a continuum, against which all service occupations may be 'measured'.

Early in the century, Abraham Flexner (1915, pp. 576—90) set forth the first systematic statement regarding criteria for a profession. According to Flexner, a profession (1) is based on intellectual activity, (2) requires from its members the possession of a considerable amount of knowledge and learning, (3) has definite and practical purposes, (4) has certain techniques which can be communicated, (5) has an effective self-organization, (6) is motivated by a desire to work for the welfare of society.

Better known, perhaps, is A.M. Carr-Saunders' later characterization of the 'professions' which is similar to, but somewhat more restrictive than Flexner's. Writing with Wilson a decade later (1944) Carr-Saunders also anticipated later sociological commentary by predicting a gradual extension of professionalism into *all* occupational fields. 'The labourer is becoming a figure of the past...and all occupations may evolve some kind of vocational association or organization' (Carr-Saunders and Wilson, 1944, p.208).

Ernest Greenwood (1962), a social worker, is yet another 'outsider' who more recently has used a sociological perspective to define a profession, in his case, in the context of proving that social work is rapidly becoming a profession. Greenwood comments that: 'After a careful canvass of the sociological literature on occupations, this writer has been able to distil five elements upon which there appears to be consensus among the students of the subject...all professions seem to possess: (1) systematic theory, (2) authority, (3) community sanction, (4) ethical codes, and (5) a culture.' Clearly, Greenwood has stated these criteria in sufficiently broad terms that the attributes do not become the exclusive monopoly of the professions but rather characteristics of all occupations. And since 'we must think of all occupations in a society as distributing themselves along a continuum', it seems clear that professionalism must be identified with the high status end of the continuum. 'Professionalism' then becomes the model against which all other occupations (especially, in this case, social work) are measured.

A much more abstract version of what is essentially the same ideal type is found in Talcott Parsons' (1937) classic article on the professions. In an early usage of pattern variable analysis Parsons depicts the professions as characterized by 'rationality', 'universalism' and 'functional specificity'. Rationality (not of course one of the pattern variables as later developed) is loosely defined as a 'scientific approach', in fact anything 'which is opposed to traditionalism' and in which the 'relative questions are, rather, objective'. A thorough reading of his discussion of rationality would seem to find Parsons identifying professionalism with the systematic use of any scientific knowledge. This, of course, is a great assist to him in establishing his basic thesis, namely, that modern businessmen will increasingly measure up to his standards of 'professional'. Parsons' other two criteria for professionalism are the two well known pattern variables of universalism and functional specificity. The professional (and therefore the businessman in Parsons' eyes) increasingly deals with his subjects and/or clients according to universalistic criteria; while at the same time their own work becomes more specialized, according to specific 'technical competencies'. In this discussion Parsons emphasizes the specialized knowledge component of professionalism, to the seeming neglect of service or organizational considerations which authors have stressed. In a particularly interesting passage Parsons emphasizes the functional importance of 'disinterestedness' to the 'modern professions'. And in a later writing, Parsons (1959, p.547) seems to closely identify professionalism with modern scholarship when he writes: 'I conceive a profession to be a category of occupational role which is organized about the mastery of, and fiduciary responsibility for, any important segment of a cultural tradition. In addition a profession *may* have responsibility for the application of knowledge in practical situations'. (Italics added).

In this heavy emphasis on the knowledge base of the professions Parsons differs dramatically from the other well known sociological commentator on professions, E.C. Hughes. Consistent with his general style of doing sociology, Hughes is typically discursive in his treatment of the concept of professional. In his most focused article on the topic, however, Hughes (1963) places heavier stress on the service and trust components of professional performance than on the knowledge component. In a deft bit of philology Hughes traces the origins of the word professional to the early meaning of the word 'profess', as in to 'take vows', so that the term professional (as well as the title of professor) is clearly related to its medieval origin in professing or taking vows to the Church. Religious identification of course implies special insight, perhaps even powers, but also suggests clear expectations of duty and service. Because of the continuity of this tradition, the professional role, Hughes implies, is uniquely identified with service to a client. In the ideal situation the professional asks to be trusted (based on a vow, a code of ethics, or some similar initial commitment), and ideally he is granted this trust. The motto of the professional should, according to Hughes, be *credat emptor* (let the buyer trust) not the traditional *caveat* of business. Friedson, a student of Hughes, has recently (1968) followed up Hughes' emphasis on the professional/client role relationship with its service and trust reciprocation as the core of the meaning of professional conduct.

Hughes (1958, 1963) also stresses the group solidarity of the professional and views it as the institutionalization of client trust. The professional group obtains, or assumes, a mandate from the client publics. 'Every profession considers itself the proper body to set the terms in which some aspect of social life or nature is to be thought of and to define the general lines of even the details of public policy concerning it'. The client-professional role set and the working out of service ideal is obviously far more important to Hughes than the extent or preciousness of the knowledge base. In fact, the use and abuse of professional exclusiveness and solidarity by aspiring professional groups (barbers, salesmen, funeral directors and so on) has been the theme pursued by several of Hughes' students (Becker, 1962; and Habenstein, 1963). Becker is probably the best known proponent of the more extreme social behaviourist position that the term professional is nothing more than an occupational status symbol (the 'honorific title' as he calls it) which is put to use either in attempting to bring about social mobility for aspiring groups, or to protect established groups from interlopers.

Besides the well known attempts by Parsons and Hughes to define the professional concept, numerous other sociologists have attempted to delineate the essential 'traits' associated with an ideal type of profession (Cogan, 1965; Barber, 1963; Pavalko, 1970; Hall, 1969, and others). But the most explicit efforts to develop a systematic ideal type are found in Wilensky (1964) and Moore (1970). Of the two, Moore's discussion is the broadest and most detailed, while Wilensky's is more parsimonious. Moore deals with six major ideal typical characteristics which are designed so as to allow each component dimension to be sub-scaled. Moore goes to considerable length to point out the social implications of his criteria and in this regard his work represents an ambitious attempt to realize Cogan's so-called 'operational definition'. Unlike Habenstein, both Moore and Wilensky certainly see 'professional' as a useful sociological category and one which can be clearly defined in analytic terms.

According to the six dimensions of Moore's ideal type a profession entails: (1) the existence of a full time *occupation*, (2) the existence of a *calling* which implies 'the treatment of the occupation and all of its requirements as an enduring set of normative and behavioural expectations', (3) a formalized occupational *organization*, (4) specialized *education* based on the acquisition of useful knowledge and skills, (5) a *service orientation*, (6) personal and collective *organization* 'restrained by responsibility'. Eliminating the first dimension as inclusive of nearly all work and translating number two to imply the existence of a more or less formalized code of ethics, it would seem that Moore's treatment subsumes all the other suggested components of 'professional'.[4]

To go one step further, it seems possible to view Moore's second and third criteria ('ethical calling' and 'organization') as marginal criteria, or more precisely, as derivative of the latter three points. They are especially

William S. Bennett Jr. and Merl C. Hokenstad Jr.

closed related to the last criteria which is the assumption of autonomy, or as Hughes says, 'trust' as granted by the public at large. With the injection of this bit of parsimony we have, then, what seems to be the *core* essentials of the ideal type: a knowledge base, a service ideal, and autonomy (trust).

These are precisely the three major criteria which Wilensky emphasizes in his earlier and somewhat shorter work. They seem to compose the dominant, and nearly consensual, version of the professional ideal type. As Wilensky (1964, p.137) writes in the summary of his article: '...those loose criteria (things like licensing and tenure arrangements) are less essential for understanding professional organization than the traditional model of professionalism which emphasizes *autonomous expertise* and the *service ideal'.* (Italics added).

It is, therefore, against this tripartite ideal type that we will compare the so-called professionalization of the human service occupations. As indicated, this comparison has the explicit intention of proposing that societal conditions under which human service workers operate make it doubtful if this ideal type can be used to deal with them. Rather, the very nature of their work makes utilization of the professional model of dubious value. To use the professional criteria to study people workers seems a bit like trying to use blue prints of an internal combustion engine to understand an electric motor: both engines involve transformation of energy, but beyond that, understanding one model is little help in working with the other. Social work and architecture are both modern forms of work which involve services, but that is nearly all that they have in common.

The characteristic way of treating people working jobs has been to see them as lesser professions because they rank somewhat lower on some or all of the major dimensions of the professional model; but to see them moving toward professional status by improving their 'position' in terms of these criteria (e.g., the possession of a knowledge base). It is this proposition, which of course has strong normative and sometimes self-seeking components to it, which is seriously disputed. On the contrary it will be argued that the entire world of work for the typical people working job is so different from that of the traditional professions (as well as from other recent aspirants such as architecture) that a different typology is necessary to deal with individual careers, occupational organization and more specific role orientations within these fields. Indeed the *differences* between people working and the traditional professions seem more important than the similarities in trying to predict the future of these growing work specialities, and their relation to the rest of society.

Dissenting Opinions

Before elaborating a dissenting model for the human services it might be well to look briefly at several other orientations which differ from the seemingly dominant position outlined above.

The Semi-Professional Perspective. Differing slightly from the position that the human service fields are in the process of acquiring professional status is the view that they are, indeed, lesser professions *but* in the nature of things must remain in the position of aspirant on a permanent basis. This position is most clearly enunciated by Etzioni (1966) and followed up by compendium of edited essays (Etzioni, 1969) which deal with the particular problems of what the author calls 'semi-professions'. In the second work these fields are implicitly defined as school teaching, nursing and social work. The main reasons why these fields cannot meet the requirements of full professional status is that they 'are more concerned with the communication than the application of knowledge', they are less likely to be guaranteed privileged communication (not as much community trust) and are 'rarely directly concerned with matters of life and death')i.e., their services aren't so important). Etzioni also points out some peripheral factors which may permanently inhibit the movement of an occupation up the 'professional' status ladder. These include a preponderance of women in the ranks (making elementary school teaching the 'archtypical' semi-profession) or working within a bureaucratic structure, as is usually the case with social work.

Putting it in more psychologistic or individualistic terms Goode (1969, pp. 267—308) writes in a companion piece that:

> ... most of the occupations that do rise to such high levels will continue to be viewed as qualitatively different from the four great *person* professions: law, medicine, the ministry and university teaching. This view will correspond to a social reality, for they will be less professional in such traits as cohesion, commitment to norms of service, percentage of members remaining in the profession throughout their lifetime, homogeneity of membership, control over professional violations and others.[5]

Although Goode seems to emphasize an almost voluntaristic orientation in which the individual workers perversely refuse to 'make the effort' to be a professional; he too returns to the basic ideal type by way of an exchange theory of human behaviour. The semi-professions will never be full-fledged professions because they do not have the knowledge (skills) or the service value to exchange for the public trust. This, of course, is an exchange version of the basic ideal type presented above. On the question of autonomy for the semi-professions Goode is most explicit. 'The crucial difference', he argues, 'is whether the substance of the task *requires* trust, and therefore *autonomy*, and therefore some cohesion through which the occupation can in fact impose ethical controls on its members'. And, 'if we place the various professions along this continuum—the extent to which the client must allow the professional to know intimate and possibly damaging secrets about his life if the task is to be performed adequately—a fairly clear ranking emerges...' Interestingly enough Goode puts one of the major people working fields ('the psychotherapies') high on his ranking list.

In an earlier article Naegle presents another version of the semi-professional position when he, too, describes psychiatry as less restricted than two other professions (teachers, clergymen) working in the community health field. Naegle (1956) (following Parsons) asserts this to be the case because of the functional specificity of the psychiatrist's role. Naegle sees functional specificity, and the absence of community restraint which it brings, as a feature clearly distinguishing among various helping roles but also characteristic of all helping roles to some extent. Wilensky (1964) is likewise sceptical about the continued rise of various occupations to professional status due to a variety of influences including careerist, political, or organizational encumbrances which take precedence over professional (i.e. knowledge and service) commitments.

There are still other authors who question the imminent professionalization of the human service fields; but what is more salient in the Etzioni-Goode position is that it sees these fields (which include our people working fields) as having a service and knowledge base which is *functionally* similar to that of the established professions (Bennett, 1972). These fields also share in and aspire to the autonomy and trust which is characteristic of the professional ideal type. The semi-professions 'merely' possess less of these qualities and cannot expect to alter their relative deprivation in the near future. As a deduction from this position, the semi-professions it is felt should settle for a secure secondary niche behind the established professions in the status competition among occupational groups. It is important to note, of course, that this implicitly concedes the point that the professional model will be the standard against which all modern work will be compared.

The Anti-Professional Perspective. Singularly distinct from minor critiques of the professional pretensions as provided by Etzioni, Goode and others are a variety of perspectives which (although they differ in many specifics) agree among themselves that professional aspirations of people workers are self-serving and totally inappropriate. One of the present authors has elsewhere discussed this perspective more extensively under the rubric 'the communard ideologies' (Bennett, 1972). It is sufficient, here, to note that a wide diversity of authors have directed considerable hostility towards all 'professional' people working fields (especially social work, education and psychiatry). In the process they have attacked the idea that the human services could (or should) meet the requirements of the core model of a profession, or most of the peripheral characteristics (licensing, formal training, privileged communication, and so on) sometimes associated with professionalization.

This polemical type of critique has most frequently been directed against education (Goodman, 1956, 1962, and many other writings; Illych, 1970; Silberman, 1970; Freire, 1970; Oliver and Newmann, 1967; and numerous others). The basic argument seems focused around the notion that teaching must be communal, personalized, and radical; none of which is embraced by the professional model, and most of which runs counter to it. These criticisms do not so much attack the notion of teachers as professionals or semi-professionals, *per se;* they simply ignore the question as irrelevant to the more critical question of what education and teaching is all about. The radical critics tend to assume sinister implications to professionalization as well as unionization of teachers. They view professional aspirations as essentially political in nature and thoroughly detrimental to humanistic and/or egalitarian goals which they hold for education.

Similar radical critics can be found for social work as well as the various new left political theoreticians who typically view social work and mental health experts as political agents whose major function is to keep minorities, the poor, college students and others in their place. Art Pearl (1972) catches the essence of this anti-professionalism as directed at social work and psychiatry when he writes:

> Mental Health interventionists tend to reinforce the feeling of uselessness...there is an exchange relationship between therapist and patient (counsellor and student, etc.) for the helper to sustain his sense of uselessness, the helplessness has to remain. The creation of a spoiled image misshapes all mental health processes at the present time but this is particularly true with the treatment offered to low income patients. The same argument can be made for the inappropriateness of the typical correctional services. These, too, victimize the poor, segregate them into a criminal way of life with the attendant destruction of persons, and expense to society.

In a similarly polemical vein Haber (1968) has argued that psychiatric skills are hereditary or culturally acquired skills which cannot be taught, but are pseudo-taught as a means of systematizing the control of the 'unworthy poor'. Szasz, of course, is associated with a polemical attack on the apolitical and non-legal pretension of psychiatry. As an insider (Szasz is a psychiatrist), he is probably the best known anti-professionalist on the mental health front.

The Counselling Ideology Perspective. There is a third perspective which differs from the conventional view of the people working fields yet presents a vivid contrast to the anti-professional perspective. This is the view that the people working professions differ ideologically from the traditional professions, and that they will eventually exert an influence on the older professions to imitate them, and in this process will have a profound influence on all of modern society. The most systematic presentation of this point of view is that given by Paul Halmos (1962; 1968). Influenced by the work of T.H. Marshall, Halmos argues that the modern 'personal service' professions generate a set of assumptions about human behaviour and a perspective for providing service of any kind which constitutes a unique form of orientation toward work and which systematically affects nearly all service occupations. He refers to this point of view as 'the ideology of the counsellor'. This ideology, it is important to point out, develops as a function of the work relations and contexts in which people workers do their jobs, and not as a result of individual personalities. In his most recent book, entitled *The Personal Service Society,* Halmos deals explicitly with the hypothesized impact of this newer ideology on traditional worlds of work. He sets forth three seminal hypotheses concerning the 'personal service professions'. First, their numbers will increase and 'go on proliferating in the coming decades'; secondly, 'the paedagogical regime of these personal service professionals, as well as their professional ethics, are influencing the self-image of the other professional workers whose calling is not in the area of the personal services ... engineers, architects, lawyers and others like them...'; and thirdly, 'the moral reformation of the professions brings with it the moral transformation of some influential leadership outside the personal service professions as well, and therefore, a major change in the moral climate of society as a whole'.

Whither the People Working Professions?

It is obvious that there is widespread disagreement on the social status and even the moral worth of the human services. But do the ideological debates (most of which are in no way true debates since the proponents never address each other directly) tell one anything about the 'real' conditions affecting people workers? It will be proposed here that they do allow one to speculate about fundamental differences between people working professions and other service type occupations, whether publicly referred to as professions or not. These differences are perhaps best approached by re-examining the ideal type of professional (as developed above) with particular concern for major discrepancies inherent in the nature of people working jobs. Our analysis owes its greatest debt to Halmos' discussion of the counselling ideology, but differs from his position in certain ways.

The Knowledge Base. One primary criticism of the people working fields as full-fledged professionals is that their knowledge basis is thin and underdeveloped. There are numerous versions of this critique. The major difference among them being in whether the knowledge claim is seen as a near total hoax as in some of the more polemical attacks (Haber, 1968; Pearl, 1972) or whether it is seen mainly as a matter of degree with a social worker simply possessing less knowledge than an architect (Etzioni, 1969; Goode, 1969; etc.)

It is quite possible that both these positions are wrong, and that the error in both forms of critique stems from a simplistic notion of 'knowledge' as it relates to 'work'. This simplistic view would tend to see only one kind of knowledge, that which is usually referred to as cognitive or which relates to the common use of the term information. Limiting knowledge to these confines clearly seems to overlook the existence of quite different types of knowledge, including intuitive knowledge, interpersonal skills, rule making knowledge (as in making rules, devising games, etc.; not just knowing the rules) techniques of helping, and perhaps several other types. All of these types of knowledge or abilities can be involved in various work contexts.

One need not get too far into broad psychological and epistemological questions here. It is sufficient to ask whether in dealing with the core people working 'professions' we cannot admit that the amount of required cognitive knowledge is indeed less than that needed in, say, architecture or medicine, but at the same time suggest that other types of knowledge and/or skills may be required.

It is helpful here to take a page from the work of Kenneth Benne on authority (1970). In work ranging over twenty years, Benne has systematically distinguished 'expert' authority from 'rule' authority and also from what he calls 'anthropogogical' authority.[6] Leaving aside rule authority for the moment, it is suggested here that we concentrate on Benne's important distinction between expert authority and anthropological authority as a major feature separating the 'traditional professions' from the 'people working professions'. Both types of authority are based on types of knowledge, or at least on the ways in which people *use* their knowledge and/or skills to exercise authority. That this is related to profound differences within service occupations is illustrated by the fact that Benne himself uses the difference in authority between the medical practitioner (expert authority) and the medical teacher (anthropogogical authority) as his root example.

Expert authority, according to Benne, has two principal characteristics. 'First, the field is independent of the will or fiat of the bearer of authority and the conscient will of the subject.' In short, the test of expert authority must be against some independent 'objective factor or forces which are distinguishable from and independent of the patient's wishes or intentions'. (See the above discussion of the 'third party' nature of the *object* of deliberations in the traditional professions.) Secondly, expert authority is based on a consistent and unbroken functional distinction between professional and client. The doctor's job is to treat, the patient's is to get well. As Benne goes on to say, 'We may contrast the relationship of a doctor to a patient with that of the doctor as teacher of a medical student. The patient puts himself under the authority of the doctor not in the hope of himself becoming a doctor but in the hope of getting or staying well. The medical student puts himself under the authority of the doctor in the hope of himself becoming a doctor and entering into the collegial community of doctors'. Benne goes on to point out how in the latter, anthropogogical relation, if the relationship is successful there becomes an increasing similarity between professional and client and a *decrease* in the differentiation of function and specialized ability of both parties.

We would suggest, here, that people working professions as they are construed here, constitute a special case of anthropogogical authority and this suggests a unique type of knowledge base underlying their authority. That is, people working as it has generally been conceived during their roughly one hundred years of existence as organized forms of work, involves the transference of knowledge, not just the use of it. They stress the methodologies of applying skills and (perhaps) more limited ranges of cognitive knowledge; and they are far more deeply involved in becoming agents catalytic of change in another *person* than any of the traditional professions. In short, they can be said to idealize growth or change in the client, so that, if he does not become a carbon copy of the worker, he at least grows in some capacity, and most importantly is able to handle functionally similar situations (a family crisis, a need for information, a future economic problem) *on his own* without the help of the workers a second time around. This kind of authority based on interpersonal skills and skills in the transferral of knowledge[7] is fundamentally absent in medicine, law, architecture, engineering or even aspiring professions like funeral directing or interior decorating. Architects do not expect that clients will build future homes on a 'design it yourself' basis. Or, has any mortician ever suggested that someone try to stage his next family funeral on his own?

Another important classical profession which helps to illuminate Benne's distinction is the clergy. Goode (1969) refers to the clergy as one of the 'four great professions', but one is tempted to ask doesn't the clergy deal with people problems, isn't the priesthood intimately and inevitably involved with human affairs? Well, yes and no; and therein lies considerable meaning. It is true that many modern clergy, and churches themselves, do increasingly define their role in anthropogogical terms; and perhaps the early Christians (indeed most embryonic churches in any complex society) did, too. But, the medieval and early modern church, which gave rise to all the 'great' professions, as Hughes points out, most certainly did not. The object of religious service was of course the supernatural which was known about and negotiated with via sacraments, a community of saints (and especially esoteric lore concerning these saints) and scripture which as every high school history student knows was read only by the professional clergy. It is not hard to see how the objectification of spiritual knowledge into expert knowledge was the foundation for the modern church. Such transformation of spiritual affairs is probably the basis of priestly power and status in all societies, the possible exceptions to this being new or marginal sects in complex societies and the modern secularized church itself.

But whether or not the modern church has become increasingly anthropogogical in its orientation is not really at issue here; what is important is that the professional concept of the clergy dates from an era when it most certainly was not so conceived. The only irony, perhaps, is that among many contemporary clergy one may find the clearest anthropogogical notion of psychotherapy and 'social work'. By their very social relation to the 'client' ministers must be more concerned that the client become more like themselves, for they have to interact with the client and possibly his family on a rather frequent basis. Naegle has perceptively observed how this 'hinders' and restricts the 'professional' role of clergy (and teachers) in comparison to psychiatrists when both participate in community mental health efforts.

But the clergy is basically an atypical case which is used here only for illustrative purposes. More to the point it seems likely that, if the conditions of work help to understand the sociological implications of work, it is important to keep in mind the different knowledge structures underlying expert authority and anthropogogical authority. Anthropogogical knowledge and skills are much less easily codified; therefore, the apparent thinness of the knowledge base for people workers. Anthropogogical knowledge or skill can be gained only through experience, therefore, explaining why 'professional' training in the human services is more sensitizing and intensive. Finally, anthropogogical knowledge is less instrumental than expert knowledge and concomitantly is more interested in change in the client than in obtaining some external goal for him. The implication of the latter is perceivable in the observation that if it is impossible to deal with a learning problem in the same manner of fact way that one deals with a diseased kidney. It makes a difference whether the person with the reading problem is black, or hostile, or has been a victim of child neglect in a basic way that these personalistic considerations are rarely vital in the case of a physician trying to heal an ailing kidney. It is likely that a reading problem can be solved only if the student existentially understands many contingencies related to the problem (he does not always have to be able to verbalize these understandings), than it is that a patient needs to understand all the causal factors involved in a kidney ailment.[8]

Autonomy. The brunt of the radical criticisms of people workers, as discussed above, has been on the clearly political nature of the human services. Radical critics of education as diverse as Paul Goodman, Ivan Illych, Art Pearl, Jules Henry, Paolo Freire, and Mario Fantini seem to find a common ground in the frequently encountered theme that the professional educator and professional education guard scarce, yet increasingly valuable, resources in modern society. This not only applies to the obvious economic rewards for those successful in the educational process, but applies as well to competition for social status. As we move toward something roughly approximating Michael Young's 'meritocracy', the role of the professional educator (and other people workers) will become increasingly important as an arbitrator of status. As society becomes more thoroughly characterized by contest mobility rather than sponsored mobility (as it will assuredly will), the particular judges of the 'contest' will increase in potential political importance. The school monks (to use Goodman's phrase) will increasingly guard the gates to a secular heaven of increased consumption and higher status. Illych goes even further when he sees the schools as propagating and defining the core values of an exploitative and consumption oriented society. The political clout of the schools, as perceived by at least some of its radical critics, is put in its most acerbic (and most sharply focused form) by Illych (1970) when he writes:

> Schools select for each successive level (of advancement) those who have at earlier stages in the game proved themselves good risks for the established order. Having a monopoly on both the resources for learning and the investiture of social roles, the university co-opts the discoverer and the potential dissenter...The university graduate has been schooled for selective service among the rich of the world.

Now it is obvious that the schooled have always been among the rich of the world, what is important in the writing of many radical critics is the perception that the schools have increasing power, perhaps eventually total power, over who joins and who does not join the 'select of the world'. Social workers and mental health workers, likewise, play the gate-keeper role in the distribution of society's material and status resources. Whether working in a public welfare agency or a state mental institution, their diagnoses and decisions have a direct effect on the access of their clientele to these scarce commodities in the present and the labels they apply can also affect future access. This influence is exerted largely through the worker's organizational location rather than because of his personal autonomy. In spite of the fact that public trust is quite low for people workers in some such settings (e.g., the public welfare workers), they do exercise considerable control over the lives of many people.

The radical critics of education (and of social work and mental health fields as well) consistently emphasize the conservation of this arrangement with its potential for social control, inhibition of individual freedom and maintenance of an unjust and vicious class system. But one does not have to accept all of the deductions and flights of fancy of a writer like Illych, to agree with the seminal sociological observation that people workers, even those relegated to low 'professional' status (like elementary school teachers), by Etzioni, will increasingly play a quasi-political role. As indivduals, but more likely as occupational groups, they will be in a position to say what kind of society will exist and what the leadership cadres will look like and how they will think. Whether seen as defenders of a bourgeoisie status quo, or as leaders of a 'personal service society' as forseen by Halmos, the people workers of the future will have political power or at least be important sources of influence (e.g., through the universities) on the uses of power. Halmos (1970) indicates how this may be true on a numerical basis alone!

In short, one cannot escape the conclusion that the people working professions will become further removed from the 'autonomy' ideal of the traditional professions. And, as one views the political implications of this shift, one has to admit that the criteria of social and political autonomy will become increasingly *irrelevant* as a way of defining what education, social work or mental health work is all about—*qua* work. It seems even less likely that personal autonomy and unquestioned public trust will be granted to people workers, and when it does it will not be a sign of 'progress' along some professional continuum but will be seen as an anachronism which will soon be reversed. In fact, it is clear to even the most casual observer that personal service workers are with rare exception deeply involved in the politics of agency bureaucracies and frequently caught up in external affairs. Very few aspects of the jobs of teachers and social workers, especially, do not come under political scrutiny. In even fewer cases do the actions of these workers fail to possess some political meaning of their own: even if these political implications are only dimly perceived by the worker. In fact, the bureaucratic and political involvement of the personal service professions must be seen as a *normal* condition of their work.

It is suggested that to understand the social relations and conditions under which people workers do their jobs, sociologists and laymen alike will increasingly recognize the inherent political nature of such work. Of course, as indicated, this will be 'political' in a broad sense, in which non-functionally specific control over access to scarce resources, and perhaps especially the intangible but nonetheless competitive struggle for social status, is distinctly political. Therefore, as in 'substituting' an anthropogogical knowledge base for expert knowledge base, it is also true that a fundamentally different 'ideal type' of professional people worker must be considered in which 'political' replaces 'autonomous' as a major dimension defining the analytic boundaries of this type of work. Whether sociologists do so or not, it is fairly clear that numerous influential intellectuals and writers, as well as those large social groups most open to political manipulation by people workers, are already making this redefinition. Sociologists, it is suggested, would be well advised to follow suit and to deal with the political implications of people work as it relates to education, careers, certification, control of organizations (e.g., school boards), role conflict, and job satisfaction in these fields).

Service Goals and the New Ideal Typical Person Workers. Only the service ideal or goal seems transferable from the model of the traditional professions to that of the people working professions. This seems to be the main tie between these two worlds of work: in both cases the goal of the

William S. Bennett Jr. and Merl C. Hokenstad Jr.

work is service for a client who is in some need or for whom in some cases a third party is seeking service (e.g., a parent for his child). Even here a significant difference suggests itself in that, as discussed above, the service in the traditional profession (new or emergent) is usually seen as repeatable, whereas in the case of human service professionals there seems to be strong assumption that the service is ideally a once-only situation. Teachers do not like to see their students return to repeat a grade; psychiatrists (except perhaps the most mercenary) do not like to see a patient return after what the psychiatrists judge as to be a 'cure' has been effected.[9] But in essence a service goal remains. As opposed to a scientist or scholar, whose basic role set is with colleagues, or for the business man whose role set is with customers (or employees), the role relation with client is quite similar for both the traditional professions and for the typical people worker.

It should be clear by now that this article is suggesting the utility of a new ideal type of personal service professional which is in no way simply a minor adjustment to the model against which the 'traditional professions' have been judged. If the notion of a 'knowledge base' is still relevant it must be a new type of knowledge that is considered 'basic'; we have chosen to suggest anthropogogical knowledge as that alternative. Similarly, we have chosen to reject the criteria of autonomy and substitute the criteria of political accountability. Only perhaps the criteria of a 'service ideal' does not need to be rewritten to provide an analytic definition of the 'personal service professional'. In short, the personal professional, in juxtaposition to the traditional professional is defined as a worker engaged in a service to some client, who works from an anthropogogical knowledge base and whose job is manifestly political in nature or which at least has strong political implications. In fact, the authors would like to suggest the necessity of developing two ideal types: (1) the *personal service professions* (described above) and (2) the *craft professions* (fitting the traditional model)[10] as two very fundamentally different modes of work which should never be directly compared and should be distinguished in sociological theory about the past, present and future of the world of work.

Hunches and Predictions

Certainly little progress in the sociology of the human services can be made utilizing an ideal typical construction which is fundamentally misapplied. If predictions are made about the future of the people working fields on the basis of the implicit continuum which has been developed for 'measuring' professionalization, these predictions may turn out to be quite inaccurate. As an illustration of this the present article will conclude by suggesting several interrelated propositions about the social contexts of the human services which are suggested by the new type of people working profession. First, it is predicted that the human services will grow even faster in scope and in number of practitioners. This is premised on the fact that anthropogogical authority and its knowledge base is by nature open and less exclusive. Its social and cultural particularism and *lack* of functional specificity will create pressures to broaden the base of the work force, to sharply decrease the social class bias in recruitment and to encourage a much more varied conception of the 'work place', e.g., the attention given to a notion of a 'classroom without walls'. In other words, more people will be doing people work, in a wide variety of settings, but with less clear social status attached to the position.

Secondly, formal educational requirements will be more flexible and increasingly particularistic. The university will substantially modify qualifying requirements for people working professions and formal training in people working careers may gravitate away from university settings. Educational requirements in social work are already being modified to place greater emphasis upon the development of methodological skills at community college and baccalaureate levels of training. New careers programmes with or without university affiliation are preparing many individuals for people working careers. In spite of a current tendency to tighten up certification requirements in teaching and social work, the long range trend towards flexibility and diversity will predominate. This is in part due to the nature of the knowledge base in these professions. Training programmes will become more anthropogogical in their own practices to match the anthropogogical knowledge base of their fields.

Finally, it is predicted that people workers will *not* become increasingly depoliticalized as suggested by the traditional professional model. Increasingly there will be visible examples of public 'control' over vital aspects of education, social work and mental health fields (as in the community school movement or in the resident dominated boards of welfare programmes). Likewise, people workers, individually and collectively, will themselves become more active politically (e.g. social work activism). There will, in short, be increased consciousness of the political nature of people working by practitioners themselves. That there is a natural tension between public supervision and political action is fully recognized and leads to a final corollary prediction; that is, that the human services will increasingly find social conflict as part of their 'ordinary' work and that this will become the most salient role characteristic attendant on people working between now and the end of the century. This endemic social conflict has already caught some people workers (school administrators, for example) by surprise. The situation will almost certainly be exacerbated if professional schools are unwilling or unable to train students for advocacy or conflict resolution roles.

These, then, are a few predictions which are stimulated by a revised conceptualization of the people working professions. Due to the possibility

William S. Bennett Jr. and Merl C. Hokenstad Jr.

for misunderstanding, it should be emphasized that these are empirical predictions, not normative exhortations. They are hypotheses for testing, and they are suggested for professional people working partially because some of the trends are clearly in evidence, but more importantly because they are theoretically entailed in a revised conceptualization of the social basis and the entailed meanings of working with people.

Western Michigan University

NOTES

1. Etzioni and Goode are, however, sceptical that certain semi-professions will ever 'make it' to full professional status.

2. The authors have been criticized for using the somewhat awkward and abrasive term 'people working' rather than established terms such as 'human services'. If there is a reason for this, other than style (or the 'feel' of the term), it is to emphasize the authors' unique stress on *work with people* (especially people defined as personalities or selves) rather than stressing *service to people* which might include parts of people (lancing a boil) or things belonging to people (repairing their auto or making their will). But this a matter of emphasis, not an absolute. For example, the medical field is seen as a *mixed* type, and is *not* totally excluded from the people working professions.

3. This is most clearly stated by Wilensky (1964); but we will review his comments only at the end of this historical review of the literature.

4. This is with the possible exception of Parsons, whose typology is on a totally different level of abstraction from all other efforts to define professional and whose concepts of rationality and universalism are difficult to put into any operational terms.

5. Two things should be pointed out concerning differences between Goode's terminology and terms used elsewhere in this paper. First, Goode is using person professions to include practically every line of work which has ever been called a profession and which have people for clients; whereas we have chosen to restrict the term people working profession to refer to those service occupations where in a fundamental sense a person may be both client and object for the service. This is an important sociological distinction from our perspective. Secondly, in addressing himself to semi-professions, a category in which he obviously firmly believes, Goode is referring to nearly all modern occupations other than the 'four great professions'.

6. Benne apologizes for introducing such an awkward neologism but defends it on heuristic grounds.

7. An important aspect of this 'authority' is the sensitivity as to when *not* to utilize one's skills; but this will not be further developed in this paper.

8. Psychosomatic ailments are, of course, critical and sociologically important exceptions to this generalization about kidneys and kidney healers.

9. Of course other medical doctors do not like to see their patient returning for exactly the same ailment, but neither do they expect never to see the patient

again, and most certainly they do not expect the patient to handle his next attack or seizure 'on his own', except with carefully prescribed physical aides.

10. These titles for our ideal types should be considered highly tentative. The term 'craft' professional has been chosen because of the objective nature of the knowledge base in traditional professions and the craft-like nature of the skills involved (surgery, drafting, design, etc.). And as ideal types, real behaviour and actual roles (jobs) will rarely, if ever, fit either ideal type exactly.

References

Barber, B. (1963), 'Some Problems in the Sociology of the Professions', in *Daedalus,* Vol. 92, no. 4 (Fall), pp. 669–88.

Becker, H. (1962), 'The Nature of a Profession', in Nelson B.H.(ed.), *Education for the Professions,* University of Chicago Press, Chicago.

Benne, K. (1970), 'Authority in Education', *Harvard Educational Review,* Vol. 40, no. 3 (August), pp. 385–410.

Bennett, W.S. (1972), 'The Communards: Counter Ideologists of the People-Working Professions'. Paper presented at the annual meeting of the American Sociological Association, New Orleans, August.

Carr-Saunders, A.M. (1928), *Professions: Their Organization and Place in Society,* Clarendon Press, Oxford.

– – and Wilson, P.A. (1944), 'The Emergence of the Professions', *Encyclopedia of Social Sciences,* Macmillan, New York.

Cogan, M.L. (1955), 'The Problems of Defining a Profession', *The Annals of the American Academy of Political and Social Sciences,* no. 297 (January), pp. 105.

Etzioni, A. (1966), *Modern Organizations,* Prentice-Hall, Englewood Cliffs, N.J.

– – (1969), *The Semi-Professions and Their Organizations,* The Free Press, New York.

Fantini, M. (1968), *Making Urban Schools Work,* Holt, Rinehart and Winston, New York.

Flexner, A. (1915), 'Is Social Work a Profession?', in *Proceedings of the National Conference of Charities and Correction,* Hildman Publishing, Chicago.

Freire, P. (1970), *Cultural Action for Freedom,* Harvard Education Review and Centre for the Study of Development, Monograph No. 1, Cambridge, Massachusetts.

Freidson, E. (1968), 'The Impurity of Professional Authority', in H. Becker *et al.* (eds.), *Institutions and the Person,* Aldine, Chicago, Illnois.

Goode, W.J. (1969), 'The Theoretical Limits of Professionalization', in A. Etzioni (ed.), *The Semi-Professions and Their Organizations,* The Free Press, New York.

William S. Bennett Jr. and Merl C. Hokenstad Jr.

Goodman, P. (1956), *Growing Up Absurd,* Vintage, New York.

–– (1962), *Compulsory Miseducation and the Community of Scholars,* Vintage, New York.

Greenwood, E. (1962), 'Attributes of a Profession', in S. Noscow and W. Form, *Man, Work and Society,* Basic Books, New York.

Habenstein, R. (1963), 'Critique of "Profession" as a Sociological Category', *The Sociological Quarterly,* no.4, Vol.4 (Autumn), pp.291–300.

Haber, A. (1968), *'Issues Beyond Consensus',* Unpublished paper presented to First National Conference on New Careers, Detroit, Michigan, June 1968.

Hall, R.H. (1969), *Occupations and the Social Structure* , Prentice-Hall, Englewood Cliffs, N.J.

Halmos, P. (1965), *The Faith of the Counsellors,* Schocken Books, New York, and Constables, London.

–– (1970), *The Personal Service Society,* Schocken Books, New York, and Constables, London.

Henry, J. (1963), *Culture Against Man,* Vintage Books, New York.

Hughes, E.C. (1958), *Men and Their Work,* The Free Press, New York.

–– (1963). 'Professions', in *Daedalus,* Vol. 92, no. 4 (Fall), pp. 647–53.

Illych, I. (1970a), *DeSchooling Society,* Harper-Row, New York.

–– (1970b), 'Schooling: The Ritual of Progress', *The New York Review of Books,* Vol. 25, no. 10, pp.20–26.

Marshall, T.H. (1965), 'The Recent History of Professionalism in Relation to Social Policy' (written in 1949) in *Class, Citizenship and Democracy,* Anchor Books, Garden City, New York.

Moore, W.E. (1970), *The Professional: Rules and Roles,* Russel Sage Foundation, New York.

Naegle, K. (1956), 'Clergymen, Teachers and Psychiatrists: A study of Roles and Socialization', *Canadian Journal of Politics and Education,* 22 (Feb.–Nov.), pp. 46–62.

Newman, F.M. and Oliver, D.W. (1967), 'Education and Community', *Harvard Education Review,* vol. 37. no. 1 (Winter), pp.61–106.

Riessman, F. and Pearl, A. (1965), *New Careers for the Poor,* The Free Press, New York.

Parsons, T. (1937), 'The Professions and Social Structure', in *Structure of Social Action,* McGraw-Hill, New York.

270

Parsons, T., (1959), 'Some Problems Confronting Sociology as a Profession', *American Sociological Review*, Vol. 24, no. 4, pp.547–59.

Pavalko, R. (1970), *The Sociology of Occupations and Professions*, Peacock Press, Itasca, Illinois.

Pearl, A. (1972), *The Atrocity of Education*, New Critics Press, New York.

Szasz, T. (1960), *The Myth of Mental Illness: Foundation for a Theory of Personal Conduct*, Harper and Brothers, New York.

Wilensky, H.L. (1963), 'The Professionalization of Everybody', *American Journal of Sociology*, Vol. 70, no. 2 (September), pp. 137–58.

Part VI
STRATEGIES OF INNOVATION

24. THE MANAGEMENT OF EDUCATIONAL CHANGE: TOWARDS A CONCEPTUAL FRAMEWORK

Ray Bolam

From V. Houghton, R. McHugh and C. Morgan, *Management of Organizations and Individuals,* Reader 1, Open University (E321 Management in Education), (Ward Lock, London, forthcoming).

[Educational innovation is a rapidly expanding field of study. This overview of the field attempts three tasks: (1) to provide an organizing framework for reviewing the literature on educational innovation: (2) to provide a heuristic framework as an aid to understanding management of change in education: (3) to suggest guidelines for people involved in the management of change.]

1. Introduction

The literature on innovation in general and on educational innovation in particular is already extensive and is growing rapidly. Some of this work dates back to the early fifties but most has been written since the mid sixties. One American reviewer (Havelock, 1969) identified 4,000 studies and estimated that at least 1,000 more were being carried out each year. In fact these figures were certainly too low since his review included very little European work. Moreover, this literature '...comes from many fields of enquiry, both within and outside of education, and covers a great range of topics. It is also characterised by a wide variety of publications, sources, research traditions and contributions to research knowledge.' (Chin and Downey, 1973). Thus, writers often adopt widely different theoretical perspectives and, in consequence, the reader is faced by a bewildering variety of models and theories and by frequent terminological and conceptual overlap and confusion.

It is, of course, beyond the scope of this paper to try to review this wider literature or to attempt any significant clarification of issues and theories arising from such diverse fields as knowledge diffusion and utilisation, curriculum innovation, educational administration, organisation theory, systems theory, the management of planned change, phenomenological sociology, etc. My purposes are more modest: first, to provide an organising framework for this wider literature as it relates to educational innovation; second, to provide a heuristic framework which may act as an aid to understanding some key problems, tasks and procedures associated with the management of change at several levels in consideration than any researcher or administrator can reasonably be expected to take into account. More fundamentally, it has been criticised the educational system; third, to suggest guidelines for practitioners engaged in the management of change.

In any innovation process we can usefully distinguish between four major factors: the change agent, the innovation, the user system and the process of innovation over time. These four factors are represented in

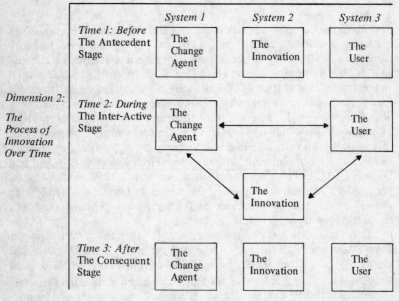

Figure 1. A Conceptual Framework for the Study of Educational Innovation

Figure 1 as a two-dimensional conceptual framework. The various components in this framework are drawn from the literature on change. Havelock, 1969, highlights some key factors in the knowledge diffusion process by asking the simple question: Who (the change agent) says what (the innovation) to whom (the user system)? Hull *et al.* (1973), also working within the knowledge diffusion tradition, distinguish between the antecedent, inter-active and consequent stages. Several writers suggest the value of conceptualising the user as a social system (e.g. Katz and Kahn, 1964; Fullan, 1972) and by using the same approach with the change agent and innovation, we can explore the systemic implications and consequences of an innovation as the three factors interact with, change and are changed by each other during the process of innovation over time. We also have to recognise that the way in which individual members of these three systems perceive their own system, the other two systems and the process over time, may crucially affect the fate of the innovation (Silverman, 1970; Esland, 1972).

A model of this kind is bound to be over-simplified. Its prime purpose is to provide a framework which may be of help in focussing our thinking about and understanding of the innovation process. In the following sections, the four factors are explored in greater detail and then the limitations and strengths of the conceptual framework are considered in relation to an actual complex innovation.

2. Dimension 1. The Three Major Systems

It is a fundamental assumption of this paper that most changes in education take place in an organisational context. Classrooms, schools, teachers' centres, colleges of education, universities, local education authorities, the Schools Council, the Department of Education and Science, etc. may all be thought of as organisations. Accordingly it should be helpful to look to organisation theory as an aid to understanding what happens when these various educational organisations become involved in the process of education innovation.

Although theorists from different disciplines have conceptualised organisations in a variety of ways, there now appears to be some consensus that, with the qualifications outlined below, general systems theory has much to offer as a means of ordering data from various social sciences, as a model of an organisation and its environment and as a powerful heuristic device (Hoyle, 1969). Within this tradition the closed system approach has been criticised because it devalues the importance of external or contextual factors (Eggleston, 1969; Hall, 1972). The common characteristics of open systems include input, throughput, output, differentiation and finality (Katz and Kahn, 1964). The open systems approach has been criticised because it introduces more factors for because it ignores the motives of individuals (March and Simon, 1958). This has led to the formulation of an alternative approach — the action frame of reference — which argues that systems should not be reified; that they do not determine the behaviour of their members; and that only individuals, and not systems, can have needs and goals or take decisions. Writers in this tradition stress the need to look to the causes as well as the consequences of actions and advocate the use of qualitative research methods, like the analytic case-study, as a means of understanding the part played by individual perceptions, motives and actions in particular organisations (Silverman, 1970; Greenfield,1974).

The view taken here is that the systems and action frames of reference can be treated as complementary (cf. Cohen, 1968; Dawe, 1970). Hence three of the major factors in the innovation process — the change agent, the user and the innovation — have been conceptualised as open systems but particular account is taken of the way in which individuals and groups within those systems construct their own phenomenological worlds and thus affect all aspects of the organisation, including its innovation activities.

(i) The Change Agent System

The change agent system is also often referred to in the literature as the change advocate, consultant or innovator and may be analysed in terms similar to that suggested below for the user system, although those dimensions will not always be relevant. The change agent may thus be, for example, an individual teacher, head or adviser, a teachers' centre, a local authority or a national government. It may be a part of the user system (e.g. the head of a school) or outside it (e.g. a project director working with a pilot school). Both its internal and external characteristics may influence and be changed by any particular innovation process. It will probably be perceived differently by the user and innovation systems according to its status, location and the change strategies it adopts.

Perhaps the most important basic characteristic of the change agent as far as innovations are concerned is its *authority relationship* with the user system. This authority may be based either upon administrative status, professional colleagueship, external consultancy or a combination of the three. For example, in his administrative or inspectorial role an LEA adviser has the power to assess teachers and schools on behalf of their employers whereas in his professional advisory role he seeks to advise them as a respected professional colleague. This inevitably causes difficulties and effectively debars most advisers from carrying out the consultancy role described below (Bolam, Smith and Canter, 1975). Several writers have devised change agent role typologies (e.g. Jones, 1969; Hoyle, 1970). Havelock's 1969 linkage role typology distinguishes between nine roles: conveyor, consultant, trainer, leader, innovator, defender, knowledge builder, practitioner and user. He recognises that such roles rarely exist in their pure form and that in the real world any one linkage agent may play several roles simultaneously or sequentially. The typology is nonetheless useful in clarifying the way in which, for example, knowledge about innovations may be transmitted to teachers by various educationists. Thus we can analyse the 'linkage' role played by colleagues, heads, LEA advisers, teachers' centre wardens, etc.

The change agent system may have access to a number of innovation strategies. We may adopt Dalin's, 1973, broad concept of strategy as 'all available procedures and techniques used by individuals and groups at different levels of the educational system to reach desired objectives'. Bennis, Benne and Chin, 1969, offer the following well known typology of innovation strategies:

(a) *Power-coercive* strategies depend upon access to political, legal, administrative and economic resources. Typically they involve the use of legal or administrative power. Governments, local education authorities, inspectors, head teachers and teachers all employ such strategies at some time or other.

(b) *Empirical-rational* strategies assume that men are reasonable and will respond best to rational explanation and demonstration. Typically they involve the use of education, training and publications to disseminate knowledge and research findings.

(c) *Normative–re-educative* strategies assume that effective innovation requires a change of attitudes, relationships, values and skills and, therefore, the activation of forces within the client system. They typically involve a consultant/change agent who works in co-operation with a client system and uses behavioural skills.

Although these categories are helpful for purposes of analysis, they are inevitably somewhat arbitrary and rarely exist in their pure form. For instance, innovations frequently require changes in both curriculum and organisation and innovators frequently employ both power-coercive and empirical-rational strategies. At the national level, the major strategy used by governments to disseminate *policy* is probably a power-coercive or political-administrative one. In both centralised and de-centralised systems, governments usually attempt to change their educational system's goals and structure by political-administrative means, but such policy directives are probably generally followed by empirical-rational strategies of information dissemination and training; latterly, empirical-rational strategies of research and development often precede policy directives. It seems likely that in most countries the problems of changing role relationships and attitudes have been underestimated when introducing, say, curriculum innovation and that, accordingly, normative-re-educative strategies have rarely been used. At the school level, a typical variant on

277

Ray Bolam

the power-coercive strategy is one which Hoyle, 1970, calls administrative and Dalin, 1973, political-administrative. It involves, for instance, the use of various forms of incentive (Pincus, 1973; Becher, 1974).

In considering the *diffusion of knowledge* rather than policy, Havelock, 1969, provides many insights into the workings of empirical-rational and normative–re-educative strategies. (Though his work is not, it should be emphasised, very relevant to an understanding of power-coercive strategies.) He seeks to explain the way knowledge diffuses through social systems by formulating four models of the knowledge diffusion and utilisation process:

(a) The *Social-interaction* model describes a process which is probably historically the earliest approach to knowledge by individuals along informal networks of professional colleagues and friends. It is unsystematic and unplanned, though the original source of the knowledge (or innovation) may nowadays be research-based. Although it may be categorised as an empirical-rational process, it derives its strength from the well-documented fact that we are more likely to be influenced by people whose judgements and opinions we share or respect. In decentralised systems, this was, until fairly recently (i.e. until about 1960 in the UK), probably the principal way in which knowledge about innovations in curriculum and pedagogy diffused through the system.

(b) *The research, development and diffusion* (RD & D) model describes a process with several major stages: basic research; applied research; development and testing of prototypes; mass production and packaging; planned mass dissemination; receipt by the user. It is essentially an empirical-rational strategy and has come to be widely adopted over the last fifteen to twenty years as the principal approach to curriculum development and innovation. In this context, we can point to the establishment of the various national organisations, e.g. the Schools Council in the UK, Research for Better Schools Inc. in the USA and the National Council for Innovation in Education in Norway (CERI, 1973, Vol. 1). The RD & D approach has recently provoked increasing scepticism because of its apparent lack of success in bringing about change at the user level (see (iii) below).

(c) The *problem-solver* model is presented by Havelock as a single model but, arguably, consists of three quite distinct sub-models. The first, which we may call the *problem-solving user* model, is based upon empirical-rational assumptions. It describes a user, say a school, which employs a cyclic, problem-solving strategy: felt need; problem diagnosis; search and retrieval of resources, from within and without the school; fabrication of solution; application; evaluation; re-start of cycle (cf. Stufflebeam *et al*, 1971). The second sub-model, which we may call the *task consultant* model, is also an empirical-rational one, and describes the role of an outside change agent who seeks to help a school with a specific task, e.g. curriculum development. The third sub-model, which we may call the *process consultant* model, is based upon normative—re-educative assumptions and describes the role of a non-directive outside change agent who typically seeks to help a school with its decision-making and problem-solving procedures. Recent suggestions that in-service training should adopt a system-focused approach rather than withdrawing individuals for off-the-job training indicate the problem-solver perspective is finding increasing support (Hoyle, 1973a). In the UK, consultancy approaches are only just beginning (e.g. Richardson, 1973), but in the USA organisation development consultancy is being increasingly used (Schmuck and Miles, 1971), though not uncritically (Chesler and Lohman, 1971).

(d) The *linkage* model is Havelock's attempt to unify and integrate the three preceding models by emphasising the need for linkage procedures and agencies which both offer resources to users and link them with more remote resource agencies. These resources could consist of curriculum materials from a central agency, consultancy, or information about other users with related experience or interests. In the UK the proposed professional centres provide an obvious example of a linkage agency (Hoyle, 1973a).

Finally, according to Havelock, 1969, whatever strategy it adopts, the change agent may have access to several communication modes (e.g. written media, television, etc.), training techniques (e.g. survey feedback, micro-teaching, etc.) and feedback techniques (e.g. evaluative research, observation, etc.).

(ii) The Innovation System

Key terms like 'change' and 'innovation' are often used in different senses in the literature. Following Hoyle, 1972, it is, therefore, worth defining 'change' as a generic term embracing a family of concepts (e.g. innovation, development, renewal, etc.). We can also distinguish between innovation as being an intentional and deliberate process and change which can also include accidental or unintentional movements and shifts, though it must be conceded that this distinction is frequently not adhered to in the literature. A quotation from Edmund Burke, 1796 — 'To innovate is not to reform' — reminds us that there is nothing inherently good about any innovation. Following Esland, 1972, therefore, it seems sensible to treat newness or goodness as characteristics which are likely to be perceived differently by the various people involved and, since these perceptions may have a crucial bearing upon the fate of an innovation, to ensure that they are adequately taken into account in studying any particular innovation process. This leads to a fourth preliminary consideration which relates to what I shall call the systemic nature of innovations. Innovations do not exist in any unchanging, objective sense: they are constantly being defined, changed and redefined as a result of experience and the differing perceptions of the people who handle them (cf. Shipman *et al.*, 1974). Even within a project team, fundamentally different notions of the 'innovation' may co-exist. Hence I am suggesting it may be helpful to define an innovation as an open system (cf. Reynolds, 1972).

Innovations have been analysed along a number of sub-dimensions with two broad purposes in mind: first, simply as an analytic aid to understanding; second, as an attempt to explain why they succeed or fail. At the most basic level Havelock, 1969, distinguishes between four *types of knowledge* from which innovations may be derived: basic knowledge, applied research and development knowledge; practice knowledge; and user feedback knowledge. Hull *et al.* (1973) says that innovations come in three broad *forms;* information documents, training materials and an installable system. We can add to this that many of the innovations generated at the user level come up in the form of untested, and often vaguely formulated, ideas. An innovation is usually aimed at a particular *target* system (see (iii) below) but it is important to note that this may differ from the user system which actually takes it up. This may well explain some of the problems encountered by a user system. An innovation will also usually *focus* upon a particular aspect of the target user system; upon, for example, aims, values or perspectives; organisation and administration; role relationships; curriculum, pedagogy and evaluation (see Hoyle, 1970; Dalin, 1973).

We now move to a consideration of those factors which appear to have a more direct bearing upon the success or otherwise of an innovation. Most of them are very subjective and are often referred to as perceived characteristics since they are likely to be judged differently both between *and* within the user, change agent and innovation systems. Perhaps the first question likely to be asked by members of a user system about an innovation would be to do with its *relevance.* Their answers would probably be dependent upon the extent to which they considered it to have some *relative advantage* over their current practice (Rogers and Shoemaker, 1971), upon its *competitive strength* as against other innovations or activities requiring scarce resources, and, finally, upon its *feasibility* within a particular organisational context.

The answers to all these questions may well turn upon considerations of the *magnitude* of any particular innovations (Hull *et al.*, 1973). This dimension would include several sub-dimensions: the *scale* of change involved, e.g. one teacher, a department, a school staff, all LEA staff, etc.; the *degree* of change, i.e. fundamental or superficial (see Hoyle, 1972; Bernstein, 1971); its *trialability/divisibility*, i.e. the extent to which it can be experimented with on a limited basis (Rogers and Shoemaker, 1971). All of these factors will have implications for the innovation's *communicability* which in turn will depend upon its *complexity*, i.e. the extent to which it is perceived as being difficult to understand and use, and its *observability*, i.e. the extent to which others can observe it in action or observe its results and ideas (Rogers and Shoemaker, 1971).

Next, we need to consider a group of *normative* factors. The perceived *compatability* of an innovation with existing values and practices in a user system is, according to Rogers and Shoemaker, 1971, a crucial factor. An aspect which is rarely mentioned in the literature is *adaptability*. Research and development agencies understandably deplore the fact that their materials are adapted, but from the user's viewpoint this may be the chief strength of the innovation. The problem is to decide when an adaption is so significantly different from the original that it ought not to bear the same name. Some innovations may be valued less for their own sake than for their *gatewayability* or the opportunities which they create for the introduction of other, more highly valued, innovations (Zaltman and Lin, 1971).

Finally, we come to some fundamentally important factors to do with the *costs and benefits* of an innovation. These can be either actual or perceived, material or non-material, and initial or continuing (Havelock, 1969). Material costs and benefits may relate to finance, output, time, space, personal, training and equipment. Non-material costs and benefits may relate to organisational and administrative changes, decision-making procedures, psychological discontent or reward, working conditions, career opportunities, status and prestige. Any one or more of these costs and benefits may loom large for a particular innovation and may have a significant impact upon the other factors identified above and, ultimately, upon the fate of the innovation.

(iii) The User System

This is the system which is either inventing or adopting an innovation or is being aimed at by a change agent. Several other terms are commonly used in the literature, e.g. receiver, client, adopter, target and consumer. In education the user may be an individual teacher, a departmental team, a school, a local education authority or a national education system. In the past, there has been a tendency for work in the diffusion and adoption tradition to focus upon individuals to the neglect of groups and organisations. There is now general agreement that individuals in educational settings are rarely free to choose whether or not to adopt an innovation since they are constrained by the need to obtain the co-operation and support of professional colleagues, pupils, parents, administrators etc. (Gross *et al.,* 1971). It follows that schools, colleges, departments, etc. have to be viewed as open-systems if the fate of an innovation is to be understood. There is also considerable agreement amongst writers from several countries (Hoyle, 1970; Fullan, 1972; Dalin, 1973) that the research, development and diffusion strategy of change has

Ray Bolam

made very little impact upon the curricula and organisation of schools: hence, attention is now increasingly being paid to the user system's view of the innovation process and its associated problems.

Individuals, whether they be teachers, pupils, parents, administrators, advisers, etc. are likely to respond differently to innovation. Guskin (1969) refers to enduring and difficult to change characteristics, like authoritarianism, and to less endurable and easier to change characteristics, like a sense of threat. He regards open-mindedness and the use of incentives as important factors but concludes that the most critical variable is the extent to which enduring personality characteristics are aroused by an innovation. 'If they are highly activated then the new knowledge will be accepted if it is congruent with them, rejected if it is not. If they are not activated, then congruence to personality is only one of many variables influencing the decision' (pp. 4–39). A number of writers have tried to explain the way in which key individuals respond to innovations in educational settings (e.g. Carlson, 1964, on American school superintendents and Hughes, 1973, on British headmasters). Hoyle (1974) hypothesises two ideal-types of teacher – the restricted professional, who is mainly interested, for example, in children and classroom teaching, and the extended professional, who is, in addition, also interested in, for example, attending courses of a theoretical kind and participating in decision-making. Although the typology has not been verified empirically, it does draw attention to the phenomenological world of the teacher as an important variable in the innovation process (cf. Jackson, 1968). It seems unlikely, for example, that restricted professionals will respond favourably to the requests of central curriculum developers to adopt their complex technical terms and concepts or want to spend time participating in decision-making.

Significant characteristics of organisations have been summarised by Hall (1972) in terms of their functions and goals (both operative and official): their effectiveness; their general contextual environment (e.g. technological, legal, political, economic, demographic, ecological and social); their specific contextual environment (e.g. the people and organisation with which a school was in frequent contact); their structure (e.g. size, complexity, degree of formalisation); their processes (e.g. power and conflict, leadership and decision-making, and communications). In this context it is worth recalling Silverman's 1970 critique of the systems perspective: he argues that the way in which individual members of an organisation perceive and react to its context, inputs, structure, processes and outputs will vary and that their views and behaviours may well affect both the organisation itself and the fate of an innovation.

With specific reference to the key *internal* factors which affect innovations in educational organisations, a number of writers have commented on the problem of defining both goals and outputs (Miles, 1967; Hoyle, 1973b), though this has not deterred advocates of the application of management by objectives (cf. Harries, 1974) or of planning, programming and budgeting systems (Eidell and Nagle, 1972) to schools. Several writers, too, have sought to identify the characteristics of innovative organisations in terms of such concepts as organic and mechanistic systems (Burns and Stalker, 1961), open and closed systems (Bernstein, 1971), organisational health (Miles, 1965), organisational climate (Halpin, 1966) and knowledge dissemination and utilisation in organisations (Havelock, 1969). All of these approaches have considerable heuristic and sensitising value but they tend to be difficult to operationalise and, especially in a UK context, to be difficult to use because of their central focus upon sensitive professional issues. Furthermore, they frequently tell us little either about the way in which particular people and interest groups see each other or about ongoing processes within, say, a school. For instance, they say little about the problems of curriculum development, innovation management or participation at the school level (see Bolam, 1974).

Two recent OECD projects have highlighted many of the issues associated with the user system's perspective of educational innovation. The first was on the creativity of the school which was defined as 'its capacity to adopt, adapt, generate or reject innovations' (Nisbet, 1973). This project built upon ideas similar to the problem-solving user concept (Havelock, 1969) in the context of practical international educational experiences. It summarised, and to some extent synthesised, certain key ideas concerning the major internal system variables and also identified some of the key external or *contextual variables*. For example, it stressed the importance of such constraint upon innovation as LEA regulations, the examination system and the views of parents (cf. Taylor *et al.*, 1973). It also pointed to the importance of an external support structure for the innovative school, e.g. teachers' centres, the inspectorate, in-service training, etc. The second OECD project has also focussed on these external factors by stressing the importance of training educationists to manage the change process.

3. Dimension 2: The Process of Innovation Over Time

The second dimension of the conceptual framework is a time dimension. A number of writers have stressed the notion of innovation as a dynamic, social process which takes place over a period of time during which the innovation may be redefined and modified as a result of that social process (Gross *et al.*, 1971; Eslane, 1972). This dimension can be analysed in terms of three major stages: the antecedent, interactive and consequent stages (Hall *et al.*, 1973). Of course, these distinctions are somewhat arbitrary but they are useful for analytic purposes.

Ray Bolam

Time 1: Before: The Antecedent Stage

It is vital to have a clear understanding of the situation before the innovation process begins (Greiner, 1967; Gross, 1971). At this stage the three systems — change agent, innovation and user — may be said to exist separately, though each may have a relationship with, or opinion of, the other. The relationship between the change agent and user system may be of particular significance, especially if the former is a member (e.g. the head) of the latter (e.g. a school). The characteristics and relationships of the three systems at this stage may be analysed in terms of the dimensions outlined above.

Time 2: During: The Interactive Stage

During the innovation process the three systems may be said to be in interaction with each other. This period is both the most critical and the most complex as far as understanding the outcome of the innovation is concerned. The general aim should, therefore, be to identify and monitor what precisely happens during this stage (Stufflebeam *et al.*, 1971). The interaction probably begins during the dissemination or awareness stage and is certainly taking place during the trial and implementation stages (Guba and Clark, 1965). Key questions here relate to the change agent's strategies and communication modes and the user system's initial response to them and the innovation.

Time 3: After: The Consequent Stage

After the completion of the process, the three systems may be said to be separate again and some assessment can then be made of the impact of the interactive experience on all three systems, using the dimensions discussed above. They will almost certainly be different. For example, the teachers in the user system may have changed their teaching methods (though not necessarily as much as, or even in the same direction as, the change agent intended), their opinion of the change agent (who could be their head) and their opinion of the innovation materials. The change agent head may have learned some new techniques in the management of change and be more wary about introducing an innovation without careful planning (cf. Gross *et al.*, 1971). The innovation itself may have undergone some change and may subsequently be radically revised by, say, an external project team. The overriding consideration will probably be the impact upon the user system. It is likely that an evaluative research approach (Weiss, 1972) will provide the most satisfactory mode for handling the complexities and uncertainties of the innovation process, especially with respect to its unintended consequences.

The user system may respond in a variety of ways during both the interactive and consequent stages. First, it may reject the innovation for one or more reasons (Eicholtz and Rogers, 1964). Since the worthwhileness or desirability of an innovation is not here being taken for granted then rejection is not necessarily a cause for concern; on the contrary it will be an inevitable and desirable fate for some innovations in a creative or problem-solving user system. Second, it may resist the innovation for one or more reasons (Watson, 1966) but here, too, this is not necessarily a bad thing: Havelock, 1969, argues that 'defenders' are essential for the creative or problem-solving system. An important variant on resistance is the 'facade phenomenon' (Smith and Keith, 1971) in which those involved (e.g. teachers, heads and inspectors) unintentionally collude to present an image to each other and to the outside world which suggests that an innovation is working successfully although 'objective' outsiders report otherwise. Third, the user system may adapt an innovation, usually to the dismay of the outside project team (Macdonald and Ruddock, 1971), though its adaptability may be its chief strength from the user's standpoint. Fourth, the innovation may be fully institutionalised as an integral part of the system (Guba and Clark, 1965). Fifth, an enthusiastic user system may become an advocate of an innovation. Finally, account has also to be taken of the terminal relationship between the change agent and the user system. This may range from co-operation to conflict (Hull *et al.*, 1973).

4. Applying the Conceptual Framework

In essence, the framework generates four sets of questions about the change agent, innovation and user systems:

1. What are their significant characteristics with respect to any particular innovation process?
2. What were they like before the process began?
3. What happened when they inter-acted with each other during the process?
4. What were they like at the end of the process?

The ultimate purpose of the framework is to deepen our understanding of any educational innovation but, of course, it falls far short of that aim at present. Perhaps we may best explore its strengths and limitations by applying it to a complex innovation like the Teacher Induction Pilot Schemes (TIPS) project.

The problems of beginning or probationary teachers have been the focus of concern in the profession for some time past. In a recent White Paper (DES, 1972), the Government proposed some quite radical improvements in the procedures for inducting new entrants into the profession. The proposals can be summarised as follows: probationers to receive special help during their first year and to be released for not less

Ray Bolam

Table 1. The TIPS Project: Major Components

Level	No.	1. The Change Agent System	2. The Innovation System	3. The User System
National	1	Minister + DES Administrators	National Scheme: Finance and Logistics	The National System: LEAs; professional associations; colleges; universities; polytechnics, etc.
	2	Minister + HMI	National Scheme: Professional Aspects	" "
LEA	3	LEA Administrator	Finance + Logistics of the whole Induction Scheme in the LEA	The LEA: local politicians, administrators; professional associations; schools; colleges, etc.
	4	LEA Adviser	Professional Aspects of the whole Induction Scheme in the LEA	The LEA: professional associations; schools; colleges, etc.
Professional Centre	5	Warden	Creation of a new role: professional centre warden	The professional centre and its catchment area
	6	Director of Training Course/Programme	Teacher tutor training programme	All teacher tutors in an LEA
	7	Director of Induction Course/Programme	Probationer induction courses: outside school	All probationers in an LEA
School	8	Head	Probationer induction programme: inside school: logistic aspects	All staff in a school
	9	Teacher tutor	Creation of a new role: teacher tutor	All staff in a school
	10	Teacher tutor	Probationer induction courses: inside school: professional aspects	All probationers in a school
	11	Teacher tutor	Professional induction of one probationer	One probationer
	12	One probationer	Creation of a new role: beginning teacher	One probationer

than one fifth of their time for in-service training; their overall teaching timetable to be lightened; sufficient replacement teachers to be made available; the profession to play a full part in the induction process; teacher tutors to be appointed in each school and to be trained; professional centres to be established; regional co-ordinating committees to replace the present University-based area training organisations. As a result of these proposals, two official, government-funded pilot schemes were set up in Liverpool and Northumberland and other local authorities were encouraged to set up their own unofficial experiments in preparation for the introduction of a national scheme. The two official schemes and several unofficial schemes are being monitored on a national basis using the conceptual framework outlined above (Bolam, 1975).

The TIPS project is essentially concerned with the introduction of a massive and complex innovation which in itself consists of several sub-innovations. Each sub-innovation involves a different change agent and user system and each is implemented on a different time-scale. In Table 1 these parameters of the project are explored at four levels and twelve significant sub-innovations are identified. The identification of the significant sub-perspectives are to be adopted within it. Its principal message is that all four factors are relevant to an understanding of the way in which changes do or do not take place. Both students and managers of change should, therefore, beware of their ignoring or underestimating the importance of any one of these factors.

REFERENCES

Becher, R.A. (1974), *Incentive Systems for Teachers*, Working paper for the 'Creativity of the School' Project, CERI/CS/74.06.

Bennis, W.G. (1969), 'Theory and method in *applying* behavioural science to planned organisational change', in W.G. Bennis, K.D. Benne and R. Chin, *The Planning of Change*, 2nd edition, Holt, Rinehart and Winston, New York.

Bennis, W.G., K.D. Benne and R. Chin (1969), *The Planning of Change*, Holt, Rinehart and Winston, New York.

Bernstein, B. (1971), 'On the classification and framing of knowledge', in M.F.D. Young, *Knowledge and Control*, Collier-Macmillan, London.

Bolam, R. (1973), *Induction Programmes for Probationary Teachers*, The University of Bristol School of Education, Bristol.

—— (1974), *Teachers as Innovators*, DAS/EID/74.53, OECD, Paris.

—— (1975), 'The Teacher Induction Pilot Schemes (TIPS) Project', *London Educational Review*, Vol. 4, no. 1.

Bolam, R. , G. Smith, and H. Canter (1975), *The LEA Adviser and Educational Innovation*, The University of Bristol School of Education, Bristol.

Burke, E. (1796), 'A Letter to a Noble Lord'.

Burns, T. and J. Stalker (1961), *The Management of Innovation*, Tavistock Publications, London.

Carlson, R.O. (1964), 'School superintendents and the adoption of modern math: a social structure profile', in M.B. Miles (ed.), *Innovation in Education*, Bureau of Publications, Teachers College, Columbia University, New York.

Centre for Educational Research and Innovation (1973), *Case Studies in Educational Innovation*, Vol. 1, OECD, Paris.

Chesler, M. and J. Lochman (1971), 'Changing schools through student advocacy', in R. Schmuck and M. Miles (eds.), *Organisation Development in Schools*, National Press Books, Palo Alto, California.

Chin, R. and L. Downey (1973), 'Changing change: innovating a discipline', in R.M.W. Traverse, *Second Handbook of Research on Teaching*, Rand McNally & Co., Chicago.

Cohen, P.S. (1968), *Modern Social Theory*, Heinemann, London.

Dalin, P. (1973), *Case Studies in Educational Innovation: Strategies for Innovation in Education*, OECD, Paris.

Dalin, P. (1974), *International Management Training for Educational Change (IMTEC)*. Paper given at the Third International Intervisitation Programme on Educational Administration, London, England.

Dawe, A. (1970), 'The two sociologies', *British Journal of Sociology*, Vol. 21, no. 2, pp. 207–18.

Department of Education and Science (1972), *Education: a Framework for Expansion*, HMSO, London.

Eggleston, S.J. (1969), 'The social context of administration', in G. Baron and W. Taylor, *Educational Administration and the Social Sciences*, Athlone Press, London.

Eicholz, G. and E.M. Rogers (1964), 'Resistance to the adoption of audio-visual aids by elementary school teachers: contrasts and similarities to agriculture innovation', in M. Miles (ed.), *Innovation in Education*, Teachers College, Columbia, New York, pp. 299–316.

Eidell, T.L. and J.M. Nagle (1972), *SPECS: School Planning, Evaluation and Communication System: Second Progress Report*, University of Oregon Centre for the Advanced Study of Educational Administration, Eugene, Oregon.

Esland, G. (1972), 'Innovation in the school', in P. Seaman, G. Esland and B. Cosin, *Innovation and Ideology*, Open University Course E282, Units 11–14 (Unit 12, pp. 95–126), The Open University Press, Bletchley.

Fullan, M. (1972), 'Overview of the innovative process and the user', *Interchange*, Vol. 3, nos. 2–3, pp.1–46.

Greenfield, T.B. (1974), *Theory in the Study of Organisations and Administrative Structures: a New Perspective*. A Paper read at the International Intervisitation Programme for Educational Administrators in Bristol, England.

Greiner, L.E. (1967), 'Antecedents of planned organisational change', *Journal of Applied Behavioural Science*, 3:1, pp. 51–85.

Gross, N., J.B. Giacquinta and M. Bernstein (1971), *Implementing Organisational Innovations*, Harper and Row, London.

Guba, E. and D.L. Clark (1965), 'An examination of potential change roles in education', National Education Association Committee for Study of Instruction Symposium – Innovation in Planning School Curricula, Airlie House, Va. Oct. 2–4, 1965, quoted in *Strategies for Educational Change Newsletter No. 2*, October 1965, Ohio State University.

Guskin, A. (1969), 'The individual' in R.G. Havelock, *Planning for Innovation*, The University of Michigan, Institute for Social Research, Ann Arbor, Michigan.

Hall, R.H. (1972), *Organisations: Structure and Process*, Prentice Hall Inc., Englewood Cliffs, New Jersey.

Halpin, A.W. (1966), *Theory and Research in Educational Administration*, Macmillan, New York.

Harries, T.W. (1974), 'M. B. O.: a rational approach and a comparative frameworks approach', *Educational Administration Bulletin,* Vol. 3, No. 1., pp. 42–50.

Havelock, R.G. (1969), *Planning for Innovation Through Dissemination and Utilization of Knowledge,* Centre for Research on Utilization of Scientific Knowledge, Institute for Social Research, Ann Arbor, Michigan.

Hoyle, E., (1969), 'Organisational theory and educational administration', in G. Baron and W. Taylor, *Educational Administration and the Social Sciences,* Athlone Press, London.

–– (1970), 'Planned organizational change in education', *Research in Education 3.*

–– (1972), 'Facing the difficulties', in E. Hoyle and R. Bell, *Problems of Curriculum Innovation I* (Open University Course E283, Units 13 to 15), The Open University Press, Bletchley.

–– (1973a), 'Strategies of curriculum change', in R. Watkins (ed.), *In-Service Training: Structure and Content,* Ward Lock, London.

–– (1973b), 'The study of schools as organisations', in H.J. Butcher and H. Pont (eds.), *Educ. Res. in Britain III,* London.

–– (1974), 'Professionality, professionalism and control in teaching', *London Ed. Rev.,* Vol. 3, no. 2.

Hughes, M.G. (1973), 'The professional-as-administrator: the case of the secondary school head', *Educational Administration Bulletin,* Vol. 2, no. 1, pp. 11–23.

Hull, W.L., R.J. Kester and W.B. Martin (1973), *A Conceptual Framework for the Diffusion of Innovations in Vocational and Technical Education,* The Centre for Vocational and Technical Education, The Ohio State University, Columbus, Ohio.

Jackson, P.W. (1968), *Life in Classrooms,* Holt, Rinehart and Winston, New York.

Jones, G.N. (1969), *Planned Organisational Change,* Routledge and Kegan Paul, London.

Katz, D. and R.L. Kahn (1964), *The Social Psychology of Organisations,* John Wiley and Sons, New York.

Macdonald, B. and J. Ruddock (1971), 'Curriculum research and development projects: barriers to success', *British Journal of Educational Psychology,* Vol. 42, no. 2.

March, J.G. and H.A. Simon (1958), *Organisations,* John Wiley and Sons, New York.

Miles, M.B. (1965), 'Planned change and organisational health: figure and ground', in R.O. Carlson, *Change Processes in the Public Schools,* University of Oregon Centre for the Advanced Study of Educational Administration, Eugene, Oregon.

Miles, M.B. (1967), 'Some properties of schools as social systems' in G. Watson *Change in School Systems,* National Training Laboratories, National Education Association, Washington.

Nisbet, J. (1973), *Strengthening the Creativity of the School.* Working paper for the 'Creativity of the School' Project, CERI/CD(73)7, OECD, Paris.

Pincus, J. (1973), 'Incentives for innovation in the public schools', *Review of Educational Research,* Vol. 44, no. 1, pp. 113–43.

Reynolds, J. (1972), 'Geography 14–18: A framework for development', in R. Bell, *Perspectives on Innovation.* Unit 14 of Course E283, The Curriculum: Context, Design and Development, The Open University, Bletchley.

Richardson, E. (1973), *The Teacher, the School and the Task of Management,* Heinemann Educational Books Ltd., London.

Rogers, E.M. and F.F. Shoemaker (1971), *Communication of Innovations: A Cross-Cultural Approach,* Collier-Macmillan, London.

Schmuck, R.A. and M. Miles (1971), *Organization Development in Schools,* National Press Books, Palo Alto, California.

Shipman, M.D., D. Bolam and D. Jenkins (1974), *Inside a Curriculum Project,* Methuen, London.

Ray Bolam

Silverman, D. (1970), *The Theory of Organisations,* Heinemann, London.

Simon, H.A. (1957), *Administrative Behavior,* Macmillan, New York.

Smith, L. and P. Keith (1971), *Anatomy of Educational Innovation: An Organizational Analysis of an Elementary School,* Wiley, London.

Stufflebeam, D. *et al.* (1971), *Educational Evaluation and Decision Making,* F.E. Peacock Publishers Inc., Itasca, Illinois.

Taylor, P.H., W.A. Reid, J.B. Holley and G. Exon (1974), *Purpose, Power and Constraint in the Primary School Curriculum,* Macmillan Educational, London.

Taylor, J.K. and I.R. Dale (1971), *A Survey of Teachers in Their First Year of Service,* University of Bristol, School of Education Research Unit, Bristol.

Watson, G. (1966), 'Resistance to change', in G. Watson (ed.), *Concepts for Social Change, Co-operative Project for Educational Development Series, Volume 1, National Training Laboratories, Washington, D.C.*

Weiss, C.H. (1972), *Evaluation Research — Methods for Assessing Program Effectiveness,* Methods of Social Science Series, Prentice Hall Inc., Englewood Cliffs, New Jersey.

Zaltman, G. and N. Lin (1971), 'On the nature of innovations', *American Behavioural Scientist,* Vol. 14, pp. 651–73.

25. PLANNED ORGANIZATIONAL CHANGE IN EDUCATION

Eric Hoyle

From *Research in Education*, Vol. 3, May 1970, pp. 1–22.

[Innovation depends upon changing people and providing means of improving receptivity to change. Hoyle discusses several types of change strategy and their application to educational organisations. In particular, the notion of the 'change agent' is outlined.]

It is a basic assumption of this paper that the process of educational innovation is rapidly becoming institutionalised. It is the basic argument of the paper that this process of institutionalisation has reached a point where we must consider potential strategies of *planned* organisational change in education.

It is now becoming widely accepted that educational innovation is not a temporary process, a rather tiresome interlude between long periods of peace and stability. The rate of social, economic and technological change outside the educational system is too persistent for that, and the educationist, whilst continuing to perform *some* relatively unchanging tasks, will need to readjust many of his functions in response to their broader changes. The shift from crescive to deliberate change has been one of the most interesting features of British education in recent years. We have seen the emergence of such bodies as the Schools Council, the Nuffield Foundation, the National Council for Educational Technology, the North West Curriculum Development Project, the Goldsmiths Curriculum Laboratory, the University of Sussex Centre for Educational Technology and many other institutions commited to furthering educational change (Hoyle, 1969a). These bodies have made very valuable contributions at certain points in the change process, but the need for planned organisational change goes beyond what they are presently able to accomplish with existing resources. This point can perhaps be clarified by means of the following taxonomy of change processes proposed by Guba and Clark (1965):

Research
Development
Dissemination
Demonstration
Implementation

Installation

Institutionalisation

It can be argued that only the first four of these processes are being fully pursued with respect to curriculum change at the present time. New curricula, materials, technologies, teaching methods and forms of school organisation are being researched and developed, disseminated and demonstrated by the innovating institutions, but less attention has been given to the strategies of implementation. Educational innovation still proceeds largely by diffusion (Rogers, 1962; Miles, 1964; Carlson, 1965; Bhola, 1967), or perhaps more precisely by 'assisted' diffusion, than by a process of planned organisational change. Yet the cost, complexity and radical nature of current innovations perhaps renders inappropriate the reliance upon the rather *ad hoc* and individualistic response that one has had in the past. The writer has argued elsewhere that a basic problem in educational change is that of 'tissue rejection' whereby an innovation, although it is formally 'adopted' by a school, does not become an effectively functioning part of the system (Hoyle, 1969b). One thinks here particularly of such innovations as de-streaming, team teaching and discovery-learning, which require a positive commitment by teachers if they are to improve upon previous practices. Indeed, a review of the literature on the effectiveness of various educational innovations underlines the importance of this factor, as it often appears that the commitment of a teacher to a method, new or old, is as important as the method itself. It would thus appear that strategies of implementation are complementary to, but different from, strategies of research, development and dissemination. It is probable, as the work of Lippitt and his associates shows, that different skills are required (Lippitt *et al.*, 1967). Moreover, whereas diffusion relies upon the individual response of heads and teachers, many current innovations require a school response and therefore the school itself, conceptualised as a social system,[1] becomes the target of change.

Underpinning much recent debate on planned organisational change are two basic assumptions. First, technical, organisational and, in the case of education, curricular changes require concurrent efforts to change *people*. Second, there is a need for social units, intermediate between the research and development units and the target system (school or college), which would be concerned with improving receptivity to innovation. These assumptions have become widely accepted in industry, and whilst many educationists resent the smell of the factory pervading the discussion of schools it would seem worth while at least to consider strategies of planned change wherever they are developed. This article will therefore discuss various types of change strategy and the problems associated with their application to educational organisations.

Strategies of Change

It is interesting to note that several independent attempts to develop a typology of change strategies reveal a high degree of consensus. Their comparative terminologies are as shown in Table 1.[2] We can briefly examine the implications of these strategies of change before proceeding to discuss their relevance to the field of education, and for the sake of simplicity Chin's terms will be used.

Table 1

Chin	Jones	Miles	Walton
Power-coercive	Coercive	Power-solution	Power
Normative-re-education	Normative	Relationship-attitude	Love-trust
Rational-empirical	Utilitarian	Problem-process	Problem-solving

Power–coercive. The exercise of power to alter an existing situation is undoubtedly the most common form of change strategy. Goldhamer and Shils (1939) write: 'a person may be said to have power to the extent that he influences the behaviour of others in accordance with his own intentions'. Strictly speaking, all the three strategies under discussion are power strategies, differing only in the manner of their use, but here we are concerned with the use of that form of power which ultimately has coercion as its legitimate sanction. Change occurs *via* the deliberate restructuring of the situation by a superordinate having the necessary authority. Of course, legal coercion is the sanction of the last resort and usually remains latent. For the most part the superordinate has to gain compliance by the more immediate exercise of personal influence and persuasion.[3] In education there is a tendency for reliance on legal power to decrease with the size of the unit. Table 2 illustrates this. It is generally assumed in education that coercion becomes less appropriate at the level of the school and its sub-systems, but even at this level the use of coercive power is often considerable.

Table 2

Initiator	Unit	Example	Power-Influence ratio
Government	National system	Raising the school-leaving age	Power
LEA committee	LEA	Secondary reorganisation	
Head teacher	School	De-streaming	
Head of department	Department	New science scheme	
Teacher	Class	Discovery learning	Influence

Normative—re-educative. Fundamentally, this strategy is concerned with changing people – their perceptions, attitudes and behaviours – by means of group techniques. This approach owes much to Kurt Lewin's work on group approaches to attitude change. Lewin's injunction to would-be change agents—'unfreeze, change, re-freeze'—remains the basic paradigm and has influenced the pioneers of the application of group methods to curriculum change such as Benne and Muntyan (1951). The uses of group techniques are varied, and can be ranged upon a continuum from person-change to problem-solving. The use of group techniques to heighten the individual's self-awareness, often termed *sensitivity training,* owes much to the work of the National Training Laboratories, which since 1947 have held sessions for representatives from industrial and other types of institutions. The major technique is the T group, a group of ten to fifteen people plus one or more 'trainers', which meets together without agenda, rules or structure. In this unstructured situation the group members are encouraged by the trainer to observe and discuss problems of interpersonal relationships in an effort to enhance self-knowledge, especially about the impact of one's personality upon others. Although a T group session could become part of a programme of organisational change, its target is the individual rather than the organisation. Initially, T group members came from different organisations, but in recent years the technique has been used with members of the same organisations; the groups have consisted of either a 'horizontal slice', i.e. individuals occupying roles at the same level of the hierarchy, or of a 'vertical slice', i.e. individuals occupying roles at different levels of the hierarchy. Clearly, T groups comprising people from the same organisation have greater control difficulties but, if successful, they should have a considerable impact upon future relationships in the organisation. However, the effectiveness of T groups is still a matter of debate. One can move along a continuum of group techniques, from the T group concern with individual change through the group therapy techniques practised within organisations by the Tavistock Institute (Jaques, 1951) and through other group techniques of attitude change to a use of group methods for the solving of a specific organisational problem. In the latter case a group comprising all organisational or work-group members meet together for the purpose of identifying problems, discussing possible solutions and deciding on future actions. Changes in personal relationships are a likely by-product of this activity, but not its central aim as in the case of sensitivity training. It will be clear that group techniques can occur within or away from the organisation. Each approach has its advantages and disadvantages, but a strong case has been made for the value of what the National Training Laboratories termed a 'cultural island' and Miles (1964) a 'temporary system', whereby the groups meet in a 'country house' situation away from the actual work setting in order that this insulation will to some extent overcome the hierarchical relationships, conflicts and the pressure of immediate problems which tend to inhibit change.

Normative—re-educative techniques have been used in the fields of education by Miles, Lippitt and other American behavioural scientists with an interest in education. But it is somewhat paradoxical that although approaches to change are underpinned by many of the values which are, at least notionally, accepted in education, they have been so little used in effecting educational change. Although considerable amounts of time, effort and resources are devoted to promoting change in education *via* courses, lectures, workshops, etc., the approach is highly individualistic. The relevance of the work-group as the target of change can be substantiated by any teacher who returns to his school after attending some course, full of enthusiasm for the new approach which he has acquired, only to be rapidly deflated by the scepticism and resistance of his colleagues who did not attend the course. Groups are not lacking in education—staff meetings, academic boards, committees and working parties abound, but the normative—re-educative approach, especially in its deliberate use of a behavioural scientist to facilitate group learning, has seldom been used in this country.

Rational—empirical. This approach is characterised by Chin in the following terms: 'The primary task is seen as one of demonstrating through the best known method the validity of the new mode (the proposed changes) in terms of the increased benefits to be gained from adopting it.' The terminology of Miles, Walton and Chin suggests that at the centre of this change-strategy is the concern of all parties to resolve a particular problem and that men respond rationally to the demonstrated superiority of an innovation over previous practice. This change-strategy takes a variety of forms.

Applied research is a form of research whereby the researcher not only produces findings but participates in the process of implementing the policies suggested by the findings. One form of applied research is, of course, *action research,* wherein there is an intimate relationship between the change process itself and the evaluation of its effects upon the system. *System linkage* is a process whereby an interactive relationship is established between a development unit—say, an agency concerned with the creation of new curriculum packages—and a target system such as a school. This clearly goes beyond a dissemination process whereby the exchange takes place, as it were, at the door of the school, to involve an interpenetration of the two social systems. This approach has been increasingly based upon the techniques of systems analysis, and a developing approach in the educational field is the planning-pro-gramming-budgeting system (PPBS) (see Hartley, 1968). *Consultancy* involves the use of a change agent whose function is to assist the organisation to identify and solve particular problems. The consultant may function to assist the organisations to arrive at a decision with regard to a specific innovation or he may function to improve the effectiveness

Eric Hoyle

more generally in a manner which is likely to make it more open to innovation.

Each of these approaches is characterised by the involvement of an external change agent in the internal affairs of the organisation. As a strategy it has been considerably more widely used in industrial, commercial and welfare organisations than in schools and colleges and a considerable literature on the role of the change agent exists.[4] *Planned change* is viewed as 'a deliberate and collaborative process involving a change agent and a client system which are brought together to solve a problem or, more generally, to plan and attain an improved state of functioning and applying valid knowledge' (Bennis, 1966).

The valid knowledge referred to is the knowledge of the behavioural scientist. Bennis discusses seven desiderata of such knowledge, which indicate that it is a body of knowledge relating to the behaviour of persons performing roles in an organisation which yields empirically testable propositions incorporating variables which are relevant to a particular situation. The protagonists of the change agent role emphasise that it is essentially a collaborative process voluntarily entered into by both parties and founded upon a relationship in which each party has an equal opportunity of influencing the other and which is permeated by a spirit of enquiry.

The Potentiality of Planned Organisational Change in Education

In this section the discussion of the potentiality of planned organisational change focuses on the school as the target system. Much of the discussion is also relevant to other forms of educational organisation, for example the college and the university, and to educational units of different sizes, for example the college department, or the local education authority. But it will simplify the discussion if the school is taken as the central focus and the reader left to draw inferences relevant to other forms of educational organisation. One of the reasons why the school has not been regarded as the target of change is that until recently it has been characterised by a low interdependence of parts. The teacher has had a high degree of autonomy in the classroom but a low degree of interaction with other teachers, either at the level of his day-to-day teaching or at the level of decision-making regarding the educational policies of the school. But recently schools have been more frequently conceptualised as social systems comprising sets of interdependent parts, partly because of the growth of systems thinking and partly because certain organisational trends and administrative practices have in fact led to a greater interaction of teachers in pursuit of the goals of the school. This emphasis on the systemic quality of the school enhances the importance of involving in the change process some outside party capable of taking a perspective on the system as a whole.

This section will be largely concerned with strategies of planned change which use a combination of rational—empirical and normative—re-educative techniques, but the realities of the present situation in Britain—particularly the degree of power inhering in the role of the head teacher—make it necessary to begin by discussing the possibilities of change through the use of a modified power—coercive strategy which we will term *administrative change*. It is difficult to determine where innovation, in the sense of the generation of new ideas and techniques, occurs in education. Many of them no doubt occur at the classroom level, but it would seem as though they tend to be systematised and developed outside the school before they become the objects of diffusion. Thus Griffiths (1964) includes as two of his propositions relating to change: 'The major impetus for change in organizations is from the outside.' And: 'When change in an organization does occur, it will tend to occur from the top down, not from the bottom up.' One does not wish to under-estimate the innovativeness of individual teachers with respect to their own teaching, nor with respect to school-wide innovations, although this is likely to be less. Schools probably benefit considerably from the activities of the 'robber baron', the 'heretic' or the 'committed nut', who often have to disrupt established bureaucratic procedures in the pursuit of educational goals. But one must recognise that the head teacher occupies the key role in initiating (or resisting) innovation. The functions of the leadership behaviour of the head teacher in creating an innovation climate can be inferred from several research reports (e.g. Halpin, 1966; Gross and Herriott, 1964). Miles (1965) has listed some of the criteria of what he terms 'organizational health', i.e. goal focus, communication adequacy, optimal power equalisation (between subordinates and superordinates), resource utilisation (technical and human), cohesiveness, morale, innovativeness, autonomy, adaptability,, and problem-solving adequacy (appropriate techniques for handling the conflicts which inevitably arise in any organisation). Miles notes that one-shot innovations are unlikely to be effectively adopted in schools if the schools are not receptive to innovation by being in a good state of organisational health. One can surmise that organisational health in the school is to a large extent the function of the manner in which the head teacher performs his role.

The head teacher is thus in a strong position to initiate innovation, but has at his disposal only his own skill in using administrative strategies, with the persistent danger that he will inhibit the acceptance of innovation, or achieve the form without the substance, if he misperceives the situation or lacks appropriate leadership skills. Theoretically there are a number of ways in which the head can create a receptiveness to innovation by his staff. Some of these ways are very fundamental and include striving for an optimum degree of communication within the school and striving for the optimum degree of teacher involvement in decision-making which balances motivation and efficiency. One could also suggest ways in which a specific innovation might be introduced into a school. A theoretical series of stages is the following: awareness of innovation—creation of staff interest—encouragement of staff knowledge—preliminary evaluation—involvement of staff in decision regarding tentative adoption (or rejection)— limited trial—feedback—evaluation—involvement of staff in decision on complete adoption (or rejection)—provision of support to ensure effective adoption. Such strategies might be regarded as highly desirable, but it must be remembered that they are founded upon an unequal power distribution. The crucial decision by the head and his staff would be to invite the collaboration of a change agent who would be the captive of neither the head nor his staff, but would interact with both on the basis of 'power equalisation' (Strauss, 1963).

The functions of the change agent, in the fullest sense of that term, would be so novel in the British school, owing to the nature of its power structure, that one can perhaps pause before proceeding to a discussion of this role to consider intermediate roles which have less radical implications for the power structure and which might provide opportunities for experiments in consultancy which, although falling short of complete power equalisation, would perhaps provide the necessary experience leading to an increase in confidence (or otherwise) in the change agent function. These are set out in Table 3.

The role of the change agent, in the fullest meaning of the term, can be considered in terms of overall strategy, functions, and the skills required. The most explicit statement of the strategy of the change agent occurs in the pioneering study by Lippitt, Watson and Westley (1958), where the following elements are identified: '(1) diagnosing the nature of the client system's problem; (2) assessment of the client system's motivations and capacities to change; (3) appraising the agent's own motivations and resources; (4) selecting appropriate change objectives; (5) choosing an appropriate type of helping role; (6) establishing and maintaining the helping relationship; (7) recognizing and guiding the phases of the change process; (8) choosing the specific techniques and modes of behaviour which will be appropriate to each progressive encounter in the change relationship; and (9) contributing to the development of the basic skills and theories of the profession.' To these elements can be added two more: achieving an appropriate terminal relationship with the client system and providing or recommending forms of support for the ongoing innovation.

Before the change agent can pursue this strategy a relationship must, of course, be established with the school. The school, for example, might be about to change from a secondary modern school to a junior high school for children of all abilities aged 11—14, and on the basis of a joint decision the head and the staff invite a change agent to advise on the problems created by the change and assist in the change process. The change agent would have preliminary meetings with the staff of the school and suggest how they might help. If these suggestions were accepted by the staff, the strategies outlined above could then be developed. It need hardly be stressed that there will be considerable suspicion of the change agent even on the part of a school staff which is initially willing to consider using his

Table 3

Role	Potential incumbent	Function	Relationship to change process
Researcher	(a)	Evaluation of curriculum, teaching methods, technological innovations, and form of organisation	No direct relationship. Any change occurs through the operation of the Hawthorne effect
Catalyst	(b) (c)	Trials of curriculum or methods innovation (with or without evaluation) involving full-time or part-time participation in the school	No direct relationship. Change occurs via stimulation of interest, informal persuasion, demonstration of effectiveness of an innovation and Hawthorne effect
Resource	(b) (c) (d) (e) (f)	Makes systematic knowledge of curriculum or social science knowledge available to school on an *ad hoc* basis or through regular visits	No direct relationship. Influence on change variable and dependent upon persuasion or access to the power–coercive sanctions available to some roles
Counsellor	(b) (c) (d) (e) (f)	Makes systematic knowledge of curriculum or social science knowledge available to school with respect to specific problem. Perhaps carries out research or other form of analysis at the request of the school. Proposes solutions	Propose change but does not participate in change process
Change agent	(b) (c) (f)	Provides a basis of theory, analysis, research, and support functions related to change in staff perspectives, staff relationships, school organisation and curriculum.	Direct relationship. Collaborates with staff in identifying problems, evolving solutions and achieving change

(a) Research worker from university or research foundation
(b) Lecturer in college or university with curriculum knowledge
(c) Curriculum development specialist, e.g. centre leader, field officer[5]
(d) Local education authority's inspector or adviser
(e) H.M. Inspector[6]
(f) Social scientist from university, polytechnic or other organisation

Eric Hoyle

services. These services will be more acceptable in the situation described above, where the school is forced by external circumstances to accept change, than where no such external factors are operating. In the latter case the change agent will meet the resentment which will follow from the implication that the school is not functioning effectively, and if he does not meet resentment he will probably meet complacency.

In order to achieve an appropriate diagnosis of the problems of the school and its individual members the change agent must clearly possess the personal skills to facilitate open communication between the teachers and himself and amongst the teachers themselves. A useful distinction here is that made by Gouldner (1956) between 'engineering' and 'clinical' approaches to change. In the case of the former the change agent accepts the diagnosis of the problem offered by the elite of the organisation who request his services. Thus a firm might call in a team of 'management consultants' to conduct a survey which would provide the information required to develop a new wages policy. In the case of the latter the organisational members themselves define their own problems. Advocates of the 'clinical' approach to change frequently draw analogies with Carl Rogers' theory of 'client-centred therapy', which holds the function of the therapists to be the creation of situations in which the client has an opportunity of changing his self-concept with the support of the therapist, but not on the basis of the latter's evaluation. It can be suggested that an early task of the change agent in the school is to make it clear to the staff that he has adopted a 'clinical' rather than an 'engineering' approach and that their definitions of the situation are central to the process of change, the outcome of which has been in no way predetermined except where a basic need for change has been proved from without, as in the case of secondary reorganisation. The research for solutions is a collaborative enterprise with no restriction upon the alternatives discussed, but ultimately the alternatives must have apparent feasibility. Once possible solutions have been jointly determined, in order of priority, it is a function of the change agent to assist in their implementation. This is perhaps the most important and most difficult step in the change strategy, since it is one thing to discuss change and another actually to change. Change frequently has its less palatable aspects: it induces uncertainty, creates anxiety about competence, status and adaptability, sometimes disrupts long-standing informal relationships, and not infrequently adds to workload—at least in the initial period. In spite of all the skills of the change agent, there will frequently remain resisters (see Klein, 1966), who must always be given full opportunity to persuade colleagues to reject a change, or a specific form of change; but the ultimate decision must be based upon the wishes of the majority. Some functions of the change agent will be common to all situations but others will vary with the specific problem. The tentative classification of these functions shown in Table 4 groups them on one dimension in terms of the *targets* of change and on the other hand in terms of the *procedures* of change:

Table 4

Targets	Procedures			
	Theory	Analysis	Research	Support
Perspectives	1	2	3	4
Relationships	5	6	7	8
Organisation	9	10	11	12

Procedures

These can be outlined briefly as follows:

Theory. Although there is as yet no well developed theory of organisational change, there are relevant research findings and conceptual frameworks through which the change agent can improve the understanding of the members of the organisation.

Analysis. This refers to the diagnostic processes undertaken by members of the organisation in collaboration with the change agent in an effort to identify problems and alternative solutions. It includes:

(a) Discussion amongst members of the organisation within the organisation itself. In the case of the school, the groups would vary in size depending upon the relevance of a particular agenda. They would normally meet at various times of the school day or out of school hours.

(b) Discussion amongst members of staff in the context of a 'temporary system'. Many local education authorities now have teachers' centres and residential centres which are largely used for courses, but which could be used for this purpose.

(c) Reports by members of the staff, which form the basic discussion. The value of written reports is that they permit a more logically developed argument than can often be achieved in a discussion.

Research. Research competence is one of the skills of the change agent which is not usually possessed by members of a teaching staff (although the number of teachers with research experience is increasing). There are a number of ways in which research can provide data relevant to decisions regarding change. Two basic distinctions can be made:

(a) Research can take various forms in the degree to which it approaches the 'pure' or 'applied' ends of the continuum.

(b) With considerable oversimplification we can identify two main forms of relevant research:

(i) Experimental research, which is concerned with the evaluation of a change in curriculum, methods, group structure, organisational structure, administrative practice, etc. (Fairweather, 1969).

Eric Hoyle

(ii) Survey research, which collects data relating to individuals, groups, the organisation, and the organisational environment.

Support. The change agent has the function of providing the school with certain resources which will support the change process. The change agent team will either possess the necessary support skills within its own number or will have the knowledge and contacts to mobilise resources from elsewhere. The following are examples of the types of support which can be provided:

(a) Team training (the change agent acting as group trainer himself or calling upon the resources of some outside training agency).
(b) 'Temporary systems' geared to problem-solving rather than sensitivity training.
(c) Role workshops in which the incumbents of a particular role meet to discuss problems attaching to the role. 'The main focus here is on role clarity, effectiveness, and improved fit between the person and the role' (Miles, 1965).
(d) Simulation techniques of various kinds: in-tray, case study, role-playing, etc.
(e) Courses, lectures, seminars, tutorials and workshops, which provide the organisation member with knowledge which is relevant to proposed changes in the curriculum, method, technique or organisation.
(f) Programmes of reading designed to provide knowledge relevant to proposed changes in the above areas.

Targets

These are the potential objectives of change. As they are numerous, only a limited number of examples can be given under each heading.

Perspectives. Under this general heading can be included the properties of the school staff which might undergo change:
(a) Knowledge, e.g. about curriculum, methods, pupils.
(b) Perceptions, e.g. of the expectations of colleagues, administrators, parents.
(c) Attitudes, e.g. towards educational objectives, organisational means, proposed changes.
(d) Aspirations, e.g. with respect to future status, salary, professional qualifications.

The function of the change agent is to clarify these for the individual, convert them into data for group discussion, point out discrepancies etc.
Relationships. Under this heading are included relevant social

relationships within the school, and between members of the school staff and interested parties outside the school:

(*a*) Between head and staff.
(*b*) Between other members of staff.
(*c*) Between staff and pupils.
(*d*) Between staff and other components of the role set.

The function of the change agent is to determine the nature of these relationships and provide facilities for change.

Organisation.[7] This group includes the major dimensions of school organisation and its relationship with its environment:

(*a*) Goals, e.g. the official goals, conflicting goals of individuals or sub-systems, working commitments.
(*b*) Formal structure, e.g. staff hierarchy, organisation for instruction,[8] the flow of pupils through the school.
(*c*) Administration, e.g. the process of communication, role allocation, decision-making, recruitment.
(*d*) Informal structure, e.g. the unplanned patterns of association between members of staff (this analytically and not substantively distinct from staff relationships).
(*e*) Informal processes, e.g. joking relationships, polite rituals, secrecy (again, these are intimately associated with relationships).
(*f*) Culture, e.g. values and norms, and their symbolisations, administrative climate.
(*g*) Organisational environment, e.g. the social, economic, administrative and political influence upon the internal activities of the school.[9]

The function of the change agent is to assist the school staff to identify organisational strains, critical decision points, discrepant commitment, etc., and to propose solutions.

The Skill Requirements of the Change Agent

The change agent can be an individual or a team. In some situations where the problem is limited and highly specific the necessary functions could be carried out by one person, but in most cases it is likely that a team would be required. Fundamentally, two kinds of knowledge are needed by the change agent—whether individual or team—involved in planned organisational change in education.

Curriculum knowledge is possessed by the individual experienced in the area of curriculum development. It includes a knowledge of objectives, content and teaching methods together with a familiarity with methods of evaluation and the relevant body of research findings. As planned organisational change will usually be concerned with curriculum change, a team would include curriculum development specialists, perhaps with special interests in certain areas, e.g. science, programmed learning, team teaching. *Behavioural science knowledge* relevant to planned organisational change would be possessed by social psychologists, sociologists, political scientists, anthropologists and economists who had interested themselves in this particular area. Each would bring to the situation the distinctive perspectives and methods of his discipline which could have a relevance to a particular school problem, but there is evidence of a considerable convergence of approaches amongst those behavioural scientists concerned with organisational change. In addition to the diagnostic skills of the behavioural scientist the change agent—individual or team—will usually require group-work skills.

At the present time there will be few people in this country who combine both forms of knowledge, and it is likely that a team would include educationists and behavioural scientists—preferably with each having at least an acquaintance with the theories and methods of the others. But the number is probably growing and the need is perhaps a pointer to the sort of training required by future curriculum development specialists. There is a growing awareness of the need for a specific training for the incumbents of certain non-teaching roles in education. The best courses for head teachers are now firmly based in the social sciences (perhaps even to the neglect of broader educational concerns) and this approach might be applied to training for other roles (see Taylor, 1966, 1968). Currently it is unusual for those involved in curriculum development—e.g. HMIs, local education authority advisers and inspectors, curriculum development leaders—to have had a social science training, but the growth of appropriate courses in university departments of education, management and social administration is now making such training available.

Lippitt, Watson and Westley (1958) list the following under the heading of 'what change agents must learn':

Conceptual—diagnostic training.
Orientation to theories and method of change.
Orientation to the ethical and evaluative functions of the change agent.
Knowledge of sources of help.
Operational and relational skills.

These suggest a useful curriculum for the change agent in education. Hilda Taba (1962) noted that one could not change a curriculum without changing both people and institutions. As this becomes widely recognised in education there is likely to be an impetus to acquire these skills.

Problems of the Change Agent Role in Education

Much of what has gone before may strike the practising educationist as totally inappropriate to the British situation, or impractical, or even impertinent. It must be conceded that considerable problems attach to the process of planned organisational change in education, and the purpose of this article is to generate discussion and to propose experiment rather than to advocate wholeheartedly this approach to change. Clearly there are considerable barriers to be overcome before this approach could be expected to yield dividends.

The head of an educational organisation has a considerable degree of autonomy. It might be the case that he tends to under-estimate the problems of his school. If he does recognise malfunctions within his school he will be reluctant to believe that an outsider can be of help—especially where the outsider is not himself involved in teaching or in running a school, as there is a strong tendency in education to believe that only those who are involved in the day-to-day operation of a school can fully understand its problems. There is sufficient justification in this belief to suggest that an over-enthusiasm for planned organisational change is inappropriate at the present time. The protagonists of this approach suggest that *valid knowledge* is essential but that our understanding of educational organisations and of curriculum development are so limited at the present time that it would be inappropriate for anyone to put himself forward as an 'expert', least of all as an expert who guarantees a solution.

In an illuminating discussion on the use of sociology in the management of educational establishments, Gross and Fishman (1967) draw upon their own experiences in consultancy work and upon discussions with sociologists who have played a variety of roles as consultants to individual schools, school systems and state systems, and with educationists who have had experience from the other side. They are neither over-optimistic nor over-pessimistic regarding the potential value of the sociologist in planning change. They argue that sociologists have been especially useful to school executives in the following respects: they '(1) sensitized them to organizational and interpersonal forces that influence the functioning of schools; (2) provided them with a greater sense of reality about the actual conditions that exist in schools and their external environments; (3) offered them clues to cope with some of their basic problems; and (4) provided them with knowledge about research techniques that may be useful to them in their administrative assignments.' In short, they believe that the main contributions which the sociologist can make at the present time are to sensitise teachers and administrators to the significance of social factors, and to carry out research.

Gross and Fishman's discussion relates to the sociologist who is employed by administrators to help some problem *as they have defined it*. But it will be clear from the earlier discussion of the role of the change agent that he cannot function effectively if he is merely the tool of the administrator. It is essential for the problem to be defined by all parties with the assistance of the change agent, but it must be admitted that there is little basis at present for such a degree of confidence by the head or by the teachers. This confidence can be built up only as social scientists effectively carry out the consultancy tasks outlined in Table 3, which fall short of the equal balance of power required for planned change.

Conclusion

This paper has been concerned with the basic problem of why so many apparently promising educational innovations show little, if any, improvement on existing practices when they are objectively evaluated. It has been argued that these failures could be accounted for by a failure to develop appropriate input strategies. A sociological perspective suggests that the manner in which an innovation is introduced is as important to its effectiveness as the qualities of the innovation itself, and that the sponsor of any innovation must consider the implications of the fact that it must be adopted by *social systems* rather than by unrelated individuals. It has been proposed that innovations might be more effective if schools, and especially head teachers, developed administrative strategies less power-coercive in nature. It has been further proposed that individuals or groups outside the school can facilitate the adoption process, and of the many roles which could be played by the outsider the 'extreme' role of change agent has been discussed in some detail. As the major concern of the paper has been to outline the potential functions of the change agent in planned organisational change, some basic problems have not been discussed and can be mentioned only briefly in the context of *values, theory* and *research*.

Planned organisational change raises fundamental questions of a value-free social science. The pretence of a neutral social science which some practitioners continue to affirm cannot be sustained where the social scientist is actively involved in the change process and not merely in supplying research data from the outside. The debate surrounding the distinction between 'sociology of education' (value-free, objective and defining problems from a sociological perspective) and 'educational sociology' (normative, prescriptive and concerned with the problems identified by educationists) is relevant here. Planned organisational change in education clearly contributes to 'educational sociology'.[10] The change agent bases his activities on certain values relating to education and, more generally, to a mode of problem-solving (democratic and participatory).

Planned organisational change presupposes an articulated theory, or set of distinctive theories, which provide a guide to strategy. It must be conceded, however, that social scientists are only part way towards developing such theories. As is often the case in the social sciences, presumptions, concepts, typologies and clusters of hypotheses are more apparent than formal theories. On the other hand, students of organisational change have refused to be rushed into the premature development of change theories and are currently concerned with delineating the *requirements* of a theory of change (e.g. Bennis, 1966; Chin, 1967).

Research on planned organisational change is equally problematical. Not only are the usual problems of sampling, instrument construction, control of variables, and experimenter bias heightened in this area of research, but the change agent must make some basic decisions about the purpose of his research. Chin (1960) identifies the following types of research relevant to organisational change:

1. *Evaluative:* assessing the effectiveness of a programme.
2. *Predictive:* for making decisions.
3. *Technique:* testing a method.
4. *Action:* affecting conduct.
5. *Practitioner theory:* building practitioner basic science.
6. *Science:* building and testing basic social science.

Fundamentally, the problem lies in the choice between 'pure' and 'applied' (action, operational) research. The former may supply verified but useless knowledge; the latter unverified but relevant knowledge. This is the dilemma which faces the social scientist who would act as a change agent.

NOTES

1. Argyris (1964) has provided the following definition of an organization as social system: (1) a plurality of parts, (2) maintaining themselves through their interrelatedness and (3) achieving specific objectives, and (4) while accomplishing 2 and 3 adapt to the external environment, thereby (5) maintaining their interrelated state of parts. The utilization of systems models has been a recent trend in many disciplines (see Grinker, 1967; Mackenzie,1967). The overarching *general systems theory* has provided a perspective and range of concepts for understanding organizations, but the relationship between theory and research is often unclear (see Hoyle, 1969c). On the use of systems approaches in industry, see Carzo and Yanouzas (1967) and in education Griffiths (1964), Immegart (1969) and Hartley (1969).
2. Chin (1967) has suggested the similarity between these typologies. Discussions appear in Chin (1967), Miles (1965b) and Walton (1965). Garth Jones' typology is based upon Etzioni's (1961) model of complex organizations. I am grateful to Dr. Jones for access to a number of working papers prepared by himself and colleagues at the University of Southern California School of Public Administration. These papers contain a detailed classification of change strategies and form the basis of a book by Jones (1969).

   Although there is clearly much in common between these typologies, there are some points of potential difference. For example, according to the Etzioni model there is a congruence between *utilitarian* strategies and calculative involvement which might not square with the types of involvement implicit in the other models. This raises interesting problems with regard to teachers' motivation and professionalism with regard to change which cannot be discussed here (see Hoyle, 1969d).

3. There is a considerable sociological literature relating to modes of power and influence. A particularly valuable approach is that of 'exchange theory' (Homans, 1961; Blau, 1965), which has been applied to educational organizations by Anderson (1967).

4. There is a considerable literature on planned organization change, and an excellent bibliography is contained in Ali and Jones (1966). Some of the more important and interesting theoretical discussions and research reports are contained in the following: Argyris (1957, 1962, 1964); Bennis (1966); Bennis, Benne and Chin (1961); Burns and Stalker (1961); Ginzberg and Reilly (1957); Lawrence and Seiler (1965); Leavitt (1964); Lickert (1961); Lippitt, Watson and Westley (1958); McGregor (1960, 1966); Mann and Neff (1959); Sofer (1961) — which contains an interesting account of planned change in a British technical college — Spencer and Sofer (1964); Schein and Bennis (1965).

5. I am grateful to Dr.W.A.G.Rudd, Director of the North West Curriculum Development Project, and his initial team of centre leaders for the opportunity of discussing this typology and broader questions of modes of influence and problems of access.

6. HMIs and local inspectors have been omitted from the list of potential change agents. Although these roles have been considerably modified in the direction of consultancy in recent years, the difficulty is that they are still perceived by teachers as part of a 'punishment-centred administration'. They could in the future change sufficiently to permit incumbents to function as change agents in the sense of the term as used in this paper.

7. Discussions of the school as an organization are contained in Bidwell (1965), Corwin (1967) and Hoyle (1965). It must be conceded, however, that there has been much more theoretical discussion than actual research.

8. Until fairly recently, schools have been characterised by a low degree of technological resources, but this situation is now changing. There are many accounts of the social influences of technical change in industry (e.g. Trist and Bamforth, 1951; Walker and Guest, 1952). It is a deficiency of this paper that it contains no discussion of the social implications of technical innovation. Useful discussions are contained in Austwick (1969) and Janowitz and Street (1966).

9. An interesting case of the evolution of a change agent role which mediated between the school and the community and evaluated their linkages occured in the Great Cities Improvement Project in Detroit. Descriptive and theoretical accounts are given in the following: Deshler and Erlich (1968); Litwak and Meyer (1965, 1967); Marburger (1964).

10. On the implications of the distinction between 'sociology of education' and 'educational sociology', see Hansen (1967), Jensen (1956) and Taylor (1967).

References

Ali, S. and Jones, G.N. (1966), *Planning, Development and Change: an annotated bibliography on developmental administration,* University of Punjab, Lahore.

Anderson, J.G. (1967), 'The authority structure of the school: a system of social exchange', *Educational Administration Quarterly,* 3(I).

Argyris, G. (1957), *Personality and Organization.* Harper, New York.

— (1962), *Interpersonal Competence and Organizational Effectiveness,* Dorsey Press, Homewood, Ill.

— (1964), *Integrating the Individual and the Organization,* Wiley, New York.

Austwick, K. (1969), 'Administration and educational technology', in G. Baron and W. Taylor, (eds.), *Educational Administration and the Social Sciences,* Athlone Press, London.

Benne, K, and Muntyan, B. (1951), *Human Relations in Curriculum Change,* Dryden Press, New York.

Bennis, W.G. (1963), 'A new role for the behavioural sciences, affecting organizational change', *Administrative Science Quarterly,* 8.

——(1966), 'Changing Organizations: essays on the development and evaluation of human organisation', McGraw Hill, New York.

Bennis, W.G., Benne, K. and Chin, R. (1961), *The Dynamics of Planned Change,* Holt, Rinehart & Winston, New York.

Bhola, H.S. (1967), 'A configuration theory of innovation diffusion', *Indian Educational Review,* 2 (I).

Bidwell, C. (1965), 'The school as a formal organization' in J.G. March, *Handbook of Organizations,* Rand McNally, New York.

Blau, P.M. (1965), *Exchange and Power in Social Life,* Wiley, New York.

Burns, T. and Stalker, C.M. (1961), *The Management of Innovation,* Tavistock, London.

Carlson, R.O. (1965), *Adoption of Educational Innovations.* Eugene, Oregon: University of Oregon Centre for the Advanced Study of Educational Administration.

Chin, R. (1960), 'Problems and prospects of applied research' in Bennis, Benne and Chin, op. cit.

——(1967) 'Basic strategies and procedures for effecting change,' in E.L. Morphet and C.O. Ryan (eds), *Designing Education for the Future,* Citation Press, New York.

Carzo, R. and Yanouzas, J.N. (1967), *Formal Organization: a systems approach,* Irwin Dorsey, New York.

Corwin, R. (1967), 'Education and the sociology of complex organizations', in D.A. Hansen and J.E. Gerst, *On Education: sociological perspectives,* Wiley, New York.

Deshler, B. and Erlich, J.L. (1968), 'The school community and the agent of change', *The Record,* Vol.69, no.6.

Etzioni, A. (1961), *A Comparative Analysis of Complex Organizations,* Free Press, New York.

Fairweather, G.W. (1967), *Methods for Experimental Social Innovation,* Wiley, New York.

Ginzberg, E. and Reilly, E.W. (1957), *Effecting Changes in Large Organizations,* Columbia University Press, New York.

Goldhamer, H. and Shils, E.A. (1939), 'Types of power and status', *American Journal of Sociology,* 45.

Gouldner, A.W. (1956), 'Explorations in applied social science', *Social Problems,* 3. Reprinted in part in Bennis, Benne and Chin, op. cit.

Griffiths, D. (1964), 'Administrative theory and change in organizations', in Miles (1964), op. cit.

Grinker, P. (1967), *Towards a Unified Theory of Human Behaviour* (second edition), Basic Books, New York.

Gross, N. and Herriott, R. (1965), *Staff Leadership in the Public Schools,* Wiley, New York.

Gross, N. and Fishman, J. (1967), 'The management of educational establishments', in P. Lazarsfeld, W.H. Sewell, and H.L. Wilensky, *The Uses of Sociology,* New York.

Guba, D. and Clark, D.L. (1965), 'An examination of potential change roles in education', *Strategies for Educational Change, Newsletter No. 2,* Ohio State

Eric Hoyle

University. (The scheme is given in full in W. Taylor, *Society and the Education of Teachers*, Faber, London, 1969).

Halpin, A.W. (1966), *Theory and Research in Administration*, Macmillan, New York.

Hansen, D.A. (1967), 'The uncomfortable relation of sociology and education', in Hansen and Gerstl, op. cit.

Hartley, H.J. (1968), *Educational Planning, Programming, Budgeting: a systems approach*, Prentice Hall, Englewood Cliffs, New Jersey.

Homans, G.C. (1961), *Social Behaviour: its elementary forms*, Routledge and Kegan Paul, London.

Hoyle, E. (1965), 'Organizational analysis in the field of education', *Educational Research*, 7(2).

—— (1969), 'How does the curriculum change? (1) A proposal for enquiries,' *Journal of Curriculum Studies*, I (2).

—— (1969b), 'How does the curriculum change? (2) Systems and strategies', *Journal of Curriculum Studies*, I (3).

—— (1969c), 'Organisation theory and educational administration', in Baron and Taylor (eds.), *Educational Administration and the Social Sciences*, Athlone Press, London.

—— (1969d), 'Professional stratification and anomie in the teaching profession', Pedagogica Europaea.

Immegart, G.L. (1969), 'Systems theory and taxonomic enquiry into organizational behaviour in education', in D.E. Griffiths (ed.), *Taxonomy of Organizational Behavior in Education*, Rand McNally, Chicago (in Press).

Janowitz, M. and Street, D. (1966), 'The social organization of education' in B.J. Biddle and P.H. Rossi (eds.), *The New Media and Education*, Aldine, Chicago.

Jaques, E. (1951), *The Changing Culture of a Factory*, Tavistock, London.

Jensen, G. (1965), *Educational Sociology: an approach to its development as a practical field of study*, Centre for Applied Research in Education, New York.

Jones, G.N. (1969), *Planned Organizational Change*, Routledge and Kegan Paul, London.

Klein, D.C. (1966), *Dynamics of Resistance to Change: the defender role*, Human Relations Centre,Boston University, Boston.

Lawrence, P. and Seiler, J.A. (eds.), (1965), *Organizational Behavior and Administration: cases, concepts and research findings*. Irwin Dorsey, Homewood, Ill.

Leavitt, H.J. (1964), 'Applied organizational change in industry,' in W. Cooper *et al., New Perspectives on Organizational Research*, Wiley, New York.

Lickert, R. (1961), *New Patterns in Management*, McGraw Hill, New York.

Lippitt, R., *et al.* (1967), 'The teacher as innovator, seeker, and sharer of new practises', in R.I. Miller, *Perspectives of Educational Change*, Appleton-Century-Crofts, New York.

Lippitt, R., Watson J. and Westley, B. (1958), *The Dynamics of Planned Change*, Harcourt, Brace, New York.

Litwak, E. and Meyer, H.J. (1965), 'Administrative styles and community linkages of the public schools: some theoretical considerations', in A.J. Reiss, (ed.), *Schools in a Changing Society*, New York.

—— (1967), 'The school and the family: linking organizations and external primary groups', in P. Lazarsfeld, W.H. Sewell and H.I. Wilensky, *The Uses of Sociology*, Basic Books, New York.

McGregor, D. (1960), *The Human Side of the Enterprise*, McGraw Hill, New York.

—— (1966), *Leadership and Motivation*, M.I.T. Press, Cambridge.

MacKenzie, W. J. M. (1967), *Politics and Social Science*, Penguin Books, London.

Mann, F.C. and Neff, E.W. (1959), *Managing Change in Organisation*, Foundation for Research on Human Behavior, Ann Arbor.

Marburger, C.L. (1961), 'Considerations for educational planning', in A.H. Passow, (ed), *Education in Depressed Areas*, Teachers' College, New York.

Miles, M.R. (ed.) (1961), *Innovation in Education*, Teachers' College, New York.

——(1965a), 'Planned change and organizational health; figure and ground', in Carlson *et al.*, *Change Processes in the Public School*, University of Oregon Centre for Advanced Study of Educational Administration, Eugene, Oregon.

——(1965b), 'Some propositions on research utilization in education' (cited by Chin, op. cit.).

Rogers, E.M. (1962), *Diffusion of Innovation*, Free Press, New York.

Schein, E.H. and Bennis, W.G. (1965), *Personal and Organizational Change through Group Methods*, Wiley, New York.

Sofer, C. (1961), *The Organization from Within*, Tavistock, London.

Spencer, P. and Sofer, C. (1964), 'Organisational change and its management', *Journal of Management Studies*, I.

Strauss, G. (1963), 'Some notes on power equalization', in H.J. Leavitt (ed.), *The Social Science of Organizations*, Prentice-Hall, Englewood Cliffs, N.J.

Tara, H. (1962), *Curriculum Development: theory and practice*, Harcourt, Brace and World, New York.

Taylor, W. (1966), 'The sociology of education', in W. Tibble, *The Study of Education*, Routledge and Kegan Paul, London.

——(1968), 'Training the head' in B. Allen, *Headship for the Seventies*, Blackwell, Oxford.

Trist, G.L. and Bamforth, K.W. (1951), 'Some social and psychological consequences of the long-wall method of coal getting', *Human Relations*, 4.

Walker, C.R. and Guest, R.H. (1952), *The Man on the Assembly Line*, Harvard University Press, Cambridge.

Walton, R. (1965), 'Two strategies of social change and their dilemma', *Journal of Applied Behavioural Science*, I (2).

26. THE UTILISATION OF EDUCATIONAL RESEARCH AND DEVELOPMENT

Ronald G. Havelock

Program Associate in the Centre for Research on Utilisation of Scientific Knowledge, University of Michigan

From *British Journal of Educational Technology*, 2(2), 1971, pp. 84–97. An earlier version of this paper entitled 'Assembling the Pieces of the Educational Revolution' was prepared as an address to the President's National Advisory Council on Supplementary Centres and Services Conference on Innovation in Washington, D.C., 31 March 1970.

[Havelock looks at the confusion surrounding many new developments in education. Using three models of knowledge utilization – the Research, Development and Diffusion Model, the Social Interaction Model and the Problem-Solver Model – he concludes that a strong link between source systems and user systems needs to be created and suggests a national system manned by 'change agents' to link research and practice.]

The United States appears to be on the brink of an extraordinary educational revolution, but as one well-known educator said recently, the pieces of that revolution are lying around unassembled (Brown, 1970). There are indeed a lot of pieces: considering only what has happened in the last five or six years, we find five new 'R & D Centres', twenty new 'Regional Laboratories', private non-profit development organisations, private profit organisations' subsidiaries, a set of Educational Resource Information Centres (ERIC), over 1,000 locally-based innovation centres of every conceivable size, description and function, information systems and centres of various sorts, and new university programmes and centres for research, development, and dissemination on every aspect of curriculum, pedagogy, and administration. Largely financed by new federal legislation in the mid-1960s, these developments are rapidly changing the landscape in the educational research community (National Centre, 1970).

At the same time the schools are bursting their doors and are submerged in crisis from blacks and whites, striking teachers and rebellious taxpayers. Things are happening. The resources are blossoming and so are the needs. It is usually very hard to discern a clear pattern in all this. Sometimes it appears that we have only created chaos: a muddle of organisational forms with no cohesion, no joint purpose, no relationship to each other, and no relevance to real educational needs.

But in this paper I want to suggest some alternative perspectives that will help us make some sense out of these developments. I propose that all these forms and projects and programs that have been developing over the last five years are truly pieces of an educational revolution, a giant mechanism which has the potential of generating continuous educational reform and self-renewal based on scientific knowledge. The key words in arriving at this understanding are 'dissemination' and 'utilisation'.

Three Models of Knowledge Utilisations

In 1966 I undertook a three-year review of literature to find out what scholars, researchers and practitioners had to say about dissemination and utilisation (Havelock). I looked at several hundred studies from a number of fields; not just from education but also from medicine, agriculture, industrial technology, and so forth. From this review I concluded that there are three main models or orientations which are used to describe the utilisation process. Each of these is valid in a different way but each represents a special perspective. I have labelled them as follows:

1. The RD & D Model
2. The Social Interaction Model
3. The Problem-Solving Model

First consider the *RD & D* (*Research Development and Diffusion*) *Model*, which is portrayed by Figure 1. The most systematic categorisation of processes related to educational innovation is that evolved first by Brickell (1961) and later by Clark and Guba (1965) under the headings 'Research, Development, and Diffusion'. This orientation is guided by at least five assumptions. First, it assumes that there should be a *rational sequence* in the evolution and application of an innovation. This sequence should include research, development, and packaging *before* mass dissemination takes place. Second, it assumes that there has to be *planning,* usually on a massive scale over a long time span. Third, it assumes that there has to be a *division and coordination of labour* to accord with the rational sequence and the planning. Fourth, it makes the assumption of a more or less *passive but rational consumer* who will accept and adopt the innovation if it is offered to him in the right place at the right time and in the right form. Fifth and finally, the proponents of this viewpoint are willing to accept the fact of high initial development cost prior to any dissemination activity because of the anticipated long-term benefits in *efficiency* and *quality* of the innovation and its suitability for *mass audience dissemination.*

313

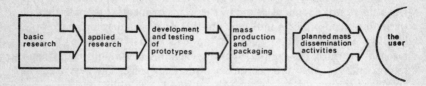

Figure 1. The Research, Development and Diffusion Model

This RD & D model is presumed to be operational in the space and defence industries and in agriculture. Figure 1 provides an outline of its major components. In broad terms RD & D is a grand strategy for planned innovation. At its best, when it really works, R & D can be a process whereby ideas and tentative models of innovations are evaluated and systematically reshaped and packaged in a form that ensures benefit to users and which eases diffusion and adoption. In this process most of the *adaptation* and *translation* problems of the user are anticipated and adjusted for. The final outcome is therefore 'user-proof', guaranteed to work for the most fumbling and incompetent receiver. To some degree the Regional Laboratories supported by the US Office of Education have been established to carry forward this strategy of high-performance product development (Boyan, 1968).

The second of the three models, the *Social Interaction Model* is depicted in Figure 2. Advocates of this approach place emphasis on the patterns by which innovations diffuse through a social system, and they are able to support what they say with a great deal of empirical research. The overwhelming body of this research tends to support five generalisations about the process of innovation diffusion; (1) that the individual user or adopter belongs to a network of social relations (Mort, 1964) which largely influences his adoption behaviour; (2) that his place in the network (centrality, peripherality, isolation) is a good predictor of his rate of acceptance of new ideas; (3) that informal personal contact is a vital part of the influence and adoption process; (4) that group membership and reference group identifications are major predictors of individual adoption; and (5) that the rate of diffusion through a social system follows a predictable S-curve pattern (very slow rate at the beginning, followed by a period of very rapid diffusion, followed in turn by a long late-adopter or 'laggard' period).

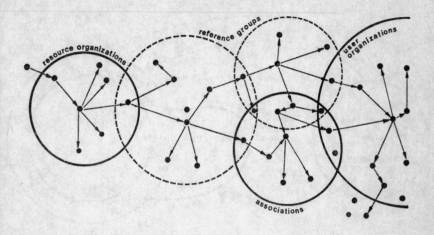

Figure 2. The Social Interaction Model

Although the bulk of the evidence comes from rural sociology, these five propositions have been demonstrated in a remarkably wide range of situations in every field of knowledge and using every conceivable adopter unit including individuals, business firms, school systems and states. Figure 2 suggests the types of variables usually considered by the social interactionists (e.g. characteristics of senders and receivers, social relationships, memberships, leadership and proximity). They have also looked at the relative effectiveness of different media and message forms. In education major advocates of the Social Interaction perspective have been Mott (1964), Ross (1958), and Carlston (1965).

Because of the strong empiricist orientation of this group it has generated relatively few explicit strategies or action alternatives. Social Interaction theorists generally prefer to observe and ponder the 'natural' process without meddling in it. Therefore, the relevance of their work for policy makers and practitioners has not become evident until very recently.

Most in favour with practitioners in education is the third model, which I call the *Problem-Solving Model*, and which is represented by Figure 3. This orientation rests on the primary assumption that innovation is a part of a problem-solving process which goes on inside the user or client system. This designated client system may be of any size and

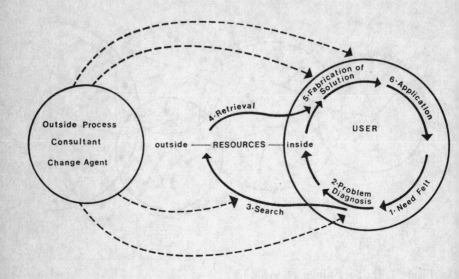

Figure 3. The Problem-Solver Model

complexity, e.g. the school district, the school building, the classroom teacher or even the student.

Problem-solving is usually seen as a patterned sequence of activities beginning with a *need* which is sensed and articulated by the client system. This need must be translated into a *problem* statement and *diagnosis*. When he has thus formulated a problem statement, the client-user is able to conduct a meaningful *search and retrieval* of ideas and information which can be used in formulating or selecting the innovation. Finally, after a potential solution is identified, the user needs to concern himself with adapting the innovation, trying it out and evaluating its effectiveness in satisfying his original need. The focus of this orientation is the user, himself: *his* needs and what he does about satisfying his needs are paramount. The role of outsiders is therefore consultative or collaborative as suggested by the dotted lines in this figure. The outside change agent may assist the user either by providing new ideas and innovations specific to the diagnosis or by providing guidance on the process of problem-solving at any or all of these problem-solving stages.

At least five points are generally stressed by advocates of this orientation: (1) that user *need* is the paramount consideration; this, they say, is the only acceptable value-stance for the change agent, what the user needs and what the user thinks he needs are the primary concern of any would-be helper; (2) that *diagnosis* of need always has to be an integral part of the total process; (3) that the outside change agent should be *nondirective,* rarely, if ever, violating the integrity of the user by setting himself up as the 'expert'; (4) that *internal resources,* i.e. those resources already existing and easily accessible within the client system itself should always be fully utilised; and (5) that *self-initiated* and self-applied innovation will have the strongest user commitment and the best chances for long-term survival. A few of the major advocates of this orientation are Ronald Lippitt and his co-workers (1958), Goodwin Watson (1967), Charles Jung, and Herbert Thelen (1967).

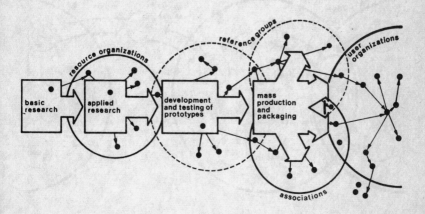

Figure 4. RD & D takes place in a social context

Most of those who belong to this school are social psychologists in the group dynamics human relations tradition.

Although the various orientations to innovation discussed above are espoused by different authors and represent different and often competing schools of thought, the pragmatic change agent should see each of them as illustrating different but equally important aspects of a total process. Consider for example Figure 4 which shows the figures for RD & D and Social Interaction superimposed in one another. Here we see the flow of

Ronald G. Havelock

knowledge from research to practice, both as a logical sequence of steps and as a natural flow from person to person and group to group. This figure probably comes a little closer to what happens in real life. There *are* logical steps but there are human senders and receivers who behave more like social animals than like logical elements. Research is not merely a series of operations, it is also a community; and the same holds true for development and for practice. As separate communities they have boundaries and barriers to sending and receiving knowledge.

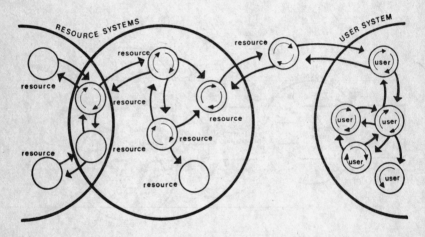

Figure 5. Users and resource persons are social interactors and problem solvers

Now looking at this same array from closer range we see in Figure 5 that information is not merely passing from point to point but also from person to person, and inside each person there is an internal problem-solving process going on, determining in part whether or not information will flow in and through and out to others. Moreover, social interaction is not merely a matter of passively receiving from others; it is also a matter of give-and-take, of mutual influence and two-way communications.

318

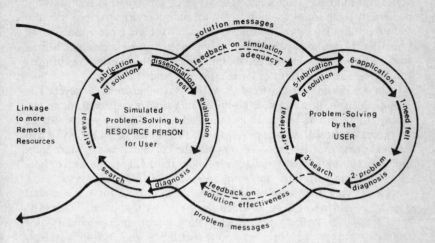

Figure 6. The Linkage Process

To consider this two-way feature in more detail let us look at Figure 6 where one resource person and one user are in interaction with each other. On the right we have the user trying to help himself like a good independent problem-solver. He identifies a need, he decides on a potential solution; he tries out the solution, and if it works, his need is met. But let us not forget that there is a man on the left, too. Where does the man on the left fit into this picture? That is the number one linkage question: anybody who wants to be effective as a resource person, as a helper, or as a linker to resources has to know when, where and how he fits in. Therefore he needs to have information from the user, not just about what the user needs but also about how the user goes about solving problems. He has to be able to simulate the user's problem-solving process so that he can feed him solutions and solution ideas that are both relevant and timely.

To co-ordinate helping activities with internal user problem-solving activities, the outside resource person must be able to recapitulate or simulate that internal process. Technically speaking, the resource person needs to develop a good 'model' of the user system in order to 'link' to him effectively. Clinically speaking, we could say that he needs to have empathy or understanding. At the same time, the user must have an adequate appreciation of how the resource system operates. In other words he must be able to understand and partially simulate such resource system activities as research, development and evaluation.

In order to build accurate models of each other, resource and user must provide reciprocal feedback and must provide signals to each other which are mutually reinforcing. This type of collaboration will not only make particular solutions more relevant and more effective but will also serve to build a lasting relationship of mutual trust and a perception by the user that the resource person is a truly concerned and competent helper. In the long run, then, initial collaborative relations build effective channels through which innovations can pass efficiently and effectively.

Linkage is not seen merely as a two-person process, however. The resource person, in turn, must be linked in a similar manner to more and more remote expert resources as indicated in previous diagrams. As the advocates of the RD & D approach hold, there must be an extensive and rational division of labour to accomplish the complex tasks of innovation building. However, each separate role-holder must have some idea of how other roles are performed and some idea of what the linkage system as a whole is trying to do. In particular, there is a need for some central agency, as shown in Figure 7, which has a primary task of 'modelling' the total innovation building and disseminating system and which acts as a facilitator and coordinator, seeing to it that the 'system' is truly a system, serving the needs of the user.

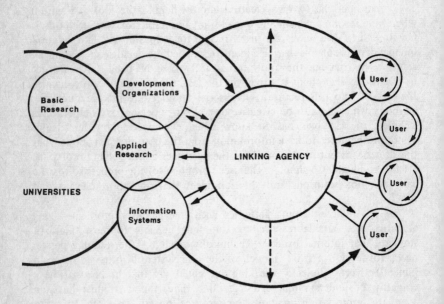

Figure 7. The Central Linkage Agency in the Macrosystem

This brings me to the main point I want to make in this paper: we need to build national systems which allow any school district to plug into the most sophisticated sources of information in such a way that they get knowledge and materials which are relevant and timely and truly cost beneficial.

As I view the landscape, trying to put pieces together, I usually find that there is one important missing piece. Many scholars have talked of the need for dissemination and utilisation of what we now know and many have talked of the need for a better problem–solving process in schools which would make adequate use of available resources, but we have not provided the institutional mechanisms that would allow these things to happen. We have research organisations, universities and R & D centres; we now have some impressive product development centres (e.g., the regional labs) and a few privately-funded organisations which are similarly engaged, but what we do not have and what we need so badly is a network of regional centres which can serve as truly comprehensive resource centres and resource linking centres with the skills and the staff to be an effective mediating mechanism between R & D on the one hand and operating school districts on the other.

Though such a network does not presently exist, there are, nevertheless, isolated cases of successful linkage agencies, and I would like to describe one of these as an example of the type of agency which I feel is needed. There is an organisation in Albuquerque, New Mexico called the South-western Co-operative Educational Laboratory. This is one of the 15 currently surviving laboratories set up by the US Office of Education in 1966 to carry out programmatic development work. This particular laboratory wanted to specialise in language arts programmes for preparing young children from Indian, Spanish-speaking and very poor families to participate in and take advantage of the established school system on a par with middle–class whites. This was a very ambitious goal, but they are very serious about it and very methodical about what will be achieved, when and at what cost. This laboratory started on this mission by adapting an 'oral language programme' for elementary school children who did not hear English spoken in the home. The programme had been sketched out by Dr Robert Wilson at the University of California at Los Angeles. The laboratory took Wilson's model and developed a prototype programme, evaluating and testing two or three advanced models with a large number of school districts throughout the southwest. They made certain that their oral language programme was producing results to specification before going on to each additional stage of development. Their prototype included complete teacher's manuals with behavioural objectives, materials and a complete in-service training package. The training package, itself, was also evaluated and improved from year to year. They have also gone beyond the teacher-training problem to look at the total question of *diffusion and installation* considering the kinds of institutional safeguards and conditions that have to be built-in to insure the programme's success in a given setting. They are currently working to develop a new kind of role in school settings which they call the 'Quality Assurance Specialist', someone who is trained to work at the school level to make sure that innovations such as the 'Oral Language Program' are used in the way they were designed to be used.

The Key Role of Regional Service Centres

A very significant aspect of the Albuquerque Laboratory's programme is its growing relationship with a network of regional service centres in west Texas. These centres are assuming the installation function for the language arts programme in their region, leaving the laboratory to concentrate on its assigned mission which is 'development'. Now, in addition, the laboratory has a contractual relationship with New Mexico State University to train teachers in this programme, once again illustrating this budding-off process from development into viable continuous operations. From the University of California to the Laboratory to the teacher-training at New Mexico State University to the Texas service centres to the operating school districts there is a true knowledge chain based on genuine collaboration and two-way communication. In this chain the regional service centre was the key link to the educational consumer; without a national network of regional centres which operate in this manner, educational research, development, disseminaton and utilisation cannot be coordinated as a system. Really significant improvement in education in the 1970s will depend largely on the emergence of these service centres as comprehensive resource linking agencies. They are the vital bridge between a very complex array of resource systems on the one hand and the operating school districts on the other.

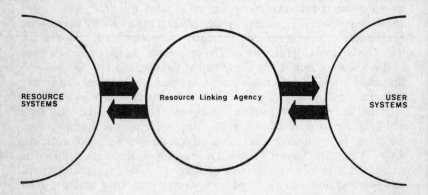

Figure 8. The Resource Linking Agency has two major linking tasks to perform

The service agency therefore has two major tasks, as shown in Figure 8: first, to build and maintain adequate linkage to resource systems: and second, to build and maintain adequate linkage to the educational users in its region. Let us consider each of these tasks in turn.

1. *Linking to Resource Systems*

The task of building linkage to resource systems may be outlined in three steps. As a first step, shown in Figure 9, the agency should develop a wide span of *awareness* of potential resource systems, who they are, where they are, which ones seem to be more relevant or less relevant, more accessible or less accessible. The array of resources identified in this diagram is, of course, only partial and sketchy. Figure 10 represents the second step, in which the agency begins to make contact with the most relevant and accessible resources, initiating two-way interchanges to promote mutual awareness and to learn about their potential resource-giving capacity. Finally, as a third step the agency begins to develop joint projects, testing out the *actual* resource giving capacity of outside agencies.

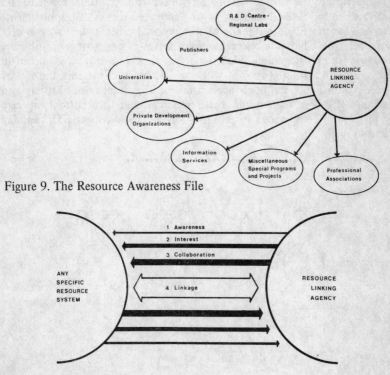

Figure 9. The Resource Awareness File

Figure 10. Building linkage to resources

Ronald G. Havelock

This process of building linkage to resource systems is exactly what took place between the west Texas centres and the Albuquerque Laboratory. What I describe in that case was an example of how the RD & D model works when it really works (which is far more rare than some of its advocates would have us believe). There are very few fully developed and fully evaluated innovations of such quality that are actually ready for installation. Most of the time the information is partial and it is scattered; it has to be retrieved from a number of sources, screened and pulled together in some sort of order before it can really be used by anybody. This pulling together can be a very complex and costly process which requires very sophisticated resource linkage. However, the successful linking agency knows how to enlist help from the above mentioned array of resource systems to do the job which it cannot do itself. Thus, it increases its linkage to resource systems and simultaneously increases its capacity to serve clients.

2. *Linkage to User Systems*

Let us turn to the second side of a service centre's activities, linkage to and service to the school districts in its designated region. To approach its service function on a rational basis the regional centre must first conceive of itself and all of the client groups it serves as one system for utilising knowledge and upgrading educational practice. This system is shown in Figure 11. As with the inventory of potential resource systems, the agency needs to make a thorough accounting of the number of districts and schools it serves, their needs, their resources, and their current capacity and level of competence in problem-solving, resource retrieval, planning and so forth.

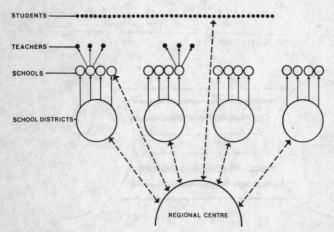

Figure 11. The Linking Agency and its users together are one system

324

Once they have defined the systems they are trying to serve, the agency staff can begin to develop a step-by-step programme for establishing a truly linking role; these steps are shown in Figure 12. The first step is creating awareness, letting the users know you exist, that you are there to help them as a general resource in their problem–solving efforts. The agency's staff create this awareness by visiting the clients, asking them what they see their needs to be, letting them see and feel the service centre as a real organisation. The centre should also have a newsletter which goes out to every key educator in the region: this can get to far more people than can be reached personally and it is a periodic reminder to them that the centre is a going concern, trying to do some things that are relevant to local educational needs in a helpful non-threatening way.

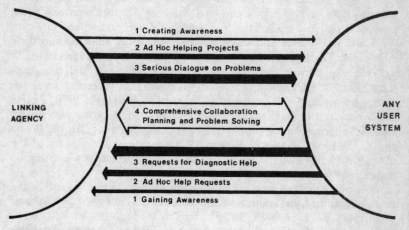

Figure 12. Building linkage to users

Beyond awareness the centre must start to become directly involved on a project-by-project basis. The Oral Language Program described previously in this paper is one good example of an *ad hoc* 'project' approach to linkage, a very visible co-operative activity on something that will be concretely helpful in some specific area. It does not have to be large but it must be *successful*. These specific successful projects, however small they are, are terribly important in building the utilisation chain because each project builds trust, builds interest, builds knowledge of each other, and builds competence and confidence on both sides. These are the beginnings of the linkage process I described earlier where resource and user understand each other's internal process, simulate one another, and thereby co-ordinate their behaviour for mutual gain.

As a third step, the centre begins to develop a serious dialogue with client systems on what their problems really are. This is very difficult to do in a systematic system-wide way, and there must be a basis of trust with the schools before one can really get very far with this. Once the schools are thinking about problems, then the service centre can start some major *ad hoc* problem-solving, using its capacity as a helper and linker to more remote resources.

It is only after the centre has started getting some success in *ad hoc* problem-solving that it can start to get schools and school districts to work in a more comprehensive way about planning, working out behavioural objectives and generating the kind of continuous monitoring and programmatic upgrading that the systems analysts tell us we need.

If this is how an ideal service centre would work, the next question is: How do we build a set of agencies which are real linking organisations? I suggest that this can be done through a systematic application of what we know about dissemination, utilisation and the planning of change. First we need to train and recruit a core staff of people who understand these processes, who understand the four models I described and can integrate them and incorporate and apply them in their daily thinking and their daily work. There are training programmes now under development which will start to provide many of the necessary skills and understandings (Havelock, 1971). There are manuals on the change process, written for change agents and administrators. (Glaser, 1971; Havelock, 1970; Rogers and Svenning, 1969). There are also books and articles which cover every aspect of dissemination and utilisation and change planning (Bennis, Benne and Chin, 1969; Havelock; Rogers, 1971) and there are reports of the actual field experience of many educational change agents which can be drawn upon (Hearn, 1969).

So many problems seem to be crowding in on us in this last half of the twentieth century, and again and again we hear that the key to solving these problems is education. Well, the key probably *is* education, but what is the key to the key? What can we do to change education so that it can deliver? I propose that the key to the key must be national systems for coordinated research, development, dissemination and utilisation, systems which are simultaneously national, regional and local and in which there is a continuous chain of interdependence and two-way linkage from researcher to developer to practitioner to consumer. The pieces of the educational revolution are lying around unassembled; we need to build systems that would link the research world and the practice world to each other on a continuous basis for their mutual gain. We need to start putting these pieces together, finding out what pieces are still missing and fashioning those new pieces. From my work, I have come to believe that there is a need for a new type of agency right in the heart of this system, an agency manned by people — 'knowledge brokers', 'linkers', 'change agents', call them what you will — people who can work in the middle between research and practice. There is a set of skills in this area which can be taught and learned, but very, very few people have them today. This is a critical task for the 1970s.

REFERENCES

Bennis, Warren G., Kenneth D., and Chin, Robert (eds) (1961, 1969), *The Planning of Change,* Holt, Rinehart and Winston, New York.

Boyan, Norman J., 'Problems and Issues of Knowledge Production and Utilization', in T.L. Eidell and J.M. Kitchel (eds), *Knowledge Production and Utilization in Educational Administration,* Centre for Advanced Study of Education Administration, University of Oregon, Eugene, 1968.

Commissioner of Education, State Education Department, Albany, New York.

Brown, B. Frank (1970), Address to *Educational Press Association,* Atlantic City, New Jersey, 17 February.

Carlson, Richard O. (1965), *Adoption of Educational Innovations,* University of Oregon, Eugene, 1965.

Clark, David L. and Guba, Egon G. (1965), *An Examination of Potential Change Roles in Education.* Paper presented at the Symposium on Innovation in Planning School Curricula, Airlie House, Virginia, October.

Glaser, Edward M. and staff at the Human Interaction Research Institute, Los Angeles, California, are under contract with the National Institute of Mental Health to develop a manual on research utilization, which should be available in 1971.

Havelock, Ronald G. (1970), *A Guide to Innovation in Education,* a handbook on the innovation process for change agents, Institute for Social Research, University of Michigan, Ann Arbor.

Havelock, Ronald G. in collaboration with Guskin, Alan *et al.,* Planning for Innovation through Dissemination and Utilization of Knowledge, Institute for Social Research, University of Michigan, Ann Arbor.

Havelock, Ronald G. *et al.* (1971), *Designs for Change Agent Training in Education.* Report on the Conference on Educational Change Agent Training, High/Scope, Clinton, Michigan, May 1970. Sponsored by the Centre for Research on Utilization of Scientific Knowledge, University of Michigan. Available from the Institute of Social Research, Ann Arbor, Michigan.

Hearn, Norman E. (1969), *Innovative Education Programs: A Study of the Influence of Selected Variables upon their Continuation Following the Termination of Three-Year ESEA Title III Grants.* Dissertation for Doctor of Education Degree, Washington D.C., George Washington University, September 30.

Jung, Charles, Research Utilizing Problem Solving: *An Instructional Program for School Personnel,* North-West Regional Educational Laboratory, Portland, Oregon.

Lippitt, Ronald, Watson, Jeanne and Westley, Bruce (1958), *The Dynamics of Planned Change,* Harcourt, Brace and Company, Inc., New York.

Mort, Paul R. (1964), 'Studies in Education Innovation from the Institute of Administrative Research', in Mathew B.Miles (ed), *Innovation in Education,* Bureau of Publications, Teachers College, Columbia University, New York.

National Center for Educational Research and Development (1970), *Educational Research and Development in the United States.* Superintendent of Documents, Catalogue No. HE5.212.12049, US Government Printing Office, Washington, D.C.

Rogers, Everett M. with Shoemaker, F. Floyd (1971), *Communication of Innovations: A Cross-Cultural Approach,* Free Press of Glencoe, New York.

Ronald G. Havelock

Rogers, Everett M. and Svenning, Lynne (1969), *Managing Change,* Operation PEP. San Mateo County Superintendent of Schools, San Mateo, California.
Ross, Donald H. (1958), *Administration for Adaptability: A Source Book Drawing Together the Results of More than 150 Individual Studies Related to the Question of Why and How Schools Improve.* Metropolitan School Study Council, New York.
Thelen, Herbert A.(1967), 'Concepts for Collaborative Action-Inquiry', in *Concepts for Social Change.* Moran Printing Service. Published by N.T.L., National Education Association for COPED, Baltimore, March.
Watson, Goodwin (1967), 'Resistance to Change', in G.Watson (ed), *Concepts for Social Change.* Moran Printing Service. Published by N.T.L., (National Training Laboratories), National Education Association for COPED, Baltimore, March.

27. THE CREATIVITY OF THE SCHOOL IN BRITAIN

Eric Hoyle

Paper prepared for CERI Workshop on 'The Creativity of the School', unpublished (copyright with author).

[Schools in Britain are willing to introduce innovations but difficulties occur in sustaining or institutionalising them. Hoyle explores the link between the capacity to sustain innovation (creativity) and the 'social organisation of the school'. He then considers recent strategies for innovation — the problems in constitutionalising innovations, the changing nature of the social system of the school, and ways of supporting innovatory schools.]

The topic chosen for special consideration in the British position paper is the relationship between creativity, i.e. the capacity to sustain innovation, and the social organisation of the school. The reason for this choice is that within the relatively decentralised British educational system the school enjoys a high degree of autonomy in such matters as curriculum, method and pupil-grouping, and, therefore, must be regarded as the most significant innovating unit. The quality and extent of its innovating capacity is, therefore, of some interest.

The fact that the British system is relatively decentralised does not, of course, mean that the school is entirely free from external constraints. These arise from the policy decisions made at the levels of national and local government. Moreover, the school is most certainly open to influence exerted by the administration at national and local levels and by a variety of other agencies. The point is, however, that although the possibility of *influencing* is high, the possibility of *coercion* is very low. We can, perhaps, illustrate this with one or two examples. An individual school has no control over whether or not it becomes comprehensive. But to create comprehensive *schools* is not necessarily to create comprehensive *education* insofar as this term implies a particular educational approach. One can have comprehensive schools which do little more than perpetuate the type of education which was purveyed under the old selective system, or one can have comprehensive education based on a different concept involving mixed ability grouping, flexible organisation and pupil choice, counselling and pastoral work, etc. The *educational* response to *structural* reorganisation is largely a matter for the school, although, in fact, comprehensive reorganisation has generated considerable innovation in curriculum, method and pupil grouping as schools have responded to the challenge. Local Education

329

Authorities, which have responsibility for the day-to-day administration of education, naturally have a considerable influence on what goes on inside the schools. It is no accident that certain LEAs are associated with particular forms of innovation. This influence is achieved through the allocation of resources, the selection of head teachers and other staff, the guidance given to schools by inspectors and advisers, and the nature of the in-service training provided. But even LEAs do not intervene directly in the internal activities of the school, and individual schools can choose to withstand such influences and decide upon different objectives, curriculum, or internal organisation. The same applies to the expectations of the community and the influence of such agencies of innovation as the Nuffield Foundation and the Schools Council. Although there is within the Department of Education and Science considerable knowledge of curriculum matters, central government has in the past traditionally remained detached from questions of curriculum and method. Some years ago one Minister of Education claimed that he was the wrong person to ask about the curriculum as he knew nothing about such matters. Another Minister of Education referred to 'the secret garden of the curriculum' when initiating the process which led to the establishment of the Schools Council. The function of this Council is to initiate research and development on curriculum and examinations. Its publications are naturally influential but it has no powers of direction whatsoever. Even so, the teachers' associations were unhappy about the establishment of the Curriculum Study Group which preceded the Council, seeing it as the thin end of the wedge of Government interference in the curriculum. The Schools Council itself, with a majority of teachers on all its committees, was more acceptable to the teachers' associations, but was, nevertheless, greeted with some reservations.

One must mention the external examining boards as having a significant influence on the internal activities of the school. External examinations are held to exert one of the most potent constraints upon the internal activities of the British secondary school. In any system where secondary schools act as agencies of selection, and where this is achieved through examinations conducted by agencies outside the school on the basis of curricula which they decide, the school inevitably loses a degree of autonomy. This is true of the British system where external examinations restrict the autonomy of the school in matters of curriculum and method with regard to the more able children at the upper end of the secondary school. On the other hand, not all initiative disappears from the school. The fact that there are a number of examining boards for the General Certificate of Education enables the school some choice in syllabus. Moreover, the examination boards have become much more flexible in their approach to examinable subjects and curricula and are prepared to give sympathetic consideration to innovations suggested by groups of schools or even by individual schools. There is a much greater degree of flexibility in the examination procedures for the Certificate of Secondary Education, the examination taken at the age of sixteen by roughly the second quartile of the ability range. It is possible under this system for a school to have its own syllabus approved and to set its own examination with external moderation, but surprisingly few schools have taken advantage of this opportunity. This may, however, be due to the fact that teachers were in any case crucially involved in setting examinations at the regional level.

Finally, one must consider the significance of the growing influence of parents. There is little doubt that in some schools parental pressures have been not inconsiderable factors leading to constraint in organisational and curricular development. Doubt and distrust regarding changing school policy are evident in some areas, particularly among parents of more able pupils, although in the main parents have appeared ready to trust the judgment of schools and content to wait and see the ultimate effects of change. As teachers, through their membership of local committees and groups, become more involved in the work of curriculum innovation and development, the importance of publicity and of rapid dissemination of information within the educational service is being clearly realised. In several areas regular bulletins and papers are issued for circulation among teachers. It is something of a paradox, however, that at a time when schools are consciously extending their activities beyond the confines of the classroom into the community at large, they are failing to make clear to the community — in particular, employers and parents — the nature of the change taking place in the aims, organisation and methods of the schools and the reasons for them. While schools generally acknowledge the interests and concerns of parents, comparatively few have as yet shown themselves prepared to take them fully into their confidence.

In sum, although there are very definite external constraints on the school, and although it is exposed to a number of sources of influence, the degree to which the school is innovative is to a large extent a function of its own 'organisational character'.

An assumption made in this paper is that autonomy is conducive to creativity if the internal organisation of the school is such that it sustains an innovative orientation. In recent years the British school has been open to new ideas and practice. Examples of the innovations which have been adopted by British secondary schools are:

New curricula in the sciences and humanities
Interdisciplinary enquiry
Team teaching
Mixed ability grouping
Resource-based learning
Flexible grouping
New modes of pupil assessment.

The rate of innovation is such that one might say that teachers are suffering from 'innovation fatigue'. But there are some indications that this innovation is often short-lived. It is *adopted* by schools but not *institutionalised*[1] to become a fully functioning part of the school system. It is suggested that the reason for this is that, although schools have invested a great deal of effort in curriculum innovation (using that term widely) and have responded enthusiastically to the challenges which have been made, the success of these efforts has been limited by the fact that schools have not generally used their freedom to innovate to bring about changes in their own structures, decision-making procedures, professional relationships, etc. which may be a prior condition of successful innovation in curriculum and method. Thus, the dilemma faced by the school can be expressed as follows:

> Curriculum innovation requires change in the internal *organisation* of the school.
> Change in the internal organisation of the school is a major innovation.

This paper will explore the implications of these two propositions. The paper falls into four main parts. Part 1 considers the strategies of innovation which have emerged in recent years. Part 2 discusses the problems of institutionalisation. Part 3 considers the ways in which the social system of the school is changing and the barriers encountered. Part 4 suggests ways in which the school might be supported in its change efforts.

1. Strategies of Curriculum Innovation

In this context the term 'curriculum' is used in a broad sense to include the totality of what is taught in school, the relationship between school subjects, teaching materials, teaching methods, technological and other aids, and the organisation of teaching/learning. One of the most significant developments in recent years has been not only an increase in the degree of innovation but also the emergence of a more systematic approach to development, dissemination and implementation. Earlier, innovation had proceeded by means of the rather haphazard diffusion of new ideas and practices via networks of interested groups and individuals. This occurred through the courses and conferences arranged by the Department of Education and Science, Local Education Authorities, universities and colleges, through the visits to schools made by members of Her Majesty's Inspectorate and the inspectors and advisers employed by Local Education Authorities, and through the educational press, radio and television. The adoption of new ideas by schools was dependent upon the enthusiasm of individual teachers. Where the innovation could be adopted by an individual, then his own commitment was sufficient. Where, however, the innovation involved the school as a whole, or a substantial segment of it (as with mixed ability grouping, for example), the commitment of the head teacher was essential.

He might initiate the innovation himself or be persuaded to do so by members of his staff. Using the classifications suggested by Havelock, we can term this the *social interaction* pattern of innovation.

A more systematic approach to innovation emerged in the 1960s, especially in relation to the production and dissemination of curriculum materials. The initiative was taken by such central agencies as the Nuffield Foundation and the newly-established Schools Council. In Havelock's terms the dominant strategy was that of Research, Development and Dissemination (RD & D). Materials were devised by a project team, developed in a number of trial schools and then made generally available for purchase by other schools. Some of these materials diffused widely. It has been estimated, for example, that Nuffield Science materials for pupils taking O level of the General Certificate of Education had been adopted by over 45 per cent of potential consumer schools within five years of publication. (One should note here the support of examining boards.) The great advantage of the RD & D approach is the high quality of the materials produced. On the other hand, teachers are more or less passive recipients of the packaged materials.

Tony Becher, Assistant Director of the Nuffield Foundation, who has studied trends in the strategies of innovation, has noted that an alternative to the RD & D model began to emerge in the 1960s which he compares with the *social interaction* model of Havelock. It is, in fact, a development of the unplanned pattern of diffusion referred to above having become a much more systematic approach through the co-ordinating function of the various agencies of curriculum development. These agencies supported and serviced networks of teachers in developing their own materials. Teachers met regularly, usually on a local or regional basis, to reconsider particular parts of the curriculum and to collate and publish exemplars of good practice. This was the approach used, for example, in Project Technology of the Schools Council. This approach appealed to a number of Local Education Authorities who had felt that local needs were best met by local initiatives rather than through the RD & D agencies. They supported 'networks' of local teachers, which were often based upon the Authorities' own Teachers' Centres which were established during the 1960s. An interesting example of collaboration between a university and a number of Local Education Authorities occurred in the North West Curriculum Project. This was financed by the Schools Council and the participating LEAs and was based upon the University of Manchester School of Education. A particular problem was selected for consideration – the curriculum of the extra year after the raising of the school leaving age – and a particular approach was taken towards curriculum development based upon Bloom's taxonomy. Panels of teachers, with college or university consultants, were established, to consider curriculum objectives and to develop new approaches in the various aspects of the curriculum. Central to the scheme was a cadre of Teachers' Centre Leaders who worked with the project leader to establish the general direction of the project and then participated in panel meetings and acted as local agents of dissemination through their Centres.

There is little doubt that these strategies have made a considerable impact upon education in Britain, but it should be pointed out that they apply only to certain aspects of what has been included within the concept of 'curriculum' which has been adopted in this paper. They have been particularly effective in the dissemination of materials. They are also app-ropriate to innovation in certain aspects of the organisation of teaching/learning as, for example, discovery learning principles. But other inno-vations in the organisation of teaching/learning have been dependent upon the initiative of the school. We can consider the examples of mixed ability grouping and team teaching. There has been a strong trend to mixed ability grouping in the primary schools, but a proportion of secondary schools also instituted the practice, usually in the first or first and second years. It is difficult to say how this particular innovation originated. No doubt some schools decided on the basis of experience that mixed ability grouping would be of general benefit to pupils. But certainly an impetus came from research published during the 1960s which indicated the 'self-fulfilling prophecy' of streaming by ability. This research encouraged the imple-mentation of mixed ability grouping. As more schools began to adopt this mode of organisation, various agencies arranged courses, conferences and workshops on this innovation. A similar pattern occurred in the case of team teaching, although in this case the support of research was not avail-able. Groups of enthusiastic teachers who saw virtues in team teaching secured its adoption by their schools and the innovation spread through the medium of courses and conferences. In fact, the strategies involved were little different from the unstructured social interaction model of change which depended upon diffusion amongst interested teachers making what use they could of existing forms of external support. Yet this sort of innovation, especially where it involved a fundamental change in pro-fessional relationships amongst teachers as in the case of team teaching, is difficult to accomplish and perhaps even more difficult to sustain. [See Lortie, p. 230.]

2. The Problem of Institutionalisation

The major problem which has been encountered in the attempt to intro-duce innovations in curriculum and method has been that of institutional-isation. British schools have been very eager to innovate, but they have ex-perienced considerable difficulty in sustaining the innovations adopted until they have passed that tipping point whereby they have become a fully functioning part of the social system of the individual school. Thus, inno-vations have been dropped altogether or they have been so adapted to the prevailing modes of education that they have been robbed of their inno-vativeness. The motto of 'adopt and adapt' is generally sound in that it indicates the necessity of modifying an innovation in the light of local circumstances. But where the adaptation involves 'knocking off the corners to get it through the door of the school' — in other words, adapting the innovation to prevailing patterns of curriculum, method, or organisation — the innovatory aspect is often lost. Thus, materials designed to be used in the context of discovery learning are used in traditionally didactic ways, the purpose of mixed ability grouping is undermined where teachers effectively 'stream' within a single class, and interdisciplinary work founders when individual teachers insist on maintaining their monodisciplinary approach. There are perhaps two fundamental reasons why innovations fail to 'take' — a lack of resources and 'tissue rejection' by the school.

The question of resources will not be dealt with in any length, but one or two brief points can be made. The first is that resources are often needed for a longer period than anticipated. Innovations need extensive 'after-care' if they are to be fully institutionalised. The RD & D agencies have not always had the necessary resources to provide this after care over a lengthy period — even for a small number of schools involved in the initial development — and other agencies have not emerged to provide this support. Secondly, perhaps the most important resource for the support of innovation is *time*. In particular, at the school level teachers often require time free from teaching duties to acquire new knowledge and skills, and, importantly, to collaborate with other teachers. Thirdly, to innovate 'on the cheap' can often be frustrating for teachers. Head teachers and Local Education Authorities may be reluctant to invest in expensive materials or equipment and rationalise this by claiming that it is appropriate that teachers should produce their own. It is true that teachers can often produce innovations which are suited to their special problems, but innovation 'on a shoestring' can often lead to strain. The importance of the investment factor should not be underestimated, but it is not the central concern of this paper.

Finally, we can briefly touch upon the role of non-teaching personnel in supporting innovation. The actual and potential roles cannot be given in detail here, but perhaps two functions can be identified. One is the release of teaching personnel from non-professional or semi-professional activities in order to allow them the *time* which is so essential to the planning and implementation of innovation. Examples would be the nursery assistant in the nursery school, women helpers in the primary school, and the laboratory assistant in the secondary school. The other function is much more directly related to innovation and involves a professional service to teachers. An example would be the Inner London Education Authority's introduction of the Media Resources Officer, a well-trained and professional person skilled in providing teachers with learning resources in non-print media. Yet, although it would appear that non-teaching personnel of various kinds could make a valuable contribution to the school's capacity to innovate, the extension of this practice is dependent upon its acceptance by the teachers' associations. Hitherto, these associations have expressed reservations about the employment of non-professional or para-professional people in schools, fearing that they might eventually take on some of the fully professional tasks of the teacher. There are also reservations about changing the balance between teaching and non-teaching personnel in schools. The teachers' associations would want to be assured that any developments of this kind would not be at the cost of expanding the teaching force.

'Tissue rejection' occurs where there is a discrepancy between innovation and the 'pedagogical code' of the school. Many current innovations are underpinned by a 'code' which is quite radically new as far as the adopting school is concerned. This 'code' may perhaps place an emphasis on *openness* and *flexibility* in matters of curriculum, methods and the organisation of learning. There are problems of institutionalisation at two levels. At the more superficial level there is the problem of institutionalising the 'medium', e.g. materials, hardware, pupil-grouping. At a more fundamental level there is the problem of institutionalising not only the medium but also the 'message' which it carries and which is derived from the new pedagogical code. The media can often be readily adopted by one part of the school; the 'message' requires a switch in code on the part of the school as a whole.

The problem of institutionalisation at these different levels has been illustrated in some of the studies which have been carried out on the process of innovation. Shipman studied the Integrated Studies Project financed by the Schools Council and based upon the University of Keele. Thirty-eight schools were involved and the strategy was of the 'network' or 'systematic social interaction' pattern referred to in the previous section. The direction of change was towards the integration of subjects, learning by enquiry and team teaching. Shipman found that the innovating teachers experienced anxieties arising from those elements of innovation which were characterised by what has been termed 'openness', e.g. loss of the security formerly to be derived from subject teaching, classroom teaching, and established modes of evaluation. The teachers experienced a variety of pressures, some of which arose from the fact that their schools continued to function in traditional ways. The key issues determining the success of the innovation were: the degree of initial investment made by the teachers and their schools, the degree of support from outside agencies, and the degree of support from the head and other teachers in the school.

Although not the only factor determining the success of this particular innovation, the support given by the school as a whole and its adaptive, creative capacity appears to have been most important. One might surmise that the support of the school for an innovation carrying a radical 'message' is likely to be forthcoming where the underlying pedagogical 'code' of the school is shifting. Where this is occurring, the institutionalisation of any innovation underpinned by the openness/flexibility code will be relatively easier to accomplish. But does the 'code' change as the result of the adoption of a number of 'message-carrying' innovations, in spite of the apparent difficulties of institutionalisation? Or does the prior innovation of a switch in the pedagogical code from within result in the successful institutionalis-ation of innovations already available?

Present evidence suggests that the major impetus for change comes from outside the school. At the same time there are indications that some schools are seeking to establish a positive attitude to innovation from with-in the school which is congruent with its pedagogical code. Such schools have been compared with the 'learning systems' described by Schon. They utilise the strategy which Havelock has termed 'problem-solving'. This approach identifies the *need*, translates this into a *problem*, conducts a *diagnosis*, and institutes a *search* and *retrieval* process for information which can be used in formulating or selecting an innovation. Set out thus, the procedure is perhaps described in terms which are too tidy. Problem-solving is rarely as neat as that. But it does at least indicate the approach which some schools are seeking to adopt where innovation is self-initiated on the basis of felt needs. But again, this approach is in itself quite a major inno-vation in the social system of the school.

3. Innovation and the Social System of the School

It is a major assumption of this paper that the school as a social system can be creative. This is not to deny the significance of the creative individual. Creative teachers and head teachers have been very important in the deve-lopment of educational innovation in Britain. They have been the prophets, the pathfinders — and often the rebels, who have caused educational institutions to take a look at themselves. But education is a shared enter-prise and even the rebels have had to persuade colleagues to adopt their proposals (and there have been some notable cases where rebels have been unable to gain this co-operation and their innovative efforts have not succeeded. — at least in that place at that time). But in the ordinary run of educational life it is the quality of the school as an institution which is the important factor since perhaps the majority of educational innovations involve groups of teachers if not entire schools. It is also an assumption of this paper that creativity requires the various components of the social system of the school to be, as it were, in phase and that there is no great discrepancy between values, internal organisation, authority patterns, curriculum and modes of teaching. One of the problems leading to the tissue-rejection of innovations is that there has been a lag between the new materials or methods and the organisational changes, finance, equipment and training facilities required to support them. In this section we can con-sider in turn several components of the social system of the school. In each case we can look at the traditional schools, identify the changes required to sustain a creative approach, examine some of the barriers encountered and suggest necessary changes. Although these dimensions are considered separately, it is important to appreciate that they are closely interrelated.

Authority

Any discussion of authority within the school must inevitably begin with a consideration of the role of the head teacher. It is frequently affirmed that the British head teacher has a greater degree of authority than his counterpart in other systems. This can be seen as a corollary of the relative freedom of the school from external control by outside bodies which gives the head teacher a high degree of responsibility for the internal affairs of the school. The head teacher combines in the one role both policy-making and administration functions. He heads the two hierarchies of the school: the academic hierarchy based upon subject departments in which the heads of department play a key role, and the pastoral/administrative hierarchy based on the administrative subdivisions of the school (e.g. houses) in which the head of division plays a key role.

Although the head teacher enjoys a considerable degree of authority, it should also be noted that the assistant teacher enjoys a considerable degree of autonomy. This is especially true where the unit of instruction is one teacher per class. Behind the closed doors of his classroom the teacher functions in a relatively private setting, observed by his pupils but not by other teachers. This isolation is supported by a strong professional norm which affirms the teacher's freedom from interference by other adults. His major constraint is the syllabus for his subject which he may or may not have been involved in devising. But he enjoys considerable autonomy in matters of teaching style, method and relationships with pupils. We thus have the situation where the head has a high degree of authority over matters of policy, but little control over the teacher's classroom work. On the other hand, the teacher has his classroom freedom but may be little involved in the policy decisions of the school.

The relative classroom autonomy of the teacher puts a premium on the head teacher's leadership skills. School policies have ultimately to be operationalised by teachers and this requires the head to perform his role in a manner which is sufficiently motivating. This is particularly relevant to innovation since leadership is essentially concerned with changing the school's goals or the procedures for attaining existing goals. The key role of the head teacher in the school is central to innovation. He has the necessary authority to introduce innovations into the school, he has the opportunity to view the school as a whole and hence to see the need for innovation, he has the contact with the 'messengers' of innovation (e.g. inspectors), and he controls the resources which innovation usually requires. Thus, not only does the head have the opportunity to initiate innovation himself, but, where an individual or group of teachers wishes to introduce an innovation into school, the support of the head is essential, for he must make the necessary resources available and arrange for any reorganisation in the school which may be involved. Thus, the innovativeness of schools has been very much a function of the leadership style of the head and his capacity both to initiate innovation and secure its implementation and also to encourage innovative activities on the part of teachers.

Given the key role of the head in the school, it would be easy to see the answer to the problems of innovation in terms of the leadership training of the head. This is undoubtedly important but is perhaps not sufficient. It is currently argued that a change in the authority *structure* of the school is necessary. This is based on the view that the present authority structure inhibits the innovativeness of teachers. There is this pressure for a move towards a *collegial* pattern of authority whereby professional equals govern their affairs by internal democratic procedures. This move has two major sources. It is partly the outcome of changes in the social and political climate with its growing emphasis on the participation in the decision-making process by those whom the decisions will affect. It is also partly suggested by changes in the nature of teaching which are bringing teachers into closer collaboration and hence involving more lateral decision-making in the school.

Many heads, especially in large schools, have created decision-making structures which involve teachers in policy making, and the very size of the newer secondary schools has necessitated more delegation than in the past to subject departments and school divisions. In some large schools the heads of lower, middle and upper 'schools' have delegated to them responsibility for most of the day-to-day running of their 'schools'. But it is argued that authority is still hierarchical and teachers are involved in decisions about the educational policy of the school to a lesser degree than they are involved in the administrative matters.

The greater involvement of teachers in decision-making may enhance the creativity of the school. On the other hand, there are some unanswered questions concerning the viability of collegial authority. One major question concerns the role of the head. At the present time he is responsible to his governors and to the LEA for the internal affairs of the school and must retain ultimate authority unless his responsibility is to pass formally to the staff as a collective to be exercised through an elected chairman. There are few signs of this possibility at the moment, although some schools have established 'academic boards' which debate school policy but do not usurp the final authority of the head teacher. The other question concerns the leadership role of the head with regard to innovation. There is little doubt that innovation owes much to the most progressive of British head teachers. The question must be asked whether the same initiative can be given by the collective leadership of teachers or whether self-cancelling 'veto groups' might not inhibit innovation. A further question concerns the willingness of teachers to participate in the exercise of collegial authority, since this would be an additional burden and perhaps detract from their work satisfaction which is mainly derived from the activity of teaching.

Eric Hoyle

There must remain open questions. What is required at the moment are experiments in different forms of decision-making patterns in schools. One notable experiment is being carried out at Countesthorpe College in Leicestershire [see the case study of Countesthorpe, page 347]. The school was established with a specific mandate to incorporate many of the current innovations in education within a single project. Its first warden, Tim McMullen (now with CERI) was appointed from the Nuffield Resources for Learning Project and two of his colleagues on the Project became members of the Countesthorpe staff. The curriculum innovations introduced included some interdisciplinary studies and the widespread use of self-instructional materials. Close relationships with the community were established and teacher-pupil relationships were liberalised. However, we are concerned here only with authority patterns. McMullen yielded his head's authority to the staff meeting (or 'moot') which met weekly to discuss the overall policy of the school. Although still formally responsible for the internal affairs of the school, the warden (headmaster) regarded himself as the chief executive of the policy board of the school which elected an executive committee of senior staff to be responsible for decisions which had to be taken in between meetings of the policy board [cf. Elizabeth Richardson's description of Nailsea School, p. 170].

Professional Relationships

The traditional structure of the British school involves the isolation of the teacher from his colleagues at the level of day-to-day work. The emphasis has been on specialised subject teaching with one teacher to one class as the basic form of organisation for instruction. Collaboration between teachers has been confined to deciding the content of the subject syllabus by members of an academic department – although this has been on a limited scale in some cases with the syllabus simply being handed down.

The trend is now towards a greater degree of interdependence amongst teachers. This is occurring at a number of levels. The breaking down of subject barriers and the increase of interdisciplinary enquiry has led to increased collaboration across subject departments. This has often been accompanied by team teaching. This term has, of course, many connotations, but it is used here in a broad sense to include those forms of teaching which involve a collaboration between teachers involving either the simultaneous teaching of a single group of pupils or the joint responsibility for a large number of pupils who may be learning in groups of different size. Another trend in the case of interdisciplinary teaching, and also in the case of discipline-based work, is for teachers to collaborate in the formulation of educational objectives. Finally, as noted in the previous section, as the pattern of authority in schools moves towards collegiality, teachers become increasingly involved with each other in formulating school policy.

The greater interdependence of teachers is in many ways conducive to

340

the creativity of the school. Under the system of independent class teaching the innovativeness of the individual teacher could go unnoticed. In a collaborative enterprise this would be observed by colleagues leading to the possibility of building up a body of good practice. Teachers bring to the joint enterprise different forms of knowledge and skill and different perspectives which are advantageous in two ways. The interplay of these individual differences is in itself creative in that it is mutually broadening for the teachers. And in a team situation it is possible to capitalise upon the particular strengths of individuals who can thus make different sorts of contribution to the enterprise as a whole.

The major problem which arises from interdependent professional relationships — as many reports have indicated — is that it is likely to generate anxieties in the teacher. He loses the anonymity of the classroom and must demonstrate his professionality to an audience of peers. It is necessary for him to acquire new knowledge and skills in a public setting. He loses the freedom to follow his mood and the opportunity to 'rest on his oars' from time to time which he has to some degree in a system of class teaching. And, since the main source of the secondary school teacher's professional identity is his subject, this is threatened as subject boundaries are broken down. The teacher may also see this loss of identity as a threat to his career prospects.

We thus see again the dilemma which is the central concern of this paper. Innovation requires a collaborative professional relationship, but a collaborative relationship is itself an innovation. It can only be slowly established over time if anxiety is to be reduced and it is related to changes in the professionality of teachers, to which we can now turn.

Professionality

Since professionality is an attribute of the individual, its inclusion in this section on the social system of the school might be queried. But professionality is not simply an input of the school. The school itself is a crucial agency of professional improvement — a point which will be stressed in the final section. It is for this reason that teacher professionality is here conceptualised as an aspect of the school.

Although a considerable oversimplification is involved, only two forms of professionality are hypothesised here.

The *restricted professional* can be hypothesised as having these characteristics amongst others:

A high level of classroom competence
Child-centredness (or sometimes subject-centredness)
A high degree of skill in understanding and handling children
Derives high satisfaction from personal relationships with pupils
Evaluates performance in terms of his own perceptions of changes

in pupil behaviour and achievement
Attends short courses of a practical nature

The *extended professional* has the qualities attributed to the restricted professional but has certain skills, perspectives and involvements in addition. His characteristics include the following:

Views work in the wider context of school, community and society
Participates in a wide range of professional activities, e.g. subject panels, teachers' centres, conferences
Has a concern to link theory and practice
Has a commitment to some form of curriculum theory and mode of evaluation

The movement from restricted to extended professionality would be considerable in the case of many teachers. There is evidence that many teachers who have an intuitive approach to teaching would find the requirements of extended professionality too rationalistic for their taste. Similarly, many teachers derive predominantly intrinsic interests from the activity of teaching and would not in the short term find satisfaction in the non-teaching activities which extended professionality involves.

We are thus, yet again, faced with our fundamental dilemma: innovation begets the need for innovation. It is tempting to see the answer to the problem of professionality in terms of the initial training of teachers where new patterns can be induced. There is much in this and the institutions of initial training are moving somewhat in that direction. But the inculcation of extended professionality is perhaps the concern of the institutions of in-service training, since it must arise out of experience. It will, therefore, be suggested in the final section of this paper that new modes of in-service training may be required to induce extended professionality.

Although this paper is concerned with secondary schools, it is instructive to look briefly at recent developments in the British primary school which caters for pupils up to the age of eleven years. The creativity of these schools had drawn very favourable comments from educationalists from many countries. The basic approach is developmental in that the stress is upon nurturing the growth of individual children through shifting the balance from formal class teaching to the creation of informal learning situations with an emphasis on exploration. The curriculum trend has been towards the integration of subjects, with the pupil's own environment taken as the starting point for much of this work. This shift in curriculum and method in the schools has been accompanied by a number of curriculum projects such as the Nuffield schemes for Mathematics and Science.

In spite of the existence of national curriculum projects for primary schools, the transformation has been an informal, relatively unplanned and more or less a spontaneous movement. In order to understand how creativity in the primary school has perhaps been less problematic than in the secondary school, it is necessary to look at their different structures. Firstly, primary education is founded upon class teaching and very limited specialisation. Then, the target of change is the individual teacher rather than the subject department or interdisciplinary team, and the fact that the class teacher is responsible for most aspects of children's learning means that a change in curriculum and method are likely to proceed as a piece and in phase. A second point to note is that the head teacher in the primary school, because of its relatively small size, and the greater opportunity for face-to-face contact, is perhaps in a stronger position than the head of a large secondary school to induce a more creative school environment. And there is little doubt from the available evidence that primary school head teachers, supported by LEA advisers, have played a key role in the recent transition. Thirdly, the relatively greater ease of pupil control in the primary school than in the secondary school is likely to be more conducive to the creativity – although one would not want to press this difference too far. Finally, as the primary schools in Britain have gradually shed their selective functions, they have come to enjoy a degree of freedom from external pressure which the secondary school still experiences in the form of the examination system and other forms of external expectation.

The secondary school can certainly take lessons from the primary school in terms of its general educational approach, but it is unlikely that the process of change in the primary school has a great deal of applicability to the secondary school – at least, given its present structure. Its problems are so different that it must work out its own solutions.

4. Support for the School

The argument of this paper so far has been that, although there has been considerable innovation in British schools in recent years, institutionalisation has been a problem since there has been a lag between innovations in curriculum, method and the organisation of teaching/learning and necessary changes in what might be termed the 'deep structure' of the school. This is inevitable, since such radical change must be a slow process. Changes in this 'deep structure' are being stimulated by the curriculum innovations themselves, but it is suggested that attention should be given to the supports which the school may need to effect this more fundamental shift without undue strain and anxiety for the staff. In this final section we can consider some aspects of the support which can be given and which, in some cases, is beginning to emerge. The focus will be upon the school itself and the immediate support which it might receive. The assumption is made that the target of this support should be, to a greater degree than in the past, the school itself. The professional development of the individual is, of course, also vital, but it is part of the argument of this section that professional development of the individual and the improvement of the creativity of the school proceed simultaneously.

There has been a considerable expansion of in-service training in Britain in recent years. This is likely to be further increased if the report on the James Committee on the training of teachers is implemented. This report recommended a further increase in provision with a proposal that every teacher should be entitled to one term's sabbatical leave for every seven (and, in time, every five) years served. In-service training at the present time takes many forms, varying from one-day courses on purely practical aspects of teaching, to courses of one or more years' duration leading to academic qualifications. For the most part, this in-service training involves teachers attending courses away from their schools *as individuals*. The argument advanced in the earlier sections of this paper might be seen as indicating the need for modifications in this pattern. Four propositions can be advanced.

1. In-service training should, to a greater extent than in the past, be linked with specific innovatory activities undertaken by the school. This happens to some degree at the present time where teachers attend courses to acquire knowledge and skills relevant to a particular innovation. But this can be extended and linked with the proposals below.

2. The focus of in-service training should be to some degree a functioning group, e.g. a school staff, a subject department, interdisciplinary teams. The training would thus concern itself not only with the content of change, but with procedures for implementing it.

3. In-service training should ideally begin in the school. The school should establish its own staff development programme. This should be a necessary preliminary to staff becoming involved in in-service training in outside institutions, since this outside support should build upon the requirements of the school which the in-school training will have generated. Ron Pepper, Headmaster of the Thomas Calton Comprehensive School in London, has given an account of the in-school programme developed at this school which, amongst other activities, was concerned with preparing to participate in a new team-based integrated studies scheme. At Codsall Comprehensive School, Staffordshire, the Resource Centre is also an agency for curriculum innovation and in-service training on the shop floor. Although time is inevitably a problem, staff are released from normal duties for periods of one week in order to think, talk and begin to prepare their own materials. Hartcliffe School in Bristol has recently appointed to its staff a person with special responsibility for this task.

4. The in-school training schemes should have access to the facilities and resources of a professional centre, e.g. libraries, resource centre, residential accommodation

One of the most interesting developments in the British educational system in recent years has been the Teachers' Centre. The majority of LEAs have established at least one of these in their areas. These centres function in very different ways but they generally act as a resource centre, a base for in-service courses and a place where teachers can hold meetings, conferences, etc. There is, perhaps, a case for considerably extending the functions of some of these centres to give a greater degree of support to innovating schools. The following can be suggested as possible functions:

(a) Linkage. This term is used to cover those functions which involve linking various institutions by acting as a resource centre (for project materials, research findings, etc.), an information centre, and a liaison between colleges, schools, etc., where a connection would be mutually advantageous.

(b) Project support. One of the difficulties of the RD & D approach to innovation is to ensure continuing support for a school project after the withdrawal of the development team, or where a school has not been involved in the development stage. The professional centre might provide support for these projects and also for projects initiated in a single school and in the process of local diffusion.

(c) Consultancy. The professional centre might be a base for permanent consultants or act as an agency putting schools in touch with consultants. It can be argued that, in order to innovate successfully, a school may need the support of an external consultant who might work with the school in a non-directive manner. The consultant might assist changes in the curriculum, the attitudes, skills and knowledge of staff members, relationships within the school, and school organisation.

(d) In-service training. The professional centre could be to provide in-service training. (It should be noted that the James Report recommends the establishment of professional centres based on universities, colleges or teachers' centres for the purpose of providing in-service training. The report does not, however, go into details as to what other functions such a centre would provide).

Finally, we can consider the roles of the HMI and local inspectorate. Inspectors of both kinds have played a most important role in curriculum innovation in this country in recent years, by advising schools on specific innovations, arranging courses and conferences, and generally acting as resource persons. They have not, however, usually performed the consultancy role as described above — although there has been a move in this direction. We do not, at the moment, have a great deal of information on the functions performed by inspectors, but the indications are that they are too involved in other duties — particularly administration — to give the sort of help which many of them feel that they have to offer. There might be a case for developing this into a distinctive consultancy role based upon a professional centre.

Eric Hoyle

Conclusion

The main argument of the paper has been that, although British schools have been willing to introduce innovations, there have been problems in their institutionalisation. This is, perhaps, due to the discrepancy between requirements of the innovation and the quality of the social system of the school. A school which is free to establish its own staff—staff relations, forms of pupil grouping, arrangements for teaching and curriculum; its own form of staff-pupil relations, of school—social environment co-operation and so on, including influence over the promotion of its own educational ideology and a measure of involvement in the in-service education of its staff, is more likely to innovate than a school which does not have this autonomy. At the same time it is suggested that, in order to effect internal changes, a school should have access to a variety of supporting agencies.

NOTES

1. As used throughout this paper, the term *institutionalisation* implies that the school is to some degree transformed by the innovation and a new level of functioning achieved. It does not imply that the school adopts the innovation to fit to its own value system and procedures. It is also assumed that the innovation itself may, in time, undergo further change as circumstances alter.

Part VII

CASE STUDY

28. COUNTESTHORPE COLLEGE

Gerald Bernbaum

From *Case Studies of Educational Innovation: III. At the School Level* (CERI/OECD, Paris, 1973).

Countesthorpe College is a secondary school in Leicestershire which opened in 1970. Although intended ultimately as a school for 14–18-year-old pupils, it began with pupils aged 11–14.

The Director of Education, Stuart Mason, wanted to build a secondary school which would promote some of the practices which he admired in primary schools: the emphasis on individual learning and group work, interdisciplinary studies, and a more flexible timetable.

The case study — written soon after the school opened — concentrates first on the goals of the school as seen by administrators, teachers, parents and pupils. Next the management of the innovations is considered. Finally, four innovations (individualized learning, the interdisciplinary curriculum, staff democracy, and the move to greater equity in pupil/teacher relationships) are considered in their social context. These very early impressions by Bernbaum should be compared with later studies, e.g. 'Portrait of Countesthorpe', Case Study in the Open University course E203 *Curriculum Design and Development,* Open University Press, 1976, and *Countesthorpe College; the first five years,* edited by John Watts, George Allen and Unwin (forthcoming).

The Goals of the School

In much contemporary writing on educational administration and the sociology of the school it is common to talk of the 'goals of the school'. In reality, however, it is difficult to see how these can be explicated except in terms of the goals and purposes of individuals or groups of individuals. It follows therefore, that different individuals or different groups might hold different goals with respect to the nature and work of the school. Clearly the investigation of these different goals is a major empirical task. Nevertheless, the goals of the administrators, teachers, pupils and parents will be discussed in the light of the overall work and design of the school.

Administrators

It should be noted that, given the long tradition of the autonomy of English schools, it is extremely difficult for detailed interference by the local authority to occur on a day-to-day basis. Thus, as Mason [the Director of Education] pointed out, the establishment of the school, its design, and the appointment of its headmaster were to a large degree technical and professional matters which concerned his department only. Once the head was appointed he had almost complete freedom in appointment of staff. As a result, therefore, any political or educational opposition to the school can only make itself felt after the school has been established and its working pattern is known. It follows that it is important to understand fully the goals, or more general aspirations, of Stuart Mason, the Director of Education for the County of Leicestershire, and Tim McMullen, the Headmaster, or Warden, as he prefers to be known.

As far as Mason is concerned, the discussion of the design of the school has shown the generally progressive orientation of his goals. It is not only a question of Mason believing that his job as an educational administrator is to build schools which will be able to keep pace with more general changes in education. It is also the case that Mason believes in fostering and encouraging what might be termed progressive changes. Thus, at interview Mason denied that he was neutral with respect to these developments. 'I take sides', declared Mason, 'but I hope I take sides open-mindedly, fairly, so to speak...I think educational administration fares better if it is positive rather than negative...' In his own words Mason is anxious to establish in the schools 'the kind of atmosphere where people can have a go... it's much better to have had a go and failed than not to have had a go at all.' Mason claims that he is not anxious to prescribe the sort of things which people should do but he does 'believe in the general kind of trend...I mean I do believe that individual learning...is a better thing than class learning.' Moreover he argues 'that anything that moves towards a development of all the talents and interests of each individual is basically good.' In the setting up and establishment of the school at Countesthorpe, Mason clearly recognizes his own contribution and the diffuse origins of his ideas; thus he claims that as far as the conception of the school goes, 'it is awfully difficult to claim that it is me or that it's someone else; I think that a lot of the basic ideas probably originated from me, though I don't mean that I invented them. For whenever I thought that I invented anything I immediately observed...that somebody else thought of it and that it's happening somewhere else.' Thus as far as Mason was concerned, his main goal in establishing the school at Countesthorpe was to provide the conditions under which all kinds of opportunities would be available to the teachers and pupils of the school. It was vitally important, therefore, that great care was taken with the appointment of the headmaster. As the headmaster has a great deal of control over the choice of staff and the internal organization of the school, his goals and orientation with regard to education can be a significant determinant of the work and ethos of a school. Mason clearly recognized this, for he argued that, 'Having built a school that is so obviously on the side of the trends in which education appears to be moving...quite obviously we would be looking for somebody who was in sympathy with the changes...and we would very much like to have somebody who is a bit ahead'.

Headmaster

From a very large number of applicants, Tim McMullen was chosen to be Headmaster. He has had a crucial influence on the early life of the school and it is imperative that his ideas, goals and objectives are examined in detail. Fortunately it is possible to do this, utilizing three main sources. In 1968 McMullen published an article entitled 'Flexibility for a Comprehensive School' in the journal *Forum*, in which he set forth, in great detail, the objectives he would have if he were to be put in charge of a comprehensive school.[1] Moreover, he reflects on the changes that have occurred in his own thinking since he was appointed to his first headship, ten years previously, in 1958. This article will be used as a major source of data in relation to McMullen's ideas. Secondly, in February 1971 McMullen lectured to a group of postgraduate students of the University of Leicester School of Education about his school at Countesthorpe. This lecture was tape recorded and will also be used in the ensuing discussion of McMullen's goals, purposes and aspirations. Finally, for this research project McMullen was interviewed at length in order to probe, in depth, his views and attitudes on education, and his part in establishing the school.

When McMullen first became a headmaster of a school in the late 1950s, he claimed to have three major aims. His first objective was to develop the intellectual ability of every child through exposure to academic work. McMullen was convinced that more children were capable of success at the public examinations of Ordinary and Advanced Levels than was normally thought possible. Thus, he emphasized the importance of examinations for career success and encouraged organizational arrangements in the school which differentiated children by academic ability. His second aim was to ensure that each child was looked after as an individual. He wished to be confident that someone knew each child's personal and social background, and to achieve this a member of staff with a reduced teaching load was given special responsibility for the pastoral care of 150–250 children. Finally, McMullen was anxious to establish a relaxed and friendly atmosphere in the school; to create this, authority was to be related to the person of the teacher and his activities rather than to the teacher's position as such.

In the decade of the 1960s, however, McMullen's thinking changed radically, and he now no longer looks upon his initial objectives as adequate. Important in his redefinition of the situation has been the awareness of the need for a clear set of objectives, which almost certainly stems from his work on curriculum and resources development. Nevertheless, accompanying the substantive changes in his ideas has been his growing concern with what he sees as the increasing rapidity of social change. McMullen is particularly impressed by the importance for education of changes coming in the world between 1975 and 2025, which is the time during which the present generation of schoolchildren will live their adult lives. McMullen emphasizes especially the immense potential changes in technology which will, he believes, have the effect of rendering particular skills out of date. The aim of education, therefore, should be to develop general abilities in the children. At the same time, McMullen attaches great importance to the increased leisure which will be available to people in the future. Simply, McMullen's argument is that change is coming about in schools because of a growing awareness that traditional education does not fulfil the needs of the students in a changing society. As he has said, the old style education is inappropriate, as 'the country is changing, society is changing and the changes are coming fast'.

In his article in *Forum,* McMullen has set out clearly his ideas on the possible future relationship between education and society. According to McMullen, the rapidity of change implies

> that the individual who will achieve satisfaction over this coming half century must have a clear sense of his own identity and ability, must have developed intellectual and emotional strategies that make for adaptation to change. Emotional satisfaction must come entirely from his relationships with the small groups he lives, plays and works with, but these may change over his lifetime and may involve others from differing social and racial backgrounds. He is unlikely to develop an absolute ethos that will serve him for the fifty years of his adult life; he will need to decide on ethical guide lines at any given moment, but he must also be prepared to re-examine them in the light of changing social structures and organization. In the face of shorter working hours and less exacting or stimulating work, he will have to develop a full life outside his working hours, one that allows him intellectual, emotional and physical actions that bring satisfaction.[2]

This lengthy quotation offers an impression of the overall goals which McMullen has for a school and a system of education. Inevitably, since they were presented at a very high level of generality, they required more particular explication if they were to be operationalized in a practical fashion, a task which has been undertaken by McMullen in a recent article, 'The Clarification of Aims and Objectives as an Aid to Making Decisions', in *Teachers as Managers,* edited by George Taylor.

McMullen approached the question of operationalizing the generalized goals by looking at the content of education and the methods of teaching. He asked, 'What is the most relevant knowledge to the 16-year-old? and provided the answer that the 16-year-old should know about himself, about his relationship with people and about the various parts of society which he is going to go into. A major objective was therefore 'to give the individual knowledge about himself, his relationships to the small groups he works, lives and plays with and the relationship of these groups to the larger societies.[3] Similarly, McMullen has urged that children have to be given the chance to develop various attitudes, and also their personalities, but he has insisted it is for 'them to develop, not us to instil'. Thus it was important that the school encouraged the children to study independently for a distant objective, planning their 'own work and overcoming immediate pressure from drives that would divert them from their goal'. Equally, though, McMullen wanted the children to be able to work as members of a group for a corporate end, subduing their own drives for a common end.

In order to foster the capacity to cope with new situations, McMullen advocates strategies that 'include both the ability to deduce principles from data and ability to induce instances from general principles'. Moreover, these strategies 'must also include strategies for problem solving which embrace both scientific proof and judgment'. In all of this, though, McMullen reminds us to remember always 'that it is the principles and concepts governing relationships rather than information about the structure that is important'.[4] In terms of pedagogy, therefore, McMullen is led to advocate individualized learning in order that each child can proceed at his own pace, develop his own motivation, and hence study independently. Similarly, McMullen favours giving the opportunity to pupils of choice and options, in order that individual motivation and responsibility might be increased.

It is not only in the curriculum and the teaching arrangements that McMullen has made a leading innovative contribution to Countesthorpe College, since one of the most novel aspects of the school is the staff democracy. It is this feature which has been the subject of much attention and for which McMullen can claim most of the responsibility. He suggests that an important factor which brought about a change in his thinking, and which led him to reconsider his own fairly autocratic views on being a headmaster, were the events in Paris in which the students questioned the basis of many of the traditional forms of authority. Essentially, what McMullen is anxious to achieve is a 'position where the policy of the school is decided by the staff as a whole', and he justifies this, as he does many of his other ideas, in terms of his estimates of the future. 'If you actually really believe, as I do believe, that the development of the next fifty years will be to mix a central elective democracy such as we've got at the moment with a great increase in the rate of grass roots participatory democracy...(then) we shall increase very considerably the people controlling effectively the matters that effect their everyday lives...then you've got to start it in a school.' Moreover, McMullen is confident that greater staff participation in the government of the school will tend to improved efficiency in the overall organization and management of the academic and social arrangements.

McMullen makes few claims to be the absolute originator of the ideas which he is attempting to operationalize and practise at Countesthorpe. He indicates that many of the innovations in respect of the curriculum can be traced to his experience with the *Nuffield Resources for Learning Project* in which he was associated with a large team, and which in turn drew many of its proposals from the United States. As far as individualized learning is concerned, a major influence has been Taylor's book *Resources for Learning.*

Nevertheless, it is not only important to consider McMullen's goals and their intellectual origins at a personal level, but is equally vital to see how the objectives and goals have been established at an organizational level within the school. Fortunately, there are good documentary sources for doing this as the Warden and his staff have produced papers which are designed to explain the purposes of the school to parents, and to applicants for teaching posts at the school.

Central to the arguments in these documents is that the opportunity is being offered by the foundation of the new school to rethink the total process of learning within the school, for according to authors 'it should mean that we do not automatically repeat an established practice without considering why'. At the same time, however, it is regarded as essential that the *relative* importance of the objectives is established, because they are not looked upon as being of equal significance. Therefore it is argued that 'the major over-riding consideration is to provide children with the desire to achieve the objectives we consider essential, the motivation'. This is seen as being of two kinds (1) Internal — that is, the arousal of interest in the work for its own sake; (2) External — the pupils' desire to achieve some distant goal — e.g. an examination or career success, though here it is argued that the staff need to stress the importance of all objectives aimed at in relation to working, living and enjoying, rather than concentrating on the narrow concept of the examination. Also, the pupils' desire to please or not displease peers, staff and parents is regarded as a potent source of motivation. From these general propositions five classes of objectives are derived, and described as the most important features of the educational process — knowledge; skills; creative and expressive actions; personality factors and attitudes.

In the area of knowledge the main point is considered to be that the curriculum should be directed clearly to the 'student's knowledge of himself, his relationships with others, both individuals and groups, of groups and their behaviour, of local, national and international aspects of society — in that order of importance'. Similarly, the student must come to understand his environment and man's interaction with it. Again, though, the perspective is interdisciplinary, as it is suggested that there is 'a clear need for the selection of those principles and concepts which have a *direct* bearing on the pupil's understanding of the environment, not on the further development of the subject discipline itself'.

As far as 'logical processes' are concerned the emphasis here is to be on problem-solving, particularly the recall and selection of relevant principles, the construction of hypotheses and the testing of hypotheses against the data. In the long run, therefore, this should lead to a much more problem-based curriculum. The authors then move on to consider a set of objectives relating to 'skills' and 'creative and expressive actions'. The relevant sections are quoted in full in order to show the difficulties of attempting to translate general aspirations into precise goals.

Skills

    (i) Communication skills

        (*a*) Oral Communication
        (*b*) Social Communication
        (*c*) Reading
        (*d*) Writing
        (*e*) Numerical and symbolic communication
        (*f*) Graphical communication and communication by a static visual image
        (*g*) Communication by a moving visual image – as in film and T.V.
        (*h*) Communication as in (*a*) and (*d*), in a foreign language

    (ii) Skills related to other objectives – i.e. performance skills in music, craft skills, physical skills.

Creative and Expressive Actions

    (i) Ability and desire to carry out such actions in some of the following fields:

        (*a*) Two and three dimensional arts and crafts

        (*b*) Words, music, drama and movement

        (*c*) In applied science 'invention' and construction

        (*d*) In the field of athletic and sporting activity

    (ii) In all areas, an ability to produce 'new' ideas and concepts; to think laterally rather than convergently.

Finally, there is a long statement of objectives which relate to 'Personal Characteristics and Attitudes'. Thirteen separate items are listed, including such things as 'An ability to understand, as well as possible, one's own behaviour and the motives that lie behind it', 'The ability to organize one's own work and play', 'A development and recognition of one's own moral code', 'An ability to recognize the nature of social situations and to find the right reactions for them'. It is clear, as the staff recognize, that there are likely to be many difficulties in translating the generalized goals into precise behavioural objectives. Indeed, in the early months of the school's life all who work in it have been very much involved in this task. Work which it is recognized will have to be continued in the coming years. A great deal of attention has been given to the objectives set out by Tim McMullen because he has played the most important part in establishing the school and in the appointment of the staff. The statements of formal goals obtained from him in different contexts represent significant clues to our understanding of the organizational climate of the school.

Teachers

In discussing teachers' goals, expectations and self-perceptions it is important to remember that the school at Countesthorpe is the microcosm of the county of Leicestershire. Just as the county recruits teachers who might be especially interested in educational experiment, so Countesthorpe College attracts teachers who are especially committed to change and innovation. Indeed, as Mason approved McMullen's appointment because of the latter's orientation to new ideas in education so, in turn, McMullen has recruited to the staff teachers who are anxious to innovate. Thus 61 per cent of the staff perceive themselves as having been involved in innovations in the syllabus at schools before they came to Countesthorpe and 55 per cent in innovations in methods of teaching. If it is noted that 22 per cent of the staff had no previous teaching experience, then the high proportion of innovators amongst the staff who came from other schools is clear.

The selection procedures for the new school, therefore, seem likely to lead to staff being chosen who would reflect the goals for the school set out by McMullen. Thus, over 90 per cent of the teachers in the school agree that Countesthorpe can be seen 'as the school of the future' and that it will be 'influential in bringing about change in educational organization'. Similarly, an examination of staff responses to the open-ended sections of the questionnaire dealing with the objectives of their own teaching shows clearly that McMullen's perspectives are shared by many members of staff. Thus a young science teacher designates as her main objectives making 'the science taught here more relevant to everyday life than that usually taught'. Similarly, an experienced teacher in the science area describes his objectives as getting 'a genuine enthusiastic interest in science', and encouraging pupils 'to look at all things in a enquiring way'.

Other teachers also align themselves with McMullen's goals when they speak of their own aims in terms of firing 'children's interests to do work on their own by choice, not as a pointless chore', or in 'developing for the children's interest, understanding and enjoyment in the subject rather than on proficiency in mathematical skills'. It is surprising, however, that not one of the teachers listed his definite objectives in precise behavioural terms such as is usually done in modern work on curriculum development. The majority could only describe their goals with respect to the curriculum very generally. Evidence of this kind, along with careful observation of the staff, suggests that they are interested in the expressive features of their work rather than in the cognitive and instrumental aspects of it. Support for this argument can be drawn from the fact that when the staff were invited to indicate which one innovation they regarded as the most important, the largest single group, 45 per cent, chose 'greater equality in social relations between staff and children'. Only 11 per cent, for example, selected the 'inter-disciplinary curriculum', and just 25 per cent chose 'individualized learning'.

Evidence such as this suggests that the teachers at Countesthorpe are not representative of the teaching profession as a whole. Musgrove and Taylor [5] in their study of teachers, parents and pupils found that 'all groups of teachers placed the greatest emphasis on teaching and saw others placing great weight on this function'.[6] There are other studies which suggest that secondary school teachers tend to identify with the subjects which they teach and to give less importance to their relationship with pupils. Musgrove and Taylor's work, however, is especially relevant in that they argue that the head teacher is a particular source of anxiety and conflict to the ordinary class teacher. Thus, they write, 'in comparison with pupils, head teachers are seen as attaching little importance to friendly, sympathetic and understanding personal relationships'.[7] At Countesthorpe, though, this cannot be the case, for, as has been shown, the quality of inter-personal relationships in the school is one of McMullen's major concerns; as he has stated in a policy document for parents.

> the system of governing the school and the relations within it...are different and have two main aims; to develop a sense of real democracy in deciding on the policy of the school; and secondly, to replace, as far as possible, the sense that adolescents and adults are two armed camps, by a feeling that we are all people of the same kind co-operating in trying to make a reasonable life.

At Countesthorpe, therefore, there is unlikely to be the marked incongruence between head teacher, pupils and teachers in respect of their perceptions of the quality of personal relationships which Taylor and Musgrove suggest exists elsewhere. As one very experienced teacher put it,

Gerald Bernbaum

'This is the very first place I've been in where people have really cared for every child'.

Before concluding this section dealing with teachers it should be noted that, as in many other social contexts, there is the possibility that differences might exist between the stated goals and the real goals as they turn out to be held in practice. This possibility is likely to increase when the statements of goals are of a very generalised kind and perhaps of an ideological nature. There is some evidence that this is the situation at Countesthorpe, where the long term educational objectives of the staff discussed earlier are occasionally submerged beneath the more immediate concerns with control, motivation and activity of pupils. This is particularly the case with those pupils with low achievement and who do not share the dominant values of the staff. That there might be a shift from the overtly educational goals described above to goals more immediately concerned with social control can be seen from one teacher's comment about these difficult pupils that 'though they're great big tough boys they'll sit and play with Lego for hours;[8] I'm quite prepared to let them play with Lego – but I don't know about their parents.'

Forty years ago in his classic analysis of *The Sociology of Teaching,* Willard Waller maintained that 'parents and teachers are natural enemies, each predestined for the discomfiture of the other'.[9] Since that time, however, it is possible that teachers and parents may have moved into closer accord. The problem is to discover the degree to which they recognise this movement.

Biddle and his associates have recently conducted a large international comparative study of teachers' role conceptions and conflicts in England, Australia, New Zealand and the United States of America.[10] Teachers in all four countries placed comparatively little emphasis on social advancement as an object of instruction, yet all saw parents as placing the greatest emphasis on this objective. Moreover, the largest gap between teachers and perceived parental expectations occurred in England. Teachers in England thoroughly disagreed with parents over the emphasis to be given to social advancement. More accurately, they thoroughly disagreed with what they *thought* was the emphasis that parents gave. These findings are strongly supported by those of Taylor and Musgrove, who also found that 'teachers take an unflattering view of parents...seeing them as indifferent to moral training but very concerned with social advancement'.[11] In fact, though, the teachers perceived the parents wrongly and the parents really were in some agreement with the teachers. Thus Taylor and Musgrove conclude, 'teachers in all types of school see their role in moral and intellectual terms and are comparatively indifferent to the more specifically social aims of education'. They go on to emphasize the great importance attached by both teachers and parents to instruction in school subjects.

356

Parents

Now, these findings are useful in arriving at an understanding of the parents' attitudes towards Countesthorpe. Many parents have already expressed their anxieties that the school might not meet their expectations with respect to both instruction in subjects and social advancement. Their concerns have been expressed in private and in public and there have been many questions put to McMullen and his staff about these issues. Indeed, the teachers regarded it as one of their most important tasks to put over to the parents the nature and purposes of the school and the long-term goals held by the staff. Clearly, many parents do not find the practices of the school familiar to them and suspect that their children may be disadvantaged as compared with those who are being educated in more formal situations.

In many respects, what the teachers are experiencing is very similar to those problems faced by those who introduced progressive educational innovations in the junior schools. There is a sense, nevertheless, in which the parental anxieties might be well founded. Evidence from the junior school does suggest that children taught by informal methods progress more slowly at the beginning, but that they catch up as they get older. If, however, this pattern is reproduced in the secondary sphere then the parents are likely to express initial anxieties. Furthermore, though middle-class parents are likely to understand more readily the abstract and long-term goals associated with educational innovation, they are also likely to be those who are most capable of understanding the demands and constraints imposed by the occupational and economic systems upon the schools, and the necessity for their children to achieve the kind of success in education which can be publicly measured. Equally, they will be the parents who can articulate their demands and anxieties to the school, both individually to their children and their teachers and corporately through the Parents Association and the local authority. The working-class parents, in so far as they have clearly defined objectives for their children at school, may be totally unable to articulate these through any form of voluntary association. There is a real possibility, therefore, that through parental differences in social class the main focus for experiment and innovation in the long run may be the non-achieving working-class pupils.

Pupils

Finally, consideration must be given to the expectations of the pupils. There is a great deal of evidence which suggests that under conventional, traditional arrangements, the pupils expect teachers to teach. They value lucid exposition, the clear statement of problems and guidance in their solution. Personal qualities of kindness, sympathy and patience are secondary, appreciated by pupils if they make the teacher more effective in carrying out his primary, intellectual task. As Musgrove and Taylor argue, 'there appears to be little demand by pupils that teachers shall be friends or temporary mothers and fathers. They are expected to assume an essentially intellectual and instrumental role'.[12] Moreover, enquiries conducted in England and America over fifty years have pointed to this conclusion. As long ago as 1896 Kratz showed that schoolchildren demanded 'help in study' as the first requirement of their teachers. In the 1930s Hollis studied over 8,000 children in a variety of schools, finding that the characteristic of teachers which they valued most highly was the ability to explain difficulties patiently. In the early 1950s Michael, in the United States, found that the older adolescent pupils regarded the teacher's method of teaching as his most important attribute. Of less importance were the teacher's personality and his mode of enforcing discipline. These findings are similar to those of Allen in English secondary modern schools. Both boys and girls were found to value most highly the teacher's competence as an instructor, his pedagogical skills.

There is little evidence from the general studies that pupils are encouraging their teachers to adopt goals which are less specifically pedagogical. Home rather than school is still the main source of expressive, emotional satisfactions. Musgrove has shown [13] that the school and its teachers are expected to meet instrumental (mainly intellectual) needs. His study of adolescents' demands of home and school has shown this sharp contrast in expectations for the two institutions. At the moment, remembering that all the Countesthorpe pupils have come from conventional schools, there is some evidence to suggest that the children are not very different from those reported in the major studies quoted. Obviously, it is the hope and the intention of the staff that exposure to the new teaching methods and procedures for control will quickly modify the expectations of the pupils as they go through the school. Meanwhile it is interesting to note that when the staff were asked which factors most constrained them in the innovations they might wish to introduce in their teaching, the two items chosen most frequently were 'Lack of Adequate Teaching Material', and 'Previous Educational Experience' of children. Together these two items accounted for 55 per cent of the choices from a list of nine. It is possible to argue, therefore, that the teachers are facing difficulties precisely because their own concern with the expressive, pastoral side of their work is not matched by the pupils', who are anxious for their teachers to teach. Informal discussions with pupils suggest that this is the case; some seem uncertain in the more unstructured situation and those who have goals which relate to academic qualifications, educational success and social advancement feel that they run the risk of having them thwarted. Similarly, it is worth noting that only 8 per cent of the staff are dissatisfied with the nature of relationships between children and staff in the school, yet in the cognitive, instrumental areas, 55 per cent are not satisfied with the operation of individualized learning in the school, and 75 per cent are not satisfied with the operation of inter-disciplinary schemes of work in the school.

In many respects the nature of the staff dissatisfactions can be attributed to the difficulties associated with establishment of a new school. Particularly important in this case was the fact that the builders were still on the site when the school opened, and that supplies and materials from the local authority were held up owing to unusual difficulties in the relevant department at the central supplying agency. Difficulties of this kind may well have exaggerated the problems facing the staff in respect of their teaching roles.

Future Pupils

Another perspective on the expectations and goals which pupils have for Leicestershire upper schools can be gained by referring to some comments made by those young people of 14 who are in the high schools and are approaching the point of transfer to the upper schools. Such an investigation was conducted to run parallel to the present study.[14] The pattern of results is remarkably similar to those in the large-scale studies already reported. The children who are potential pupils at Countesthorpe indicate that they have goals in the area of social mobility and recognize the part that academic qualifications will play in realizing the goals. Consequently, some are anxious about the nature of teaching and the orientations of the teachers at Countesthorpe. Thus they maintain 'that it will not be as good because at Countesthorpe you do not have to work if you don't want to. If you're the sort of person who wants a good job yet you cannot be bothered to work, then it is not really going to do you any good, whereas here you have to work, or else you've had it ' (14-year-old boy). Similarly a 14-year-old girl does not think that Countesthorpe will be better than her present school, 'because a lot of my friends who attend Countesthorpe say that you have no homework and that you are not worked hard. This is all needed if you want to study 'O' levels.' Others emphasize anxieties about learning – 'I don't think you will learn as much, it seems a very carefree school', 'It will not be as good as here, because we will not have set work', 'It will not be as good because most of the teachers don't help you.'

It should be noted that this kind of evidence only tells us about pupils' perceptions and does not give us real information about the learning undertaken by children at Countesthorpe. Nevertheless, it is very helpful in explaining some of the dissatisfactions felt by the staff, especially in the light of their own orientations towards education, and their emphasis on the expressive relationships with pupils. Many years ago Waller argued that the effective teacher should maintain a marked social distance from his pupils, and that he must be relatively meaningless as a person. More recently, the foremost sociologist concerned with the study of organizations has asserted that when expressive relationships are emphasized unduly, whether in a school or factory, instrumental relationships may be impaired. [15] Insistence on getting the job done might put at risk the friendliness between subordinates and those in authority; too much concern with friendliness may mean that the more difficult tasks are never seriously attempted. At Countesthorpe, in the initial stages, there are suggestions that the staff recognize the problem. One female teacher indicates her realization of the dilemma when she notes that what the staff have to resolve is whether they 'want to be liked more than they want to be respected for what they teach or get kids to do'.

Innovation and Management

So far the discussion of innovation at Countesthorpe has concentrated upon the establishment and design of the school, and upon the examination of the goals, objectives and expectations of those teachers, pupils and parents who are associated with the school. Now, however, the study will describe and explain the nature of the innovations at Countesthorpe, and later discussion will investigate the working of the innovations in practice. It is important to remember that the school is, at the time of writing, little more than six months old and some of the innovatory features are not yet fully operational; also, it is important to note that in the initial stages at least, the senior members of staff had the opportunity to exercise their power to innovate according to their own predispositions. It might be helpful, therefore, to be reminded of the aspirations of those who were instrumental in preparing the initial plans for the operation of the school.

> We hope, they wrote in an early document, to educate children for the world they will live in, the world of 1975 to 2025 – not for the world of the last fifty years; we believe this means the all-round development of brain, personality and body. To think rather than to memorize; to develop high skills in all forms of communication – in speech, in social communication as well as in writing and reading; in attitudes to themselves and to others that will enable them to cope with, and contribute to, the changes in standards of private and public behaviour; to earn a living in a world in which work, for some, becomes increasingly technological – and in itself subject to change – for others, involves greater contacts with people, and for yet others, becomes duller in content and shorter in duration; to develop interests and abilities of all kinds to enrich their leisure time; and finally, to enable them to participate in making sensible decisions in their work and play, and in the community.

In order to attain these wide-ranging and multifarious aims a variety of new ideas has been put into practice at Countesthorpe. Each on its own is probably not totally novel, though the accumulation of innovation in one school most certainly is. The innovations may be considered under broad titles; the learning, the curriculum (subjects and contents), the organization, staff relationships, staff—pupil relationships, and relationships with the local community.

Learning

The innovations in respect of the curriculum and timetable arrangements have been far-reaching. The timetable has been set up so that the chronological teaching unit is longer than in most schools. The day is split into four periods, two morning and two afternoon, whereas the normal division in English schools is into six or seven periods a day. At Countesthorpe, therefore, each lesson is about eighty minutes long. In the initial planning stages most of the staff accepted that long spans of time would be more appropriate to the kind of work they wished to undertake, for it would enable more integrated subject material to be studied and also make for greater flexibility in the grouping of the pupils.

Furthermore, in order to encourage children to work independently and to exercise choice in their own work, certain periods of the week have been set aside for 'independent non-timetable study time'. As the staff proposed in their early plans, 'this is to encourage the ability in children to work by themselves, to show initiative, and to plan work; it is therefore necessary to ensure that this does not involve too much staff guidance and supervision'. In fact, this policy of independent work time only serves to symbolize the great emphasis within the school on individualized learning and group work. In the school as a whole, class teaching on a didactic fashion is at a minimum. As a document dealing with suggested practical applications of the overall organization of the school indicates, though class teaching might be efficient for imparting knowledge of a limited nature to homogeneous groups, it will not achieve adequate results when the full range of objectives are to be achieved, and where the groups are not homogeneous. It also limits the kind of motivation that can be aroused. It should be noted that there are hardly any academically homogeneous groups at Countesthorpe. The staff, then, postulate three main learning situations:

(a) The student works by himself from or on various media.
(b) A small group of children work together: a pair up to five making a small group.
(c) A seminar group work with a teacher; perhaps up to fifteen children, and occasionally large teaching groups for films or lectures.

Various mixtures of the arrangements are recommended in this initial advisory document for staff, it being argued that the exact mixture of methods desirable will certainly vary from subject to subject, from group to group, and even from individual to individual. Now, individual or group methods for teaching have been proposed by many different educationalists throughout this century, but although in the last twenty years such methods have been widely adopted in English primary schools, it is unlikely that any secondary school has embraced the principles of individualized learning to the extent of Countesthorpe College.

Inevitably, such an approach to learning relies very heavily upon the production of materials upon which the children can work. At Countesthorpe, individualized learning in all fields is closely dependent upon the production of work sheets. In some cases these work sheets are available from commercial sources, or have been made available through some central educational agency. When this is the case then the teachers can use what is presented or modify the worksheets for their own purposes. Thus the Mathematics Department is using material based on modified School Mathematics Project materials and a BBC programme. The teachers in the humanities areas are using both Nuffield and American materials. One fourth year option on control technology is based upon Project Technology, and another on computers on a course built up by the computer firm itself. As has already been indicated, a very high proportion of the staff with teaching experience perceived themselves as having been involved with innovation in their previous schools. In the majority of cases these innovations were concerned with the production of materials upon which the children could work. In many respects therefore, both in terms of the earlier experience of the staff and the widespread use of centrally produced pre-packaged material, many of the plans at Countesthorpe are made possible as a result of the innovation that has already happened in schools in the past few years. Nevertheless, since Countesthorpe takes these plans very much further, and the existing materials are not as yet sufficient for their operation, it is a vital part of the staff's task at Countesthorpe to produce new materials. Clearly this is viewed as a major concern, as the document already quoted on the practical application of the advice for staff sternly reminds the teachers that 'it is important that the initial generous staff ratio, which is given to all new schools for the first three years, is *not* used to reduce group size but to make materials'. Nevertheless, the shortage of technical staff at the school has placed even greater responsibility for the production of materials upon the teaching staff.

The emphasis on individualized work sheets stems from the goals of the staff with respect to the motivation of the children, and the concern to let the pupils work at their own pace. The pupils can proceed through the work sheets at their own rate, under the guidance and supervision of the staff. Those who are capable of quick and accurate work will cover more material, or the staff will have the flexibility to provide them with more detailed and advanced work in the fields in which the rest of the group are engaged. Obviously the content of the work sheets will differ between the various subject areas, but the aim is to achieve a full coverage of approaches to learning. Thus, some work sheets are almost 'self-contained', the sheet offering the pupil certain types of information and following this up with questions designed to explore the child's understanding of the information and, perhaps, provide him with the opportunity to discuss the material in a new context. Alternatively, the latter part of the work sheet might suggest a short project for the pupil to follow up the original information. The project will be such that the pupil will be required to draw upon his own initiative and motivation in order to pursue material contained say, in the resource area and library. In science the work sheets are frequently more practical. They enable the pupil to set up an experiment and guide him through the observations and measurements necessary for its completion. Moreover, the work sheets can be developed in such a way as to enable a group of students to work collectively on a project. Obviously, in terms of the stated goals of Tim McMullen and many staff, individualized learning of the kind described is an important educational innovation. It is well to remember, however, that its success or failure is very dependent on a range of technical facilities being available for the reproduction, storage and retrieval of material, upon the skill and energy of the staff in preparing new and stimulating work sheets, and upon ancillary staff. In fact the school is excellently equipped to handle the production and retention of the necessary sheets, though short of technicians to support the teaching staff. At a technical level there are a few problems, though at a creative and operational level individualized learning and the preparation of material have brought many difficulties. These will be discussed later, when a description of all the major innovations in the school has been completed.

Curriculum

Associated with the move to new perspectives in learning there have been many changes in the curriculum of the school, mostly involving moves to more inter-disciplinary work. Since the curriculum has been planned to a large extent by McMullen, it reflects his views that have already been discussed. In its most novel aspects McMullen has actually invented new descriptions for certain parts of the curriculum. The whole point of the innovations, says McMullen, 'is to avoid giving the traditional message'. Essentially, the curriculum is divided into seven areas, four of which are recognizable in conventional terms – Mathematics, Science, Languages and Physical Education – and three of which embody radical moves to inter-disciplinary activities. In the language of the school these three areas are C.W.; 2D and 3D; and I.G. C.W. represents Creative and Expressive

Words, Music and Drama and encloses that group of studies normally associated with English and Literature. 2D and 3D stands for Creative and Expressive two and three dimensional Arts and Crafts (which includes Home Economics). I.G. stands for the Study of the Individual and the Group which has replaced the conventional History, Geography and Social Studies. In addition to the inter-disciplinary approach through the merging of traditional subjects within the new boundaries, it is hoped by McMullen and his colleagues that there will be much co-operation between departments. Thus the document of practical advice for staff reminds teachers that,

> Timetable and accommodation make staff co-operation easy; what form it takes can be left to the groups concerned − it can vary from interchange of material and ideas to planned team-teaching. It would, however, be a waste if staff did not find ways of sharing their expertise and knowledge; it would also be a pity if the opportunity that exists for children to exercise some choice of whom they find easiest to relate to was lost.

According to this argument, therefore, the inter-disciplinary work has not only academic advantage but is clearly seen as a means of enhancing pupil-teacher relationships in the school. Background papers, prepared by the staff, setting out in great detail the purposes and nature of the inter-disciplinary work in the school are evidence of their interest in this area. The staff are anxious, in their initial aspirations, to prevent the new areas building up walls around themselves, and the working paper explicitly urges the Warden, Tim McMullen, and the Director of Studies for each area to take means to prevent this happening. In addition, the staff are presented with ways in which the interconnections between the areas of study can be demonstrated. The document expresses hopes that the C.W. and I.G. departments should be working together and sharing staff, and suggests that they will ultimately merge. It indicates the links that might exist between the teaching of foreign languages. More particularly, however, the possible areas of co-operation between the two main sides of the curriculum − the Humanities and the Sciences − are clearly stated:

(i) Between the Biological Sciences and the Study of the Individual and the Group − both from the point of view of the physiology and psychology of man, and also the nature of the environment − particularly in relation to the pollution of the environment.

(ii) Between the Physical Sciences and the Design section of the Creative/Expressive Arts and Crafts work, in creative technology and design.

(iii) Between the Mathematics studies and the study of the individual and the group in relation to statistics.

Furthermore, the staff document dealing with the academic organization gives more detail of the work and structure of the I.G., C.W. and 2D and 3D. The study of the Individual and the Group is envisaged as embracing the student's understanding of himself, of his relationships with those he works, plays and lives with, both present, past and future. It will, therefore, include the understanding of the society he lives in — its social groupings, its political structure, its legal system, its general ethical and moral system and the relation of this to the pupil's personal moral code. Other fields of study will include the economic organization of society, and its relationship to the international world. Finally the course will pay 'particular attention to the current major problems: prejudice and tolerance; war and peace; pollution of the environment'.

In the field of Creative and Expressive Work in Words, Music and Movement the main emphasis is to be on actions, in writing, speaking, acting, making music, dancing and movement. The staff document reminds all that 'the main point about this area is that the content is not of much importance compared to the actual activity of the students'. As a result of this emphasis in integration, the staff recognize that they face particular challenges to work out the balance of teaching arrangement between the specialist teacher's requirements and his need to work in co-operation with others to develop activities that use all the skills. Finally, the advice document for staff explores in more detail the inter-disciplinary possibilities of the 2D and 3D department. Again the main emphasis is to be on action. It is noted that though there can be work which is specialist in the sense of using one medium or one craft, such an approach should be interspersed with either the creation of artefacts or environments using many media and techniques. Furthermore it is pointed out that design, technological design and construction are related and that together these will involve the Physical Sciences also. It has already been noted that certain architectural features of the school have been designed to encourage such co-operation.

It is clear, therefore, that the curriculum and many pedagogic arrangements in the school are aimed at fulfilling the goals set out earlier by McMullen and his staff through the operation of inter-disciplinary and co-operative perspectives. Nevertheless, it must not be assumed that, at this early stage in the life of the school, the objectives of the teachers are achieved in practice. And later discussion will illustrate some of the problems and constraints facing the staff as they attempt to develop their integrative concepts.

Organization

Perhaps the innovations at Countesthorpe which have engendered the most widespread interest have been those concerned with the government of the school, particularly the staff democracy and the nature of the control relationships between staff and pupils. In one respect, of course, Countesthorpe College is like any other maintained school, that is, the external control of the school is in the hands of the local education authority, the county of Leicestershire, and the Board of Governors which it has appointed to help in the overall direction of the school. Nevertheless, there is a powerful tradition in English education of autonomy for individual schools. Usually this means that considerable freedom is vested in the individual headmasters, who have a great deal of control over the internal organization of their schools. This is exactly the situation at Countesthorpe, where Tim McMullen has a great deal of independence in his handling of the internal affairs of the school. The great novelty at Countesthorpe, however, is that McMullen has refused to take on the traditional headmaster's authority. As was made clear in the earlier analysis, he is anxious to establish a participatory democracy in the school, and by so doing he hopes to achieve a number of aims: to increase the personal satisfaction of all members of the College; to increase pupil motivation through giving them the opportunity to influence or decide their own actions in school; to provide a model to the students of a desirable form of government; and finally, to increase staff motivation by giving them the opportunity to influence or decide their own actions in the school.

Staff relationships

The initial paradox at Countesthorpe, therefore, is that McMullen has employed the traditional authority of his status to divest himself of his authority within the bureaucratic organization of the school, and though, at this early stage, pupil participation in school government is limited, there is a very strong framework of staff democracy. There are arrangements which enable the full staff to meet weekly to discuss overall policy for the school. This assembly which is the main legislative body in the college is known as the 'Moot', and within the broad lines established by the meetings of the senior staff before the school opened, it is responsible for the policy-making in the school. McMullen's relationship to this body is that of chief executive and he looks upon himself as the executive agent of the Moot responsible for efficiently implementing the decisions made by the collectivity of the staff. And, of course, McMullen is accountable to the local education authority for the collective decisions which the staff make.

It is obvious, however, that a weekly meeting of the total staff is an unwieldy body and to supplement its work there is an Executive Committee of senior staff which is responsible for more immediate decisions. The actions of the Committee are of course subject to the approval and ratification of the Moot. The relationships between the

Committee and the Moot are not yet fully developed, and have been the subject of an almost continuous debate within the staff. Nevertheless, the uncertainties in this respect should not be allowed to obscure the thoroughgoing nature of the democratic arrangements already established. The Moot has already made a large number of decisions which in any other school would be clearly within the prerogative of the headmaster. On occasions, the decisions taken by the Moot have been different from the personal views of McMullen. Already, the Moot has taken significant steps by making decisions on the nature of sanctions in the school, children's dress, the modes of address between pupils and staff. Even more important, perhaps, the Moot has overall responsibility for the appointment of new staff and the distribution of additional salary allowances. This is a major innovation, since in almost all English schools decisions of that kind are in the hands of the headmaster and, moreover, are regarded as amongst the most vital aspects of their work by headmasters.[16] At Countesthorpe the Moot decides upon the appointment to be advertised and a committee of the staff act as the appointing body. The committee is made up of those with a special interest in the appointment either in terms of the teaching department, or in terms of the pastoral organization of the school. McMullen is available to the appointing committee, which can employ his experience and expertise to assist in the questioning of candidates.

The overall democratic organization of the school is reflected in the small democracies within each department, so that though each academic area and pastoral section has its own head, these leaders are expected to be controlled by the overall policies of the Moot and also to consult fully with the junior members of staff in their charge. Though the arrangements for the pastoral care of the children are not novel, they do show a very careful concern for the individual child. It is regarded as very important that each child is known with respect to his 'whole' activities rather than just in terms of the specific skills which are likely to be demonstrated to a particular teacher. Such an attitude is regarded as especially important in a school where there is much individual and small group work and where there is independent untimetabled time, all of which could make it easier for the child to be lost or to stagnate. In order to prevent this from happening a yearmistress or yearmaster has been appointed to be associated with each year group in the school. These teachers have been chosen for their special interest in children, and their responsibility for the children in their year group is similar to that of a headmaster in a small school. They are expected, therefore, to fulfil a variety of responsibilities – knowing the academic and social progress of each child, knowing the parents' and the child's family history, dealing with parents and, if necessary, visiting their homes, helping with careers advice, establishing relationships with the local social, medical and welfare services. In order to assist the yearteachers in their work, there are also a number of group tutors, each of whom will be responsible for about 20—25 children and will be teachers who normally teach those children in one of the major subject areas. They are responsible for the daily registration of their children, for getting to know their children very well and looking for early signs of emotional, social and academic disturbance, and are generally expected to assist the yearteacher in his pastoral work.

Staff–pupil Relationships

The pastoral organization of the school and the staff democracy are both associated with an almost total revolution (at least in the state sector of education) in the nature of pupil/teacher relationships. Pupil participation in the government of the school is at the moment restricted, partly because it is unclear as to what part they should or could play, and partly because the oldest pupils in the school are only fifteen, and pupil participation is being seen by the staff essentially in terms of Sixth Form students. Nevertheless, amongst the earliest decisions of the staff, both in their preliminary meetings and later in the Moot, were many which have transformed the nature of pupil/teacher relationships in comparison with other secondary schools.

At the time of writing there are no formal conventional sanctions at Countesthorpe. Amongst the staff there is a generalized notion of what constitutes 'anti-social behaviour' on the part of the pupils. A child who is regarded as having been anti-social will be subjected to moral exhortation by the staff but without the employment of any of the usual controls available in a school — corporal punishment, extra work, detention and the like. Anti-social pupils will perhaps be made to work alone for a set period of time or will be sent to report their activities to their tutor. At the very extreme, persistent offenders at Countesthorpe might be sent home for the remainder of the day if their behaviour interferes too greatly with the work of the school. Moreover, amongst the staff there is a very great tolerance of those pupils who are most likely to be troublesome and they are especially likely to be handled most sensitively by the teachers.

The absence of formal sanctions and the attempt to obtain egalitarian pupil/teacher relationships in the school are reflected in a whole variety of symbolic forms. There are no separate lavatories for staff, and both pupils and teachers are expected to take their turn in the queue for lunch. More significantly, perhaps, pupils call teachers by their Christian names, and pupils are welcomed into the staff room, where they are frequently invited by teachers for coffee. In other respects also the school is markedly unconventional. No effort is made to keep the children out of the school at lunch or break times; indeed, the lunch time discotheque, with pop music, soft drinks, table-tennis and darts is seen by the staff as offering a teacher-controlled alternative to the potential deviance of the middle school pupils. Finally, the attempt at staff-student democracy is symbolized by the egalitarian dress of pupils and staff. In the majority of English schools both pupil and staff dress is carefully regulated by the headmasters and is frequently taken as an index of attitudes to the school. At Countesthorpe there is no uniform for the children and no regulations concerning dress for the staff. Moreover, the document on suggested practical applications for staff seems to emphasize the democratic role of the teacher *vis-à-vis* the pupils. Thus the teacher's main role is seen as 'a guide to the individual students through the learning situation, the provider of stimulus and excitement'. Staff are advised to enforce the rules by a process of *constant,* friendly insistence, rather than by draconic punishment or threats of such punishment, and are recommended to avoid giving the impression that children are morally deficient while the teachers are full of virtue.

As has already been suggested, the quality of relationships with, and the treatment given to, the pupils who are especially difficult are of special concern to the staff at Countesthorpe. Like any large secondary school Countesthorpe has a small proportion of pupils who have extreme emotional or academic problems and do not fit readily into the everyday routine of the school. The problems arising from these pupils can be particularly acute in Leicestershire where there is below-average provision in special schools for educationally subnormal and maladjusted children. Any ordinary secondary school, like Countesthorpe, will have to cope with a few pupils who have severe learning or emotional difficulties.

In most schools such pupils are extremely troublesome, sometimes functionally illiterate and therefore unable to participate in normal classroom activities, or totally unable to adjust to the pattern of authority and control in a school. At Countesthorpe, special arrangements have been made for children of this kind. An extremely experienced teacher has been appointed to be responsible for them. The teacher has no formal time-table duties and these difficult, 'non-involved' children, therefore, can be given specialist attention. More important, they can on occasions be part of a normal academic teaching group if they wish, or can be withdrawn at very short notice from school routines as the specialist teachers are readily available. Two large rooms are set aside for these pupils and the teacher in charge is involved in modifying and rewriting material produced by other staff in order to make it more suitable for the children she is concerned with. In this work she is greatly aided by three synchrofax machines which the school has and which enables a highly individual approach to be adopted with these children. The tapes last only four minutes and are much easier to handle than cassette types. Perhaps one should note that the teacher in charge of these children does not make great claims about the novelty of anything she does with the children, but chooses to emphasize her availability 'to take, take and take, until the children trust you as a person − the approach is not unique but the amount of time spent on them is.'

Gerald Bernbaum

Relationships with the Local Community

Finally, the school at Countesthorpe has been designed to serve as a community college, and to make an important impact on the local village. The concept of a community college is not new, and several authorities, most notably Cambridgeshire, have experimented in this direction. Although Leicestershire itself already has several in operation, in the main the community college work is confined to the latter part of the day; after the children have left the school, evening classes for adults begin and these are not necessarily taught by members of the school staff. At Countesthorpe the arrangements will be different and to some extent are already so. There is a section of the College designated for special, but not exclusive, use by the adults, and facilities for refreshments and recreation exist. It is anticipated, therefore, that adults will use the facilities of the school during normal school hours, and that to some extent they will work alongside the pupils. When the plans are fully developed it is hoped that such activities will make a notable contribution to the understanding of the innovations which the staff propose for the children, and also enable closer teacher/parent contact. At the same time, of course, a notable encouragement will have been given to community life.

The main innovations, as defined by the staff, have been carefully described in the preceding sections. It is essential to remember, however, that whatever are the ideologies, goals or even definitions of education their transmission occurs in a social context. It is vital therefore to understand the operation of the innovations in the social context of the school, in order to fully comprehend the constraints, problems and achievements involved in the new practice.

The social context of innovation

The study so far has examined Countesthorpe College in the context of the administration of the County of Leicestershire and the social background of the village of Countesthorpe, and has given an account of the ideologies, goals and objectives of those who work in the school, most especially of those who have power and autonomy, namely the Warden and the staff. In addition, it has described in detail the major innovative features of the school. As the school is, at the time of writing, designed for innovation from the beginning, it is impossible to examine how the innovations have changed the roles and behaviours of the personnel. However, consideration can be usefully given to several significant factors relating to the major innovations: the degrees of satisfaction they have brought their proponents; the constraints that have been operative in modifying initial plans and aspirations: and the unintended consequences that have been brought about by some of the proposals. At all times this examination will be made not only in the context of the school and neighbourhood, but in the light of the theoretical frameworks and empirical studies of the relevant social sciences. For this purpose, then, four major innovations have been chosen for closer inspection – individualized learning, the inter-disciplinary curriculum, staff democracy, and the move to greater equality in pupil/teacher relationships.

Throughout, however, it must be remembered that this exploratory study was undertaken in only the second term of the life of the new school. In its early months the school was faced with many unusual problems. Notably, the delay in the completion of the building which meant that major works of construction were still being undertaken when the pupils had already arrived, and that not all the school was available for use. At the same time it should be remembered that the local authority supplies department was going through an unexpected administrative crisis which severely curtailed delivery of vital materials to the school. In both these respects, therefore, the school started in a very disadvantaged position as a result of circumstances completely beyond the control of those who worked in it. Moreover, for its first few years Countesthorpe College is in an unusual situation. The school has been designed for pupils between the ages of 14 and 18, and will eventually be for such pupils. At the beginning, however, the school contains pupils between 11 and 14. Consequently, the immediate arrangements are somewhat temporary. It is very likely, therefore, that all these circumstances have combined to present a typical problem to the staff. Certainly, any analysis of problems, constraints and dissatisfactions must, at this stage, be of only a tentative nature.

Individualized Learning

Over half the teachers (55 per cent) at Countesthorpe are not satisfied with the operation of individualized learning at the school. Significantly the evidence[17] suggests that it is the older, more experienced teachers who are less satisfied in this respect than the young teachers, and that male teachers are less satisfied than female teachers. Sources of dissatisfaction fall into two categories, doubts about the ability and opportunity of the teachers to prepare adequate material, and doubts about the effectiveness of the material prepared, particularly in its usefulness to motivate all the children. Over and over again the staff give indications that there are problems of preparing the work sheets so vital for individualized learning – 'In our department, we have not enough time to prepare enough interesting and varied material', 'Nowhere near enough time or resources to adequately occupy all the children all the time according to their individual needs.' Problems of this kind should not be underestimated. The production of imaginative and stimulating work sheets on a regular basis requires immense skill and a considerable sense of purpose over a long period, and demands of the teacher a long-standing commitment and involvement with a large part of his professional personality.

Furthermore, there are difficulties with the individualized approach to learning even when the work sheets have been produced. Essentially these difficulties arise because the motivation of the pupils cannot be taken for granted. It appears, then, that these approaches demand from the pupils an equivalently high degree of readiness for commitment, and it must be questionable whether it is reasonable to hold a uniform perspective on all pupils in this respect. If the pace of learning is to be virtually in the pupil's control then the conditions which are operative to determine the pacing are very important. In turn, these conditions are likely to be a function of the previous socialization of the child. What is often ignored in this respect is that middle-class family socialization of the child is a hidden subsidy, providing both a physical and psychological environment which immensely facilitates, in diverse ways, school learning. Where the school system is not subsidized by the home, the pupil often fails. As one teacher neatly puts the problem, 'Some children just can't discipline themselves to work...the drawback with our system is that the children who need to do the extra work are the ones who don't do it; the children who are interested and are good are the ones who go on and do more.'

There is evidence that McMullen is aware of the problems in this area, for he has observed that, at this very early stage, he thinks that the school is working well for the most able and motivated pupils, and that the care and attention devoted to the minority of pupils with severe emotional or learning difficulties is having its reward. He is, however, anxious that the great mass of the children 'in the middle' are not ignored as they can readily be when so much depends upon their own initiative. The problem of motivation in a system of individualized learning is crucial and unless the teachers are remarkably skilful, energetic and imaginative real differences will appear in the children's academic performance largely on lines determined by social class differences. As has been suggested, there are signs that the teachers are already experiencing some of these phenomena, as is indicated by their expressions of anxiety over work sheets and the problems over the motivation of the children. Thus, when offered nine items from which to choose those factors which might constrain them in the innovations they wished to adopt, 30 per cent of the choices were for 'lack of adequate teaching material', and 25 per cent emphasized 'the previous educational experience of the children'. Together, therefore, the two items account for 55 per cent of the choices, the remaining seven factors only receiving 45 per cent of the selections. As an experienced teacher suggests, 'It must be an enormous shock for the children to have to think for themselves.' There is, however, a risk that the pupils in the school will show a tendency to polarise — some getting on with the academic work as the staff have prescribed, and these will contain a large proportion from middle-class homes where the notions of learning and individual self-control are encouraged, others making little academic progress, because they find little support for this in their immediate subculture, or may have arrived from their previous educational experience deficient in the necessary skills. This second group is likely to contain a large proportion of children from the homes of the unskilled manual working class. It should be noted, however, that as the school gets older some of these difficulties might diminish. Firstly, the present intake of the school contains an unusually large proportion of working-class children; as under a special arrangement with the City of Leicester, the children from a nearby council housing estate have been temporarily admitted. Secondly, as the school becomes established the proportion of new entrants to the total population will drop.

Nevertheless, even when the school operates under more normal circumstances the individualized learning will involve something of a withdrawal by the teachers from the role as it might be defined in terms of the pupils' expectations. The pupils tend to emphasize strongly the instrumental features of the teacher's role; simply, they expect him to teach and to be responsible for control, and are less concerned with the teacher's personality or the expressive aspects of perspectives. Nevertheless, they are real and powerful and can only be ignored at risk to the learning climate of the school. Clearly it is possible to argue that the pupil's expectations must be modified, but it is a complex empirical question to decide how this is best done, and under what conditions attitudes most readily change. It means, of course, that one of the major long-term empirical tasks will be to examine the way in which the new relationships established in the school will modify the expectations and assessments of the pupils.

As has been seen, also, a further important feature of the work at Countesthorpe is that the teachers see themselves as models for the young, in that they wish to achieve their objectives by example. Thus, as has been argued, if the staff are seen to be rational, liberal, democratic and co-operative then their influence will spread to the pupils. The studies, however, of this modelling process do not testify to its overwhelming effectiveness. Wright [18] investigated the self-concepts and the perceptions of parents and teachers among 105 15- and 16-year-old secondary modern school children. He concluded that, 'in their last year at school secondary modern pupils are a good deal less identified with their teachers than with their parents'. The pupils, it seems, value their teachers mainly for their intellectual abilities; they are little concerned with their more general human qualities. Thus Wright points out that, 'In so far as the pupils do identify with teachers, it is restricted to those aspects of personality which relate to academic achievement. They admire teachers for their cleverness and knowledge. But they do not seem to value them highly as persons'. Wright emphasizes the influence of parents rather than teachers; 'it is of interest to note', he writes, 'that the opinion sometimes expressed that adolescents are, in general, rejecting parental influence, receives no confirmation'. Finally, Wright is sceptical about the efficiency of the wider, less specialized role that is frequently ascribed to teachers, an ascription which has been shown to be central to the functioning of the arrangements at Countesthorpe. He points out that 'there has been a tendency in recent years to place increasing responsibility on the teacher for such things as mental health, attitudes, values and social awareness of adolescents. Yet there are no indications that pupils expect those services from their teachers or that when they are rendered they have much effect'.

The studies, therefore, tend to emphasize the influence of parents and to devalue the potential impact of schools and teachers. In emphasizing parents the research findings are, of course, implicitly and explicitly pointing to the links between social class and the socialization of the child. There are numerous enquiries which reveal the differences in socialization between the social classes and the way in which position in the social structure and induction into certain value systems offer different opportunities to profit from the educational system. Critical to this process might be the future orientation of the middle class, whose elaborated language codes not only make the language of learning more readily available to them, enabling their children to be more flexible in the learning situation and to switch roles more readily in response to new contexts, but also provide the greater sense of uniqueness and individuality developed by a middle-class socialization. As argued, therefore, there is a real possibility that the teachers at Countesthorpe might encounter problems from those working-class children whose academic success is not likely to be great, whose values will not embody large elements of rationalism, liberalism, or tolerance, who will not be able to perceive, or at least realize, the long-term goals inherent in the pedagogy and curriculum of the school, and who will not be able to manifest that flexibility necessary to switch roles in new situations. There are signs that this is already the case.

The problem of motivation with respect to individualized learning has been considered and the difficulties of the staff discussed. It is clear that this method of learning, in which the pacing is essentially that of the pupils, alters the balance of power between teacher and taught. The nature of teacher-pupil relationships at Countesthorpe and particularly the absence of traditional sanctions possibly serves to generalize this problem, since, without a formal structure of support, the teachers must rely on their personalities to manipulate and control the pupils. In turn, this can give rise to much anxiety and, frequently, doubt.

Pupil—teacher Relationships

It is important to recognize from the beginning that the nature of relationships between children and staff in the school, and the sanctions available to staff are the matters which present difficulties to the staff. Thus, although about 28 per cent of the staff claim to be very satisfied with the nature of the relationships in the school, exactly the same proportion claim to be not satisfied with the sanctions available. It is interesting to note that in the second three months of the life of the new school much attention has been given to the question of sanctions, the result being a general 'stiffening' of the staff's approach to pupil–teacher relationships and the insistence on sanctions. Nevertheless, there are distinct differences between the sexes in these areas. Whereas half the women teachers are very satisfied with the pupil–teacher relations in the school, only about 15 per cent of the men are. Similarly, the men are less satisfied than the women with the sanctions available in the school. These findings must be seen in the light of the fact that females choose 'greater equality in social relations between staff and children' as the most important innovation in the school. Their satisfaction in this area, therefore, is likely to be a reflection of their orientation towards teaching in an expressive rather than an instrumental fashion. They have probably come to the school precisely because it offers the opportunity to enter into more expressive relationships with children. As one young female teacher succinctly remarked, 'It's becoming increasingly obvious to me that I'm far more concerned with children than I am with mathematics.' Since, as has already been shown, it is the men who place more emphasis on learning, it is not surprising that they are less satisfied with the absence of sanctions and the quality of pupil–teacher interaction, because it is these factors which they are likely to perceive as inhibiting and restricting the extent and quality of academic learning in the school. Repeatedly the staff, other than those who claim to be satisfied in these respects, express their anxieties over the question of sanctions: 'The present situation on sanctions is absurd and unrealistic, given the society in which the children live and the present age range of children'; 'My own personal relationships...are O.K. – but when it comes to enforcement of social behaviour, things grind a bit'; 'The teacher has been deprived of all means of enforcing his authority in the learning situation with the result that a few children can effectively destroy whole lessons for the rest'; 'More positive sanctions are required'. Other teachers, especially in the 2D and 3D practical subjects, indicate that the absence of sanctions can create particular problems for them in dealing with dangerous tools and machinery; as the Head of Design put it, 'We have found some very real problems in simple control. I'm thinking of things like safety when dealing with craft work, for instance. Can we maintain standards of safety and a general agreement with the ethos of the school?' It is reasonable to suggest, however, that this particular difficulty symbolizes a more general dilemma arising from the absence of traditional sanctions and the operation of the staff democracy – a dilemma which was particularly acute in the earliest weeks of the school's existence. For in such a system, there are no clearly defined arrangements which can serve to guide the staff in their relationships with pupils. As already suggested, much depends on the individual qualities and attributes of the teacher, and in the terms of their earlier analysis, upon the individual qualities and attributes of the pupil. There is a sense therefore, in which much more of the personalities of the participants is made public than under traditional systems of school authority which reinforces that which was indicated earlier in reference to individualized learning, that it is likely to involve more of the pupil's character being open to inspection and to manipulation — more of his thoughts, feelings and values. Yet the same is true for the teachers, as they are increasingly beginning to realize.

The realization on the part of the teachers at Countesthorpe that, in the earliest stage, the idiographic elements in social relationships counted for more than the nomethetic arrangements in the school took two forms. There was their awareness of their own isolation, and growing out of this, their dependence on the involvement, commitment and skill of all their colleagues. Yet just as these qualities could not be taken for granted in their pupils, equally they could not be guaranteed in colleagues. The teachers recognized the situation:

'Any discipline here has to come from the personality of the member of staff concerned'; 'Some are worried because it is not structured enough here. Some people cannot stand on their own feet'; 'I think it all depends on the teacher, how expert he is at handling the situation'; 'Natural approach combined with freer structures means that often chaos is the result. My own relationships with children probably better in a more formal set up'. The teachers also recognized the way in which the system placed additional responsibilities upon them, 'Technique of constant insistence on social behaviour more wearing for staff and having mixed success'; 'There is doubt about what is "on" and what is "not on" which makes for confusion and leads to general laxness'; 'The absence of sanctions tends to obscure the essential responsibilities of a teacher. We are not always honest and consistent in our jobs...A lot of teachers need to achieve self-discipline before they can impart it to the children'.

Occasionally, a teacher's comment goes right to the source of the problem. Thus, one teacher noting the lack of sanctions on the part of the staff dealing with children, also draws attention to McMullen's denial of traditional authority by his refusal to sanction staff; 'It must be very difficult for Tim, he's got to rely on people's good will. Psychologically, for him it must be very demanding especially having been a head previously. The whole thing puts much more on people's self-discipline, in which we fall down all of us. We get tired, and do not do what we agreed to do'. Clearly circumstances such as those described have been very instrumental in bringing about a greater availability of sanctions in the school and a greater willingness to operate them, both of these developments being features of the more recent changes at Countesthorpe.

The Interdisciplinary Curriculum

Just as the lack of sanctions and the absence of the traditional authority of the head place greater emphasis on the commitment and ability of the individual teacher, so the inter-disciplinary and group teaching schemes tend to expose the teacher to public view and to emphasize his dependence upon the others in the team. The main point about integrated arrangements is that there must be some relational idea, a supra-concept, which is designed to draw students' attention to knowledge at a high level of abstraction. Whatever the relational concepts are, they will act selectively upon the knowledge within each subject which is to be transmitted. The particulars of each subject are likely to have reduced significance. In turn, this will lead to an emphasis upon, and the explorations of, general principles and the concepts through which these principles are obtained. As has been shown, these are the goals held for learning at Countesthorpe, where the programmes of work are such that the children are not meant to be given too much detailed information or too many facts, but are encouraged to explore the principles involved and perhaps 'experience' the subject. What is not always recognized, however, is that this, in turn, is likely to affect the orientation of the pedagogy, which will be less concerned to emphasize the need to acquire states of knowledge, but will be more concerned to stress how knowledge is created. In this way integrated arrangements, at least at an ideological level, make readily available to pupils the principles for generating new knowledge. Part of the underlying theory of the integrated code is to encourage learning which is self-regulated, a feature which is demonstrated at Countesthorpe. The inherent logic of the integrated curriculum tends to create a change in the structure of teaching groups towards the adoption of considerable flexibility. In this way also therefore, integrated codes come to modify authority relationships by increasing the rights of the taught. Such developments are clearly anticipated at Countesthorpe where the document on practical applications for the staff describes the role of the teacher as 'one of a group, comprising students, ancillary staff and colleagues creating a learning situation...one of the very many, and by no means main, sources of information and explanation'.

It is likely, however, to be just these aspects which present most problems to the staff at a practical level. In an earlier section it was shown that the expression of objectives set out for the various parts of the curriculum provided no real guide in behavioural terms to what could be expected from pupils and staff. In a sense this is to be expected, for, as with work sheets, it requires great skill and knowledge as well as

Gerald Bernbaum

commitment to devise a truly integrated scheme of work. Detailed knowledge of a range of subjects and the concepts which make up their organization of knowledge is essential, if the integration is to be effective. Moreover, the teachers must be prepared to yield some of their identity in terms of their original socialization by subject, and to genuinely recognize the enhanced power position of the pupil in the learning situation. At Countesthorpe these things have been difficult to achieve. That only 11 per cent of the teachers rate it as the most important innovation suggests that the inter-disciplinary curriculum has not been rated highly by staff. More significantly, perhaps, 75 per cent of the staff are not satisfied with the inter-disciplinary schemes in the school, and not a single teacher admits to being 'very satisfied'. Thus the teachers comment: 'There is no inter-disciplinary work here, and no real concept of what it is or involves'; 'Each area has tended to be so intent on establishing itself that it has not been able to look outwards yet'; 'Relieved that integration has gone no further at this stage'; 'Very little integration is taking place between science and other things. Between the sciences there are problems with teachers not having enough knowledge in the other fields to integrate'. Moreover, there is a certain ambivalence on the part of the staff to the inter-disciplinary activities, perhaps because they define them as the least successful innovation. Thus, at an interview session with a group of teachers being considered for a vacancy at the school, a very senior member of the staff describing the curriculum to the candidates noted mockingly that 'I.G. is staggeringly similar to Humanities and C.W. is remarkably similar to English'.

Thus, it has not been easy to move the school in the direction of inter-disciplinary activities despite all the original aspirations. Most of the effective inter-disciplinary work is *within* the departmental areas, as yet; it is the departments which have been unable to establish a real co-operation and dialogue *between* each other. The traditional subject loyalties die hard. It is into these that the teachers have received their adult socialization. It is their subjects which have given them their sense of identity and which, in the main, they are forced to utilise in the wider society to establish and promote their careers. Moreover, from the pupil's perspective, most public examinations are in traditional subject areas and there will be constraints upon the teacher not to move too far from these, especially as the pupils get older. To move wholeheartedly into fully integrated work, therefore, perhaps exposes the teacher to the greatest risks.

Staff Democracy

Finally, consideration must be given to the operation of the staff democracy. Though many teachers are very excited about the democratic arrangements, 'I love it...absolutely unique', they nevertheless look upon it as the least important of the innovations at the school, in fact only 5.5 per cent regard it as the most important innovation. Furthermore, there are clearly problems in the operation of a staff democracy, as only 5 per cent of the teachers claim to be 'very satisfied with it, whereas 45 per cent are positively 'not satisfied'.

The sources of dissatisfaction are various. Many teachers resent the cumbersome and time-wasting machinery that is part of the democratic process. 'Committed to staff democracy but find the time consumed by unwieldy process very worrying'; 'Long, laborious, time-consuming'; 'It has a negative value in terms of efficiency. It needs streamlining'; 'There is so much time consumed in decision-making'; 'Staff democracy does go to the head of some staff who behave as if they are in the Oxford Debating Society rather than a school!'

Part of this problem undoubtedly stems from the fact that the arrangements are newly established and there has been a period of trial and error. Even more important, perhaps, has been the novelty of the situation for the majority of staff. For most of them the experience is unique and it is bound to take time before they can establish command of the form and principles of debate in this new context. One of the difficulties is that the democratic—liberal principles underlying the establishment of the Moot have been carried forward into its operation; this has, inevitably, blurred the process of decision-making and produced a sense of unreality. Because there is no regular chairman, and no regular secretary, the form of debate is frequently unclear and there are inadequate minutes and records of decisions. Traditional procedures tend, in fact, to be reversed at Countesthorpe; the actual agenda is sometimes disregarded while the important matters of an immediate kind are discussed first at the Moot, under the heading of Any Other Business. As one experienced member of staff notes, 'I'm very disappointed at the way the Moot is run, too many ideas are given off the cuff, we don't know what's going to come next'. Staff opinion such as this has been important in bringing about recent changes in the Moot. It now meets less frequently but operates on a more formal level, with a carefully prepared agenda and minutes.

Another problem deriving from the arrangements described is that it is very difficult for the whole of the staff to take anything but radical educational decisions. As has been shown, the staff have been recruited partly because of their progressive and innovative orientations, which means that, overall, they are likely to be committed to educational change. Moreover, as has been shown, the staff are, above all, involved in the nature of social relationships between teachers and pupils, an involvement which makes them unwilling to resist radicalism overtly in this field. It is, apparently, awkward for those who have doubts about the rapidity of some of the changes to state them, let alone make their doubts effective in action, without appearing conservative and traditional, and in some sense striking at the whole foundation of the school.

Gerald Bernbaum

This pervasive radicalism becomes a source of a twofold set of problems both outside and inside the school. As has been shown, the most extreme radicalization has taken place in the field of staff—pupil relationships and the withdrawal of sanctions, and it is these features of the school which have attracted the most criticism in the local community and press. On the one hand, the response of the extreme progressives amongst the teachers is that they must not react to 'every nervous twitch in the local community'; on the other hand, Stuart Mason and McMullen have expressed anxieties that there might be a local 'backlash' which would endanger all the worthwhile educational works of the school.

A second consequence of the Moot's radicalization of staff—pupil relationships is that it starkly emphasizes the commitment and skill of each individual teacher, in the manner described earlier. This cannot be guaranteed, as one teacher observes, 'the staff do not *act* on what is decided'. The consequence is, therefore, that interpersonal relationships within the staff can become subjected to severe strain, as teachers are accused, privately and publicly, of inadequately performing their responsibilities, and so making the work more difficult for everybody else. Group teaching and open architecture only serve to highlight the problem. Moreover, the tension is likely to be greatest in precisely those areas, which because of the control element involved, are the 'dirty work' of teaching and most likely to bring the teachers into contact with the deviant pupils — supervision of pupils in classes, at play, at dinner, observation and control of truants from class and school, admission of pupils to the staff room. In conventional and traditional schools such problems also arise. They tend, however, to be focused upon the role of the headmaster, and especially what the staff regard as his inadequacies and weaknesses. In a sense, therefore, the difficulties may serve to unite the staff in their hostility to the head. At Countesthorpe the staff democracy ensures that the responsibility is that of the teachers. As they increasingly find, responsibility can be difficult and problematical as well as rewarding.

Some staff are disturbed by certain oligarchic tendencies which are manifest in the operation of the democracy. As a young female science teacher puts it, 'I think it began well, but as time goes on the "Chiefs" find it harder not to slip back to old habits'. Complaints about oligarchies are commonplace in most democratic systems, and at Countesthorpe some of the staff are prepared to express them. As shown in an earlier section, there are difficulties in the relationships between the Moot and the Executive, and McMullen with his much greater experience and expertise is clearly deferred to in a way in which other members of staff are not. There is a real sense in which he is 'primus inter pares'. Nevertheless, certain aspects of the democracy, like the appointment of staff, are very thorough-going and unique, a feature which many of the teachers appreciate. In these initial stages, at least, more of the staff are worried that democracy is endangered by demagoguery than by oligarchy!

In examining in detail the social context of four of the major innovations this study has attempted to look at some of the realities of innovation in order that those who wish to follow the progress at Countesthorpe might be made aware of the kinds of problems and difficulties which are likely to arise. This seems to be the real purpose of a case study and accounts for the attention given to the social and organizational constraints upon innovation. It is possible, as is shown by other studies, to describe the ways in which traditional schools adjust to their internal and external realities.[19] None of what has gone before is meant to decry or deplore innovation at Countesthorpe College, but only to set it in its social context...

NOTES

1. T. McMullen, 'Flexibility for a Comprehensive School', *Forum,* Spring 1968, x 2, pp. 64—6.
2. Ibid., p.65.
3. Ibid., p.66.
4. Ibid., loc. cit.
5. F. Musgrove and P.H. Taylor, *Society and the Teacher's Role* (Routledge and Kegan Paul, London, 1969).
6. Ibid., p.50.
7. Ibid., p.56.
8. Lego is a child's toy of interlocking small plastic bricks.
9. W. Waller, *The Sociology of Teaching* (John Wiley, New York, 1960 Edition), p.68.
10. Bruce J. Biddle, *Role Conflicts of Teachers in the English Speaking Community:* paper presented at the 40th Congress of the Australian and New Zealand Association for the Advancement of Science, Christchurch, New Zealand, January 1968.
11. Musgrove and Taylor, op. cit., p. 67.
12. Ibid., p.17.
13. F. Musgrove, 'The Social Needs and Satisfactions of Some Young People', *British Journal of Educational Psychology,* 1966, 36, Parts I and II.
14. J.S. Gott, 'High School Pupils' Perceptions of Progressive Upper Schools', an unpublished dissertation for the award of the University of Leicester. Postgraduate Certificate of Education, 1971.
15. A. Etzioni, *A Comparative Analysis of Complex Organisations* (Free Press of Glencoe, New York, 1971), p. 181.
16. G. Bernbaum, *The Headmasters* (Social Science Research Council Research Project).
17. There are 50 teachers on the staff. The breakdown into various categories, therefore, yields very small cells. As a result only simple analysis of the data is presented.
18. D.S. Wright, 'A Comparative Study of the Adolescent's Concepts of his Parents and Teachers', *Educational Review,* 14, 1962.
19. See, for example, D. Hargreaves, *Social Relations in a Secondary School* (Routledge and Kegan Paul, London 1967); J. Partridge, *Middle School* (Gollancz, London, 1966).

INDEX

Adelman, Clem, on open education, iv, 162-8
Adolescents, 358, 374
Allen, 358
Argyris, C., 192, 196, 198
Assessment: examining boards and, 107, 116, 117, 118, 119, 124; Schools Council and, 84; teachers and, 122, 123, 177-8
Assistant Masters' Association, 105
Assistant Mistresses' Association, 105
Assistant teachers, autonomy, 338
Association for Science Education, 39, 77, 105
Association of Head Teachers in Secondary Schools, 48, 50
Australia: innovation research, 7, 11, 13: teachers' role, 356
Austria, curriculum development, 23, 24
Authority, 261-3; change agents', 276; and innovation, 230-40; in schools, 338-40; teachers', 178-9, 217-29

Banks, John, 42
Bantock, G.H., 75
Barber, B., 255
Bauersfield, Heinrich, 26
Becher, R.A., on curriculum development and innovation, ii, iii, vi, 15-29, 42, 96, 278, 333
Becker, Howard. S.: on professionalism, 255; on teacher authority, iv, 217-29
Behaviour: objectives, 11, 326, 354; science, 304
Belgium, curriculum development, 22-3
Bell, R., 59, 95
Beloe Report, 95, 115
Benne, Kenneth D., 261-2, 277, 294, 326
Bennett, William S. Jnr., on professionalism, v, 250-68
Bennis, Warren G., 277, 296, 307, 326
Bernbaum, Gerald, on Countesthorpe College, 347-81
Bernstein, Basil: on educational change, 280; on open education, iv, 155-61, 164, 167, 283
Bhola, H.S., 292
Biddle, Bruce J., 356
Black Paper, 75, 92

Blake, R.R., 198
Bloom, Benjamin S., 333
Bolam, Ray, on educational innovation, v, 273-87
Boyon, Norman, J., 314
Brickell, Henry M., 313
Bristow, Adrian, 63
British Broadcasting Corporation, educational programmes, 39, 362
Broudy, Harry, 211
Brown, B. Frank, 312
Brown, M., 49
Bruner, Jerome, 77
Burke, Edmund, 279
Burns, T., 283
Butler, R.A. (Lord), 59, 89

California University, 321
Cambridge: classics project, 107; examinations, 108
Cambridgeshire, community colleges, 370
Canada: curriculum development, 15, 28; educational system, 24; innovation research, 7
Canadian Studies Foundation, 28
Canter, H., 276
Careers programmes, 267
Carlson, Richard O., 192, 282, 292, 315
Carr-Saunders, A.M., 253
Carroll, John R., 144
Case Studies of Educational Innovation, 347
Caston, Geoffrey, on Schools Council, ii-iii, 73-85, 88
Centre for Education in Humanities and Social Science (Univ. of East Anglia), 84
Centre for Science Education, 84
Centres Regionaux de Documentation Pedagogique, 21
Certificate of Extended Education, 89
Certificate of Secondary Education; 67-8, 95, 115-19; examination procedure, 97, 98, 330-1; syllabuses, 96, 112
Change, defined, 279
Change agents, 276-9, 295-6, 298-300
Change Processes in the Public Schools, 192
Chesler, M., 279

Chicago: public schools, 218; university, 217

Chin, Robert, on change and innovation, 273, 277, 293, 295, 307, 326

Churchill, Sir Winston, 59, 60

Clark, David L., 284, 285, 291, 313

Classrooms, life in, 205-15

Codsall Comprehensive School, Staffs, 344

Cogan. M.L., 255

Cohen, P.S., 276

Commission on the Organisation of Curriculum Development (COLO), 27

Community relations in schools, 48, 49, 340, 370

Community schools, iv, 267

Comprehensive schools, 60, 329; Austrian. 24. Belgian, 22; in-service training, 344; West German, 25, 26;

Consultancy, 9, 295-6, 298, 345

Cooley, Charles H., 215, 219

Corbett, Anne, on teachers and Schools Council, iii, 87-93, 97

Corwin, R.G., on teaching reform, v, 242-9

Council of Europe, innovation research, 7

Countesthorpe College, iv, vi, 340, 347-81

Creative and expressive studies, 353, 363-4, 365

Creativity, of British schools, v, vi, 283, 329-46

Crosland, C.A.R., 59, 60, 65, 88

Crowther Report, 102

Cultural studies, 49

Culture, of schools, 144-5

Curriculum: control, 15-16, 19, 28, 96; examinations and, 104-25; extra year, 333; government influence, ii-iii, 34-5, 59-71; innovation, 329-47, 363-5, 377-8; integration, iv, 377; materials, 18, 23, 279, 333, 334; objectives, 333; Schools Council and, ii, 29, 39, 49, 75, 77, 90, 91-3, 95-103. 278, 330, 333; study groups, 91, 179; teachers and, 34, 70, 87-8, 97, 331

Dainton Report on further education, 70

Dalin, P., 277, 278, 280, 281

Dawe, A., 276

Decision making, in schools, 279, 340

De-streaming, 292

Discovery learning, 292, 334

Division of Labour in Society, 155

Douglas, Mary, 160

Downey, L., 273

Duane, Michael, 80

Dublin, Robert, 239

Durkheim, Emile, 155-6, 161

Education: Act (1944), 32, 97; agencies, 23; innovation, 1-13, 230-40, 273-307, 312, 337-43; publishers, 18, 19, 22, 24, 26, 27, 29, 36, 39-40; resource information centres (ERIC), 312; research, 8, 200, 312-26; White Paper (1972), 69

Education and Science, Department of: and curriculum, 38, 39, 59-71, 95, 330, 332; and open plan primaries, 162; and Schools Council, 79, 88; and teacher training, 41

Educationists, 70, 283

Eggleston, S.J., 68, 275

Eicholtz, G., 285

Eidell, T.L., 283

Employers, 33, 331

England, curriculum development, 30-46

English teaching, 55-6, 104, 109, 111

Esland, G., 275, 279, 283

Etzioni, A., 250, 257, 258, 260, 264

Exemplars of Teaching Method, 211

Experimental schools, 23, 26

Examinations: and curriculum, 104-23; McMullen on, 349; Schools Council and, 68, 95-103; Secretary of State and, 87, 101-2

Fairweather, G.W., 301

Fantini, Mario, 263

Finland, curriculum development, 16, 17

First Three Years (Schools Council report), 53

Fisher, Sam 89

Fishman, J., 305

Flexner, Abraham, 253

Fowler, Gerry on government and curriculum, ii, iii, 34, 59-71

France: curriculum control and development, 15, 20-2, 96, 103; educational system, 23

Freinet schools, 21

Freire, Paulo, 258, 263

Friedson, E., 254
Fullan, M., 275, 281
Further education, 62-7; curriculum, 70-1

Gage, N.L., 198
General Certificate of Education (GCE), examining boards and curriculum, 70, 104-13, 116-19, 330
General studies, 48, 63
Germany, Western, educational system, 24-6; curriculum, 15, 96
Glaser, Edward M., 326
Goldhamer, H., 293
Goldsmith's College, curriculum laboratory, 291
Goode, W.J., 250, 257, 258-9, 260, 262
Goodlad, John I., on staff development, 143-52
Goodman, Paul, 258, 263, 264
Gouldner, A.W., 300
Greenfield, T.B., 276
Greenwood, Ernest, 253
Greiner, L.E., 284
Griffin, Gary A., 149
Griffiths, D., 297
Gross, N., 281, 283, 284, 297, 305
Group teaching, 361-2, 377, 380; tutors, 369-70
Guba, Egon G., 284, 285, 291, 313
Guskin, Alan, 282

Habenstein, R., 255
Haber, 259, 260
Hall, E.T., 168
Hall, R.H., 255, 275, 283
Halmos, Paul, 250, 251, 259, 260, 265
Halpin, A.W., 283, 297
Harries, T.W., 283
Hartcliffe School, Bristol, 344
Hartley, H.J., 295
Haslegrave Committee, on technical education, 65
Havelock, Ronald G.: on educational research, v, 312-26, 333; and innovation, 273, 275, 276-7, 278, 279, 280, 281, 283, 285
Head teachers: authority, 171, 178-9, 222-7, 338-40; and curriculum, 8, 97; and innovation, 297-8, 304-5, 332-3
Headmistresses' Association, 105
Hearn, Norman E., 326
Henry, Jules, 263

Hentig, Prof. von, 26
Herriott, R., 297
High School Certificate, 108
Hockenstad, Merl C., Jnr., on professionalism, v, 250-68
Hollis, 358
Houghton, V., 273
Howarth, Tom, 80
Hoyle, Eric; 275, 276, 278, 279, 280, 281, 282; on educational change, v, 289-307; on school creativity, vi, 329-46
Hughes, Everett C., 254, 255, 256, 262
Hughes, M.G., 282
Hull, W.L., 275, 280, 285

Illich, Ivan D., 258, 263, 264
Independent Television Authority, schools programmes, 39
Individual and the group, study of, 364-5
Individualised learning, 351, 355, 358, 361-3, 371-4, 376
Industrial training boards, 63
In-service education and training. See Teachers: education and training
In-Service Training: Structure and Content, 127
Inspectors: and curriculum, 59, 60, 64, 66, 67, 332, 345; and teacher education, 69
Institut Pedagogique Nationale, 21
Institute for Development of Educational Activities Inc (IDEA), 146-8
Institute for Development of Mathematical Instruction (IOWO), 27
Institute of Educational Sciences, (Klagenfurt), 24
Institute for Educational Study (ICE), 23
Institutionalisation, of British schools, 334-7, 343, 346
Integrated Studies Project, 336
Interdisciplinary enquiry (IDE), 121, 124, 340; teaching, 117, 335, 340, 347, 355, 363, 364, 377-8
Ireland, curricular development, ii, 47-50

JACT ancient history course, 107
Jackson, Philip W., 282; on classroom teaching, iv, 205-15
Jahoda, M., 192
James Report: and in-service training,

384

344; and professional centres, 127, 136, 137, 345; on teacher education and training, 69, 128
Jacques, E., 294
Jarvis, Fred, 89
Joint Matriculation Board, 108
Jones, Garth N., 276, 293
Joyce, Bruce R., 147
Jung, Charles, 317

Kahn, R.L., 275
Karmel Report, 9, 13
Katz, D., 275
Keele University, 48, 336
Keith, P., 285
Kettering, Charles F., Foundation, 146, 148
Kiel University, 26
Klaffki, Prof., 26
Klein, D.C., 300
Knowledge: behavioural, 296; diffusion, 160, 275, 278, 283; types, 280; utilisation, 313-22
Kogan, M., 87, 88
Kratz, 358

League of Cooperating Schools, iii, 146-51
Learning: by enquiry, 75, 336; systems, 337
Leicestershire: community colleges, 370; upper schools, 359
Lewin, Kurt, 294
Liberal studies, 63, 65
Likert, R., 194
Lin, N., 281
Linkage, 279, 320, 345
Lippitt, Ronald, 292, 295, 298, 304, 317
Liverpool, teacher training pilot scheme, 287
Local education authorities: advisers, 41, 276, 332, 343; and curriculum, 87, 97, 330; and further education, 64, 65; and teachers' centres, 90, 128-31, 333, 345
Lohman, J., 279
London University entrance, 108
London Association of Teachers of English, 111
Lortie, Dan, on team teaching, iv-v, 230-40, 334
Lytle, W.O. Jnr., 199

McConnelgue, P., 50

Macdonald, Barry, vi, 13, 285
McHirgin, R., 273
Macintosh, Henry G., on examinations and curricula, 113, 115-25
Mackenzie, R.F., 5
Maclure, Stuart; on curriculum development, ii, iii, vi, 15-29, on Schools Council and examinations, 95-103
McMahon, H.F., on curriculum development in N. Ireland, ii, 47-50
McMullen, Tim, 340, 348-57, 363-7, 372, 376, 380
Malmo Educational Development Centre, iii, 138-42
Malone, J.M., 48
Management of Organisations and Individuals, 273
Manchester University: Area Training Organisation, 128; School of Education, 333
Mann, F.C., 198
March, J.G., 276
Marshall, T.H., 250, 259
Mason, Stuart, 347, 348, 354, 380
Mathematical Association, 105
Mathematics: primary, 26, 27, 35; secondary, 52, 54-5, 107
Media resources officer, 335
Michael, 358
Michigan University, 312
Midlands Mathematics Experiment, 107
Miles, Matthew B.: and innovation, 282, 292, 293, 294, 295, 302; on school organisation, iv, 192-201, 283, 297
Mixed ability grouping, 334, 335
Moore, W.E., 250, 251, 253, 255
Moral education, 40, 48
Morgan, C., 273
Morrell, Derek H., 42, 76-7
Morse, N., 199
Mort, Paul R., 314, 315
Motivation, and learning, 352, 372, 374
Mouton, J.S., 198
Muntyan, B., 294
Musgrove, F., 75, 355, 356, 358

Naegle, K., 258, 263
Nagle, J.M., 283
Nailsea School, iv, 92, 170-90, 340
National Association for the Teaching of English, 39
National Association of Schoolmasters (NAS), 88

National Centre, 312
National Certificate, 62
National Council for Innovation in Education (Norway), 17, 278
National Council for Educational Technology, 291
National Foundation for Educational Research (NFER), 84, 129
National Training Laboratory, 294
National Union of Teachers (NUT), 88, 89, 91, 97
Netherlands, educational system, 26-7
Newman, F.M., 258
New Mexico State Unviersity, 322
New Zealand: curriculum development, 7, 12; teachers' role, 10, 356
Nisbet, John: on curriculum development in Scotland, 52-7; on innovation, ii, iv, vi, 1-13, 283; on Schools Council, 93
Non-teaching personnel in schools, 335-6
Northumberland, teacher training pilot scheme, 287
North West Curriculum Project, iii, 91, 127-37, 291, 333
Norway, curriculum development, 7, 15, 16, 17-18, 19, 96
Norwood Committee, 95, 101
Nuffield Foundation 48; and curriculum reform, 39, 77, 333; language courses, 107; projects, 99, 340, 342, 352
Nursery education, 35, 39, 49

OECD: innovation research, 7, 283; Lisbon seminar, 6
Oliver, D.W., 258
Ontario Institute for Studies in Education (OISE), 28
Open education, v, 155-68
Oral language programme, 322
Owen, J.G., on curriculum development, ii, 10, 30-46
Oxford Delegacy, examinations, 104, 108
Oxford and Cambridge Schools Examination Board, 108

Palmer, John, 211
Parents: and curriculum, 33, 331; influence on children, 373-4; and innovation, 5, 10, 11; and open schools, 159, 357; relations with teachers, iv, 218-22, 228, 229, 356
Parsons, Talcott, 253-4, 255, 258
Pavalko, R., 255
Pearl, Art, 250, 259, 260, 263
People workers, 250-68
Pepper, Ron, 344
Personal Service Society, 260
Piaget, Jean, 167
Pincus, J., 278
Pluralism, iii, 73, 88
Polytechnics, 62, 65
Prescott, W., 59, 95
Primary schools: in Belgium, 23; curriculum, 23, 35, 50, 115, 342-3; group learning, 334, 362; in N. Ireland, 50; open plan, 162
Principals *See* Head teachers
Problem solving, and innovation, 278-9, 315-16, 325-6, 337, 353
Professionalisation and Social Change, 250
Professionalism, 73, 74-5, 88, 250-68
Public curriculum, 96, 97, 100, 101
Pupils: attitude to teachers, 357-9, 373, 374-7; behaviour study, 144; difficult, 189
Purity and Danger, 160

Q and F examinations, 89, 98, 102
Quality assurance specialist, 322

Race relations curriculum project, 93
Raising school leaving age (ROSLA), iii, 37, 66, 90, 91, 127, 129
Ralphs, Sir Lincoln, 92
Reform and Organisational Survival, 242
Regional Advisory Council for Further Education (RAC), 64
Regional centres, 23
Regional coordinating committees, 287
Regional Laboratories 312, 314
Regional service centres, 322-6
Regional staff inspector (RSI), 64
Reimer, E., 199
Research for Better Schools Inc., 278
Research, development and diffusion (RD & D), 278, 313-14, 320, 333, 345
Resources for learning projects, 49, 352
Reynolds, J., 280
Richardson, Elizabeth, iv, 5, 9, 92, 279, 340; on staff problems, 170-90
Riessman, F., 250
Robertson, A.G., 54, 55

Rogers, Carl, 300
Rogers, Everett M., 280, 281, 285, 292, 326
Role workshop, 198-9
Ross, Donald H., 315
Rowntree Charitable Trust, 49
Rudd, W.A.G., on curriculum development, iii, 91, 127-37
Ruddock, J., 285

Sanctions for pupils, 188, 189, 367, 368, 374-5, 376-7, 380
Scandinavia; curriculum development, 15, 16-19, 24
Scenning, 326
Schachtel, E.G., 196
Schmuck, R.A., 279
Schon, 337
School: building, 39, 67; culture, 144-5, 146; governors, 68, 69, 87, 267; organisation, 17, 19, 92, 192-202, 297, 329, 332; regulations, 68
School Certificate, 108
School Mathematics Project (SMP), 99, 107, 362
Schools Council: committees, 75, 88, 93, 105, and curriculum, ii, 29, 39, 49, 75, 77, 90, 91-3, 95-103, 278; and examinations, 95, 103, 117; and in-service training, 89-90; and moral education, 48; and school leavers, 75; and teachers, 60, 87-93; projects, 9, 48, 93, 99, 123, 333, 336, 362
Schools Council: a Second Look, 59, 95
Science: innovation failure, III, teaching reforms, 105, 106
Science Masters' Association, 105
Scotland, curriculum development, ii, 52-7
Secondary schools: curriculum, 68-9, 115; examinations, 68, 330; government, 68-9; and innovation, 160, 334; social control, 157-9; White Paper, 68
Secondary Schools Examination Council (SSEC), 95, 98, 104, 109, 110, 111
Shils, E.A., 293
Shipman, M.D., 280, 336
Shoemaker, F. Floyd, 280, 281
Silberman, Charles E., 258
Silverman, D., 275, 276, 282
Simon, H.A., 276
Sixteen-plus examination, 89, 102, 107, 116, 119

Sixth form reform, 70, 80-1, 97, 100, 101, 102
Skellefteo projects (Sweden), 18
Skilbeck, Malcolm, 49
Skills, 353
Smith, G., 276
Smith, L., 285
Smith, L.A., 123
Smith, Leslie, on curriculum reform, 115-25
Smith, W.O. Lester, 66, 71
Social interaction, and innovation, 278, 313-15, 333, 334, 336
Sociology and education, 305, 306
Sociology of Teaching, 356
South Western Cooperative Educational Laboratory (Albuquerque), 321, 322, 324
Spain, curriculum development, 23
Staff development, 143-52, 170-90, 340, 351, 366, 378-81
Stalker, J., 283
Standing Conference on University Entrance (SCUE), 100, 102, 111
State School, a Question of Living, 5
Stenhouse, Lawrence, 84, 96
Strauss, G., 298
Straw, Jack, 61
Streaming, 60, 159, 334, 335
Stufflebeam, D., 278, 284
Sussex University, Centre for Educational Technology, 291
Swann Report on technological employment, 70
Sweden, curriculum development, iii, 7, 15, 16, 17, 18-19, 77-8, 85, 96, 138-42
Szasz, T., 259

Taba, Hilda, 304
Tavistock Institute, 294
Taylor, George, 350, 352
Taylor, Philip H., 42, 283, 304, 355, 356, 358
Teacher Corps, v, 242-9
Teacher Induction Pilot Schemes (TIPS), 285-7
Teacher tutors, 184-5, 287
Teachers: associations, 39, 88, 89, 90, 91; authority patterns, 217-29, 230-40; centres, 49, 79, 90, 127, 128-9, 333-4, 345; classroom attitudes, 205-15, and curriculum, 34, 50, 70, 87-8, 97, 127-37, 331; education and training, 36, 41, 69, 89-90, 128, 344-5; and examinations,

91, 115-251; professionality, 282, 341-3; professional relationships, 218-29, 334, 340-1; and Schools Council, 87-93; relations with pupils, 359-60, 368-9
Teachers as Managers, 350
Team teaching, iv, 230-40, 292, 334, 336, 340-1
Team training, 197-8
Technical education, 63-5
Texas, West, regional service centres, 322
Thatcher, Mrs Margaret, 97
Thelen, Herbert, A., 317
Thomas Calton Comprehensive School (London), 344
Timetable innovation, 361
Tutgen, Prof., 26
Tyvaskala University, Institute of Educational Research, 17

UNESCO: curriculum survey, 26; innovation research, 7
Ulster University, education centre, 49
United States: curriculum development, 24, 25, 28, 77; educational research, 312-26; teaching reform, 242-9

University Grants Committee (UGC), 69
Universities: 69-70, 100, 101, 151

Vocational education, 24, 65
Volkswagenwerk Foundation, 26

Walker, Rob, on open education, iv, 162-8
Waller, Willard, 356, 359
Walton, R., 293, 295
Watkins, R., 127
Watson, Goodwin, 285, 317
Watson, Jeanne, 298, 304
Weiss, C.H., 284
West African Examinations Council, 104
Western Michigan University, 250
Westley, Bruce, 298, 304
Wicksteed, Joseph H., 173
Wilensky, H.L., 255, 256, 258
Wilson, P.A., 253
Wilson, Robert, 321
Wiseman, S., 34
Women teachers, 22, 375
Work sheets, 362-3, 371, 372
Working class pupils, 357, 373, 374
Wright, D.S., 373-4
Wrigley, J., 42, 92

Wyatt, T.S., on examining boards, iii, 98, 104-13

Yearmasters/mistresses, 367
York University, modern language teaching centre, 84; general studies project, 48
Young, Brian, 42
Young, Michael F.D., 61, 89, 263

Zaltman, G., 281
Zand, D., 199
Zander, A., 199